ALSO BY RONALD T. TAKAKI

A PRO-SLAVERY CRUSADE:
The Agitation to Reopen the African Slave Trade (1971)

VIOLENCE IN THE BLACK IMAGINATION:
Essays and Documents (1972)

IRON CAGES

RONALD T. TAKAKI

IRON CAGES

Race and Culture in
Nineteenth-Century America

University of Washington Press
Seattle

Copyright © 1979 by Ronald T. Takaki

Originally published in hardback by Alfred A. Knopf Inc., 1979. University of Washington Press paperback edition published by arrangement with Alfred A. Knopf, Inc., 1982.

Second printing, 1985
Third printing, 1988

All rights reserved. No part of this publication may be reproduced or transmitted in any form or by any means, electronic or mechanical, including photocopy, recording, or any information storage or retrieval system, without permission in writing from the publisher.

Library of Congress Cataloging in Publication Data

Takaki, Ronald T., 1939-
  Iron cages.

  Originally published: 1st ed. New York: Knopf, 1979.
  Bibliography: p.
  Includes index.
    1. United States—Race relations.   2. United States—Civilization—19th century.   3. Minorities—United States—History.   I. Title.
  E184.A1T337   1982   973'.04   81-21940
  ISBN 0-295-95904-5 (pbk.)   AACR2

Printed in the United States of America

Contents

A Note of Appreciation

The vast amount of documents housed in our repositories is awesome and sometimes overwhelming, and historians have a singular reliance on librarians. While many librarians assisted me, two of them deserve special acknowledgments. Helen Slotkin, archivist of the Massachusetts Institute of Technology, sent me detailed descriptions of the Francis Amasa Walker Papers at MIT and also checked collections in Washington to see whether they contained documents of interest to me. Richard J. Wolfe, director of the rare book room at the Countway Library of Harvard Medical School, allowed me to reproduce all the materials I needed for my research on the controversy over the Harvard Medical School admissions of 1850.

This book, while in the making, served as a focus for the sharing of information and ideas. Michael Rogin and Lawrence Friedman were involved in this study in a special way: Over the years our meetings to discuss our research and analyses constituted a rare seminar. Both of them read drafts of chapters time and again, offering thoughtful and heuristic criticisms that helped me conceptualize the three "iron cages." Charles Sellers read critically the entire manuscript in one of its many drafts. Alexander Saxton showed me how and where I had changed ("grown," he insists) over the years and my manuscript (parts of which were written some time ago) had not. I hope the study in its published form is closer to where I am at this time. Martin Van Buren referred me to studies of Protestant thought and republican ideology which influenced my understanding of both. Herbert Hill, Charles B. Dew, and Herbert G. Gutman kindly responded with bibliographical suggestions for my research on black labor. James Y. Henderson, Clara Sue Kidwell, and Terry Wilson provided bibliographical help for the section on the Dawes Act; Ling-chi Wang guided me to documents so I could develop certain linkages in my analysis of United States expansion into Asia and the use of Chinese labor in America. Ricky Rodriguez, Jere Takahashi, and Roberto Haro recommended readings which opened the way to new intellectual vistas. Carol Takaki read the manuscript as I was preparing its final form; her criticisms were so complete and withering I was compelled to rework entire chapters and to keep it much longer than I had planned. Consequently, Ashbel Green, already a patient and understanding editor, had to wait for it a bit longer.

Self-renunciation, the renunciation of life and of all human needs, is its principal thesis. The less you eat, drink and buy books; the less you go to the theatre, the dance hall, the public house; the less you think, love, theorize, sing, paint, fence, etc., the more you save—the greater becomes your treasure . . . your capital. The less you are, the less you express your own life, the greater is your alienated life, the more you have, the greater is the store of your estranged being.
        —*Karl Marx,*
            "The Meaning of Human Requirements"

The White Whale swam before him as the monomaniac incarnation of all those malicious agencies which some deep men feel eating in them, till they are left living on with half a heart and half a lung. That intangible malignity . . . Ahab did not fall down and worship it . . . but deliriously transferring its idea to the abhorred whale, he pitted himself, all mutilated, against it. . . . All evil, to crazy Ahab, were visibly personified, and made practically assailable in Moby Dick. He piled upon the whale's white hump the sum of all the general rage and hate felt by his whole race from Adam down; and then, as if his chest had been a mortar, he burst his hot heart's shell upon it.
        —*Herman Melville,*
            Moby-Dick

Preface

Unlike other books on the history of racism in America, this study seeks to offer a comparative analysis of racial domination within the context of the development of capitalism and class divisions in nineteenth-century American society. Where scholars have examined separately the oppression of blacks, Indians, Mexicans, and Asians, I have tried to analyze the ways the experiences of these different groups related to each other. Where scholars have tended to isolate racism as a history of attitudes, I have attempted to relate it to the broad political, social, and economic developments that occurred during this formative and crucial century. Both of my efforts have a common purpose: to understand how the domination of various peoples of color in America had cultural and economic bases which involved as well as transcended race.[1]

When I began this book many years ago, I became increasingly aware of the fragmentation evident in the scholarship on the history of race. I realized my own study of the southern defense of slavery had been too narrow in focus: *A Pro-Slavery Crusade: The Agitation to Reopen the African Slave Trade* located racism in the South and failed to comprehend its national character, and it analyzed racism only in relation to blacks, apart from Indians, Mexicans, and Asians in nineteenth-century society. Like many other scholars, I had parceled out white attitudes toward different racial groups almost as if there were no important similarities as well as differences in the ways whites imaged and treated them. Yet I knew that the reality of white America's experience was dynamically multiracial. What whites did to one racial group had direct consequences for others. And whites did not artificially view each group in a vacuum; rather, in their minds, they lumped the different groups together or counterpointed them against each other. Indeed, as Winthrop Jordan noted, it would be "impossible to see clearly what Americans thought of Negroes without ascertaining their almost invariably contrary thoughts concerning Indians: in the settlement of this country the red and black peoples served white men as aids to navigation by which they would find their safe positions as they ventured into America." And I could see how brown and yellow peoples also became "aids to navigation" as white Americans established and expanded the new nation in the nineteenth century.[2]

More importantly, I felt the need not only to bring comparative analysis to the study of racism but also to overcome the excessive specialization characteristic of contemporary historical scholarship. As historians, many of us have fragmented the past; and in our study of the parts—politics, labor, economics, literature, religion, technology, relations between men and women, race relations, foreign affairs, ideology, and institutions—we have written about each in isolation from the others and the whole. Our very "fields of specialization" have become paddocks for our research and imagination. Rarely have scholars sought and seldom have they achieved an integrated analysis of the past. This recognition led me to take steps toward the study of the past as something organic and to approach American society as a total structure. Thus, in this work, I have analyzed racial domination in America, from the time of the American Revolution to the Spanish-American War, in order to understand its relationship to the development of American culture as well as to the political, social, and economic institutions the culture helped to spawn and sustain.[3]

By culture, I essentially mean what Antonio Gramsci has called cultural hegemony, "an order in which a certain way of life and thought is dominant, in which one concept of reality is diffused throughout society in all its institutional and private manifestations, informing with its spirit all taste, morality, customs, religious and political principles, and all social relations, particularly in their intellectual and moral connotation." Culture or the superstructure of ideology had a dialectical relationship to the development of particular circumstances or material conditions in nineteenth-century society: It both sprang from and shaped material reality. The "phantoms" of the mind and the "sublimations of man's material life-process" constituted a shared set of ideas, images, values, and assumptions about human nature and society. Hegemonic in terms of the way men and women viewed the world around them, culture also served an important class function, for it provided the ideology necessary for the legitimation and development of the mode of production and the order of social relations in American society.[4]

Employing Gramsci's concept of cultural hegemony, I have focused on the culture-makers and policy-makers, or the white men in positions of influence and power: political leaders, editors, novelists, educators, ministers, military leaders, doctors, and businessmen. Their ideas and decisions mattered, for they were consequential. In order to be certain that this analysis of culture and ideology is not abstract or remote from human life and drama, it is grounded in the biographies and thoughts of specific men, and seeks to take us toward C. Wright Mills' concept of the "sociological imagination"—the study of the intersection between biography and history within society. Thus chapters that contain general analyses are buttressed concretely by chapters on Benjamin Rush, Thomas Jefferson, Robert Montgomery Bird, Andrew Jackson, Henry Hughes, Oliver Wendell Holmes, Francis Amasa Walker, George Armstrong Custer, George Washington Cable, Henry W. Grady, Bret Harte, Henry George, Josiah Strong, and Alfred Thayer Mahan. Since culture has "private" as well as institutional manifestations, I have examined not only public documents such as books, messages to Congress, editorials, newspapers, magazines, and speeches, but also private documents such as letters, notebooks, and journals. Diffused throughout society, ideology must be studied everywhere, even in personal correspondence and diaries. Although their role as culture-makers did not preclude criticism of certain aspects of American capitalism, the men analyzed in this study shared a basic commitment to the system and its values, and participated in its maintenance and advancement in varying degrees and ways. They were what Karl Mannheim described as the "intelligentsia": Their special task was to provide an "interpretation of the world" for American society. As intellectuals or interpreters of social reality, most of them were agents or members of a class that owned property used for production, appropriated labor from workers either through enslavement or wages, and possessed an inordinate degree of control over institutions which had the power to disseminate information and ideas, make laws, punish in the courts and use the instruments of state violence. What white men in power thought and did mightily affected what everyone thought and did.[5]

As a study of cultural hegemony, this comparative analysis of race in America is concerned with more than the need to understand how slavery in the South and anti-black discrimination in the North were related to Indian removal; or how the destruction of Indians and the war against Mexico were related to the exploitation of Chinese laborers in the American West as well as New England; or how "internal colonies"* were developed in the United States as people of color, particularly blacks, Mexicans, and Asians, were exploited for their labor and subordinated to caste/class domination; or how racial oppression was part of a larger "labor-repressive system"† and a general class structure; or how racism within the United States expressed itself in international racial conflict and violence. As we shall see, all of these racial developments interfaced not only with each other but also with the republican ideology of the American Revolution (part 1 of this book), enterprise and the Market Revolution of the age of Jackson (part 2), the emergence of American technology and industrialization or the transformation of the United States into the locus of the "modern world-system"‡ and the development of an urban industrial working

* Mario Barrera, "Colonial Labor and Theories of Inequality: The Case of International Harvester," *Review of Radical Political Economics,* vol. 8, no. 2 (Summer 1976), pp. 1-18; Robert Blauner, *Racial Oppression in America* (New York, 1972). According to Barrera, "colonialism is a structured relationship of domination and subordination among groups which are defined along ethnic and/or racial lines, where the relationship is established or maintained to serve the interests of all or part of the dominant group" (p. 3). "Internal colonialism" refers to this relationship of domination, which involves both class exploitation and caste hegemony, within the United States.
† The term "labor-repressive system" is from Barrington Moore, Jr., *Social Origins of Dictatorship and Democracy: Lord and Peasant in the Making of the Modern World* (Boston, 1967). I am using it in a broader sense than Moore, in that I extend it to industrial labor. The labor-repressive process, whether in agricultural or industrial production, involves reliance on "strong political methods to extract the surplus, keep the labor force in its place, and in general make the system work." See Moore, p. 434.
‡ For the development of world capitalism, see Immanuel Wallerstein, *The Modern World-System: Capitalist Agriculture and the Origins of the European World-Economy in the Sixteenth Century* (New York, 1974). In Wallerstein's framework, the modern world-system has three parts or areas: the core areas (such as England) where capitalist agriculture and a degree of industrial production had developed, the semi-peripheral areas (such as Spain) which were primarily engaged in agricultural production based on share-crop labor, and the peripheral areas (such as Hispanic America) where coerced labor produced cash crops for export, especially to the core areas. In *The Triumph of the Middle Classes: A Political and Social History of Europe in the Nineteenth Century* (Garden City, N. Y., 1968), Charles Moraze observed that by 1880 "the capital of the seas had shifted westwards towards America . . ." (p. 549; see also pp. 385-408, 545). In a breathtaking sweep, Moraze covers the modernization of Europe and what he calls the triumph of the middle classes, in which businessmen and industrialists used scientific techniques and modern credit systems to overthrow the old courtly society.

class (part 3), and finally American expansion toward Asia (part 4). All four parts build on each other and come together in a final chapter, "Down from the Gardens of Asia"—a title taken from Walt Whitman's *Passage to India*.[6]

Underlying all of these concerns, in a paraphrase of both Karl Marx and Herman Melville, is the question: How did white men in nineteenth-century America repress or "mutilate" themselves, become "less" than they "were," and construct a culture of "self-renunciation" and "alienation"? And how did this process of domination produce a rage so intense it overwhelmed even rationality itself?[7]

During the years between the American Revolution and the Spanish-American War, "iron cages," to borrow and expand Max Weber's graphic metaphor, emerged in American society as the self was placed in confinement, its emotions controlled, and its spirit subdued. As white men in power separated themselves from the king during the War of Independence and as they set themselves even further apart from blacks and Indians, they promoted a republican ideology rooted in the Protestant ethic and devised what may be called republican "iron cages" to help Americans rule the emotional part of themselves. Rational, ascetic, and self-governing individuals, republicans were expected to fear spontaneity and to resist serendipity. As enterprising whites expanded the market and "civilization" during the age of Jackson and afterward, as they appropriated Indian and Mexican lands and exploited black and Asian labor, and as they channeled white workers into the factories, they opened the way for the domination of the corporate "iron cage" of bureaucratic capitalism. And, as the nation advanced toward the Far East in the late nineteenth century and developed overseas colonies and an awesome military complex with ties to the new industrial order, American expansionists became imprisoned in an even more terrifying "iron cage": Demonic in force and nature, it took them into an imperialistic war and an irrational quest for power and destruction—a quest described metaphorically in Melville's *Moby-Dick*.[8]

All three "iron cages" were not separate entities. Rather, they dynamically interacted in an organic continuum as the United States was transformed from an agrarian-commercial to a highly technological and bureaucratic capitalist economy. Republican ascetic self-control and individualism isolated people from each other and helped to make possible the ascendancy of bureaucratic corporate capitalism; both, in turn, in their domination of the instinctual life and their denial of human completeness generated the discontent and rage which gave power to the demonic "iron cage." The final cage, promising white Americans regeneration through violence and carrying death to Asia during the Spanish-American War, rendered corporate rule at home even more formidable as it extended the market into the Far East and integrated industrial interests and state power. Throughout this entire process, "the vast, surging, hopeful army of workers"—men and women of all races—were denied the class consciousness, the feeling of community, and the power of collective action they needed in order to respond effectively to what Max Weber has called the "tremendous development" in the modern age of "victorious capitalism," the hegemony of a powerful rational capitalist bureaucracy. For us, living in this Weberian world, we still do not know for certain whether "entirely new prophets" will arise at the end of this development to help us create a new critical vision; or whether civilization will reach a level never before achieved, where "mechanized petrification," "specialists without spirit," and "sensualists without heart" will characterize the new nullity; or whether the fate of the men on board the *Pequod* may indeed be ours.[9]

Ronald T. Takaki
Berkeley, California

PART ONE

REPUBLICANISM

Seeking to conquer a larger liberty, man but extends the empire of necessity.
—Herman Melville

CHAPTER I

THE "IRON CAGE" IN THE NEW NATION

Now is your chance, Europe. Now let Hell loose and get your own back, and paddle your own canoe on a new sea, while clever America lies on her muck-heaps of gold, strangled in her own barbed wire of shalt-not ideals and shalt-not moralisms. While she goes out to work like millions of squirrels in millions of cages.

—D. H. Lawrence

O the joy of my spirit—it is uncaged—it darts like lightning!

—Walt Whitman

Nowhere in American history were love for virtue and hatred for vice proclaimed so aggressively and yet so anxiously than during the era of the American Revolution. For many Revolutionary leaders, the War of Independence had a great moral as well as political purpose: Unless the conflict involved the reformation of American society and unless the people of the new nation were as virtuous as their Puritan ancestors of the "City upon a Hill" had been, independence would be merely sound and fury. Theirs was a struggle not only for home rule but also for moral rule at home. The Revolutionary society had to make war against both the tyranny of England and the profligacy of the American people themselves.

Within months after the Declaration of Independence, John Adams was complaining that there was "too much Corruption, even in this infant Age of our Republic." "Virtue" was not in fashion, and "vice" was not infamous. A year later, Adams harbored an almost treasonous wish that it should be the "Will of Heaven" and the "Design of Providence" that the

3

British army would punish the Americans for their waywardness. If "our Army should be defeated, our Artillery lost, our best Generals kill'd, and Philadelphia fall in Mr. Howes [sic] Hands," the foundations of American independence would be laid deeper and stronger. Such military disasters "would cure Americans of their vicious and luxurious and effeminate Appetites, Passions and Habits, a more dangerous Army to American Liberty than Mr. Howes." Here was the language of Puritanism and the Great Awakening again bursting forth, demanding moral regeneration and separation from sin and corruption. Indeed, due to the Great Awakening, America in 1750 had become what Richard Hofstadter has called "a concentrated repository of the Protestant Ethic" and "a center of ascetic Protestantism." During the Revolution, moral asceticism and republicanism were melded together, and self-governing men were expected to restrict the range of experiences they could have in their pursuit of liberty.[1]

The war against England involved more than a struggle for moral purity, independence, and the formation of a national identity: Separation from England and the destruction of the crown gave Americans market freedom. The American Revolution not only severed the colonies from British corruption, it also freed American business from British economic regulation and domination. Colonial merchants, manufacturers, land speculators, and planters had economic interests in independence from England. The Proclamation of 1763, which restricted settlement west of the Appalachian Mountains, erected a barrier to westward expansion and the activities of land speculators. British regulations imposed limitations on manufacturing in the colonies in order to keep them dependent on British industries for manufactured goods. Legislation prohibited the manufacture of articles such as hats, shoes, and finished ironware in the colonies. British merchant houses also increasingly bypassed colonial merchants and sold goods at auction or directly to shopkeepers. "I would have you not bee [sic] too forward in pushing goods upon people," Philadelphia importer John Kidd wrote to the London House of Neate and Neave. "I shall also take the liberty to inform you that your supplying the shopkeepers at all is more harm than good to you. . . ." Such warnings went unheeded as British merchants flooded the American market with goods, forced prices down, reduced the profit margins of colonial merchants, and even drove some of them into bankruptcy. American businessmen were also alarmed by the Currency Act of 1764, which threatened the issuance of colonial currency: Both farmers and merchants relied on land banks to issue bills of tender to provide loans and working capital. Meanwhile, Tidewater tobacco planters increasingly found themselves indebted to Scottish banking firms and under the political influence of Scottish traders and agents. When credit in

England collapsed in 1762, Scottish banking houses pressed Virginia plant-ers for payment of debts and cut down the amount of credit available. The War of Independence, in short, liberated capitalism in America: It secured for American enterprisers freedom to convert Indian lands west of the Appalachians into private property, trade whenever and with whomever they pleased, import goods like tea and molasses without payment of taxes imposed by an external authority, issue their own currency, develop their own industries, and in general expand the market.[2]

All this they hoped to do as a virtuous people. What they achieved in the end was more than mere market freedom. In their overthrow of the king in America, they advanced an ideology which irrevocably separated white Americans from feudal traditions and provided the cultural superstructure for a new bourgeois order. And as the Revolutionary leaders labored to define precisely who Americans were or should be as virtuous people and as republicans, they were establishing a national identity which had signif-icant implications for race in America. Whites were no longer Englishmen in America, set apart from Indians and blacks, as they had been through-out the colonial experience. The success of the Revolution required patriot leaders and culture-makers to confront a vexatious concern which had impinged on the consciousness of whites for nearly two centuries as they cleared the forests and erected civilization in America: More than ever before, as Americans, they had to determine what the relationship should be between nationality and race.

The Birth of a Virtuous People

Vice was something men of the Revolution, like their Puritan forefathers, were able to identify without difficulty: It was the domination of what Adams called the "vicious and luxurious and effeminate Appetites, Pas-sions and Habits." The key word used to describe vice was *luxury*. In the list of grievances against the king of England issued in his electrifying *Common Sense,* Thomas Paine charged that the monarch was guilty of oppression, corruption, and "luxury." For the leadership of the Revolu-tionary generation, *luxury* was an obsessive term, referring to "dull animal enjoyment" which left "minds stupified, and bodies enervated, by wallow-ing for ever in one continual puddle of voluptuousness." The problem was not luxury itself, but its power to appeal to the senses and to give men pleasure, drawing off their energy and making them "effeminate" and weak. One way in which the Revolution tried to handle the problem was to suppress luxury. In his support for the nonimportation and nonconsumption of English goods, the editor of the *Boston Evening Post* reminded Americans that they had been lately "insensibly drawn into too great a degree of *luxury* and *dissipation.*" What Americans had to do was to boycott the "Baubles of Britain" and "banish the syren of LUXURY with all her train of fascinating pleasures, idle dissipation and expensive amusements." In their call for a boycott in 1774, the Continental Congress insisted that Americans encourage frugality, economy, and industry, and refrain from every form of extravagance and dissipation, especially horse racing, cockfighting, shows, plays, and expensive entertainment.[3] The play element had to be repressed in the Revolutionary society.

Yet, to the dismay of many men of the Revolution, play was not easily denied. The Boston Tea Assembly, organized in 1785, allowed cardplaying and dancing, and one angry Bostonian protested: "We are prostituting all our glory as a people for new modes of pleasure." During the war years, Samuel Adams was distressed to receive reports that Boston appeared exceedingly gay. "I would fain hope this is confined to Strangers," he wrote to a friend. "Luxury & Extravagance are . . . totally destructive of those Virtues which are necessary for the Preservation of the Liberty and Happiness of the People. Is it true that the Review of the Boston Militia was closed with an expensive Entertainment?" If it were, he added, the militia would never become formidable to its enemies. Thus many Revolutionary leaders themselves betrayed a lack of confidence in the ability of Americans to resist the temptations of pleasure. Their fear of human disposition only intensified their demand for honest industry, sober frugality, and simplicity of manners, and also their demand for separation from England.[4]

During the struggle for independence, England was condemned as a source of luxury, dissipation, licentiousness, and extravagance. Writing from London in February 1775, Benjamin Franklin observed: "When I consider the extreme corruption prevalent among all orders of men in this old rotten state, and the glorious public virtue so predominant in our rising country, I cannot but apprehend more mischief than benefit from a close union." Looking around them, Americans thought they saw the symptoms of the British disease. Luxury and effeminacy seemed to be appearing everywhere, and "Venality, Servility, and Prostitution" seemed to be spreading like a "Cancer." Determined to protect and isolate Americans from the disease of British corruption, patriot leaders sought to enact sumptuary laws to check the growth of luxury and to prohibit plays and extravagant dress and diet. But they feared that every restraint of this kind was sure to be met with the royal negative. They felt they had to rebel, or else they would become lost in imitation of British prodigality, idleness, and false refinements. Their ability to criticize the "*constitutional errors* in the English form of government" was interpreted by the patriot leaders as a sign of their moral character. "As a man who is attached to a prostitute is unfitted to choose or judge of a wife," Paine argued, "so any prepossession in favour of a rotten constitution of government will disable us from discerning a good one."[5]

American condemnation of British sexual and political impurities focused on the king. Idleness, wealth, and power had corrupted him, Paine charged; the ruler had "little more to do than to make war and give away places. . . ." Here was a "pretty business" indeed: The king had no business and no work, yet he was paid eight hundred thousand sterling a year and "worshipped in the bargain!" One "honest man" was worth more to society and in the sight of God than "all the crowned ruffians that ever lived." To his fellow Americans, Paine cried out: "If ye wish to preserve your native country uncontaminated by European corruption, ye must in secret wish a separation." Thus the solution to the problem of luxury and vice appeared plain and simple: Virtue demanded Americans separate themselves from England. This was only "common sense."[6]

In their castigation of the king, patriot leaders used a rhetoric which revealed familial politics. The king had, Paine asserted, the "pretended title" of "FATHER OF HIS PEOPLE." As a parent, the king had lost all virtue, for he had failed to control his passions and threatened the safety of the children. In England he had "swallowed up" the power and "eaten out" the virtue of the House of Commons, which represented the republican part of the constitution. This rendered him worse than a brute or savage, for even brutes did not "devour their young, nor savages make war upon their families." The struggle to separate themselves from a "devouring" father involved the consciousness that the colonists had grown up and no longer needed their father/king. Unless they declared their independence and formed a new government in America, Paine argued, they might as well assert "that because a child has thrived upon milk, that it is never to have meat. . . ." Americans should no longer run three or four thousand miles with a petition and wait four or five months for an answer; they should look upon such behavior and such a way of conducting their business as "childishness." Even in terms of physical size, there was "something absurd, in supposing a Continent to be perpetually governed by an island."[7] Americans had grown up, had become bigger than the father. The time had come for them to separate and govern themselves.

As the patriot leaders rebelled against their father/king, they transferred his authority and power to the "people" and instituted a republic. The 1776 rebellion against royal authority was a logical climax of the forces unleashed during the Great Awakening. The religious excitement of 1740 had opened the way to republicanism: It was, as Perry Miller observed, "the point at which the wilderness took over the task of defining the objectives of the Puritan errand." Jonathan Edwards and other revivalists had aroused the masses and created a momentum they could not control. They had been forced "not only to admit all those who would come, but to excite and to drive as many as possible, by such rhetorical stimulations as 'Sinners in the hands of an Angry God,' into demanding entrance." The result was "the end of the reign over the New England and American mind of a European and scholastical conception of an authority put over men because men were incapable of recognizing their own welfare."[8] Thirty years later, this destruction of the traditional concept of authority took a political form as the American Revolution asserted the belief that men were capable.

This new belief compelled patriot leaders to establish a government without a king. In America the king would not be the law; rather the law would be king and derived from the people. During the violence of the Revolution, Americans symbolically expressed the destruction of the father/king and the relocation of authority in the people. "Let the Crown . . . be demolished," Paine urged, "and scattered among the people whose right it is." In Boston, the cradle of the Revolution, "the King's Arms were taken down and broken to pieces in the street, and carried off by the people." Thus, the American Revolution was no mere war for independence: It wrecked the traditional hierarchical structure of authority and removed the king from the Great Chain of Being, the order from God to the lowest creature. To remove the king was to break the entire chain. If men had previously felt a sense of community rooted in tradition and symbolized by the king, now they were free individuals and relationships among them would be contractual. If in the beginning all the world was like America, or in a state of nature, as Locke theorized, in America men would enter into a social contract and form government. They would be free, created "equal," a new people without a king, a feudal past, or a spirit of connectedness. Henceforth, to borrow from D. H. Lawrence, they would be "masterless." "No kings, no bishops maybe," they would be "masterful men."[9]

In the republic, the people would no longer have an external authority over them, a father/king to restrain their passions and deny them luxury; they would instead have to control themselves. Whether or not they would be able to exercise self-control effectively depended on their virtue. "To suppose that any form of government," explained James Madison, "will secure liberty or happiness without virtue in the people, is a chimerical idea." Republicanism and virtue would reinforce each other: Moral character would enable republican man to govern himself. John Adams viewed republicanism as a reflection of virtue as well as a means of self-control. "If there is a form of government, then, whose principle and foundation is virtue, will not every sober man acknowledge it better calculated to promote the general happiness than any other form?" he asked in 1776. In the republic, Adams continued, the people would be educated and inspired with "a conscious dignity becoming freemen"; they would develop good manners and good morals and become sober, industrious, frugal, and virtuous. As republicans, Americans would resemble their Puritan ancestors, and the new nation would become what Samuel Adams called "the Christian Sparta."[10]

This fusion of Protestant asceticism and republican theory provided the ideology for bourgeois acquisitiveness and modern capitalism in the United States. The seventeenth-century belief in the covenant of grace had made it possible for the Puritan to affirm God's omnipotence while he strived to demonstrate he had the outward signs of salvation. This Protestant anxiety—the need to know how one had been predestined and to do good works and diligently follow one's calling—led ironically to the erosion of piety itself. Good works resulted often enough in worldly goods and a concern for the here rather than the hereafter. Eighteenth-century republicanism accelerated this thrust toward commodity accumulation and the primacy of the marketplace, as it disintegrated the feudal order and freed men as individuals to prove their virtue in their pursuit of possessions.

Yet, this freedom to pursue wealth created a special anxiety. Here was a "sad dilemma," William M. Smith told the Continental Congress in 1775. If wealth were to be excluded, it must be done by regulations which interfered with civil liberty; but without restraints on wealth, "the syren of *luxury*" would soon corrupt society. What was to be done in this situation? Did not wealth spring from liberty, and was there no "proper use of *wealth* and *civil happiness,* the genuine descendents of *civil liberty,* without abusing them to the nourishment of luxury and corruption?" Years after independence, John Adams also discerned this republican dilemma: "Will you tell me how to prevent riches from becoming the effects of temperance and industry? Will you tell me how to prevent riches from producing luxury? Will you tell me how to prevent luxury from producing effeminacy, intoxication, extravagance, vice and folly?"[11] Patriot leaders like Smith and Adams felt at once an intense need for the people to be free from external authority and a severe lack of confidence in their ability to control themselves. A government dependent on the character of the people would be fragile. If the people abandoned simplicity of manners and succumbed to luxury, the government would become corrupt and tyrannical. As American leaders called for the scattering of the king's power among the people and the broad dispersal of virtue, they worried about whether the people would be able to subdue their passions and shun luxury in a republic.

To overcome this dilemma, patriot leaders proposed the construction of what we have called the republican "iron cage," or, as D. H. Lawrence said, "millions of cages," one in each self. Freed from the authority of the father/king, each American had to become self-regulatory. In the new republican society, he could no longer depend on an external authority to dominate the play element and help him control the instinctual demands he felt he could not satisfy without threatening civilization. Neither could he depend on a sense of security bound in tradition and community which gave men a degree of freedom to be spontaneous and joyful and to accept as well as satisfy the complexity of their total needs. The primary source of restraint would be personal; the piece of the king's arms a man possessed symbolically represented the moral conscience and internal rational authority he must now rely on to reign over the human needs which seemed to threaten order in the new society. In his autonomy, he had no one to answer to but himself; and if he strayed toward the path of luxury, republican man would have no one to punish him but himself. This entire process involved the division and denial of each person's "wholeness," which for Karl Marx meant "seeing, hearing, smelling, tasting, feeling, thinking, observing, experiencing, wanting, acting, loving—in short, all the organs of his individual being." The fragmentization of the self—what R. D. Laing has described as "bodies half-dead; genitals dissociated from heart; heart severed from head; head dissociated from genitals"—required republican man to split off his rationality and raise it to authority. Thus, he had to curtail the range of experiences he could have in a republican society. This meant he had to devote his life to work, frugality, and sobriety, and to be the master of his passions and instinctual needs. "The only foundation of a free constitution," declared John Adams, "is pure virtue"; and Fourth of July orators would echo: "To be Free we must be virtuous."[12]

Urged to set themselves apart from their instinctual life and to make war against its needs, republicans were instructed always to be vigilant in their struggle against the passions. Indeed, nowhere were they given a more striking example of how easily men could fall to the power of the instincts and become "savages" than in the king of England himself. Referring to one of the king's speeches, Paine declared: "Brutality and tyranny appear on the face of it. It leaves us at no loss: And every line convinces . . . that he who hunts the woods for prey, the naked and untutored Indian, is less Savage than the King of Britain." Condemning the British efforts to recruit Indians and blacks to assist the king in his determination to crush the rebellion, Paine called upon Americans to "expel from the continent, that barbarous and hellish power, which hath stirred up the Indians and Negroes to destroy us. . . ."[13]

Race and Republican Society

The Revolution successfully expelled the "Savage" king, but it did not remove "savages" from America. Blacks and Indians remained. Long before whites had declared their independence from England and sought to become republicans, English culture-makers and political leaders had associated both groups with the instinctual life; and in the very way they identified peoples of color, they were defining themselves as men of "civilization." This psychological process, while it reflected some general fears of English culture, evolved in relation to the development of capitalist production in America. English definitions of Indians and blacks served as more than "aids to navigation" for Englishmen in their venture into America.[14] They also encouraged English immigrants to appropriate Indian land and black labor as they settled and set up production in the New World, and enabled white colonists to justify the actions they had committed against both peoples. This process of interaction among psychological needs, ideology, and economic interests functioned dynamically in the English settlement of America.

Even before the English migration to America was fully under way and even before the arrival of those "twenty Negars" on the coast of Virginia in 1619, Englishmen had felt a need to separate themselves from both the instinctual part of the self and from blacks and Indians. This separation may be seen in William Shakespeare's *The Tempest,* written and performed in 1611. In it, Prospero is a man of intellect, a scholar, and the antithesis of Caliban, "a savage and deformed slave." The ex-duke of Milan images Caliban as everything he believes he is not: a "bastard," a "thing of darkness," "filth," sexuality, a threat to his fair daughter's virginity. Racially, Caliban is not white: He has a dark complexion, his mother is from Africa, he lives in the "Bermoothes" or possibly the "Indes." Thus he could be African, American Indian, or even Asian; he belongs to a "vile race" and Prospero calls him a "devil, a devil, on whose nature Nurture can never stick!" Exiled from civilization, Prospero has taken the island from Caliban and forced the native to live in its rocky and desolate regions. While he segregates Caliban physically and socially, however, Prospero uses him as a slave, a worker who "serves in offices that profit" the white master. Viewing Caliban as a creature of passions, Prospero angrily condemns him for seeking to "violate the honor of my child." The master, assigning all the passions to the native, must enslave and brutalize him before Prospero realizes the "thing of darkness" is himself.[15]

In an uncanny way, America became a larger theater for *The Tempest*. As it turned out, the play was the thing: English fantasies of the stage were acted out in reality in the New World. As Englishmen made their "errand into the wilderness" of America, they took lands from red Calibans and made black Calibans work for them. Far from English civilization, they had to remind themselves constantly what it meant to be civilized—Christian, rational, sexually controlled, and white. And they tried to impute to peoples they called "savages" the instinctual forces they had within themselves. They feared, to use Lawrence's language, the "dark forest" within and the "strange gods" who came forth from the forest into the "little clearing" of their known selves and then went back. As civilized men, they believed they had to have the courage to dominate their passional impulses, and make certain those "dark gods" remained hidden. Thus, as Winthrop Jordan has pointed out, Englishmen in America

> were attempting to destroy the living image of primitive aggressions which they said was the Negro but was really their own. Their very lives as social beings were at stake. Intermixture and insurrection, violent sex and sexual violence, creation and destruction, life and death—the stuff of animal existence was rumbling at the gates of rational and moral judgment. If the gates fell, so did humanness; they could not fall; indeed there could be no possibility of their falling, else man was not man and his civilization not civilized. We, therefore, we do not lust and destroy; it is someone else. We are not great black bucks of the fields. But a buck *is* loose, his great horns menacing to gore into us with life and destruction. Chain him, either chain him or expel his black shape from our midst, before we realize that he is ourselves.[16]

This fear of the instinctual life was aggravated during the era of the American Revolution. As patriot leaders and culture-makers urged white Americans to be self-governing, they cast onto blacks and Indians those qualities they felt republicans should not have, and they denied the "black bucks" contained within themselves. On the eve of the Revolution, Arthur Lee of Virginia sharply separated blacks from republican society in his *Essay in Vindication of the Continental Colonies of America*. Negroes were cruel and cunning, he wrote; they ate like "absolute brutes" and believed in "the most gross idolatry." "Aristotle . . . declared that slaves could not have virtue, but he knew not any who were so utterly devoid of any semblance of virtue as are the Africans; whose understandings are generally shallow, and their hearts cruel, vindictive, stubborn, base, and wicked." Here, then, were a people, devoid of virtue in a society which required virtue if it were to be independent and republican. Indians, too, were viewed as creatures of passion: They were wild and primitive, and lacked the control and inclination to labor which whites believed were necessary if men were to be civilized. In an extreme view of Indians, writer Hugh Henry Brackenridge of Pennsylvania referred to them as "animals, vulgarly called Indians." Even Benjamin Franklin, a self-proclaimed "friend" of the Indian, expressed mild scorn for the original Americans. "The proneness of human Nature to a life of ease, of freedom from care and labour," he remarked "appears strongly in the little success that has hitherto attended every attempt to civilize our American Indians. . . ." Unlike whites, they did not work but depended instead on the spontaneous productions of nature to supply almost all their wants; even their hunting and fishing could not be regarded as labor when game was so plentiful.[17]

What both blacks and Indians, as they were viewed by white society, shared was clear: Like Caliban, they were not masters over their natural life. In terms of the American Revolution, they were not republicans. The rational part of the self, republican leaders insisted, must be in command. Identifying whites with rationality or mind, they associated peoples of color with the body. Thus mind was raised to authority over the other parts of the self, and whites were raised above blacks and Indians. As republicans in the new American nation, white men felt they had to guard themselves against the needs of the instinctual life which they claimed were ascendant in peoples of color.

While the Revolution contained tendencies which reinforced existing caste lines, it also provided a basis for a criticism of slavery. As they rebelled against the "slavery" of British tyranny, some patriot leaders also recognized the contradiction present within their society, and found it difficult to demand their freedom while denying it to blacks. In his pamphlet on *The Rights of the British Colonies Asserted and Proved*, James Otis bluntly asked: "The colonists are by law of nature freeborn, as indeed all men are, white or black. . . . Does it follow that 'tis right to enslave a man because he is black? Will short curl'd hair like wool . . . help the argument? Can any logical inference in favour of slavery, be drawn from a flat nose, a long or a short face?" Similarly Paine believed blacks were human beings, entitled to freedom and dignity, and condemned both the African slave trade and slavery. In 1775, even before he wrote *Common Sense*, Paine had raised the moral issue of slavery in America: "The great Question may be—what should be done with those who are enslaved already?" The states in the North which had small numbers of slaves responded positively to the question and abolished slavery. In 1780, for example, the Pennsylvania

Assembly declared its wish to extend a portion of the freedom they had won to the blacks and release them from thralldom. "It is not for us to enquire why, in the creation of mankind, the inhabitants of the several parts of the earth were distinguished by a difference in feature or complexion. It is sufficient to know that all are the work of the Almighty Hand."[18] Still, another question remained: Could all, regardless of complexion, be republicans and Americans?

Twenty-five years before the Declaration of Independence, Benjamin Franklin had already offered his thoughts on the complexion of society in America in his essay *Observations Concerning the Increase of Mankind.* He noted that the number of "purely white People" in the world was proportionately very small. All Africa was black or tawny, Asia chiefly tawny, and "America (exclusive of the new comers) wholly so." The English were the "principle Body of white People," and Franklin wished there were more of them in America. "And while we are . . . *Scouring* our Planet, by clearing America of Woods, and so making this Side of our globe reflect a brighter Light to the Eyes of Inhabitants in Mars or Venus," he declared, "why should we in the Sight of Superior Beings, darken its People? why increase the Sons of Africa, by Planting them in America, where we have so fair an opportunity, by excluding all Blacks and Tawneys, of increasing the lovely White . . .?"[19] The question was not so simple for the men of the Revolution. It was not a matter of "excluding" "Blacks" and "Tawneys": They were already in America and in large numbers.

The American Revolution made the issue immensely complicated and vexing, and compelled whites to define the relationship between race and the republic. Indeed, if the Revolutionary experiment were to succeed, many republican leaders were convinced, American society—the "lovely White"—must not be stained. Afraid of the diversity within themselves, they feared cultural and racial diversity in the society around them.

No wonder the men of the Revolution, meeting in the First Congress of the United States, enacted the Naturalization Law of 1790. In the debates, Congress affirmed its commitment to the "pure principles of Republicanism" and its determination to develop a citizenry of good and "useful" men, a homogeneous society. Only the "worthy part of mankind" should be encouraged to settle in the new republic and be eligible for citizenship. Every prospective citizen would have to go through a probationary period which would give him time to understand republican principles, acquire a taste for republican government, and demonstrate "proper and decent behavior." In this careful screening process, the nation would be able to exclude "vagrants," "paupers," and "bad men." It would admit only the virtuous, only the individual "fit" for the society into which he was to be "blended." Thus the naturalization law required him to reside in the United States for two years, and make "proof" in a common law court that he was a person of good character. But first he had to be "white."[20]

The Naturalization Law of 1790 explicitly linked race to republican nationality. It not only defined the norms of conduct and thought for Americans in the new nation: Citizenship was reserved for republicans, and citizens were expected to have republican manners and morals. It also specified a complexion for the members of the new nation as it gave expression to the hopes and fears of a republican society determined to cage the "black buck" still loose in the fields, increase the "lovely White," and carry forward the Revolution, which required virtue as the foundation of liberty and which had created a world without a king where men had to govern themselves.

This development of a republican ideology and a white national identity in the new nation may be studied in the lives and thought of two men of the Revolution—Benjamin Rush of Pennsylvania and Thomas Jefferson of Virginia. As intellectuals of the American Enlightenment and as leaders of the American Revolution, both men were philosophers of republicanism. Their prolific and widely read writings, especially Rush's *Medical Inquiries and Observations upon the Diseases of the Mind* and Jefferson's *Notes on the State of Virginia,* provided instructions on republican conduct to Americans. Critics of slavery yet slaveholders themselves, both men were white nationalists. Though Rush favored including blacks in American society and Jefferson insisted on their exclusion, both wanted to transform America into a homogeneous white society. Both were men of great power and influence—Rush as the mover and shaker of medicine in America, and Jefferson as the President of the United States. Each of them left behind a legacy for future generations: Rush established the asylum in America, the place where men would be re-formed, and Jefferson purchased Louisiana, the place where men would find "vacant lands" and regenerate themselves. The asylum and the Louisiana Purchase expanded what both Rush and Jefferson regarded as the empire of liberty.[21]

CHAPTER II

"DISEASES" OF THE MIND AND SKIN

Of every hue and caste am I, of every rank and religion,
A farmer, mechanic, artist, gentleman, sailor, quaker,
Prisoner, fancy-man, rowdy, lawyer, physician, priest.
I resist any thing better than my own diversity.
                                    —Walt Whitman

But could the "lovely White" be increased without excluding the undesirable "Black"? This was a question Benjamin Rush thought the new republic had to resolve, and he undoubtedly believed no one was more qualified than he to provide an answer. After all, he was highly respected as one of the leading thinkers of the American Enlightenment. When Rush died in 1813, Thomas Jefferson declared: "A better man could not have left us, more benevolent, more learned, of finer genius, or more honest." A reformer, Rush wanted "to spend and be spent for the Good of Mankind," and acquired a long list of accomplishments during his lifetime. He was a founder of the Pennsylvania Society for Promoting the Abolition of Slavery, a member of the Continental Congress, a signer of the Declaration of Independence, an influential educator, and a philosopher of republican ideology. Moreover, he was a doctor of medicine, surgeon-general in the Revolutionary army, professor of the theory and practice of medicine at the University of Pennsylvania, and the head of the Pennsylvania Hospital's ward for the insane. Author of seminal books on the diseases of the mind, he would later be regarded as the Father of American Psychiatry. His reform activities penetrated virtually every area of society, including race relations. Rush shared with Franklin and other white leaders a concern for the future of America as a multiracial society. Unlike Franklin, he wanted to have it both ways: He sought to increase the "lovely White" through the inclusion of blacks. No paradox seemed too challenging for Rush. Indeed, it made no difference to him whether the problem was race, child-rearing, education, politics, sex, illness, or mental disorder, for everything could be reduced to medicine in his world view. A man of medicine, Rush offered a prescription to a racially divided society: Blacks would have to be reformed and incorporated into the republican nation. But first whites themselves would have to be made into republicans.[1]

"Republican Machines"

The Revolution, for Rush, was a movement for the reformation of Americans. Convinced Americans could not become a virtuous people as long as they were subjects of the king, he was a fervent advocate of independence, and played a crucial role in composing the most eloquent appeal for separation from England. He gave Thomas Paine the idea of writing a pamphlet on independence, read and criticized every chapter as Paine composed it, and bestowed upon it the title *Common Sense.* Only independence, in Rush's judgment, would enable Americans to free themselves from "European luxuries and vices."[2]

The concerns Rush expressed as an American patriot were rooted in the Great Awakening. Like many men of the Revolution, he had grown up in an era of intense religious ferment and in a society which felt the charismatic power of preachers like Jonathan Edwards and George Whitefield. The influence of the Great Awakening upon young Rush was direct. As a boy he had attended the Reverend Samuel Finley's boarding school in Nottingham, Maryland. One of the Awakeners of the 1740s, Reverend Finley taught his students to struggle against the corruptions and temptations of the world, and inculcated in them the values of industry and thrift. Finley's impact upon Rush was profound. Many years after he had left the school, Rush reviewed the time spent under Reverend Finley's tutelage, and regretted he did not take greater advantage of the opportunities for literary and moral instruction available to him. He felt guilty about having allowed hunting and other amusements to undermine his interest in study. As a teacher, Finley used guilt and shame to punish his students. On one occasion Rush saw him "spend half an hour in exposing the folly and wickedness of an offence with his rod in his hand. The culprit stood all this while trembling and weeping before him. After he had ended his admonitions, he lifted his rod as high as he could and then permitted it to fall gently upon his hand. The boy was surprised at this conduct. 'There go about your business (said the doctor). I mean *shame* and not *pain* in the present instance.'"[3] To young Rush, the incident vividly illustrated the importance of self-control and self-punishment: Elevated to authority, the conscience would rule and inflict guilt upon the wayward individual.

After graduation from the Nottingham Academy in 1759, Rush entered the College of New Jersey, where he came under the influence of its president, the Reverend Samuel Davies. Known as the Father of the Presbyterian Church in Virginia, Davies had been one of the leading preachers of the Great Awakening. In his baccalaureate sermon, President Davies instructed Rush and his fellow students that they could never be great and good men unless they had a regenerated spirit and a new heart. Theirs must be an inner purity; otherwise it would be better for them to be "Hottentots" or even "the most abject and miserable creatures among the meanest and most noxious of the brutal tribes, than to be the sons of NASSAU HALL." The sermon was such a moving experience for Rush that he thought it deserved "to be printed in letters of gold in every young candidate's heart." Shortly after the death of Reverend Davies in February 1761, Rush cried out to fellow student Enoch Green: "Oh, my friend, you and I have lost a father, a friend. He was the bright source of advice and consolation, the focus of every earthly virtue, and alas he bore too much of the Divine image—he had too much of the spirit of the inhabitants of Heaven to be a long sojourner here on Earth. He labored fast—and soon finished his worldly task. Oh, it is an example worthy of imitation."[4]

Rush carried the moral fervor of the Great Awakening forward into the American Revolution. On the eve of the war, he worried about the widespread presence of sin and sensuality in the colonies; he saw vice and profanity prevailing in his town of Philadelphia and young men wholly devoted to pleasure. Throughout the war, Rush wondered whether Americans possessed the virtue required to establish the new moral society. Like John Adams, he hoped the war itself would serve to punish and purge Americans, making them a virtuous people. "My faith is now stronger than ever," he wrote his wife in September 1776. "I begin to hear with pleasure an outcry among some people that there is no independence to be had upon the arm of flesh. But the worst is not over—We must be brought lower. I predict a defeat or another disgraceful retreat. We stand in need of it." Rush feared an early peace would be the "greatest curse" that could happen to them. "Liberty without virtue would be no blessing to us," he wrote to John Adams in August 1777 as General Howe's campaign pressed toward Philadelphia. "It will require one or two more campaigns to purge away the monarchical impurity we contracted by laying so long upon the lap of Great Britain." The war should last until it had reestablished among Americans "the same temperance in pleasure, the same modesty in dress, the same justice in business, and the same veneration for the name of the Deity which distinguished our ancestors." The liberty of Americans was being threatened from within, for they had more to dread from the ambition, avarice, and dissolute manners of the Whigs than from the rule of the Tories. Rush insisted that virtue alone was the basis of a republic, and warned his fellow Americans to beware of their own venality, idleness, and desire for luxury. Even after the peace, Rush continued to press for the moral reformation of American society. "There is nothing more common than to confound the terms of the American Revolution with those of the late American war," he declared in January 1787. "The American war is over; but this is far from being the case with the American revolution. On the contrary, nothing but the first act of the great drama is closed. . . . The temple of tyranny has two doors. We bolted one of them by proper restraints; but we left the other open, by neglecting to guard against the effects of our own ignorance and licentiousness."⁵ Until men had been made virtuous, the American Revolution would not be completed.

Neither, Rush feared, would republicanism survive or succeed in the newly independent America. Ironically his introduction to republicanism did not occur in America but in Scotland; in 1767, studying medicine at the University of Edinburgh, he met a student, John Bostock. During their conversations, Bostock declared himself an advocate of republicanism. "Never before had I heard the authority of Kings called in question," Rush reported. "I had been taught to consider them nearly as essential to political order as the Sun is to the order of our Solar System. For the first moment in my life I now exercised my reason upon the subject of government. I renounced the prejudices of my education upon it; and from that time to the present all my reading, observations and reflexions have tended more and more to shew the absurdity of hereditary power, and to prove that no form of government can be rational but that which is derived from the suffrages of the people. . . ."⁶ It seemed to Rush that an order which had always existed was falling apart. Nine years later, the Declaration of Independence gave political expression to this disintegration of the traditional hierarchy, and established a government whose power, theoretically, was to be derived from the people.

Yet Rush had little faith in the people. "Our own citizens," he cautioned four years after the end of the war, "act a still more absurd part, when they cry out, after the experience of three or four years, that we are not proper materials for republican government. Remember, we assumed these forms of government in a hurry, before we were prepared for them. Let every man exert himself in promoting virtue and knowledge in our country, and we shall soon become good republicans." The chaos he witnessed in the mid-1780s emphasized the need to create a virtuous American people capable of self-control and self-discipline. "Is not history as full of the vices of the people as it is of the crimes of kings?" asked Rush in 1787. "What is the present moral character of the citizens of the United States? I need not describe it. It proves too plainly that the people are as much disposed to vice as their rulers, and that nothing but a vigorous and efficient government can prevent their degenerating into savages. . . ."[7]

But the virtue of the people, Rush believed, could only come from within; his zeal for the reformation of society sprang from a reformed self. His own life was one of formidable self-discipline. "From the time of my settlement in Philadelphia in 1769 'til 1775," he wrote in his *Autobiography*, "I led a life of constant labor and self-denial. . . .While my days were thus employed in business, my evenings were devoted to study." His time was to be calculated and utilized. "I lost no time in my own house. The scraps of time which interposed between the hour I returned from visiting my patients and the time of eating, I spent in light reading, or answering letters, or such pieces of business as required but little abstraction of mind." Even relationships with women, however pleasurable they might be, had to be "self-denied." As a young man, Rush found himself responsible for supporting his recently widowed sisters and their children, and he had to postpone marriage. Thus he gave up Mary Fisher, who he later said was the only woman he had ever loved. Although he eventually did marry and have children, Rush was determined that no woman would tempt him into matrimony until he had extended his studies so far that a family would not impede his further progress. Yet he was not always able to control his emotions. As a student at Edinburgh, Rush fell in love with Lady Jane Leslie. While visiting her at Melville, he wrote to a friend: "I cannot tell when I shall return to Edinburgh. My attachment to Melville grows stronger day by day. —how insipid are all Lectures and Studies when set in Competition with the *pleasures* of *Friendship*. . . ." There had been times when Rush was not able to deny sexual pleasure. In his *Autobiography*, he confessed that the early part of his life had been spent in dissipation, folly, and the vices to which young men were prone. In "tears and sighs before God," he deplored his wickedness: "It was from deep and affecting sense of one of them that I was first led to seek the favor of God in his Son in the

21st year of my age. It was thus the woman of Samaria was brought to a repentance of all her sins by the Son of God reminding her of but one of them, viz. her living criminally with a man who was not her husband." This confession, made again some thirty years after Rush had slept with a married woman, revealed how mightily the guilt burdened his conscience. In an earlier reference to the woman of Samaria, Rush had admitted to a close friend in 1766: "One particular *sin* lay heavy upon my conscience, which brought to my *view all the things that I ever did.*"[8]

Like Finley and Davies before him, Rush believed men must develop self-control, and this applied with even greater force in a world without a king, in the new society of the Revolution. Because the source of authority was now located within the individual, men must be converted into what Rush called "republican machines." In "An Address to the Ministers of the Gospel of Every Denomination in the United States, upon subjects interesting to morals," delivered in 1788, Rush described how people should conduct their lives in a republican society. Their paramount concern should be self-restraint and control over the passions and the demands of the instinctual life. In a list of activities to be repressed in a republic, Rush called for the elimination of fairs, horse racing, cockfighting, and "clubs of all kinds, where the business of the company is feeding (for that is the true name of gratification that is simply animal)." Play should be prohibited on Sundays. "Amusements of every kind, on Sundays, beget habits of idleness and a love of pleasure, which extend their influence to every day of the week." Sunday should be a day of rest to "wind up" the "machine" of both body and soul, and invigorate it for the labor and duty of the week ahead. Spirituous liquors were especially dangerous and had to be denied. They stimulated the appetites and rendered the temper "peevish and passionate"; they were the "parents of idleness and extravagance, and the certain forerunners of poverty, and frequently of jails . . . and the gallows." As he concluded his address, Rush echoed Puritan leader John Winthrop in republican language: "America has taught the nations of Europe to be free, and it is to be hoped she will soon teach them to govern themselves."[9] America would be a republican City upon a Hill, where men would triumph over the "animal" within them and prove to the watching world they could be self-governing.

How were men to be made into republicans? Rush delineated three ways by which this objective could be accomplished: education, motherhood, and medicine. In his recommendation for the establishment of a general and uniform system of education, Rush said schools would render the mass of people "more homogeneous" and thus "fit them more easily for uniform and peaceful government." Schools would teach children republican principles and duties of "industry" and "economy," and lead them toward the pursuit of business and wealth. The poor, especially, would have to be educated in a republican society. Foreshadowing nineteenth-century educators like Horace Mann, Rush argued: "The children of poor people form a great proportion of all communities. Their ignorance and vices when neglected are not confined to themselves; they associate with and contaminate the children of persons in the higher ranks of society. Thus they assist after they arrive at manhood in choosing the rulers who govern the whole community. They give a complexion to the morals and manners of the people." But once the poor and Americans in general had been properly educated and converted into "republican machines," they would "perform their parts properly, in the great machine of the government of the state."[10] Here, indeed, was an awesome way to produce a virtuous people.

The education of children, in Rush's view, would take place in the home as well as the school. The home was the domain of women; thus women were particularly important in the early education of children. "From the numerous avocations to which a professional life exposes gentlemen in America from their families," Rush wrote, "a principle share of the instruction of children naturally devolves upon the women." Clearly, as mothers, women had to be enlisted in the great cause. "The first impressions upon the minds of children are generally derived from the women." In a republican society, mothers had a particular responsibility for the education of their sons, for they would grow up to be the citizens and shareholders of the government.[11]

The making of republicans would take place not only in schools and the home but also in hospitals and the asylum. Medicine, for Rush, was the most important means by which men could be reformed, for it involved more than the mere care for the body. At first Rush considered medicine less important than the ministry. In a letter to a friend, written shortly after he had entered the study of medicine in 1761, he pointed out what he thought was the crucial difference between medicine and the ministry. The doctor attended the body—"this earthly frame . . . forever subject to Diseases and Death"—while the minister worked to heal the sickness of "a Soul immortal and everlasting." As a doctor, however, Rush began to view the body and soul as closely related, and he soon realized how medicine could serve as a surrogate ministry. "If the moral faculty can be injured by physical causes," he asked in 1774, "may it not be improved by the same means? . . . May not . . . a medicine be discovered which shall improve, or alter the diseased state of the moral faculty?" The possibilities medicine offered were breathtaking to Rush. "Perhaps hereafter it may be as much the business of a physician as it is now of a divine to reclaim mankind from vice."[12]

In 1786, Dr. Rush further developed his views on the interrelationship between the body and soul, health and virtue, in his "Inquiry into the Influence of Physical Causes upon the Moral Faculty." In this paper read to the American Philosophical Society, Rush argued that control of both the environment and influences on the body was the key to dominating the moral faculty—the ability to disintinguish and choose between virtue and vice. If the body were put to physical labor, even a vicious man could be reformed. The workhouses of all civilized countries had proven that labor was one of the most suitable means of reformation. Idleness was the parent of every vice, and labor favored and facilitated the practice of virtue. Cleanliness of the body also promoted virtue. Rush reported how leprosy was noted to be related to the lack of hygiene and "a dirty skin." For Rush, the importance of the body's relationship to virtue required that the cultivation of the moral faculty be the responsibility of physicians as well as ministers. "From the combined actions of causes, which operate at once upon the reason, the moral faculty, the passions, the senses, the brain, the nerves, the blood, and the heart," Dr. Rush declared, "it is possible to produce such a change in [man's] moral character, as shall raise him to a resemblance of angels; nay, more, to the likeness of GOD himself." For Rush, medicine was the way to moral perfection, and the physician represented a new priesthood.[13]

Ready to reform mankind, Dr. Rush focused his attention on the treatment of the insane, and was placed in charge of the mental patients at the Pennsylvania Hospital in 1787. In a letter to a friend, Rush wrote: "I have lately obtained exclusive care of the maniacal patients in our hospital. They amount at present to 34." His letter also contained references to his hopes for the realization of the goals of the American Revolution, education in the new republic, the use of solitude and work to punish as well as reform criminals, and the bright future awaiting the nation. Rush devoted the rest of his life to the care of the insane, and summed up a quarter century of work in a voluminous book entitled *Medical Inquiries and Observations upon the Diseases of the Mind.*[14]

In his work in the asylum and in his book, Rush related "diseases of the mind" to all other diseases of the human body. To the doctor, the mind and the body were moved by the same causes and subject to the same laws. In his diagnosis, Rush viewed illness in strikingly republican terms: Sickness was the consequence of vices such as idleness, intemperance, and the loss of self-control over the appetites of the instinctual life, especially sexuality. "This appetite, which was implanted in our natures for the purposes of propagating our species, when excessive, becomes a disease of both the body and mind," the doctor noted. The results of sexual excess, Rush warned, were horrible. Promiscuous intercourse or masturbation produced "seminal weakness, impotence, dysury, tabes dorsalis, pulmonary consumption, hypochrondriasis, loss of memory, manalgia, fatuity, and death."[15]

In Dr. Rush's opinion, the most fearful excess was masturbation. "The morbid effects of intemperance in sexual intercourse with women are feeble, and of a transient nature, compared with the train of physical and moral evils which this solitary vice fixes upon the body and mind." Here, in this "solitary vice" was the ultimate loss of self-control. In *Diseases of the Mind,* Dr. Rush listed several remedies for the problems of masturbation and an "inordinate sexual appetite." They included: "matrimony; but where this is not practicable, the society of chaste and modest women"; proper diet; temperance in drinking; "constant employment in bodily labour or exercise"; "a salivation, by diverting morbid excitability from the genitals to the mouth and throat"; and "close application of the mind to business, or study of any kind, more especially to the mathematics."[16]

As the most direct remedies for mental diseases, Dr. Rush prescribed purging and bloodletting—techniques he and many physicians employed in the treatment of physical illnesses. Purging or "artificial diarrhoea" acted as a "depleting" remedy in the "tonic state of madness"; in "manalgia" it did "good by exciting a revulsive action or disease, in a less delicate part of the body than the brain." Bloodletting was even more effective. Rush instructed that bleeding should be "copious" on the first attack of the disease: "From 20 to 40 ounces of blood may be taken at once, unless fainting be induced before that quantity be drawn. . . . The effects of this early and copious bleeding are wonderful in calming mad people. . . . [And] sometimes it cures in a few hours." To facilitate the treatment of his patients, Dr. Rush invented the "tranquilizer"—a chair with straps for the patient's hands and feet, a device for holding his head in a fixed position, and a container beneath the seat to receive excreta. The "tranquilizer" enabled the physician, Rush proudly proclaimed, to feel the pulse and to open a vein from a single arm without relieving any other part of the body from its confinement; it also allowed him to "administer purgative medicines without subjecting the patient to the necessity of being moved from his chair or exposing him afterwards to the fetor of his excretions or to their contact with his body."[17]

For Dr. Rush, the asylum at the Pennsylvania Hospital was a testing ground to determine whether medicine could make men virtuous. One

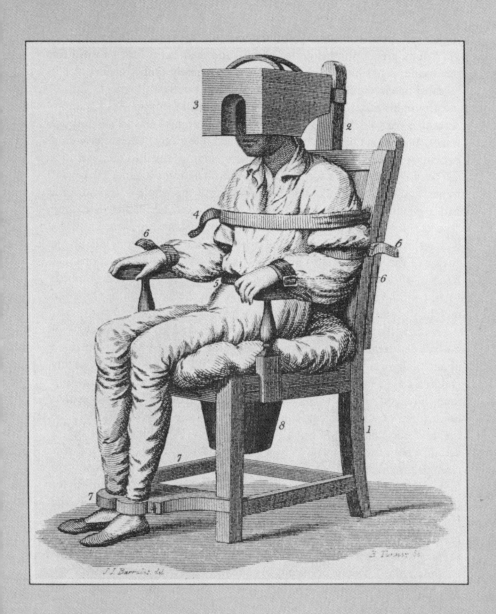

Rush's "Tranquilizer"

subject of his experiments in reforming men was his own son John. Born in 1777, John grew up in his father's house and died in his father's ward for the insane. What happened to John was not merely family history, for it revealed much about Dr. Rush's medicine and politics.

Early in his life, John became the focus of his father's special attention. As a nine-year-old, he accompanied the doctor on his visits to the hospital wards, and on one of these occasions, he had a terrifying encounter with a patient. According to Dr. Rush, a young woman chained to the floor in a cell tearfully asked John for a potato which he had in his hand. He gave it to her, and she "instantly filled her mouth with the whole of it, and for a half a minute it seemed as if it would have choked her." "Petrified" and "speechless," John did not recover from this shocking experience until he had sat down in a chair; then he asked his father questions about the "cause of the poor woman's madness." After answering his questions, Dr. Rush told his son that he seemed "devoted to physic," and John replied: "Yes, I will be nothing but a doctor." All of this the doctor/father reported to John's mother with obvious pleasure and pride.[18]

Significantly, Rush's treatment of his patients and his "management" of his own children had a striking and frightening similarity. Much is revealed about both in a letter to Enos Hitchcock: "In the management of my children I have made two discoveries. 1st, That it is as necessary to *reward* them for good as it is to *punish* them for bad actions. Nay further, that *rewards* are of immense consequence in stimulating them to industry, virtue, and good manners." Equally important was punishment, but only a certain kind of punishment. "2ly, I have discovered that all corporal corrections for children above three or four years old are highly improper and that *solitude* is the most effective punishment that can be contrived for them." Dr. Rush knew this from experience: He had employed it in the home. "I have used it for many years in my family with the greatest success." Then referring to John, he added: "My eldest son, who is now 12 years old, has more than once begged me to flog him in preference to confining him." On one occasion, he confined John in a room for two days. The impression which this punishment left upon him, Rush observed, "will never wear away, nor do I think it will ever require to be repeated." Indeed, "too much cannot be said in favor of SOLITUDE as a means of reformation, which should be the *only* end of *all* punishment. Men are wicked only from not thinking. . . . [A] whipping post, nay even a gibbet, are all light punishments compared with letting a man's conscience loose upon him in solitude. . . . A bad man should be left for some time without anything to employ his hands in his confinement. Every thought should recoil wholly upon himself."[19] In the management of his children and patients, Dr. Rush drew from the lessons of Reverend Finley and the Nottingham school.

Like his father, John attended Princeton University; he did not take a degree, however, and enrolled as a medical apprentice to Dr. Rush in September 1794. Two years later, he gave up his apprenticeship and sailed to Calcutta, carrying with him a letter from his father which warned him to avoid temptations and "youthful lusts." He was back in Philadelphia a year later and became his father's principal assistant. Shortly after a quarrel with one of Dr. Rush's medical critics, John left home again and served as a lieutenant in the United States Navy. He resigned in 1802, and on December 11, Rush recorded in his diary: "This day my son John resumed the study of medicine. So anxious was he to return to my house and business that he said 'he would supply the place of one of my men servants, and even clean my stable rather than continue to follow a sea life.' "[20] Finally, he was, or so it seemed, fulfilling his vow to be "nothing but a doctor."

In 1804, John took his medical degree at the University of Pennsylvania, dedicating his dissertation to his father. But then he turned down an appointment at the Pennsylvania General Hospital and reentered the Navy as a sailing master. In New Orleans in 1807, he fought a duel with a friend and killed him; three years later, Dr. Rush wrote in his diary: "This day my son John Rush arrived from New Orleans in a state of deep melancholy brought on by killing a brother officer in the Navy. . . . Neither the embraces nor tears of his parents, brothers, or sister could prevail upon him to speak to them. His grief and uncombed hair and long beard added to the distress produced by the disease of his mind." Three days later, "unsuccessful" in his effort to make his son "alter his appearance," Dr. Rush had John hospitalized in his ward for the mentally diseased. Many months later, Dr. Rush wrote to Thomas Jefferson: "My son is better. He has become attentive to his dress, now and then opens a book, converses with a few people, but still discourses, with a good deal of melancholy, alienation of mind upon several subjects, particularly those which associate with the cause of his derangement. He is now in a cell in the Pennsylvania Hospital, where there is too much reason to believe he will end his days."[21] As it turned out, John died there, remaining in his father's ward for twenty-seven years.

In the hospital's ward for the insane, Dr. Rush was carrying forward the American Revolution. His ferocious determination to re-form his patients, including his own son, would have little significance for our analysis had it been a mere exercise in peevishness. His dedicated labor in the asylum had instead a highly political purpose: It constituted a formidable integration of the struggle for independence from the king, the Great Awakening teachings of Finley and Davies, the republican ideology of the Revolution, and the study and practice of medicine. A doctor, Rush had ordained himself to make men resemble "angels," even God himself. For the "Father of American Psychiatry," all the world was a "hospital," and his own asylum in Philadelphia was a laboratory where he could manufacture a virtuous people for a republican society.[22]

The "Lovely White"

Yet, as a republican theoretician and doctor of medicine, Rush felt compelled to grapple with a perplexing problem: How could the new republican society, requiring a homogeneous and virtuous people, include blacks? Or, could blacks become republicans? Here were questions that demanded attention from whites as Americans and that would loom increasingly large in the country's future.[23]

In his response to these racial concerns, Rush recognized what Franklin had already noted and what was obvious to whites in the new nation: America was a tri-racial society. Thus, for Rush, the question of race in America could not avoid the problem of the presence of "Tawneys." Relating his interest in the natives of America to his medical research, Rush referred to Indians in his writings and examined them in his study of "diseases of the mind." What impressed Rush was his failure to find "a single instance of MADNESS, MELANCHOLY, or FATUITY among the Indians." He also noted that Indians had weak "venereal desires" due to their involvement in hunting and other invigorating activities, and that they lacked envy due to equality of power and property in their society. Still, Rush observed, vices were widespread among them. "UNCLEANNESS" was a characteristic of "savages." Indians were also "strangers to the obligations both of morality and decency, as far as they relate to the marriage bed." "Nastiness" was yet another vice among them, exemplified in their "food—drinks—persons—and above all, in their total disregard for decency in the *time—place—*and *manner* of their natural evacuations." The "universal" vice of savages was "IDLENESS": Indians were not only "too lazy to work, but even to think." Claiming that Indian taciturnity was a mark of stupidity, Rush wrote: "Ideas, whether acquired from books, or by reflection, produce a plethora in the mind, which can only be relieved by depletion from the pen, or tongue." Moreover, due to his lack of temperance, the Indian had no future in America; thus Rush predicted:

The mortality peculiar to those Indian tribes who have mingled with the white people, must be ascribed to the extensive mischief of spirituous liquors. . . . It does not become us to pry too much into futurity; but if we may judge from the fate of the original natives of Hispaniola, Jamaica, and the provinces on the continent, we may venture to foretell, that, in proportion as the white people multiply, the Indians will diminish; so that in a few centuries they will probably be entirely extirpated.[24]

Rush did not apply this grim forecast to blacks: Unlike Indians, blacks had a future in America and would not eventually be "extirpated." Indeed, Rush was a critic of slavery and believed blacks had the potential for republican virtue. In his *Address to the Inhabitants of the British Settlements in America upon Slave-Keeping*, written in 1773 to support a Pennsylvania bill designed to prohibit the African slave trade, Rush insisted that blacks were not inferior to whites in their intellectual ability and capacity for virtue. Slavery, their social environment, was the cause of their inferiority. "Slavery is so foreign to the human mind," he argued, "that the moral faculties, as well as those of understanding are debased, and rendered torpid by it. All the vices which are charged upon the negroes in the southern colonies . . . such as Idleness, Treachery, Theft, and the like, are the genuine offspring of slavery. . . ." The black color of their skin, he added, should not subject and did not qualify them for slavery. Rush went on to offer a plan for the gradual abolition of the institution. All blacks who had already acquired vices would remain in bondage, while all young blacks would be educated in the principles of virtue and religion, taught to read and write, and instructed in business in order to enable them to maintain themselves. Laws would be enacted to limit the time of their servitude and entitle them to all the privileges of freeborn British subjects.[25] Within the context of American independence and the new republican society, emancipation would involve the conversion of blacks along with whites into "republican machines."

During these years of conflict between England and the American colonies, Rush viewed black emancipation in relation to the general struggle against the "monster of British tyranny." "A spirit of liberty and religion with regard to the poor negroes," he observed in 1773, "spreads rapidly thro' this country. Providence I hope is at work in bringing about some great revolution in behalf of our oppressed negro brethren." The practitioner of bleeding and purging, Rush described the abolition of slavery in medical terms: "Perhaps America like a body weakened by a plentiful discharge of blood may revive in time, and resume her wonted vigor after she has been purged of Negro slavery." After the Continental Congress had adopted a resolution to prohibit the African slave trade, Rush wrote to

British abolitionist Granville Sharp in 1774: "We have now *turned from our wickedness.* Our next step we hope will be to do that *which is lawful and right.*" This would be the emancipation of slaves in America. "If the same spirit which now prevails in our counsels and among all ranks in every province, continues, I venture to predict there will not be a Negro slave in North America in 40 years." During the 1780s, Rush urged Americans to prohibit the African slave trade permanently and prepare for the eventual abolition of slavery. "For God's sake," he exclaimed to patriot general Nathanael Greene in 1782, "do not exhibit a new spectacle to the world, of men just emerging from a war in favor of liberty, with their clothes not yet washed from the blood which was shed in copious and willing streams in its defense, fitting out vessels to import their fellow creatures from Africa to reduce them afterwards to slavery."[26] Republican men, freed from the slavery of British tyranny, should not be slavemasters themselves. Rush's ideological commitment to abolition compelled him to manumit his own slave. In his *Autobiography,* he referred to William, "a native African whom I bought, and liberated after he had served me 10 years." In 1788 Rush made out manumission papers for William; he declared it was contrary to reason and religion to hold William in bondage beyond the amount of time which would give him a "just compensation" for the price of purchase. Rush finally freed him on February 25, 1794.[27]

Dr. Rush's hopes for the abolition of slavery and the eventual incorporation of blacks into republican society were raised when his medical research on the skin color of the Negro led him to an amazing observation. Before a special meeting of the American Philosophical Society on July 14, 1792, Rush presented his findings in a paper entitled "Observations intended to favour a supposition that the black Color (as it is called) of the Negroes is derived from the LEPROSY." Based on his medical analysis, Dr. Rush prescribed an interim separation of the races in order to achieve a greater good for both races.

In a sober and scholarly manner, Dr. Rush offered "observations" intended to "prove" that the "color" and "figure" of Negroes were derived from a "modification" of leprosy. He explained that a combination of factors—"unwholesome diet," "greater heat," "more savage manners," and "bilious fevers"— probably produced leprosy in the skin among blacks in Africa. Despite their condition of leprosy, blacks were as healthy and long-lived as whites, he claimed, for local diseases of the skin seldom affected general health or the duration of life. The more visible symptoms of leprosy were the Negro's physical features—the "big lip," "flat nose," "woolly hair," and especially the black color of his skin. Negroes, Dr. Rush said, had many qualities which lepers possessed. Like them, Negroes had a "morbid insensitivity of the nerves." As an example of the Negro's ability to disregard pain, Rush cited a Dr. Moseley's claim that he had amputated the legs of many Negroes while they held the upper part of the limbs. Moreover, Rush claimed, like lepers, Negroes had remarkably strong venereal desires. "This is universal among the negroes, hence their uncommon fruitfulness when they are not depressed by slavery; but even slavery in its worse state does not always subdue the venereal appetite, for after whole days spent in hard labor in a hot sun in the West Indies, the black men often walk five or six miles to comply with a venereal assignation." This was something Dr. Rush could not imagine healthy or white men doing.[28]

Commenting on the infectious quality of leprosy, Dr. Rush explained that the disease among Negroes had to a great extent ceased to be infectious. He pointed out, however, that there were cases in which something like an infectious quality had appeared, and that it was possible for whites to be infected. "A white woman in North Carolina not only acquired a dark color, but several of the features of a negro, by marrying and living with a black husband. A similar instance of a change in the color and features of a woman in Buck's county in Pennsylvania has been observed and from a similar cause. In both these cases, the women bore children by their black husbands." Dr. Rush failed to mention whether there were instances of white men acquiring Negroid features from cohabitation with black women.[29]

After the presentation of these "facts," Dr. Rush proceeded to draw three conclusions:

> 1. That all the claims of superiority of the whites over the blacks, on account of their color, are founded alike in ignorance and inhumanity. If the color of the negroes be the effect of a disease, instead of inviting us to tyrannise over them, it should entitle them to a double portion of our humanity, for disease all over the world has always been the signal for immediate and universal compassion.

For Dr. Rush, all mankind must be viewed as "patients" in a "hospital," and the "diseased" and sick Negro deserved special concern and compassion.[30]

Compassion, yes, but not contact, Dr. Rush warned in his second conclusion. He had already given whites an implicit warning: Contact could result in infection as the cases cited had shown. And the doctor had to make clear the threat whites faced in a biracial society.

> 2. The facts and principles which have been delivered, should teach white people the necessity of keeping up that prejudice against such connections with them [Negroes], as would tend to infect posterity with any portion of their

disorder. This may be done upon the ground I have mentioned without offering violence to humanity, or calling in question the sameness of descent, or natural equality of mankind.[31]

Thus, as a physician, Rush was in effect prescribing physical separation between whites and blacks, specifically the avoidance of interracial sexual relations, in order to contain this infectious disease.

Once Dr. Rush had defined the black color of the Negro's skin as a disease, he was confident the problem of race could be solved: It simply required a cure.

3. Is the color of the negroes a disease? Then let science and humanity combine their efforts, and endeavour to discover a remedy for it. Nature has lately unfurled a banner upon this subject. She has begun spontaneous cures of this disease in several black people in this country. In a certain Henry Moss . . . the cure was nearly complete. The change from black to a *natural* white flesh began about five years ago at the ends of his fingers, and has extended gradually over the greatest part of his body.[32]

Here, then, was reason for optimism. The "diseased" Negro, as the case of Henry Moss had revealed, could be spontaneously "cured," and his black skin restored to its "natural" and "healthy" whiteness.

But, as a man of "science" and as a doctor, Rush refused to wait and let nature take its course, and he recommended the use of "artificial attempts to dislodge the color in negroes." The doctor had to take command; the improvement of mankind had to be accelerated. Curiously, the "artificial" methods Dr. Rush proposed to "cure" and whiten Negroes resembled the prescriptions he used for the treatment of his patients suffering from "diseases of the mind." Physical labor was one helpful method, for it could facilitate the discharge of the black color from their skin. In the case of Henry Moss, Dr. Rush observed, "the color was first discharged from the skin in those places, on which there was most pressure from cloathing, and most attrition from labor, as on the trunk of his body, and on his fingers. The destruction of the Black color was probably occasioned by the absorption of the coloring matter of the rete mucosum" because pressure and friction had aided "the absorbing action of the lymphatics in every part of the body." A more direct method, however, was available. "Depletion, whether by bleeding, purging, or abstinence has been often observed to lessen the black color in negroes. The effects of the above remedies in curing the common leprosy, satisfy me that they might be used with advantage in that state of leprosy which I conceive to exist in the skin of negroes."[33] Since bloodletting and "artificial diarrhoea" worked effectively to cure patients afflicted with physical as well as mental diseases, it seemed logical to Dr. Rush to prescribe them to cure Negroes.

In a way, Dr. Rush could have regarded his paper as a singular triumph. Ever since the seventeenth century, a need to explain the Negro's black skin had existed in white America, and the notion that the Negro was a descendant of Ham and carried God's curse in his color had not been an altogether plausible or satisfying explanation. While Rush could not claim that his audience found his "explanation" any more satisfactory, he could congratulate himself for bringing together his concerns over slavery, race, and color. Under his direction, science had become a tool of humanitarianism. In his analysis, he had advanced an argument for abolitionism. Thus, he could feel he had done more than Princeton Professor Stanley Stanhope Smith. The author of *Essay on Variety,* published in 1787, Smith had contended that the black skin of the Negro was a "universal freckle" resulting from the greater heat in the areas near the equator and from the "savage" conditions of life in Africa. Rush had taken Smith's environmentalist explanation one step further—and in a medical direction: Heat and "savage" conditions produced leprosy. Once Rush had defined black skin as a disease, he could boldly announce the astonishing possibilities medicine held out to society. "To encourage attempts to cure this disease of the skin of negroes," he declared, "let us recollect that by succeeding in them, we shall produce a large portion of happiness in the world." Not only would the cure of Negroes destroy arguments of their inferiority, which provided a basis for the justification of slavery, it would also add to their happiness. However well Negroes appeared to be satisfied with their color, Rush contended, they "preferred" to have the color of white people.[34] Indeed, due to the wonderful magic of medicine, a harmonious future awaited all mankind.

Yet Dr. Rush did not expect the restoration of the Negro's health to happen soon. Meanwhile, he recognized that his diagnosis actually reinforced "the existing prejudices against matrimonial connections" between whites and blacks. What seemed to be required was an interim separation of the two races until the disease could be "cured." To place "diseased" Negroes in hospitals, as he had done with the sick and the insane, was out of the question for Dr. Rush. Such a massive institutionalization would have been impracticable. Still he felt some kind of physical isolation for blacks was necessary. Significantly, after he had delivered his paper on leprosy and the Negro, he developed an increasing interest in plans to colonize blacks within the United States. One of his suggestions was to offer ten thousand or more acres for sale on moderate credit terms to blacks trained in agriculture. "The attraction of color and country is such that I think the offer would succeed," he stated, "and thereby a precedent be established for colonizing, in time, all the Africans in our country." In a letter to the president of the Pennsylvania Abolitionist Society, Rush proposed a plan for the establishment of a black farming community in Bedford County. The plan specified that each individual or family be granted a portion of land in fee simple not to exceed fifty acres, that one tract be reserved for the support of schools and churches, and that "no sale shall be made of a farm by the owner of it but to a black and an actual resident or cultivator of the soil."[35] Here was a restricted covenant: Whites would not be allowed to purchase land and live in this community. Such a colony, in Rush's view, would provide an asylum where blacks, separated from whites, could be educated and "cured," and render unnecessary what Thomas Jefferson believed was imperative—the removal of all blacks from America.

For Rush, the abolition of slavery and the establishment of black colonies would be part of a general reformation. The concern for a morally pure republican society, which he shared with Franklin, Paine, John and Samuel Adams, and other patriot leaders, was at the center of all of Rush's political, humanitarian, and medical activities. As a fervent American Revolutionary and republican theoretician, Rush was demanding no less than the reformation of all segments of society in America. He believed the possibility of "perfection" existed in this country. In America, he confidently claimed, everything was in a "plastic state," and "here the benefactor of mankind may realize all his schemes for promoting human happiness." And he believed he had the scheme once he had defined "virtue" as "health" and "vice" as "sickness," and had pulled away the shrouds of mystery surrounding the human condition, uncovering the body as the object to be regulated and reformed or "cured."[36] Once the problem had been reduced to the body, the doctor had the solution.

The reformation, for Rush, had to include blacks. If blacks could be emancipated, America—"like a body weakened by a plentiful discharge of blood"—would be "purged" of slavery and restored to "vigor." If they could be civilized and "cured," the future of the republic seemed hopeful. The entire society would be whitened; the people of the new nation would become "more homogeneous." Domination over "animal gratification" would prevail throughout the population. Blacks in a "cured" condition would be able to subdue their "venereal appetite"; like whites, they would be able to control the instinctual life pulsating beneath the surface of republican order, to become self-governing men, or "republican machines." While Rush failed to convince white society to set up colonies in America for the "cure" of blacks, he reflected not only white prejudices against blacks as abnormal and deviant (white as "lovely" and "natural") but also the anxious need for white Americans to become a virtuous people.

To be virtuous, for Rush, was to realize Protestant and bourgeois activity and success—"industry," "economy," business, and wealth. To make men so in a world without a king, where external authority had been destroyed and in a republican society where the self had to govern, everyone—blacks in colonies and whites in homes, schools, and asylums—had to be reformed. The culture of republicanism had to be hegemonic in American society. Required to be virtuous, the people had to elevate their consciences into guilt-inflicting authorities; they could not be allowed to be "Hottentots" or "degenerate" into "savages." Like Rush, they had to be worthy "sons of NASSAU HALL," the possessors of an inner purity. "Liberty without virtue," Rush exclaimed a year after he had signed the Declaration of Independence, "would be no blessing to us." No irony was intended here. Determined to bring "the principles, morals and manners" of the people into conformity with republican society, Rush was deadly serious when he proclaimed three years after the Treaty of Paris: "The Revolution is not over!" Many years later, he wrote to John Adams: "Were we to live our lives over again and engage in the same benevolent enterprise, our means should not be reasoning but bleeding, purging, low diet, and the tranquilizing chair."[37]

CHAPTER III

WITHIN THE "BOWELS"
OF THE REPUBLIC

While an enemy is within our bowels, the first object is to expel him.
              —Thomas Jefferson,
                   Notes on the State of Virginia

As he called for the expulsion of the British "enemy" from the "bowels" of the emerging nation, Jefferson used rhetoric strikingly similar to the language of Dr. Rush to express his concern for moral purity in the new republican society. His role in the overthrow of the king and the removal of the British had been even more crucial than Rush's: While the doctor had helped Paine write *Common Sense,* Jefferson had authored the Declaration of Independence. Many years after the British had been forced out, President Jefferson told James Monroe that he looked forward to distant times when the American continent would be covered with "a people speaking the same language, governed in similar forms, and by similar laws." Beneath this vision of America's future, which would shortly lead him to expand the republican nation through the purchase of the Louisiana, lay a rage for order, tidiness, and uniformity which made him recoil with horror from the possibility of "either blot or mixture on that surface."[1] The purging of the British only created greater pressures to expel other "enemies" from within the "bowels" of American society, as we shall see in an analysis of Jefferson's republican ideology, his insistence on black colonization, and his views on the assimilation of the Indian. Impinging on all three areas was his concept of the moral sense.

Head over Heart

During the Revolution, Jefferson tried to explain to the Indians what the war meant to white Americans. "Our forefathers were Englishmen, inhabitants of a little island beyond the great water, and being distressed for land, they came and settled here," he told the chief of the Kaskaskias. "As long as we were young and weak, the English . . . made us carry all our wealth to their country, to enrich them; and, not satisfied with this, they at length began to say we were their slaves. . . . We were now grown up and felt ourselves strong; we knew we were free as they were . . . and were determined to be free as long as we should exist." To be "free" involved more than independence. In their overthrow of the monarchy, Americans had to establish a republican government and to exercise republican self-rule. Indeed, Jefferson asserted, "every individual" who composed the mass of society must now participate in the "ultimate authority."[2]

Jefferson thought such responsibility both possible and imperative because of his belief in moral sense—a view he shared with eighteenth-century Scottish Common Sense philosophers. For Jefferson, man possessed the power of moral discernment, which enabled him to distinguish between right and wrong. This quality was inherent in man's nature, and it compelled him to do what was right and to feel a "love for others" and "a sense of duty to them." Moral sense was the "something" man felt "within" him, which told him what was wrong and ought not to be said or done. It was, in short, his "conscience." Moral sense operated in relation to the other faculties of the self. While it could, by itself, enable man to recognize justice and injustice, conscience relied on reason or the "head" to devise ways in which to respond to this moral awareness. And whether both moral sense and reason acted harmoniously depended to a significant extent on man's social environment—his relationship to his work, his community, and his physical surroundings.[3]

An environmentalist, Jefferson believed that the possibilities of achieving moral perfection were greatest in America, for the New World offered something Europe could not—an abundance of uncultivated land. Americans would remain "virtuous" as long as agriculture was their principal objective, and this would be the case as long as there were "vacant lands" in America. But, he warned, "when we get piled upon one another in large cities, as in Europe, we shall become corrupt as in Europe, and go to eating one another as they do there." Thus, the survival and success of republicanism required the preservation of America as an agrarian society. This view led him to write to Dr. Rush regarding disease and death in the cities. "When great evils happen, I am in the habit of looking out for what good may arise from them as consolations to us, and Providence has in fact so established the order of things, as that most evils are the means of producing some good. The yellow fever will discourage the growth of great cities in our nation, and I view great cities as pestilential to the morals, the health and the liberties of man." It is remarkable how easily in Jefferson's mind the cities themselves became a disease. Thus the environment had to be controlled and agriculture preserved as the way of life. In his comparison between America and Europe, agricultural utopia and industrial/urban society, Jefferson eloquently observed:

Those who labor in the earth are the chosen people of God, if ever He had a chosen people, whose breasts He has made His peculiar deposit for substantial and genuine virtue. . . . Corruption of morals in the mass of cultivators is a phenomenon of which no age nor nation has furnished an example. It is the mark set on those, who, not looking up to heaven, to their own soil and industry, as does the husbandman, for their subsistence, depend for it on casualties and caprice of customers. Dependence begets subservience and venality, suffocates the germ of virtue, and prepares fit tools for the designs of ambition. . . . [Let] our workshops remain in Europe. . . . The mobs of great cities add just so much to the support of pure government, as sores do to the strength of the human body.[4]

The agrarianism Jefferson advocated was derived not only from America's rejection of European urban society but also from Lockean theory, which was rebelling against European feudalism—the view of men as members of a community governed by traditional authority. Jefferson believed that men as free individuals labored on the land, transforming it into private property or extensions of themselves. This ownership of property would provide the basis of social stability and civilization, and would be particularly important in a republican society where men had to be self-governing. Jefferson made this clear in his comparison between the Old World and America. "Here every one, by his property, or by his satisfactory situation, is interested in the support of law and order. And such men may safely and advantageously reserve to themselves a wholesome control over their public affairs, and a degree of freedom, which, in the hands of the canaille of the cities of Europe, would be instantly perverted to the demolition and destruction of everything public and private."[5] The problem, for Jefferson, was that not everyone in America was a Lockean: Not everyone owned property and was interested in the support of "law and order."

Republicanism, in Jefferson's view, required a homogeneous population. Unless everyone could be converted into Lockeans or what Dr. Rush called "republican machines," the republic would surely disintegrate into anarchy. Like Dr. Rush, Jefferson believed peace with England did not mean the end of the Revolution. The people themselves still had to be made uniform and a consensus of values and interests established. This homogeneity might be achieved by discouraging the rapid increase of immigrants into the country. The members of the new republican nation, Jefferson wrote in *Notes on the State of Virginia,* must "harmonize" as much as possible in government where administration must be conducted by common consent. Immigrants, if they came from countries under the rule of absolute monarchies, would bring with them the principles of monarchy which they had "imbibed" in their early youth. And, if they were able to throw off those principles, they would do so "in exchange for an unbounded licentiousness." In proportion to their numbers, they would participate in the making of legislation and "infuse into it their spirit, warp and bias its direction, and render it a heterogeneous, incoherent, distracted mass."[6] Thus the new republic had to insulate itself from the Old World and keep out immigrants potentially capable of corrupting government in America.

But what should be done to render the people already here into a more "homogeneous" body? Like Rush, Jefferson placed much of his faith in education. Public schools must be established to diffuse knowledge more generally through the mass of the people, lay the principal foundations of future order, and instill into the minds of children the first elements of morality. Education must teach the masses how to work out their own greatest happiness by showing them that it did not depend on the condition of life in which chance had placed them but was always the result of a "good conscience, good health, occupation, and freedom in all just pursuits." Thus education would render the people—"the ultimate guardian of their own liberty"—independent and self-controlled.[7]

Such education was indispensable in a society where the people ruled. Unless they were properly educated and unless they were trained to restrain vigilantly their passions, they would constitute the greatest threat to order. Indeed, like the immigrants whom Jefferson feared, they could even explode into "unbounded licentiousness" and bring down the curtains of the new republic. After independence had been won, Jefferson noticed a "spirit of luxury" springing up, and he worried about whether his country-men would be able to maintain the self-denial and ascetic control which they had demonstrated during the war. Referring to "my extravagant countrymen," he urged them not to procrastinate in the "reformation" of American morality and conduct. He regretted how Americans in the new nation were accumulating debts and ruining themselves, and remembered how the Virginia farmer had been in a happy condition during the war. Blessed with a healthy occupation, reliant on the food he produced, and satisfied with ordinary apparel, the farmer had exercised great "self-denial" and postponed purchases until he could pay for them. Condemning the postwar extravagance as "a more baneful evil" than Toryism had been during the years of conflict, Jefferson impatiently exclaimed: "Would a missionary appear, who would make frugality the basis of his religious system, and go through the land, preaching it up as the only road to salva-tion, I would join his school. . . ." Jefferson even welcomed the destruction of American credit in Europe, for he could see nothing else which could restrain Americans' disposition to luxury and reform those manners neces-sary for the preservation of republican government.[8]

Such reformation required Americans to be industrious and active. A busy man, burdened with enormous responsibilities, Jefferson governed himself severely; like Rush, the Virginia planter devised rules to regulate conduct. "Determine never to be idle. No person will have occasion to complain of want of time, who never loses any. It is wonderful how much may be done, if we are always doing." If men acquired a habit of idleness and an inability to apply themselves to business, they were useless to them-selves and their country. Years before the publication of Dr. Rush's *Dis-eases of the Mind,* Jefferson had warned: "Of all the cankers of human happiness, none corrodes it with so silent, yet so baneful a tooth, as indo-lence. Body and mind both unemployed, our being becomes a burden. . . . Idleness begets ennui, ennui hypochondria, and that a diseased body. No laborious person was ever yet hysterical."[9]

Constantly pressing from below against the rule of reason, the passions had to be governed. For Jefferson, women represented a particularly dis-tressing threat to control and order. In his opposition to a European educa-tion for young American men, Jefferson warned that Americans studying abroad would acquire a fondness for European luxury and dissipation, and would be led by "the strongest of all human passions" into a "spirit for female intrigue" or a "passion for whores." Thus not only should immi-grants and other foreigners be kept out of America, but young men of the republic should be kept away from European women with their "voluptu-ary dress and arts." Jefferson described women in general as "objects of our pleasure," "formed by nature for attentions." Seductive, they never forgot "one of the numerous train of little offices" which belonged to them. He noticed that women in France, even while working, wore some tag of a ribbon to show that the desire to please men was never suspended in them. Thus, men must guard themselves against the "objects" of their "pleasure." How far Jefferson thought this vigilance must be extended may be seen in his remarks regarding the revision of legislation for the punishment of rape. "In the criminal law," he wrote to James Madison from Paris in 1786, "the principle of retaliation is much criticized here, particularly in the case of rape. They think the punishment [castration] indecent and unjustifiable. I should be for altering it, but for a different reason: that is on account of the temptation women would be under to make it the instrument of vengeance against an inconstant lover, and of a disappointment to a rival."[10] Thus, in the case of rape, as Jefferson viewed it, the real aggressor could be the woman.

Little wonder the behavior of women in Paris alarmed him. There the breakdown of distinct behavioral roles threatened to undermine self-control in relations between the sexes. Jefferson uncomfortably noticed how French women had developed an interest in politics, an area he assigned to men. They were different from American women, who were "too wise to wrinkle their foreheads with politics," "contented" instead "to soothe and calm the minds of their husbands returning ruffled from political debate." Women in Paris lacked what Jefferson admired in American women—"the good sense to value domestic happiness above all other." Instead they "hunted" pleasure in the streets and in the assemblies. "Compare them with our own countrywomen occupied in the tender and tranquil amusements of domestic life, and confess that it is a comparison of Amazons and Angels." Both men and women had to have their respective places. As long as women were in the domestic sphere, they were "Angels"; once they stepped out of it, they became "Amazons"—hunting pleasure and undermining sexual order. Women, Jefferson cautioned years later, "could not mix promiscuously in the public meetings with men," or else there would be "depravation of morals and ambiguity of issue."[11]

Jefferson's fear of "the strongest of all the human passions" was not based merely on philosophical abstractions or observations: It was profoundly rooted in his own experiences and the personal doubt that his head would always be able to control his heart and his own passions. Jefferson admitted that, as a young man, he had offered "love to a handsome lady." She was already married, and Jefferson eventually acknowledged "its incorrectness." Years later, in the 1780s, he felt again the "strongest passions" pounding at the walls of rationality when he fell in love with another married woman, the delicately sensuous and captivating Maria Cosway. The intensity of his passions was expressed in his reference to himself as an "oran-ootan." "How have you weathered this rigorous season, my dear friend?" he wrote to her. "Surely it was never so cold before. To me who am an animal of a warm climate, a mere oran-ootan, it has been a severe trial." There had been moments when Jefferson had yielded to his passions and found himself enjoying the pleasure he feared. "I am but a son of nature, loving what I see and feel, without being able to give a reason, nor caring much whether there be one," he exclaimed to Maria. But their intimacy had nowhere to go, as both of them were aware, and the inevitable separation was painful. "Overwhelmed with grief," Jefferson turned from his heart to his head for punishment and advice. In his letter to Maria known as the "Dialogue of the Head and Heart," Jefferson had his head declare: "I have often told you during it's [sic] course that you were imprudently engaging your affections. . . . This is not a world to live at random as you do. . . . Everything in this world is a matter of calculation."[12]

Unless men in America obeyed their moral sense and exercised self-control, Jefferson feared, they would "live at random" and destroy republican order. This was an especially frightening prospect in a slaveholding society where white men like Jefferson had to guard themselves not only against "the strongest of all human passions" but also against "the most boisterous passions." The possessor of inordinate power over black men and women, Jefferson recognized the need for slavemasters, free from the king and external authority, to exercise great vigilance against their own despotism. Both passions, he anxiously believed, would continue to undermine republican self-control as long as the new nation lacked complete purity and as long as blacks remained within the "bowels" of republican society.

Black Colonization

Slavery was a most perplexing and anxious problem for Jefferson. A "driver of slaves," he also gave in the Declaration of Independence one of the "loudest yelps for liberty." The contradiction disturbed him. "The love of justice and the love of country plead equally the cause of these people [slaves]," he confessed, "and it is a moral reproach to us that they should have pleaded it so long in vain. . . ." In a letter to his brother-in-law Francis Eppes on July 30, 1787, Jefferson made a revealing slip. Once "my debts" have been cleared off, he promised, "I shall try some plan of making their situation happier, determined to content myself with a small portion of their ~~liberty~~ labour."[13] Aware he was violating the human rights of blacks, he had written *liberty,* then crossed it out of his letter and possibly his consciousness for the moment, and excused himself for appropriating only their "labour."

Not only did slavery, in Jefferson's view, violate the black's right to liberty, it also undermined the self-control white men had to have in a republican society. In *Notes on the State of Virginia,* he described what he believed was the pernicious influence of slavery upon republican men:

> There must doubtless be an unhappy influence on the manners of our people produced by the existence of slavery among us. The whole commerce between master and slave is a perpetual exercise of the most boisterous passions, the most unremitting despotism on the one part, and degrading submissions on the other. Our children see this, and learn to imitate it; for man is an imitative animal. This quality is the germ of all education in him. From his cradle to his grave he is learning to do what he sees others do. If a parent could find no motive either in his philanthropy or his self-love, for restraining the intemperance of passion towards his slave, it should always be a sufficient one that his child is present. But generally it is not sufficient. The parent storms, the child looks on, catches the lineaments of wrath, puts on the same airs in the circle of smaller slaves, gives a loose to his worst of passions, and thus nursed, educated, and daily exercised in tyranny, cannot but be stamped by it with odious peculiarities. The man must be a prodigy who can retain his manners and morals undepraved by such circumstances.[14]

A republican committed to the idea of liberty as a natural right and concerned for the need for self-control, Jefferson believed slavery should be abolished. As a member of the House of Burgesses, he had supported an effort for the emancipation of slaves. And in *Notes on the State of Virginia,* he recommended the gradual abolition of slavery and the elimination of "principles inconsistent with republicanism." In a letter to a friend written in 1788, Jefferson asserted: "You know that nobody wishes more ardently to see an abolition not only of the [African slave] trade but of the condition of slavery: and certainly nobody will be more willing to encounter every sacrifice for that object."[15]

Yet, Jefferson was not willing to "encounter every sacrifice" to free the 200 slaves he owned. During the 1780s, after the enactment of the Virginia manumission law, some ten thousand slaves were given their freedom; Jefferson, however, did not manumit his own bondsmen. To have done so would have been financially disastrous for this debt-ridden planter. "The torment of mind," he cried out, "I will endure till the moment shall arrive when I shall not owe a shilling on earth is such really as to render life of little value." Dependent on the labor of his slaves to pay off his debts, Jefferson hoped he would be able to free them and "put them ultimately on an easier footing," which he stated he would do the moment "they" had paid the debts due from the estate, two-thirds of which had been "contracted by purchasing them." [16] Unfortunately, he remained in debt until his death.

As a slavemaster, Jefferson personally experienced what he described as the "perpetual exercise of the most boisterous passions." He was capable of punishing his slaves with great cruelty. He had James Hubbard, a runaway slave who had been apprehended and returned in irons to the plantation, whipped and used as an example to the other slaves. "I had him severely flogged in the presence of his old companions," Jefferson reported. On another occasion, Jefferson punished a slave to make an example of him in "terrorem" to others, and ordered him to be sold to one of the slave traders from Georgia. "If none such offers," he added, "if he could be sold in any other quarter so distant as never more to be heard among us, it would to the others be as if he were put out of the way by death."[17] Clearly, Jefferson himself was no "prodigy," able to retain his manners and morals undepraved by the brutalizing circumstances of slavery.

Like his fellow slaveholders, Jefferson was involved in the buying and selling of slaves and viewed them in economic terms. "The value of our lands and slaves, taken conjunctly, doubles in about twenty years," he observed casually. "This arises from the multiplication of our slaves, from the extension of culture, and increased demands for lands." His was not a merely theoretical observation: Jefferson's ownership of land and slaves made him one of the wealthiest men in his state. Yet he continued to expand his slave holdings. In 1805, he informed John Jordan that he was "endeavoring to purchase young and able negro men." His interest in increasing his slave property was again revealed in a letter to his manager regarding "a breeding woman." Referring to the "loss of 5 little ones in 4 years," he complained that the overseers did not permit the slave women to devote as much time as was necessary to the care of their children. "They view their labor as the 1st object and the raising of their children but as secondary," Jefferson continued. "I consider the labor of a breeding woman as no object, and that a child raised every 2 years is of more profit than the crop of the best laboring man."[18] Little wonder that, by 1822, Jefferson owned 267 slaves.

Yet, despite his view of slave women as "breeders" and slave children as "profits," Jefferson insisted he would be willing to make a sacrifice and free all of his slaves, if they could be removed from the United States. "I can say," he asserted, "with conscious truth, that there is not a man on earth who would sacrifice more than I would to relieve us from this heavy reproach, in any practicable way. The cession of that kind of property . . . is a bagatelle which would not cost me a second thought, if, in that way, a general emancipation and expatriation could be effected." But how could a million and half slaves be expatriated? To send them all off at once, Jefferson answered, was not "practicable" for us, or expedient for them. He estimated such a removal would take twenty-five years, during which time the slave population would have doubled. Furthermore, the value of the slaves would amount to $600 million, and the cost of transportation and provisions would add up to $300 million. "It cannot be done in this way," he decided. The only "practicable" plan, he thought, was to deport the future generation of blacks: Black infants would be taken from their mothers and trained in industrious occupations until they had reached a proper age for deportation. Since a newborn infant was worth only $25.50, Jefferson calculated, the estimated loss of slave property would be reduced from $600 million to only $37.5 million. Jefferson suggested they be transported to the independent black nation of Santo Domingo. "Suppose the whole annual increase to be sixty thousand effective births, fifty vessels, of four hundred tons burthen each, constantly employed in that short run, would carry off the increase of every year, and the old stock would die off in the ordinary course of nature, lessening from the commencement until its final disappearance." He was confident the effects of his plan would be "blessed." As for the taking of children from their mothers, Jefferson remarked: "The separation of infants from their mothers . . . would produce some scruples of humanity. But this would be straining at a gnat, and swallowing a camel."[19]

Africa, it seemed to Jefferson, would be "the most desirable receptacle" for colonized blacks. Such removal, if it could be achieved, would benefit both races. Not only would the black population be drawn off from the United States, but the colonized blacks might be the means of transplanting the "useful arts" among the inhabitants of Africa and carrying the "seeds of civilization" there. Thus colonization, Jefferson added, might render the sojournment and suffering of blacks in America a "blessing" to Africa. As President, he asked Rufus King, the minister to Great Britain, to look into the possibility of establishing an African company designed to colonize American blacks in Sierra Leone. Jefferson also considered the West Indies for the relocation of American blacks. "Inhabited already by a people of their own race and color; climates congenial with their natural constitution; insulated from the other descriptions of men; nature seems to have formed these islands to become the receptacle of the blacks transplanted in this hemisphere."[20]

Why not, Jefferson asked in *Notes on the State of Virginia,* emancipate the blacks but keep them in the state? "Deep-rooted prejudices entertained by the whites," he fearfully explained, "ten thousand recollections, by the blacks, of the injuries they have sustained; new provocations; the real distinctions which nature has made and many other circumstances, will divide us into parties, and produce convulsions, which will probably never end but in the extermination of the one or the other race." Unless colonization accompanied emancipation, whites would experience the horror of race war. Yet, unless slavery were abolished, whites would continue to face the danger of servile insurrection and the violent rage springing from "ten thousand recollections" of injuries. "As it is," Jefferson declared, "we have the wolf by the ears, and we can neither hold him, nor safely let him go. Justice is in one scale, and self-preservation in the other." The slave revolt in Santo Domingo intensified his anxieties. "It is high time we should foresee," he wrote to James Monroe in 1793, "the bloody scenes which our children certainly, and possibly ourselves (south of Potomac) have to wade through, and try to avert them." Four years later, referring to the need to get under way some plan for emancipation and removal, Jefferson cried out to William and Mary College Professor St. George Tucker, a critic of slavery: "If something is not done, and soon done, we shall be the murderers of our own children." The dread of slave rebellion, which Jefferson and other whites felt, was evident in the violent suppression of the Gabriel Prosser conspiracy of 1800. During the hysteria, twenty-five blacks were hanged. Five years later, Jefferson observed that the insurrectionary spirit among the slaves had been easily quelled, but he saw it becoming general and more formidable after every defeat, until whites would be forced, "after dreadful scenes and sufferings to release them in their own way. . . ." He predicted that slavery would be abolished—"whether brought on by the generous energy of our own minds" or "by the bloody process of St. Domingo" in which slaves would seize their freedom with daggers in their hands.[21]

Yet Jefferson could understand the violence of slave revolt. He viewed it as a natural and seemingly inevitable response to oppression, and he even tried to imagine what it must be like to be a slave. He projected himself into the slave's situation as he observed how slavery had transformed the master into a "despot" and the slave into an "enemy," the black's rights being "trampled on" and his "amor patriae" destroyed. The slave must prefer any other country in the world to America, where he was "born to live and labor for another." Unable to contain the guilt he felt, Jefferson exclaimed: "Indeed I tremble for my country when I reflect that God is just; that his justice cannot sleep forever; that considering numbers, nature and natural means only, a revolution of the wheel of fortune, an exchange of situation is among possible events. . . ." Still he hoped emancipation would be achieved through the "consent" rather than the "extirpation" of the oppressors.[22]

Even if emancipation could be achieved peacefully, colonization would still be required as one of the conditions for the liberation of slaves. Though Jefferson regarded blacks as members of humankind, endowed with moral sense, he believed that blacks and whites could never coexist in America because of "the real distinctions" which "nature" had made between the two races. "The first difference which strikes us is that of color," Jefferson explained. Regardless of the origins of the Negro's skin color, this difference was "fixed in nature." "And is this difference of no importance? Is it not the foundation of a greater or less share of beauty in the two races? Are not the fine mixtures of red and white, the expressions of every passion by greater or less suffusions of color in the one, preferable to that eternal monotony, which reigns in the countenances, that immovable veil of black which covers the emotions of the other race?" To Jefferson, white was beautiful. Even blacks themselves admitted so, he thought: "Add to these, flowing hair, a more elegant symmetry of form, their own judgment in favor of the whites, declared by their preference of them, as uniformly as is the preference of Oranootan for the black woman over those of his own species." Given these racial differences, colonization of blacks was a way to preserve white beauty and "loveliness." Commenting on the breeding of domestic animals, Jefferson asked: "The circumstance of superior beauty is thought worthy of attention in the propagation of our horses, dogs, and other domestic animals; why not in that of man?"[23]

White "superiority," for Jefferson, was also a matter of intelligence. He acknowledged that the "opinion" that blacks were "inferior" in faculties of reason and imagination had to be "hazarded with great diffidence." Evaluation of intelligence was problematical: It was a faculty which eluded the research of all the senses, the conditions of its existence were various and variously combined, and its effects were impossible to calculate. "Great tenderness," he added, was required "where our conclusion would degrade a whole race of man from the rank in the scale of beings which their Creator may perhaps have given them." Thus, Jefferson advanced it as a "suspicion" only that blacks "whether originally a distinct race, or made distinct by time and circumstances," were "inferior" to whites in the endowments of both body and mind. Jefferson stated he was willing to have his "suspicion" challenged, even refuted. To the French critic of slavery Abbé Henri Gregoire, he wrote: "Be assured that no person living wishes more sincerely than I do, to see a complete refutation of the doubts I have myself entertained and expressed on the grade of understanding allotted to them by nature, and to find that in this respect they are on a par with ourselves." In 1791, Jefferson received from Benjamin Banneker a copy of an almanac the black mathematician had compiled, and responded enthusiastically: "Nobody wishes more than I do to see such proofs as you exhibit, that nature has given to our black brethren, talents equal to those of the other colors of men, and that the appearance of a want of them is owing merely to the degraded condition of their existence. . . ." Here was "proof" demanding attention, and Jefferson promptly sent the almanac to the French scientist Marquis de Condorcet.[24]

In his investigation of the black's "inferior" intelligence, however, Jefferson was more interested in "proofs" which supported rather than refuted his "suspicion." Actually he did not take Banneker seriously, and thought the mathematician had "a mind of very common stature." While he admitted Banneker had enough spherical trigonometry to make almanacs, he suspected the black scholar had aid from Andrew Ellicot, a white neighbor who "never missed an opportunity of puffing him." Unlike Rush, Jefferson did not view black "inferiority" as a consequence of slavery or as a social rather than a biological condition. Instead he seized evidence which set blacks apart as "a distinct race," and which emphasized the importance of biology over conditions or circumstances in the determination of intelligence. In a comparison between Roman slavery and American black slavery, Jefferson remarked: "Epictetus, Terence, and Phaedrus, were slaves. But they were of the race of whites. It is not their condition then, but nature, which has produced the distinction." Evidence to support this assertion, Jefferson added, could be found closer at hand. "The improvement of the blacks in body and mind, in the first instance of their mixture, has been observed by every one, and proves that their inferiority is not the effect merely of their condition of life."[25] Thus, miscegenation itself appeared to provide "proof" of the black's racial intellectual "inferiority."

Nor did Jefferson's "suspicion" and his plea for "tenderness" restrain him from cataloging what he thought were the qualities of black inferiority.

> In general, their existence appears to participate more of sensation than reflection. To this must be ascribed their disposition to sleep when abstracted from their diversions, and unemployed in labor. An animal whose body is at rest, and who does not reflect, must be disposed to sleep of course. Comparing them by their faculties of memory, reason, and imagination, it appears to me that in memory they are equal to the whites; in reason much inferior, as I think one could scarcely be found capable of tracing and comprehending the investigations of Euclid; and that in imagination they are dull, tasteless, and anomalous.

Jefferson's descriptions of the Negro involved more than the assertion of black intellectual inferiority: They depicted blacks as dominated by their bodies rather than their minds, by their sensations rather than their reflections. They appeared to be a libidinal race. "They [black men] are more ardent after their female; but love seems with them to be more an eager desire, than a tender delicate mixture of sentiment and sensation."[26] Blacks, in Jefferson's mind, represented the body and the ascendancy of the instinctual life—those volcanic forces of passions he believed whites had to control in republican society.

Here, for Jefferson, in the midst of the society which had destroyed the authority of the king, expelled the enemy from its "bowels," and established a republic of self-governing men, was the presence of a race still under the rule of the passions, created with moral sense but without sufficient intelligence to serve the conscience. This was hardly the foundation necessary to create a "homogeneous" society. What worried Jefferson was evidence showing that blacks were proliferating at a faster rate than whites. In 1782, he noted, Virginia had 567,614 inhabitants, 270,762 slaves to 296,852 "free inhabitants," a ratio of nearly ten to eleven. "Under the mild treatment our slaves experience, and their wholesome, though coarse, food, this blot in our country increases as fast, or faster, than the whites." To Jefferson, the future of the republic seemed grim as long as it contained a "blot"—a growing one—and as long as a large segment of its population was inferior in intelligence and incapable of being self-governing.[27]

What distressed him most profoundly was the danger that the black "blot" would lead to "mixture" and the "staining" of whites. Thus he asked:

> Will not a lover of natural history then, one who views the gradations in all the races of animals with the eye of philosophy, excuse an effort to keep those in the department of man as distinct as nature has formed them? This unfortunate difference of color, and perhaps of faculty, is a powerful obstacle to the emancipation of these people. Many of their advocates, while they wish to vindicate the liberty of human nature, are anxious also to preserve its dignity and beauty. . . . Among the Romans emancipation required but one effort. The slave, when made free, might mix with, without staining the blood of his master. But with us a second is necessary, unknown to history. When freed, he is to be removed beyond the reach of mixture.[28]

Unlike Rush of Pennsylvania, Jefferson did not live in a state where blacks constituted only a small proportion of the population and an insignificant part of the work force. Feeling guilty for depriving blacks of their liberty, surrounded by them and fearful of slave insurrection, Jefferson called for their exclusion from America rather than for the formation of black colonies within the country. Where Rush proposed to segregate blacks in order to reform and assimilate them eventually into white republican society, Jefferson insisted on their complete removal.

Still, regardless of whether blacks were to be included or excluded, Jefferson was articulating a general fear. If the republican experiment were to succeed and if the new nation were to realize the vision of a "homogeneous" republic, it had to preserve what Franklin described as the "lovely White." It must not allow its people to be "stained" and become a nation of mulattoes. "Their amalgamation with the other colour," Jefferson warned, "produces a degradation to which no lover of his country, no lover of excellence in the human character can innocently consent."[29] If this mixture were to occur, it would surely mean that whites had lost control of themselves and their lustful passions, and had in their "unbounded licentiousness" shattered the very experiment in self-government which they had undertaken during the American Revolution.

This was precisely why the Thomas Jefferson/Sally Hemings relationship, whether imagined or actual, was so significant. If the philosopher of republicanism could not restrain what he called "the strongest of all the human passions" and if the author of jeremiads against miscegenation were guilty of "staining" the blood of white America, how could white men in the republic ever hope to be self-governing?

In a crucial and symbolic sense, the controversy during Jefferson's lifetime over whether or not he had fathered slave children was a means by which white men—his critics as well as his defenders—could reaffirm their faith in their republicanism. "It is well known that the man, *whom it delighteth the people to honor,*" declared James Callender in the *Richmond Recorder* in 1802,

> keeps and for many years has kept, as his concubine, one of his slaves. Her name is Sally. The name of her eldest son is Tom. His features are said to bear a striking though sable resemblance to those of the president himself. The boy is ten or twelve years of age. His mother went to France in the same vessel with Mr. Jefferson and his two daughters. The delicacy of this arrangement must strike every portion of common sensibility. What a sublime pattern for an American ambassador to place before the eyes of two young ladies!

Callender's attack evoked a defense of Jefferson as a sublime pattern. Years later, protesting the charge that Jefferson had had "commerce with female slaves," Colonel Thomas Randolph insisted that his grandfather had been "chaste and pure—as 'immaculate a man as God ever created.'"[30]

Throughout the controversy, Jefferson displayed a curious comportment. He remained silent on the entire issue, except for an oblique denial in a letter to James Monroe in 1801. After describing how Callender had "intimated he was in possession of things which he could and would make use of in a certain case" and how he had demanded "hush money" and expected "a certain office," Jefferson stated: "He knows nothing of me which I am not willing to declare to the world myself." Strangely, Jefferson acted as if the controversy did not exist at all, and as if there were no mulatto children resembling him on his plantation. Even Randolph had to admit that the Hemings's children resembled Jefferson so closely that at some distance or in the dusk one of the grown slaves "might have been mistaken for Mr. Jefferson." The likeness between master and slave was "blazoned" to all the visitors. Amazingly, Jefferson himself "never betrayed the least consciousness of the resemblance."[31]

Yet, he could not have been oblivious of it. Colonel Randolph was so aware of the resemblance that both he and his mother "would have been very glad to have them thus removed," but they "venerated Mr. Jefferson too deeply to broach such a topic to him." It is doubtful Jefferson would have behaved in such a puzzling way, unless he was the father of the children or unless he thought his Carr nephews were. There is, as historian Fawn Brodie pointed out, "excellent documentary evidence" that Jefferson was "on hand" nine months before the birth of each child. But what about his nephews? While it cannot be documented that either Peter or Samuel Carr was present at Monticello during those times, it likewise cannot be documented they were *not* "on hand." And evidence does exist implying they were present. According to Colonel Randolph, on one occasion a visitor at Monticello dropped a newspaper from his pocket or left it accidentally. Randolph opened the paper and found some insulting remarks about Mr. Jefferson's mulatto children. Provoked, he showed the article to Peter and Samuel Carr, who were lying under a shade tree. "Peter read it, tears coursing down his cheeks, and then handed it to Samuel. Samuel also shed tears. Peter exclaimed 'ar'nt you and I a couple of _____ pretty fellows to bring disgrace on poor old uncle who has always fed us! We ought to be _____, by _____!' " The fact that "by 1800 the Carr brothers had plantations and slaves of their own"—a fact which Brodie used to imply either that they were responsible gentlemen or that they had their own slave women to exploit sexually, and to exculpate them—apparently did not mean that they behaved discreetly on their uncle's plantation.[32]

Yet, as Brodie noted, one must not forget the "fact" that Sally Hemings's oldest son had been conceived in France. Clearly, the Carr brothers were not "on hand" there. In 1873, many years after the controversy itself, one of her sons—Madison Hemings, born in 1805— wrote:

> He [Jefferson] desired to bring my mother back to Virginia with him but she demurred. She was just beginning to understand the French language well, and in France she was free, while if she returned to Virginia would be re-enslaved. She refused to return with him. To induce her to do so he promised her extraordinary privileges, and made a solemn pledge that her children should be freed at the age of twenty-one years. In consequence of his promises, on which she implicitly relied, she returned with him to Virginia. Soon after their arrival, she gave birth to a child of whom Thomas Jefferson was the father. It lived but a short time. She gave birth to four others, of whom Thomas Jefferson was the father.

Madison Hemings was referring to Tom, born in 1790. Yet the facts about Tom remain unclear. According to Madison Hemings, the child "lived but a short time." Callender, however, reported in 1802 a son named Tom, "ten or twelve years of age." In his new slave inventory in 1794, Jefferson listed Sally Hemings; but he did not list her son, raising the possibility that Tom had never existed, or had already died.[33]

Yet what Jefferson did or did not do in his private life mattered little as his critics attacked him with a rage and a language suggesting that more was at stake than the conduct of one man. In their poetic descriptions of Jefferson's passions and Sally Hemings's sensuality, they exposed the libidinal fires burning within themselves.

> In glaring red, and chalky white,
> > Let the others beauty see;
> Me no such tawdry tints delight—
> > No! black's the hue for me!
>
> Thick pouting lips! how sweet their grace!
> > When passion fires to kiss them!
> Wide spreading over half the face,
> > Impossible to miss them.
>
> Oh! Sally! harken to my vows!
> > Yield up thy sooty charms—
> My best belov'd! my more than spouse,
> > Oh! take me to thy arms!

Actually Sally Hemings was a quadroon. Her mother, Betty Hemings, was a mulatto, and her father was John Wayles, Jefferson's father-in-law. Two of Sally Hemings's offspring were so white in complexion they were able to run away and "pass" into white society. Sally herself, according to slave

Isaac Jefferson, was "mighty near white," "very handsome" with "long straight hair down her back." She was, in reality, hardly the "black Sally" described in the poem. No matter. What counted, for Jefferson's critics, was the Sally of their own sexual fantasies. Indeed, in their condemnation of Jefferson, they betrayed how little faith they had in their own power to control the instinctual pressures within them.

> You men of morals! and be curst,
> > You would snap like sharks for Sally.
>
> She's *black* you tell me—grant she be—
> > Must colour always tally?
> Black is love's proper hue for me—
> > And white's the hue for Sally.
>
> What though she by the glands secretes;
> > Must I stand shil— I shall— I?
> Tuck'd up between a pair of sheets
> > There's no perfume like Sally.

In an almost ritualistic way, the detractors turned against Jefferson to curb and punish the instincts which all men had. Thus, they lashed out against this "metaphysician"

> Whom the world might take to be
> > a man whose blood
> Is very snow-broth; one who never feels
> The wanton stings and motions of the female,
> But doth rebuke and blunt his natural edge
> With profits of the mind, study and fast.

It was fearful for white men to think that one of them, especially one whose passions were in a state of frozen purity, had failed to blunt his "natural edge." One critic calculated that if the eighty thousand white men of Virginia did as much as Jefferson and each fathered five mulatto children, then there would be "FOUR HUNDRED THOUSAND MULATTOES in addition to the present swarm. The country would be no longer habitable, till after a civil war, and a series of massacres. We all know with absolute certainty that the contest would end in the utter extirpation both of blacks and mulattoes. We know that the continent has as many white people, as could eat the whole race at a breakfast."[34] As republicans, white men had to be self-governing and subordinate their libidinal desires to the authority of rationality, or else they would have to do something extraordinary.

The President's unrestrained critics were not allowed to assault and degrade him unchallenged. The editor of the *Richmond Examiner* dared Callender to publish his correspondence with Jefferson. "I am too much of a republican, and have too much faith in Mr. Jefferson's virtuous actions and designs to be tremulous for his fame in a case like this," he declared. "If he has acted improperly, which no man less wicked and designing than yourself believes, let us see to what extent the evil goes: whether it is veniel [*sic*], or whether it is so heinous, as to cut him off from the love of the people." A week later, while again demanding that Callender bring forward his evidence, the editor advanced a curious defense of Jefferson's integrity:

> In gentlemen's houses everywhere, we know that the virtue of unfortunate slaves is assailed with impunity. White women in these situations, whose educations are better, frequently fall victims: but the other class are attempted, without fear, having no defender, and yield most frequently. Is it strange therefore, that a servant of Mr. Jefferson's at a house where so many strangers resort . . . should have a mulatto child? Certainly not—And if Callender had not sworn to wickedness, he never would have twisted this occurrence into a serious accusation.
>
> Mr. Jefferson has been a Bachelor for more than twenty years. During this period, he reared with parental attention, two unblemished, accomplished and amiable women. . . . In the education of his daughters, this same Thomas Jefferson, supplied the place of a *mother*—his tenderness and delicacy were proverbial—not a spot tarnished his widowed character. . . .[35]

Here was an admission of the failure of white men to control their sexuality as well as an assertion of Jefferson's purity—his supreme control for more than two decades.

Everywhere in the controversy, there was irony. Both Jefferson's critics and his defenders were demanding what Jefferson himself had also demanded: White men must vigilantly guard themselves against their own "strongest passions" and must not "stain" the blood of the white republic. The code of white racial purity required that violators be severely punished. Black men convicted of raping white women were subjected to the cruel penalty of castration. White men guilty of violating the code should also be punished: To use the words of the *Examiner's* editor, they should be "cut off" from the love of the people. In a republican society, men had to have self-control and virtue. This was the faith the editor of the *Boston Gazette* hoped to renew during the controversy over the Jefferson/Hemings relationship. "We feel for the honour of our country," he declared. "And when her Chief Magistrate labours under the imputation of the most abandoned profligacy of private life, we do most honestly and sincerely wish to see the stain upon the nation wiped away, by the appearance on it at least of some colorable reason for believing in the purity of its highest character."[36] Yet, there was nothing Jefferson could have done to wipe away the "stain" upon the nation: He had become the receptacle of the nation's guilt as white men imputed to him the passions they could not contain and the sins they could not confess. In this process, they were reaffirming in their own minds the principles of republicanism, determined to expel the "enemy"—interracial sex and impurity—from the "bowels" of the new nation.

Red Lockeans

After all, had they not fought a war to establish a virtuous republican society? The American Revolution also compelled Jefferson and his fellow Americans to resolve the question of race in relation to the Indian as well as the black. According to Franklin's delineation of the different racial groups in America, there were three based on color—white, black, and "tawny." The question of the relationship between race and republican society could not ignore the presence of the native American. Jefferson knew this, and his racial concerns did not revolve exclusively around blacks. Still, studies of Jefferson, including even Fawn Brodie's biography, which focuses largely on race, often completely overlook the Indian, almost as if he did not exist in America or in Jefferson's life or mind. As a white expansionist and an agrarian philosopher in search of "vacant lands," Jefferson was fully conscious of the Indian's existence.

During the struggle to expel the British, Jefferson had two views of the Indian's future in the new nation: He could be civilized and assimilated, or he could be removed and possibly exterminated. Thus, Jefferson declared to the chief of the Kaskaskias that he hoped "we shall long continue to smoke in friendship together," and that "we, like you, are Americans, born in the same land, and having the same interests." Yet, at the same time, Jefferson did not hesitate to advocate removal of hostile Indians beyond the Mississippi and even total war upon them. "Nothing will reduce those wretches so soon as pushing the war into the heart of their country," he wrote angrily in 1776. "But I would not stop there. I would never cease pursuing them while one of them remained on this side [of] the Mississippi." And he went further. Quoting from the instructions the Congress had given the commissioners to the Six Nations, he continued: "We would never cease pursuing them with war while one remained on the face of the earth."[37] His two views—civilization and extermination—were not contradictory: They were both consistent with his vision of a "homogeneous" American society.

To civilize the Indian meant, for Jefferson, to take him from his hunting way of life and convert him into a farmer. As President of the United States, he told the Potawatomies:

We shall . . . see your people become disposed to cultivate the earth, to raise herds of the useful animals, and to spin and weave, for their food and clothing. These resources are certain: they will never disappoint you: while those of hunting may fail, and expose your women and children to the miseries of hunger and cold. We will with pleasure furnish you with implements for the most necessary arts, and with persons who may instruct you how to make and use them.

After the purchase of the Louisiana, Jefferson sent Lewis and Clark on an expedition to explore the western territory, and instructed them to collect information on the Indians which could be useful in the effort to educate and civilize them. To the Shawnee chiefs, Jefferson explained why the Indian had no choice but to accept civilization. "When the white people first came to this land, they were few, and you were many; now we are many, and you few; and why? because, by cultivating the earth, we produce plenty to raise our children, while yours . . . suffer for want of food, are forced to eat unwholesome things, are exposed to the weather in your hunting camps, get diseases and die. Hence it is that your numbers lessen." In order to survive, Indians must adopt the ways of the white man. They must enclose farms, acquire a knowledge of the value of property, and learn arithmetic and writing in order to calculate the value of property and keep accounts. Jefferson pointed to some wealthy Cherokees as models of success for all Indians. They had raised more cattle and corn than they needed for their own use; instead of allowing this surplus to be eaten by their own "lazy" people, they carried it to the market in Knoxville, sold it to whites, and then used the money to purchase clothes and comforts for themselves.[38] Thus, as civilized people and as farmers, all Indians would be brought into the market economy.

While Jefferson argued that humanity enjoined whites to teach agriculture to the Indian, he also recognized the important control function the civilizing process served. Commenting on Indian-white conflicts in 1791, Jefferson wrote to Charles Carroll: "I hope we shall give them a thorough drubbing this summer, and then change our tomahawk into a golden chain of friendship. The most economical as well as most humane conduct towards them is to bribe them into peace, and to retain them in peace by eternal bribes." As President, Jefferson did not use the term *bribe*. But he did urge Congress to use agriculture and commerce among the Indians rather than military force as a "more effectual, economical, and humane instrument for preserving peace and good neighborhood with them." In his request to the Senate to ratify a treaty which would authorize the federal government to establish an ironworks on land purchased from the Cherokees, Jefferson stated:

As such an establishment would occasion a considerable and certain demand for corn and other provisions and necessaries, it seemed probable that it would immediately draw around it a close settlement of the Cherokees, would encourage them to enter a regular life of agriculture, familiarize them with the practice and value of the arts, attach them to property, lead them of necessity and without delay to the establishment of laws and government, and thus make a great and important advance toward assimilating their condition to ours.

The "assimilation" of Indians was a way to pacify them. As Indians became more civilized, they appeared to become more placid. "The great tribes on our Southwestern quarter," observed Jefferson in his annual message of 1807, "much advanced beyond the others in agriculture and household arts, appear tranquil," identifying "their views with ours in proportion to their advancement."[39] Clearly, Jefferson's efforts to civilize Indians and attach them Lockean-like to property were related to a strategy designed to control them.

Jefferson's efforts to civilize Indians involved more than moral and strategic concerns: It reaffirmed Jefferson's definition of civilization and his idea of progress. It enabled him to identify "savagery" and to measure how far he and his society had advanced from the time when "the selfish passions" were dominant.

Let a philosophic observer commence a journey from the savages of the Rocky Mountains, eastwardly towards our sea-coast. There he would observe in the earliest stage of association living under no law but that of nature, subsisting and covering themselves with flesh and skins of wild beasts. He would next find those on our frontiers in the pastoral state, raising domestic animals to supply the defects of hunting. Then succeed our own semi-barbarous citizens, the pioneers of the advance of civilization, and so in progress he would meet the gradual shades of improving man until he would reach his, as yet, most improved state in our seaport towns. This, in fact, is equivalent to a survey, in time, of the progress of man from infancy of creation to the present day.[40]

To Jefferson, "progress" meant the advance from "savagery" to pastoral and urban civilization, from the past to the present. In this view, the Indian was identified with nature, the West, and the past; and the past had to be dominated. The reason why this had to be done was obvious enough to Jefferson: In the beginning, had not all the world been like America, and was not the white experience in America the struggle for freedom from the past, from the earliest stage of human existence? Thus the Indian had to be civilized and integrated into the movement of "progress" or be pushed farther westward and eventually destroyed. The Indian's survival depended on his ability to become a part of the expanding "civilization."

This ability, for Jefferson, depended on whether or not the Indian was equal to the white man. Jefferson believed that Indians, like blacks and all humankind, were endowed with an innate "moral sense of right and wrong," which, like the "sense of tasting and feeling" in every man, constituted "a part of his nature." But while Jefferson assigned conscience to both the Indian and the black, he made a crucial distinction between them in the area of intelligence. "I am safe in affirming," he wrote to the Marquis de Chastellux in 1785, "that the proofs of genius given by the Indians of N. America, place them on a level with whites in the same uncultivated state. . . . I believe the Indian then to be in body and mind equal to the white man. I have supposed the black man, in his present state, might not be so." Thus, what made the Indian "equal" or potentially so was his intelligence. "The Indians . . . will often carve figures on their pipes not destitute of design and merit," Jefferson observed. "They will crayon out an animal, a plant or a country, so as to prove the existence of a germ in their minds which only wants cultivation. They astonish you with strokes of the most sublime oratory; such as prove their reason and sentiment strong, their imagination glowing and elevated. But never yet could I find that a black had uttered a thought above the level of plain narration; never saw even an elementary trait of painting or sculpture." The implications of these remarks are clear: He thought the Indian, unlike the black, could be educated and allowed to live among whites. "Before we condemn the Indians of this continent as wanting genius," he insisted, "we must consider that letters have not yet been introduced among them." If the Indians' circumstances could be changed, white Americans would "probably" find that the native Americans were "formed in mind as well as body, on the same module with the 'Homo sapiens Europaeus.' "[41] Thus, in Jefferson's mind, Indians had a potential blacks did not have: They had the intelligence capable of development which could enable them to carry out the commands of their moral sense.

This meant that Indians did not have to be a "problem" in America's future: They could be assimilated and their oneness with white America would reaffirm the republican civilization and the "progress" Jefferson hoped to realize. Time and again President Jefferson called upon the Indians to intermarry and live among whites as "one people." To the Delawares, Mohicans, and Munries, he declared:

When once you have property, you will want laws and magistrates to protect your property and persons, and to punish those among you who commit crimes. You will find that our laws are good for this purpose; you will wish to live under them, you will unite yourselves with us, join in our Great Councils and form one people with us, and we shall all be Americans; you will mix with us by marriage, your blood will run in our veins, and will spread with us over this great island.

In 1803 President Jefferson urged Colonel Benjamin Hawkins to encourage the Indians to give up hunting and turn to agriculture and household manufacture as a new way of life. Indians must learn how a little land, well cultivated, was superior in value to a great deal, unimproved. He offered a grisly analogy to illustrate his point: "The wisdom of the animal which amputates and abandons to the hunter the parts for which he is pursued should be theirs, with this difference, that the former sacrifices what is useful, the latter what is not." The wisdom to "amputate" their land and culture would make it possible for "our settlements and theirs to meet and blend together, to intermix, and become one people."[42]

The contradiction between Jefferson's acceptance of red/white amalgamation and his abhorrence of black/white intermixture was grounded in the different sociology and material conditions of red/white *vis-à-vis* black/white relations. As slave laborers, blacks lived in white society in a hierarchically integrated situation—white over black—and amalgamation between white men and slave women was in fact happening. The presence of large numbers of mulatto children betrayed the sins of white men. Not only did whites classify the mulatto as "Negro" and thereby try to deny that sexual intercourse had ever taken place between whites and blacks; they also transferred their own lusts and their anxieties of black male retaliation to their fear of black men as sexual threats to white women. Unlike blacks, Indians lived apart from white society and had their own tribal identities; they were far from close physical and cultural contact with whites. Red women were not the victims of white male sexual exploitation as were black women, and red men did not provoke the sexual anxieties of white men as did black men. Jefferson confidently claimed that the red man would not "indulge himself with a captive taken in war." Generally, Indians were not viewed as a threat to white racial purity. These important differences enabled Jefferson to offer Indians an invitation he could never extend to blacks. Furthermore, he viewed blacks in terms of an increasing population, while he saw Indians as a population in decline. In *Notes on the State of Virginia,* he pointed out that the 1669 census indicated that Indian tribes had been reduced to about one-third of their former numbers in the space of sixty-two years.[43] Thus, for Jefferson, Indians did not seem to represent the growing "blot" blacks did: They were already the vanishing American.

The decimation of the Indian population led Jefferson to comment on its causes and at the same time defend the correctness of the transfer of lands from Indians to whites.

> Spirituous liquors, the small pox, war, and an abridgement of territory to a people who lived principally on the spontaneous productions of nature, had committed terrible havoc among them, which generation, under the obstacles opposed to it among them, was not likely to make good. That the lands of this country were taken from them by conquest, is not so general a truth as is supposed. I find in our historians and records, repeated proofs of purchase, which cover a considerable part of the lower country; and many more would doubtless be found on further search. The upper country, we know, has been altogether acquired by purchases made in the most unexceptionable form.[44]

If Jefferson's denial of guilt contained a quality of shrillness, there was a reason for it. In the original manuscript for *Notes on the State of Virginia,* he had written and then crossed out: "It is true that these purchases were sometimes made with the price in one hand and the sword in the other."

Even if the Indian population did not continue to decline, assimilation as Jefferson had defined it would be in one direction only. In the process, Indians would adopt white ways. They would be converted into Lockean people: They would own private property, obey written laws, and live in a state of society rather than in a state of nature. To the chiefs of the Upper Cherokees, Jefferson spelled out the requirements for citizenship. "My children, I shall rejoice to see the day when the red man, our neighbors, become truly one people with us, enjoying all the rights and privileges we do, and living in peace and plenty as we do. . . . But are you prepared for this? Have you the resolution to leave off hunting for your living, to lay off a farm for each family to itself, to live by industry, the men working that farm with their hands . . .?" Thus, if the Indian wished to live among whites and be an "American," and if he wished to survive and spread with whites over "this great island," he would have to "amputate" his way of life.[45]

What the Indian would be required to amputate was not only his identity and culture but also his land. The civilizing of the Indian was a crucial part of Jefferson's strategy to acquire Indian land for white settlement and the expansion of white agrarian society. As President, he gave Indians assurances that whites would respect Indian possession of land. "Our seventeen States compose a great and growing nation," he told the Choctaw Nation in 1803. "Their children are as the leaves of the trees, which the winds are spreading over the forest. But we are just also. We take from no nation what belongs to it. Our growing numbers make us always willing to buy lands from our red brethren, when they are willing to sell." Again in 1808, he declared to the Ottawas, Chippewas, Potawatomies, Wyandots, and Senecas that "your lands are your own; your right to them shall never be violated by us; they are yours to keep or to sell as you please. . . . When a want of land in a particular place induces us to ask you to sell, still you are always free to say 'No'. . . ." While he offered these assurances, President Jefferson worked to create conditions which would make the Indian "willing to sell." In a "Confidential Message" to Congress in 1803, he outlined how this could be done.

> First: to encourage them to abandon hunting, to apply to the raising stock, to agriculture and domestic manufactures, and thereby prove to themselves that less land and labor will maintain them in this, better than in their former mode of living. The extensive forests necessary in the hunting life will then become useless, and they will see advantage in exchanging them for the means of improving their farms. . . . Secondly: to multiply trading-houses among them, and place within their reach those things which will contribute more to their domestic comfort than the possession of extensive but uncultivated wilds. Experience and reflection will develop to them the wisdom of exchanging what they can spare and we want, for what we can spare and they want.

So, for whites to obtain western lands the Indians must be led to agriculture, manufactures, and thus to civilization.[46]

Jefferson's strategy involved more than the conversion of Indians into farmers and encouraging them to exchange "spare" lands for "spare" manufactures. The United States government, he explained to Andrew Jackson on February 16, 1803, must keep agents among the Indians to lead them to agriculture and advise them to sell their "useless" extensive forests in order to obtain money and purchase clothes and comforts from federal trading houses. Eleven days later in a letter to Indiana Governor William Henry Harrison, designated "unofficial and private," President Jefferson wrote: "To promote this disposition to exchange lands, which they have to spare and we want, for necessaries, which we have to spare and they want, we shall push our trading houses, and be glad to see the good and influential individuals among them run in debt, because we observe that when these debts get beyond what the individuals can pay, they become willing to lop them off by a cession of lands." To destroy financially "the good and influential" Indians, Jefferson emphasized the greater effectiveness of federal trading houses over private traders. While private business had to make profits, government enterprise could sell goods to Indians at prices "so low as merely to repay us cost and charges. . . ." By this process, he explained to Harrison, white settlements would gradually "circumscribe" the Indians, and they would in time either "incorporate" with whites as "citizens" or "remove beyond the Mississippi."[47]

The purchase of the Louisiana Territory in 1803 offered Jefferson the opportunity to pursue at once the two possibilities he saw for the Indian—removal and incorporation. The vast new territory, he calculated, could be "the means of tempting all our Indians on the East side of the Mississippi to remove to the West. . . ." In his draft of an amendment to the Constitution, Jefferson included a specific provision for such a removal: "The legislature of the Union shall have authority to exchange the right of occupancy in portion where the U.S. have full rights for lands possessed by Indians within the U.S. on the East side of the Mississippi: to exchange lands on the East side of the river for those . . . on the West side. . . ." Though the amendment remained in draft form, the Louisiana Territorial Act of 1804 did contain a clause which empowered the President to effect Indian emigration. Not all Indians would be "transplanted," however. If Indians chose civilization, Jefferson explained to the Cherokees, they would be allowed to remain where they were; if they chose to continue the hunter's life, they would be permitted to leave and settle on lands beyond the Mississippi. Calling the Cherokees "my children," he promised them that the United States would be the friends of both parties, and would be willing, as far as could be reasonably asked, to satisfy the wishes of both.[48]

Still, all Indians, whether they were farmers or hunters, were subject to removal, and even extermination, if they did not behave. Should any tribe be foolhardy enough to take up the hatchet against the United States, the President wrote Governor Harrison, the federal government should seize the whole country of that tribe and drive them across the Mississippi as the only condition of peace. As Anglo-American tensions mounted in 1808, President Jefferson told the Ottawas, Chippewas, Potawatomies, and Senecas that white Americans considered them "a part of ourselves" and looked to their welfare as "our own." If they sided with the British, however, they would have to abandon forever the land of their fathers. "No nation rejecting our friendship, and commencing wanton and unprovoked war against us, shall ever after remain within our reach. . . ." A year later, Jefferson gave his Indian "children" another warning: "If you love the land in which you were born, if you wish to inhabit the earth which covers the bones of your fathers, take no part in the war between the English and us. . . . [T]he tribe which shall begin an unprovoked war against us, we will extirpate from the earth, or drive to such a distance as they shall never again be able to strike us."[49]

Jefferson's complex feelings toward the Indian were summed up in a letter he wrote to John Adams. Childhood memories welled up as he described the times Indian chiefs stayed at his home as guests of his father, and flowed into his vision of an agrarian civilization.

> So much in answer to your enquiries concerning Indians, a people with whom, in the very early part of my life, I was very familiar, and acquired impressions of attachment and commiseration for them which have never been obliterated. Before the revolution they were in the habit of coming often, and in great numbers to the seat of our government, where I was very much with them. I knew much the great Outasette [i.e., Outacity], the warrior and orator of the Cherokees. He was always the guest of my father, on his journeys to and from Williamsburg. I was in his camp when he made his great farewell oration to his people, the evening before his departure for England. The moon was in full splendor, and to her he seemed to address himself in his prayers for his own safety on the voyage, and that of his people during his absence. His sounding voice, distinct articulation, animated action, and the solemn silence of his people at their several fires, filled me with awe and veneration, altho' I did not understand a word he uttered. That nation, consisting now of about 2000 warriors, and the Creeks of about 3000, are far advanced in civilization. They have good cabins, enclosed fields, large herds of cattle and hogs, spin and weave their own clothes of cotton, have smiths and other of the most necessary tradesmen, write and read, are on the increase in numbers. . . . On those who have made any progress, English seductions will have no effect. But the backward will yield, and be thrown further back. These will relapse into barbarism and misery, lose numbers by war and want, and we shall be obliged to drive them, with the beasts of the forests into the Stony mountains.[50]

Here, in one great outpouring, were Jefferson's love for Indians and his rage against them, his memories of childhood warmth for Indians and his angry cries for their removal to the "Stony mountains."

Ultimately, for Jefferson, it made no difference whether Indians were removed to the Rocky Mountains, "extirpated from the earth," or allowed to remain in the United States. Indians as Indians could not be tolerated in the republican civilization the American Revolution had created. The new nation must have a "homogeneous" population—a people with the same language and laws, good cabins and enclosed fields, owners of private property. Diversity itself was dangerous in the republican society, especially diversity which included groups and cultures close to nature and the instinctual life.

The black and the Indian, as they existed in Jefferson's imagination and in the political economy of America, had been separated from each other. Jefferson viewed each of them as a different problem. Constituting sources of violence and sexuality, the black was a growing and threatening "blot" to be removed to Africa. Close to nature and without government, the Indian was an obstacle to be removed to the West or to be incorporated as a Lockean property-owning farmer and become "a part of ourselves." At times Jefferson identified with both the black and the Indian, but in different ways. In his protest against British tyranny, he referred to himself and other American colonists as "slaves," and he described himself as an "oran-ootan" (an animal which, he claimed, lusted for black women) in his passionate cry of love for Maria Cosway. As a child, he had warm feelings for the Indian chief Outasette, whom he called "the guest of my father," and as the President of the United States, he addressed Indian chiefs as "my children." In one of his love letters to Cosway, he described himself as "a son of nature." The guilt Jefferson felt was different for each group: He was distressed over the brutalizing effect the tyranny of slavery had on the masters, and noted the decimating effect civilization had on the Indians. The most important basis for these differences in racial attitudes was the relationship of each group to the process of production. Jefferson and the American economy had located them in different places. The black was a slave worker within white civilization, and his labor was essential for white men like Jefferson to accumulate surplus, expand their capital, and also pay off their debts which some of them insisted, originated from the purchase of slaves. The Indian was not a laborer but an occupant of "vacant lands" which white men like Jefferson desired in order to expand their land holdings, as well as the national boundaries of white settlement, and to increase agricultural production.

Regardless of whether they were viewed in terms of their labor or their land, both blacks and Indians, for Jefferson, were under the domination of the body or the instinctual life. While both of them, like whites, were endowed with moral sense, they were both deficient in reason: Black intelligence was inferior and Indian intelligence was undeveloped. Thus both lacked the self-control and rational command Jefferson believed were essential qualities republicans and civilized men must have. In a republican society, men could not live "at random," and all behavior had to be "a matter of calculation" or else the strongest passions would overwhelm the moral sense and rationality. The hope Jefferson held for white America was the creation of a perfect society through the rule of reason and the expulsion of "enemies" from the "bowels" of the new republic. Curiously, Jefferson's language and recommendations for the realization of republican purity resembled the medical prescriptions of Dr. Rush. Turning with great ease from political to physical hygiene, Jefferson wrote: "The laws [of Virginia] have also descended to the preservation and improvement of the races of useful animals, such as horses, cattle, deer; to the extirpation of those which are noxious, as wolves, squirrels, crows, blackbirds; and to the guarding our citizens against infectious disorders, by obliging suspected vessels coming into the state, to perform quarantine, and by regulating the conduct of persons having such disorders within the state." America had to be pure—in the animal kingdom as well as in human society. "Races" of "useful" animals must be improved and "noxious" ones "extirpated." The new nation must be isolated from "diseases" of all sorts: Immigrants afflicted with infectious disorders or monarchical principles must be quarantined. Indeed, everything—British corruption, luxury, monarchical ideas, "licentious" immigrants, the instinctual life, the passions, the body, blacks, and Indians—threatening to republican society had to be purged.

Throughout his life, Jefferson believed a purged republican civilization in America had significance for the world. He gave a republican emphasis to the Puritan errand in the wilderness. "The eyes of the virtuous all over the earth are turned with anxiety upon us, as the only depositories of the sacred fire of liberty," Jefferson observed, "and . . . our falling into anarchy would decide forever the destinies of mankind, and seal the political heresy that man is incapable of self-government." In his old age, he told John Adams: "And even should the cloud of barbarism and despotism again obscure the science and liberties of Europe, this country remains to preserve and restore light and liberty to them. In short the flames kindled on the 4th of July 1776, have spread over too much of the globe to be exterminated by the feeble engines of despotism."[51] Americans had to be a pure and virtuous people if they were to maintain the trust the Revolution had bestowed upon them and remain the asylum of "liberty" in the world.

PART TWO

ENTERPRISE

Political economy, this science of wealth, *is therefore simultaneously the science of renunciation, of want, of* saving—*and it actually reaches the point where it* spares *man the* need *of either fresh* air *or physical* exercise. *This science of marvelous industry is simultaneously the science of* asceticism, *and its true ideal is the* ascetic. . . .

—Karl Marx

CHAPTER IV

BEYOND PRIMITIVE ACCUMULATION

Capital in its struggle against societies with a natural economy pursues the following ends:

> *1. To gain immediate possession of important sources of productive forces such as land. . . .*
> *2. To "liberate" labour power and to coerce it into service.*
> *3. To introduce a commodity economy.*
> *4. To separate trade and agriculture. . . .*

Since the primitive associations of the natives are the strongest protection for their social organisations and for their material bases of existence, capital must begin by planning for the systematic destruction and annihilation of all the non-capitalist social units which obstruct its development. With that we have passed beyond the stage of primitive accumulation.

> *—Rosa Luxemburg*

The patriot leaders of 1776 had little confidence in the people. Even as Jefferson urged Americans to expel the British "enemy" from the "bowels" of the new nation, he anxiously wondered whether they would be able to remain pure and virtuous. "From the conclusion of this war," he wrote in 1781, "we shall be going down hill. It will not then be necessary to resort every moment to the people for support. They will be forgotten, therefore, and their rights disregarded. They will forget themselves, but in the sole faculty of making money. . . ." Many years later, in 1808, Rush bitterly complained how the people had all become "idolators," and how they "worshipped one god . . . but that god was GOD DOLLARS." Indeed, in their old age, both Jefferson and Rush could look upon a "money-making" people, erecting factories, developing steam-powered transportation, and expanding the market.[1]

Yet economic progress could have also been viewed as a sign of American virtue: Republicanism had created a moral behavior and psychology which provided one of the dynamic bases of modern capitalism in the United States and helped to set in motion various forces leading to what George Rogers Taylor has designated the "Transportation Revolution." Rush did not overlook the relationship between manufactures and morals. In 1787 he called upon the patriots of 1776 to renew their faith and to hear the country, "proclaiming in sighs and groans, in her governments, in her finances, in her trade, in her manufactures, in her morals, and in her manners, 'The Revolution is not Over!' " Nearly half a century after independence, Jefferson surveyed the bustling enterprise of republican society; perplexed, he turned to his old friend John Adams, only to be asked: "Will you tell me how to prevent riches from becoming the effects of temperance and industry?"[2]

In the early nineteenth century, republican fathers like Rush, Jefferson, and Adams were witnessing the beginnings of the Market Revolution. In this era of entrepreneurial ferment, republican ideology and its acquisitive psychology—the inner world of the bourgeoisie—became a powerful force in American society, and the tremendous economic changes in transportation and production formed a new material basis for race relations in America.

Democracy in America: The Inner World of the Bourgeoisie

During the years of the Market Revolution, Alexis de Tocqueville visited this country and recorded his observations and reflections in *Democracy in America*. Actually, what he witnessed, in terms of "the general equality of condition among the people," was more appearance than reality. As Edward Pessen has demonstrated in his impressively detailed and systematic study of riches, class, and power in New York City, Brooklyn, Boston, and Philadelphia, the "age of the common man" was hardly egalitarian. "An inequality that was marked at the beginning of the era became even more glaring at its end," Pessen concluded, "as the share owned by the wealthiest 1 per cent rose from roughly one-quarter to one-half." Still, as Pessen himself has conceded, "the data do not wholly negate the significance of appearances or what people believed. Part of the 'reality' of the period was a surface equality that dazzled contemporaries."[3] Thus, though designed to demolish Tocqueville, Pessen's iconoclastic study underscored the importance of the French visitor's observations: They reflected a subjective reality which formed people's perceptions and influenced their actions in the real world.

Everywhere in his travels and observations in America, nothing struck Tocqueville more forcibly than "the general condition of equality." This condition exercised a "prodigious influence" on the whole course of society, giving a "peculiar" direction to public opinion, a "peculiar" tenor to the laws, and "peculiar" habits to the governed. The more Tocqueville analyzed American society the more he perceived this "equality of condition" as "the fundamental fact" from which all others seemed to be derived and "the central point" at which all his observations constantly terminated. Scanning the history of the last seven hundred years, he could not find a single great event which had not promoted equality: The crusades and the English wars had decimated the nobles and divided their property, the invention of firearms had equalized vassal and noble on the battlefield, printing had made knowledge available to all classes, and the discovery of America had opened a thousand new paths to wealth. The latest and most important event in this movement toward equality of condition was the American Revolution. During the war, "the doctrine of the sovereignty of the people came out of the townships and took possession of the state. Every class was enlisted in its cause; battles were fought and victories obtained for it; it became the law of laws."[4]

Clearly, Tocqueville saw, the Revolution was more than a war for independence: It had destroyed not only royal authority but also traditions and the sense of community which had held men together. "Aristocracy had made a chain of all the members of the community, from the peasant to the king"; democracy broke that chain and severed every link of it. The Revolution had given birth to a new man, without a past or even parents in terms of his psychology and mythology; it had erased "the track of generations." The reverence for ancient customs and traditions had previously enabled men to love their country as they loved the "mansion of their fathers." But the rebellion against the king in 1776 and the triumph of republicanism had shattered this reverence and freed men from their fathers as well as from their king. When men lived more for the remembrance of what had been than for the care of what was, and when they were more given to attend to what their ancestors thought than to think for themselves, Tocqueville noted, the father was "the natural and necessary tie between the past and the present." In aristocracies, then, the father was "not only the civil head of the family, but the organ of its traditions, the expounder of its customs, the arbiter of its manners." In the new republican society, on the other hand, as soon as the young American approached manhood, the ties of filial obedience were relaxed day by day; "master of his thoughts," he was soon "master of his conduct." Thus, at the close of boyhood, the republican son became the republican man without a struggle against his father. Tocqueville stated:

> It would be an error to suppose that this is preceded by a domestic struggle in which the son has obtained by a sort of moral violence the liberty that his father refused him. The same habits, the same principles, which impel the one to assert his independence predispose the other to consider the use of that independence as an incontestable right. The former does not exhibit any of those rancorous or irregular passions which disturb men long after they have shaken off an established authority; the latter feels none of that bitter and angry regret which is apt to survive a bygone power. The father foresees the limits of his authority long beforehand, and when the time arrives, he surrenders it without a struggle; the son looks forward to the exact period at which he will be his own master, and he enters upon his freedom without precipitation and without effort, as a possession which is his own and which no one seeks to wrest from him.

No wonder Tocqueville thought there was "no adolescence" in America. From infancy, the child in the republic had been taught to be self-governing—to rely upon his own exertions in resisting the evils and overcoming the difficulties of life. Independent from king and father, this new man owed nothing to any other and expected nothing; he stood alone, confident he controlled his whole destiny, thrown back forever upon himself alone, and confined "entirely within the solitude of his own heart."[5]

This isolation led to what Tocqueville called "dangerous propensities," for it concentrated every man's attention upon himself and promoted in him "an inordinate love of material gratification." Living in a condition of equality, Americans turned to money as the source of status and as the basis of relationships between equal men. "When the reverence that belonged to what is old has vanished," Tocqueville noticed, "birth, condition, and profession no longer distinguish men . . . hardly anything but money remains to create strongly marked differences between them and to raise some of them above the common level." Not only did money enable men to define their social place in America; it also replaced traditions and the king as the common ground upon which men interacted. "When all the members of the community are independent of or indifferent to each other, the co-operation of each of them can be obtained only by paying for it: This infinitely multiplies the purposes to which wealth may be applied and increases its value."[6] Among equals, men had to pay for services and goods received, and the market had become a central place in their existence. Thus, pastless and peripatetic, men in America were plunging themselves into a restless pursuit of money, ardently seeking to satisfy their desire for prosperity.

Always in motion, they could not relax, for they did not know for certain where they were and where they soon would be financially and socially. "In no country in the world are private fortunes more precarious than in the United States," Tocqueville noted. "It is not uncommon for the same man in the course of life to rise and sink again through all the grades that lead from opulence to poverty." Life in a condition of equality seemed always in flux, always anxious. The abolition of the privileges of birth had given men equal opportunity to secure wealth; yet this very equality had opened the door to "universal competition" and rendered all of them less able to realize their ambitions. "When men are nearly alike and all follow the same track," Tocqueville wrote, "it is very difficult for any one individual to walk quickly and cleave a way through the dense throng that surrounds and presses on him." An even greater irony seemed reserved for these democrats. In their feverish agitation for wealth, they could never accumulate as much as they desired. "It perpetually retires from before them, yet without hiding itself from their sight, and in retiring draws them on. At every moment they think they are about to grasp it; it escapes at every moment from their hold. They are near enough to see its charms, but too far off to enjoy them; and before they have fully tasted its delights, they die."[7] And the certainty of death only sharpened their anxiety to accumulate more and more goods and to cling to them as if they were certain never to die.

Yet, it seemed to Tocqueville, Americans never really lived, denying not death but life itself in their frantic pursuit of fortune. Their acquisitiveness required public order as well as "regularity of morals," for good morals contributed to public tranquility and were favorable to industry. Work was viewed as the necessary, natural, and honest condition of human existence. Thus Americans loved order, without which their affairs could not prosper, and they placed special value upon "regular conduct," the "foundation of a solid business." But self-control had damaging psychological effects. "A man who raises himself by degrees to wealth and power contracts, in the course of this protracted labor, habits of prudence and restraint which he cannot afterwards shake off." The influence of this "virtuous materialism" upon the American character was profound: It would "enervate" the soul and "noiselessly unbend its springs of action."[8]

The symptoms of this enervation seemed apparent to Tocqueville as he noticed how Americans had lost their spontaneity, their sense of joy; they seemed to be "cold and calculating," the "most serious nation on the face of the earth." Absorbed in acquisitiveness, they had developed a "serious demeanor," which had become a national habit. Anxious and full of cares, they almost always preserved a "frigid air." The "freest" and most "enlightened" men living in the happiest circumstances in the world, they were "serious and almost sad," "as if a cloud habitually hung upon their brow." All of this led Tocqueville to exclaim: "I think I see the destiny of America embodied in the first Puritan who landed on those shores. . . ." Enemies of amusements, the Puritans left deep traces on the minds of their descendants, imparting to them "extreme regularity of habits and great strictness of morals." Americans perverted even the amusements that they permitted. Thus,

> in aristocratic communities the people readily give themselves up to bursts of tumultuous and boisterous gaiety, which shake off at once the recollection of their privations. The inhabitants of democracies are not fond of being thus violently broken in upon, and they never lose sight of themselves without regret. Instead of these frivolous delights they prefer those more serious and silent amusements which are like business and which do not drive business wholly out of their minds. An American, instead of going in a leisure hour to dance merrily at some place of public resort, as the fellows of his class continue to do throughout the greater part of Europe, shuts himself up at home to drink. He thus enjoys two pleasures; he can go on thinking of his business and can get drunk decently by his own fireside.[9]

Here was, indeed, a striking portrait of the nervous American, imprisoned in his "iron cage."

Alone with his bottle and absorbed in his business and ambition, Tocqueville's narcissistic American was the epitome of the self-controlled and regulated man of enterprise—Rush's "republican machine." Always striving to improve himself and accumulate capital, he lived a life of self-renunciation. To paraphrase Marx, the American democrat "stinted" the "immediate gratification of his senses" and also "spared" himself all sharing of "general interest, all sympathy, all trust." He was driven by what C. B. MacPherson has called "possessive individualism." Freed from the king, feudal traditions, roots, and connections, he saw himself simply as an entity rather than a part of a larger social or moral whole. But this very independence and individualism led to a nervous possessiveness. The American democrat felt a compulsion to possess not only himself but also as much property and wealth as he could. For him, physical possessions became in effect extensions of the self: They determined who and what he was in a society where men were "born equal." He viewed possessions in terms of the capital he was accumulating, the "vacant lands" he was appropriating from the Indians for cultivation or speculation, and the slaves he was acquiring to raise his social status and to exploit for their labor—possessions were essential not only for his market activity but also for his personal identity.[10]

The Market Revolution and Race

Tocqueville visited America during the era of the Market Revolution or what Walter W. Rostow has called the "take-off" period in America's economy—a time of enormous and far-reaching developments in technology, transportation, communication, and manufacturing which so impressed the world between 1800 and 1860. During these years, the "forces making for economic progress," which had "yielded limited bursts and enclaves of modern activity," came to dominate society and made growth the "normal condition" of the economy. This age of economic expansion has been effectively analyzed by George R. Taylor and Douglass C. North.[11] What needs attention is the Market Revolution's relationship to the removal of Indians and the exploitation of blacks.

The Market Revolution was essentially the transformation of the American economy from a simple agrarian-commercial pattern to a highly complex economy of inter-regional specialization. In 1800, the population of the United States was approximately 5.9 million, and only 322,371 persons were listed as urban. A large percentage of the rural population sold foodstuffs occasionally to supplement their primarily self-sufficient way of life, and did not constitute a regular part of the domestic market. Living in the interior parts of the country, many of these farmers did not engage in commercial agriculture because the transportation of surplus crops was too expensive. The cost of transporting a ton of goods only thirty miles overland was as much as shipping it three thousand miles from America to Europe. Thus commercial activity was limited to the areas near the seaboard and navigable waterways, and involved mainly the exportation of staples to Europe and the importation of manufactured goods. Little trade and communication existed between the agrarian and commercial sectors of the United States.[12]

By 1860, this agrarian-commercial pattern had disappeared. The urban population had zoomed up from approximately five percent in 1800 to twenty percent in 1860. This rise was dynamic, as Table 1 shows:

Table 1. Numbers of Urban Places of Varying Sizes, 1800–1860

SIZE OF POPULATION	1800	1810	1820	1830	1840	1850	1860
500,000 to 1,000,000						1	2
250,000 to 500,000					1	0	1
100,000 to 250,000			1	1	2	5	6
50,000 to 100,000	1	2	2	3	2	4	7
25,000 to 50,000	2	2	2	3	7	16	19
10,000 to 25,000	3	7	8	16	25	36	58
5,000 to 10,000	15	17	22	33	48	85	136

The expansion of their land base and developments in transportation set the American people in motion geographically. Between 1800 and 1860, the settled area of the United States increased fivefold, and forty-five percent of the total population in 1860 lived outside the national boundary of 1800. This movement was also reflected in the statistics on place of birth. In 1860, nearly one-quarter of all free native-born whites were found living outside their state of birth; roughly one out of three persons born in Vermont, Connecticut, Delaware, Virginia, the Carolinas, and Georgia had moved to another state or territory.[13]

Moreover, advances in transportation broke down the barriers which had isolated farmers from the commercial sector, and the market became the cohesive force in society. Unlike its economy in 1800, when there were two sectors separated from each other, the United States in 1860 had three sectors—the East, West, and South. All of them were economically interdependent and represented a national division of production; each tended to specialize in the production of a specific set of commodities. The East or New England and the Middle Atlantic states concentrated on manufacturing and commerce and relied on the West for foodstuff for its growing urban population and the South for raw cotton to supply its textile factories. The West, which then constituted Ohio, Indiana, and Illinois, devoted itself to the production of grain and livestock, which it sent to the East and South, and depended largely on the East for manufactured goods. The South, mainly South Carolina, Alabama, Mississippi, and Louisiana, was the cotton kingdom, producing fiber for the textile mills of the East and England, and purchasing foodstuff from the West and manufactured goods from the East.[14]

By 1860, this pattern of inter-regional specialization was evident. In that year, the average cotton factory in New England had nearly seven thousand spindles, while its counterpart in the South and West had only two thousand. Seventy percent of the total capital invested in textile manufacturing was located in New England. The regionalism of manufacturing was also reflected in the annual value of manufactured goods for 1860. The total for the South and West combined was only $540,137,811 compared to $1,270,937,679 for the East. Receipts for flour and grain shipped from the West to Buffalo indicated the increasing dependence of the eastern urban population upon western farmers for their food supply. In 1860, 1,122,335 barrels of flour and 31,441,440 barrels of grain were shipped from the West through Buffalo to the East. Western grain and livestock were also shipped south to New Orleans, which was the major distribution center for the Southwest. Produce from the interior transported to New Orleans in 1860 was valued at $185,211,254. Cultivated exclusively in the South, cotton became the most important export product for that region and for the country. This may be seen in the following comparison of the value of total exports and cotton exports from 1815 to 1860.[15]

Table 2. Value of Total Exports and Cotton Exports

YEAR	TOTAL EXPORTS	COTTON EXPORTS
1815	$ 52,557,753	$ 17,529,000
1830	71,671,000	29,674,883
1840	123,669,000	63,870,307
1850	144,376,000	71,984,616
1860	333,576,000	191,806,555

Thus, cotton constituted thirty-nine percent of the total value of exports from 1816 to 1820, sixty-three percent from 1836 to 1840, and over fifty percent from 1840 to 1860.

The emergence of the cotton kingdom was based on the expansion of white settlement and black slavery into Indian lands of the Southwest. The major cotton-producing states—Alabama, Mississippi, and Louisiana— were carved out of Indian territory. Tribe after tribe in the Southwest was forced to sign treaties, cede or "lop off" their lands to the federal government, and move west of the Mississippi River. Eleven treaties of cession were negotiated with the southern Indians between 1814 and 1824; from these agreements the United States acquired millions of acres of lands, including one-fifth of Mississippi and three-quarters of Alabama. In the Treaty of Dancing Rabbit Creek (1830), the Choctaws ceded 10,423,130 acres to the federal government. Receipts from public land sales in five southern states shot up to $9 million between 1815 and 1820, shortly after Creek resistance had been crippled during the War of 1812, and again peaked at $7 million in 1835 during the years of Indian removal. The relationship between land sales and the increase in cotton production can be demonstrated in the data for Alabama, Arkansas, Florida, Louisiana, and Mississippi for the period 1833 to 1842:

Table 3. Land Sales and Cotton Production

YEAR	LAND SALES (ACRES)	PRODUCTION (BALES)
1833	1,816,083	559,210
1834	2,388,146	641,435
1835	5,522,474	760,923
1836	5,805,180	788,013
1837	1,259,814	916,960
1838	821,600	747,227
1839	851,586	911,913
1840	401,394	1,538,904
1841	228,699	1,231,334
1842	238,079	1,160,389

If we relate this information on Indian land cessions, public land sales, and cotton production to data on slave population in the Southwest between 1820 and 1850, we can understand more fully the dynamics of economic "flush times" in Alabama and Mississippi during the Market Revolution.[16]

Table 4. Slave Population

Year	Alabama	Louisiana	Mississippi
1820	41,879	69,064	32,814
1830	117,549	109,588	65,659
1840	253,523	168,452	195,211
1850	342,892	244,809	309,878

Thus, in order to make way for white settlement and the expansion of both cotton cultivation and the market, some 70,000 Choctaws, Creeks, Cherokees, Seminoles, and Chickasaws were uprooted and deprived of their lands, and hundreds of thousands of blacks were moved into the Southwest to work the soil as slaves.

The removal of Indians and the expansion of black slavery made possible the Market Revolution. To be sure, the tremendous economic growth which took place during this period was the result of several factors. The shipping boom of the early 1800s allowed merchants such as Francis Lowell to accumulate the capital needed to invest in manufacturing enterprises. The proliferation of banks and the expansion of the credit system enabled farmers to borrow paper money and acquire land for commercial agriculture. Government intervention in the form of protective tariffs and internal improvements also contributed to the advance of the market. Technological progress transformed manufacturing from household to factory; machinery became the main means for the production of manufactured goods and an urban population was increasingly organized around the machine. The transportation revolution laid vast networks of turnpikes, canals, and railroads throughout the country; between 1815 and 1860, freight charges for shipments of goods over land had been reduced by approximately ninety-five percent. Still, as Douglass C. North has shown, cotton was the "decisive" factor. "Cotton was strategic because it was the major independent variable in the interdependent structure of internal and international trade. The demands for western foodstuffs and northeastern services and manufactures were basically dependent upon the income received from the cotton trade." Dominant in the export trade, cotton was crucial in the development of inter-regional specialization. The income derived from the export of cotton set in motion the process of accelerated market and industrial development—the Market Revolution. The development of the cotton export sector depended on the appropriation of Indian land by white farmers and planters and the expansion of a black "internal colony" in which the dominant groups in white society exploited blacks for their labor and maintained racial hegemony over them.[17]

The Market Revolution, which propelled this country from an agricultural-commercial toward an industrial corporate economy, constituted the material basis of social relations in America. What remains to be analyzed are the racial ideology and patterns of race relations which developed within the context of this tremendous economic transformation, specifically how whites perceived and treated the red race on their "borders" and the black race in their "bosom."[18]

CHAPTER V

THE METAPHYSICS OF CIVILIZATION: "THE RED RACE ON OUR BORDERS"

Next to the case of the black race within our bosom, that of the red on our borders is the problem most baffling to the policy of our country.
　　　　　　　　　　　　　　—James Madison

No, no; bloodshed and warfare are not my real gifts, but peace and mercy. Still, I must face the enemy as well as another, and as for a Mingo, I look upon him as a man looks on a snake—a creatur' to be put beneath the heel, whenever a fitting occasion offers.

　　　　　　　　　　—Natty Bumppo,
　　　　　　　　　　　　in James Fenimore Cooper,
　　　　　　　　　　　　The Pathfinder

In 1831, Alexis de Tocqueville witnessed a "solemn spectacle" which would never fade from his memory—the arrival in Memphis of a band of Choctaws as they migrated west beyond the Mississippi River. "It was then the middle of winter," he reported, "and the cold was unusually severe; the snow had frozen hard upon the ground, and the river was drifting huge masses of ice. The Indians had their families with them, and they brought in their train the wounded and the sick, with children newly born and old men upon the verge of death." There, on the bank of the river, could be seen in brutal reality the epic process under way in America—the movement of European civilization westward. "Three or four thousand soldiers drive before them the wandering races of the aborigines; these are followed by the pioneers, who pierce the woods, scare off the beasts of prey, explore the courses of the inland streams, and make ready the triumphal march of civilization across the desert." What struck Tocqueville was how whites, in their expansion westward, were able to deprive Indians of their rights and exterminate them "with singular felicity, tranquilly, legally, philanthropically, without shedding blood, and without violating a single great principle of morality in the eyes of the world." Indeed, he remarked, it was impossible to destroy men, with "more respect for the laws of humanity."[1]

An Age of Confidence

Confidence, as Herman Melville observed in his novel *The Confidence-Man,* was one of the buoyant forces in American society during the era of the Market Revolution—"the indispensable basis of all sorts of business transactions" without which "commerce between man and man" would, like "a watch," run down and stop. Confidence in business and also in society generally involved both the need for moral self-assurance and the use of disguises. Like Melville's characters on board the steamboat *Fidèle,* white Americans had to have moral faith in themselves—to be assured they were innocent of brutality and sin even if they had to tell themselves they were so. And like Melville's confidence-man with his myriad of roles and masks, they employed disguises in their social and political relationships. Role-playing and the use of masks, David Brion Davis has noted, was widespread in Jacksonian society, where "individual success depended on effective presentation of self and on convincing definitions of new situations." Nowhere did whites demonstrate the importance of confidence as moral self-assurance and deception, especially self-deception, more than in their conduct toward Indians. In the removal and extermination of Indians, they were able to admire the Indian-killer and elevate hatred for the Indian into a morality—an awesome achievement which Melville analyzed in his chapters on the "metaphysics of Indian-hating."[2]

In this story, Melville described how disguises could be used to uncover rather than shroud reality. His confidence-man poses as a cosmopolitan gentleman in order to expose the contradictions of Indian-hating. On the deck of the *Fidèle,* a symbol of the Market Revolution, he meets a westerner who offers to tell a story about Colonel John Moredock, an Indian-hater. Though the cosmopolitan gentleman appears to be merely an interested listener, he is actually preparing to demolish the westerner's credibility in a brilliant exercise in epistemology. Even the westerner's teeth do not escape his critical scrutiny. "And though his teeth were singularly good," the confidence-man alias cosmopolitan gentleman remarks to himself, "those same ungracious ones might have hinted that they were too good to be true; or rather, were not so good as they might be; since the best false teeth are those made with at least two or three blemishes, the more to look like life." The examination of the westerner's teeth leads the cosmopolitan gentleman to ask implicitly: What is reality? Meanwhile he listens intently as the westerner tells him about Colonel Moredock.

Indian-hating, the westerner says, is "no monopoly" of Colonel Moredock but "a passion, in one form or other, and to a degree, greater or less, largely shared among the class to which he belonged." A backwoodsman, Moredock is "self-willed," "self-reliant," and "lonely," not merely content to be alone but "anxious" to be by himself. He has a "private passion" stemming from an unforgettable outrage: His mother had been slain by Indians. The tragedy has turned him into an avenger and his rage is raised to a religious zeal. He takes a "vow," settles his "temporal affairs," and has the "solemnity" of a "monk." The armed party he leads to punish the Indians are pledged to serve him for "forty days." Moredock, in short, is a pious ascetic, seeking violent revenge, fully aware that Indian-hating requires "the renunciation of ambition, with its objects—the pomps and glories of the world. . . ." Thus, Indian-hating, the westerner explains, is "not wholly without the efficacy of a devout sentiment."

Moredock's "private passion" demands that he hate and kill Indians, not only the ones responsible for his mother's death but all Indians, the westerner continues. His entire body/self is organized to destroy: His nerves are "electric wires—sensitive, but steel," his "finger like a trigger." He seldom stirs without his rifle, almost as if the weapon were a part of his body. A superb athlete and marksman, he is a master of woodland cunning, skilled in the art of tracking Indians, "ever on the noiseless trail; cool, collected, patient; less seen than felt; snuffing, smelling—a Leather-stocking Nemesis."

A killer, Moredock is, nonetheless, an example of "something apparently self-contradicting," the westerner adds. He and "nearly all Indian-haters have at bottom loving hearts." Moredock himself is "not without humane feelings"—"no cold husband or colder father, he." Indeed, with nobody, "Indians excepted," does he conduct himself other than in a courteous manner. Moredock is also greatly respected in white society; "famous" in his time, he is even pressed to become a candidate for governor of Illinois. The high regard Moredock enjoys is well deserved, for he has opened the West for settlement and American white progress, serving selflessly as the "captain in the vanguard of conquering civilization" and as the "Pathfinder, provider of security to those who come after him." After the westerner completes his story, the cosmopolitan gentleman, wondering how a monomaniac killer could be a good father and an esteemed citizen and how hatred for Indians could be a metaphysics for civilization, asks skeptically: "If the man of hate, how could John Moredock be also the man of love?"[3]

What Melville was observing here, through the confidence-man, was the metaphysics of Indian-hating. His westerner is not merely telling an interesting story about Colonel John Moredock: He is also offering a metaphysical justification for the destruction of Indians. While Melville provided a much-needed criticism of Indian-hating, he missed an opportunity to reveal an even more complex dimension to this phenomenon. Separating the westerner from Colonel Moredock, Melville failed to note a perverse possibility—the combination of both the metaphysician and the Indian-hater in the same person. Such an integration occurred in reality and could be found in the life of Lewis Cass.

A colonel under General William Henry Harrison during the War of 1812, Governor of Michigan Territory from 1813 to 1831, and Secretary of War under President Andrew Jackson, Cass led troops in battles against Indians, concluded treaties with them, and helped to remove them beyond the Mississippi River. He also articulated a metaphysics for his actions: While he was governor, Cass wrote an essay on "Policy and Practice of the United States and Great Britain in their Treatment of Indians," published in the *North American Review* in 1827; and shortly before he became Secretary of War, he wrote another essay, succinctly titled, "Removal of the Indians."

The presence of Indians in nineteenth-century America, for Cass, was a "moral phenomenon." They had been in contact with whites and civilization for two centuries, and yet they had not advanced in their "moral qualities." Cass found this condition puzzling. "A principle of progressive improvement seems almost inherent in human nature," he wrote. "Communities of men, as well as individuals, are stimulated by a desire to meliorate their condition." "Meliorate" had a republican and Jacksonian meaning for Cass: to strive "in the career of life to acquire riches, or honor, or power, or some other object. . . . " But there was

> little of all this in the constitution of our savages. Like the bear, and deer, and buffalo of his own forests, an Indian lives as his father lived, and dies as his father died. He never attempts to imitate the arts of his civilized neighbors. His life passes away in a succession of listless indolence, and of vigorous exertion to provide for his animal wants, or to gratify his baleful passions. . . . Efforts . . . have not been wanting to teach and reclaim him. But he is perhaps destined to disappear with the forests. . . .

The forests, Cass continued, could not be abandoned to "hopeless sterility," but must give way to the "march of cultivation and improvement."[4]

Thus, as it turned out, Cass—a one-time Colonel Moredock or Indian-fighter—had become a westerner or metaphysician of Indian-hating. What happened to Cass suggests the complex processes at work in Indian-white relations during the age of the Market Revolution. And like Melville's confidence-man, we realize the need to examine more closely and critically the metaphysics of Indian-hating.

But, as we turn to a scrutiny of Robert Montgomery Bird and Andrew Jackson, we quickly discover how difficult is our task and how puzzling is reality. The problem is an epistemological one. Bird and Jackson were disguise artists; they used the techniques of confidence to cover up rather than to expose the crimes and moral absurdities of the market society. As the author of the popular Indian-hating novel, *Nick of the Woods, or the Jibbenainosay,* published in 1837, Bird presented a moral justification for the extermination of Indians. As the conqueror of the Creeks in the War of 1813-14 and as the President of the United States responsible for Indian removal, Jackson developed a philosophical explanation which transformed Indian deaths into moral inevitability. In their exercise of confidence—the use of disguises in the quest for moral self-assurance—both men had formulated a metaphysics of Indian-hating that sprang from as well as sustained the material base of the Market Revolution.

Jibbenainosay: Indian-Hating in Fantasy

As a metaphysician of Indian-hating, Bird was more ingenious than Melville's westerner. In *Nick of the Woods,* published during the era of Indian removal and reprinted more than twenty-one times, he justified as well as condemned the violence and hate whites were directing against Indians. How this contradiction developed in Bird is revealed in an examination of his private letters, childhood writings, later unpublished fictional works, and the novel itself. In reality, Bird was hardly the simple anti-Indian writer he appeared to have been and even thought he was. Indeed, in his effort to degrade Indians, Bird used such a multitude of masks and deceptions that he became involved in an exercise in confidence more subtle and bizarre than he himself may have fully realized.[5]

Actually Bird did not grow up on the frontier, and his contact with the wilderness and Indians was extremely limited. He was born in New Castle, Delaware, in 1806, into a family which had lived on the eastern seaboard and in settled society for generations. A Whig, Bird identified with the gentility and order of an established social hierarchy, and felt uncomfortable in the society of the Market Revolution, where the pursuit of money and social mobility seemed to have possessed Americans. Financially unsuccessful as a doctor in Philadelphia and uncertain about medicine as a career, he gave his practice up after one year and decided to become a novelist and playwright—a decision which would lead him to reflect on the meaning of the Market Revolution and its impact on white as well as Indian society.

Writing, for Bird, was a way out of the "distasteful" world of business which prevailed in the new market society. He did not have, his wife later reported, "the American propensity and talent for making money." His "soul full of poetry" and his "brain stored with book-learning," he was "ignorant as a child or a woman of all business matters." Still, as a writer, Bird discovered he had not freed himself from the market, and found himself unhappily dependent on profit-oriented publishers. He was told it was necessary for an author to "sacrifice" his first book and give it to the publisher for "nothing." And he complained: "This seems to be a pretty state of things indeed, that an author should *give* a bookseller one book for the privilege of selling him a second. . . ." Regretting his "misfortune of being unknown," Bird viewed the market as a pernicious influence on literature and American letters in general.[6]

As a novelist in a society of enterprise, Bird believed the American writer had to overcome certain literary problems or "great disadvantages": Americans were a people without "romance," "traditions," and "antique associations," and their history was "short, meager & monotonous." They lacked the feudal ambience of the Old World where a writer could find "the truest & most fruitful gardens of romance" and the inspiration of "lofty feelings and chivalrous sentiments." In the heroes of European literature, he remarked enviously, "the human passions had their fullest sway . . . more romantically than will ever a people engaged in the levelling & unenthusiastic bustle of gain. Where shall the American novelist look for his hero?" Bird wanted America to have her own literature and her own heroes. But, in his view, Americans were in a "state of mental vassalage to foreigners. . . . Our opinions, our sentiments, our tastes, all come to us from abroad. Who, then, is to remind us of the interests and duties of Americans?" Like Ralph Waldo Emerson and Nathaniel Hawthorne, Bird had delineated one of the vexing predicaments of the American writer. He did not think America provided the materials he needed as a novelist, for he did not want to write about American enterprise—the unheroic and crass making of money.[7] Yet he was determined to throw off America's vassalage to Europe and help create a truly national literature.

In his search for a way out of this dilemma, Bird noted the significance of the Indian in the making of an American nationality and a national literature. If Americans were to be original and assert their cultural independence from Europe, he insisted, they must depend on America rather than Europe for the sources of their cultural identity. This independence should be expressed even in the names Americans gave to their villages and towns. "The hankering after the vanities of the old world," Bird wrote, "is in no way so ridiculously manifested, as in the christening of our new villages. What despicable folly it is to steal the names of the remarkable cities of ancient & modern Europe, & apply them to the several clusters of taverns, smithies, & variety stores which compose our infant hamlets." Americans should not "steal" names from Europe; rather they should take them from "the peculiar & sonorous titles which the aborigines were wont to apply to some spot in the neighborhood." Indeed, Bird added, many of the Indian names were "infinitely more beautiful than the sweetest" that could be found in any European gazetteer.[8] The Indian, for Bird, offered white Americans a means to realize their own national identity.

Yet, almost like a plot out of a Hawthorne novel, this creation of a white American nationality had its origins in greed and sin: The very use of Indian names for white villages and towns involved the destruction of Indians and seizure of their lands. Bird himself recognized this reality and felt a sense of guilt. Travelling through the South and Southwest in 1833, he witnessed the injustices whites had committed against Indians. On April 23, he wrote in his diary after visiting Macon, Georgia: "Poor Cherokees your Destiny is known—But Georgia, though she strike ye from the face of the Earth, yet has she permitted your name to rest on a humble flower. But while that flower keeps for your memory the pity & admiration of posterity, what a stench of shame shall be sent up by the foul rank weeds that have overgrown the fields of your oppressor." Bird was referring to the flower named the "Cherokee Rose." Two weeks later, after an encounter with a Creek, Bird wrote to his fiancée Mary Mayer:

Even the deserts here blossom like the rose; and the sterile woodlands, which the hand of oppression is this moment wresting from the poor Creeks, are all full of beauty. . . . Talking of Creeks, I saw one fellow, one day, stalking near some wigwams, who was really as noble in figure and carriage, and as picturesque in costume, as I have imagined a wild man to be. . . . As this creature approached me with the strut and port of a god, his head elevated, his eyes neither seeking nor shunning me, but shining now to the right and now to the left, as if he felt himself the guardian spirit of his tribe . . . and had nothing to do with looking after white men—it struck me there was something in his carriage very like such a swagger of self-esteem. . . . I had saluted the gentleman, and received no other return than a most magnificent and impartial grunt. . . . I was so tickled at his vainglory that I burst into a laugh. This insult, for which I was instantly sorry—for his pride was the only possession of which my countrymen had not robbed him—stung him. He halted, wheeled half around, falling into an attitude really majestic and Apollo-like, and gave me a look of such fierce and fiery intensity that I began to wish I had my pistols about me.

Several days later, in a letter to a friend, Bird again lamented: "Then thought I, in the solitude of the pine barrens of Georgia, I shall feel very poetical; and among the Muscogee Groves, I shall see wandering red men, and verify old visions of romance. . . . I saw proud warriors; but they always came to sell green strawberries, and beg tobacco."[9] The very materials Bird needed as a writer and as a maker of a national culture were derived from what he regarded as robbery and murder.

Actually the Indian had existed in Bird's consciousness long before he developed an interest in creating a national literature and before he had met Indians in the South. As a boy, he had fantasized about them in a short story written in his school composition book. In "The White-Washed Cottage of the Susquehanna, an Indian Story," a young white boy named Charley Merton and his family are living in peace and harmony in a cottage on the bank of the Susquehanna River. One day they are forced to flee to the blockhouse in town in order to avoid an Indian attack; but they are ambushed, and all the whites, except Charley and his mother, are killed. Their captor is a "frightful savage" chief, who to their surprise, speaks French. Charley's mother speaks to Wingenund in French and learns that his father was a Frenchman and his mother an Indian. "Oh sir," she asks, "why did you murder my husband then?" And the chief replies: "Oh you forget that I am no Frenchman, I am an Indian. Though my Father was a Frenchman, my mother was an Indian, and I am bound to revenge the injuries done upon her countrymen and mine." Charley and his mother are taken to the Indian village, where Wingenund treats them kindly. But they find out from him that a rival chief will soon be returning with his warriors, and that their lives will be in danger. Taking a canoe, Charley and his mother secretly paddle away. Their escape causes great commotion in the village; but Wingenund, discovering his canoe is missing, says nothing, allowing them to escape. They return to their cottage and find Charley's father alive; the blows he had received during the ambush had not been fatal. Thus the family is joyously reunited. Years later, Charley is sitting on his porch, and an Indian approaches him. "Votre nom, n'est ça pas Charlie M.?" the Indian asks. Charley and his parents excitedly welcome Wingenund, begging him to "live with them and be a white man." The chief declines their offer, gives Charley a handsome bow and quiver, and departs, loaded with presents they had given him.[10]

In this amazing story, written during Bird's childhood, the Indians are viewed as sources of great terror: They are disrupters of peace and harmony, "frightful savages," and killers of whites. Yet, they are also described sympathetically: Wingenund is a kind and considerate person, and the anger he feels springs from the injuries whites had inflicted upon Indians. The final episode of the fantasy indicates the possible choices the young Bird thought the Indian possessed: He could live with whites and become "a white man," or he could remain in the wilderness. Thus Charley and his parents appear to have survived the traumatic experience of Indian violence emotionally unscarred: Hate for the Indian and an impulsive rage for revenge do not seem to possess or deform them.

Many years after he had written the story about Charley, Bird returned to the theme of Indian violence and its psychological effect on whites. In "Awossagame," an unpublished story probably drafted after his visit to the South in the 1830s, Bird located Indian-white conflict in New England during colonial times and explicitly acknowledged the wrongs whites had committed against Indians. "Our forefathers of New England were strange people," Bird wrote at the beginning of his narrative. "They came, as homeless and landless exiles, among a rude but not inhospitable ~~people~~ race, whom after a few years they did not scruple to dispossess of their ~~lands~~ homes & possessions." Here, in his description of the initial encounter between whites and Indians in New England, was the language Bird had used to chastise whites in Georgia for their crimes against Indians.

In "Awossagame," Bird focused on John Gilbert, a harsh magistrate and fanatical Indian-hater. A onetime papist, he had been converted to "the true faith" and was now "foremost in the persecution of papists, quakers, and anabaptists." Like Charley's family, Gilbert had been the victim of Indian violence: His wife and two daughters had been slain during an attack on their village. The "misfortune" had frozen the "gentler feelings of his heart. . . . He had no family—he was alone in the world." Interpreting the slaying as God's vengeance against him for his sinful idolatry, Gilbert turned away from Catholicism and developed a fierce hatred for Indians. The fury of his hate is directed against an Indian girl, Awossagame, who is on trial for witchcraft. Magistrate Gilbert pours his venom on her, calling her "a lewd & devilish pagan," a member of an "accursed race," and a "loose savage." Her defender, Elliot Sherwyn, insists she is innocent, and Gilbert replies sharply: "Is she not an Indian?" He then breaks into an uncontrollable "expression of rancorous and malignant hate." During the trial, the girl is ordered to bare her arm in order to reveal an imprint of the "devil's mark." Suddenly Gilbert recognizes the popish symbol he himself had placed upon one of his daughters many years ago and rushes to her, crying aloud: "My child! My child! my Elizabeth! my lost Elizabeth!" Happily reunited with his daughter, Gilbert casts off the gloom and "misanthropy" which had sustained him in his hatred for the Indian.[11]

Bird probably wrote "Awossagame" during the period he was working on *Nick of the Woods,* for both stories have somewhat similar plots involving Indian-haters. But Bird treated Indians and their haters very differently in each story. In "Awossagame," he not only portrayed Indians sympathetically, placing their violence within the context of white possession of Indian "lands homes" and contrasting the malevolent Gilbert with the poor innocent Awossagame, but also pointed out the absurdity of racial stereotyping and the tragic consequences of racial hate. In *Nick of the Woods,* on the other hand, Bird denounced Indians almost as if he were Gilbert of "Awossagame." One of the purposes of the novel, he explained, was to destroy the popular image of noble Indians created by James Fenimore Cooper, and to depict "real Indians."[12]

"The North American savage," Bird declared in his preface, "has never appeared to us the gallant and heroic personage he seems to others. . . . [W]e look into the woods for the mighty warrior . . . and behold him retiring, laden with the scalps of miserable squaws and their babes. Heroical?" Bird insisted he was describing Indians as they actually were in their "natural barbaric state"—"ignorant, violent, debased, brutal," and as they appeared in war or the scalp hunt, when "all the worst deformities of the savage temperament" received their "strongest and fiercest development." In the novel itself, Bird spoke through a renegade, Braxley, to emphasize Indian brutality, especially in the form of Indian violence to white women. The fair Edith, one of the principal characters, is captured by Indians and taken to their village. There Braxley tells her that her cries for help are in vain: "From whom do you expect it? From wild, murderous, besotted Indians, who, if roused from their drunken slumbers, would be more like to assail you with their hatchets than to weep for your sorrows? Know, fair Edith, . . . that there is not one of them who would not rather see those golden tresses hung blackening in the smoke from the rafters of his wigwam, than floating over the brows they adorn. . . ."[13] Here, unmistakably, was the same hate Gilbert had expressed.

Yet, in *Nick of the Woods,* Bird probed the contradictions of Indian-hating more deeply than he had in "Awossagame" and critically exposed the deformities and agony hate and violence produced. Unlike Gilbert, the Indian-hater of the novel is an unusually complex person. He is a gentle and peaceful man, known as Nathan Quaker, who wanders alone in the woods with his dog; yet he is also Nathan Slaughter, a man of great hate and violence, who roves the forests with his bear, killing Indians and carving huge crosses on the chests of his victims. Among the Indians, he is known as the Jibbenainosay, or the spirit that walks, or the devil. Significantly, Bird's Indian-hater is unable to separate successfully these parts of his personality. Thus, he kills Indians but feels enormous guilt for each bloody deed he commits. As he shoots them he must assure himself again and again that he is a "man of peace." Overwhelmed by the deep remorse his own violence has generated, Nathan Quaker/Slaughter insists he is only protecting fair Edith and her companions against "bloodthirsty savages." And he cries out to his friend Roland: "And thee does not think then . . . thee is not of the opinion . . . thee does not altogether hold it to be as a blood-guiltiness, and a wickedness . . . that I did take to me the weapon of war, and shoot upon thee wicked oppressors, to the saving of thee life? . . . Truly, friend, thee sees it couldn't be helped; and, truly, I don't think thee conscience can condemn me."[14]

Nathan's torment and guilt distinguish him from Melville's Indian-hater. Yet, he is in one sense very much like Colonel Moredock, for Nathan, too, is a man with a tragic past. To Roland, he tells how his wife and children were slain by Indians. As Roland listens to the horrible details of the attack, he notices that Nathan is behaving strangely, resembling "a raging maniac," his mouth foaming and his body convulsing. Suddenly Nathan's cap falls off, revealing a hideous scar. Hiding beneath his cap the grotesque reminder of a scalping, Nathan nurtures a hate and a passion for revenge which shocks Roland. The depth of Nathan's "insanity" is exposed when Nathan Quaker/Slaughter encourages Roland to take the scalps of the dead Indians lying around them. "Truly, friend," he assures him, "if thee is of that mind, truly, I won't oppose thee." The suggestion appalls Roland; regarding himself as civilized, he draws back in revulsion. "Their scalps? *I* scalp them!" Roland exclaims. "I am no butcher. I leave them to the bears and wolves, which the villains in their natures so strongly resembled. I will kill Indians wherever I can; but no scalping, Nathan, no scalping for me!" After they leave the scene of carnage, Roland notices blood dripping from Nathan's knife sheath: Scarred, Nathan himself has become a scalper.[15]

Aware of his deformity, Nathan seems to have no choice but to isolate himself from civilization and satisfy his thirst for blood. Thus, he is doomed to a life of loneliness, unable to have human relationships, a wanderer in the wilderness. He is "houseless Nathan." Yet, he was very much needed in the society of the Market Revolution, for he was a pathfinder, clearing the way for a civilization of enterprise, busy axes, plowed fields, farmhouses, and towns and cities. He was the advance guard of settlement, where the fair Ediths of America would be safe from "murderous" and "drunken" Indians. Moreover, Nathan was also needed by the Rolands of America, for as long as he existed and embodied insanity and perverse violence, men like Roland could claim they were not "butchers," not mad-men.[16]

Still, the novel contains a curious contradiction and a profound irony: The effort to degrade the Indian shades into a condemnation of Indian-hating, the depiction of the barbarity of "real Indians" turns out to be the vivid description of the psychotic cruelty of the Indian-hater, and the liter-ary search for an American hero leads to the creation of an antihero. Unlike "The White-Washed Cottage" and "Awossagame," *Nick of the Woods* disguises the sympathy Bird had for Indians and the guilt he felt for what whites had done to them—the stealing of "~~lands~~ homes" from "the poor Creeks" and the "striking" of Cherokees from the "face of the Earth." Only four years before the publication of the novel, Bird had called his countrymen "oppressors" and "robbers" in their conduct toward the In-dian. Bird's agony—his twisting and turning—reflected the ambivalent emotions of a sensitive and informed man trying to create a national litera-ture and American identity, and to make some moral sense out of the material developments of his time—the expansion of the market and the destruction of the Indian.

Nick of the Woods was Bird's way of trying to work out this distressing dilemma. As the shrillness of the novel's attack on the image of the noble Indian would suggest, Bird himself did not believe in his portrait of the "real Indian." But he needed to believe in it. Thus he simplified white-Indian conflict into a fantasized struggle between good and evil—between innocent whites like Nathan and his family, settling in the West in search of a peaceful agrarian life, and wild Indians seeking to butcher and scalp white women and children. This kind of mythmaking enabled Bird as well as readers who shared his complicated feelings to relieve their guilt and at the same time justify violence against Indians. Yet, in the novel, the dichot-omy between good and evil quickly disintegrates into awesome ambiguity. Nathan Quaker's encounter with Indians deforms him: He is filled with hate, killing and scalping Indians while pathetically reaffirming his inno-cence. Regardless of what had happened to him in the past, Nathan, in his brutality, is forced to stand condemned, particularly in his own eyes. His bloodthirstiness and the mutilated Indian corpses betray him as a psy-chotic killer. Thus, Nathan Quaker/Slaughter in effect turns against his own creator, Bird himself, exposing the anti-Indian violence and hate Bird witnessed in his own time and tried to justify in his novel. In this strange way, Bird resembled the Americans aboard Melville's *Fidèle* but was even more complex: He was his own confidence man.

Jackson: Metaphysician of Indian-Hating

In his "Eulogy" on the death of Andrew Jackson, Washington McCartney asked: "What *was* Andrew Jackson, and what did he *do,* that he should receive such honors while living, and, when dead, should gather a nation round his tomb?" One answer must have been painfully obvious to Cherokee leader John Ross. Aware the President had been what McCartney described as the "imbodiment" [*sic*] of the nation's "true spirit" and "ruling passion," the "head of the great movement of the age," Ross had offered a bitter insight into the meaning of this symbol for an age. "I knew," he had declared, "that the perpetrator of a wrong never forgives his victims."[17]

Indeed, during the age of Indian removal, American society needed confidence. Enterprising whites had to find a way to expand the market, "lop off" Indian lands, and destroy Indians without inflicting guilt and moral agony upon themselves. Or else, as they could see in Bird's Nathan Quaker/Slaughter, they were in danger of disintegrating into foaming madness. They already knew what President Jackson had declared in his first annual message to Congress: Their "conduct toward these people" was "deeply interesting" to the "national character." Aware that the identity of white Americans as a moral people was at stake, they hoped the President would be able to resolve their dilemma. Jackson succeeded: He broke Creek resistance at the battle of Horse Shoe Bend in 1814 and helped to make the Southwest safe for white settlement. He also developed and expressed a metaphysics which provided the disguises whites needed in order to be both Quaker and Slaughter, and to do what Nathan could not—to both love and destroy Indians. For this "achievement" as well as for the Bank War, the Maysville Road Veto, and the preservation of the Union during the nullification crisis, Jackson gathered a "nation round his tomb."[18]

Born in 1767, Andrew Jackson was only nine years old when Americans like Rush and Jefferson declared their independence from the king. Yet he came to represent the republican conduct and consciousness for which the Revolution had been fought. Throughout his life, he did not allow himself to forget the "bravery and blood" of his "fore fathers" and the "independent rights" they had secured for him and other Americans; he insisted Americans be worthy of the name of "freemen." As President, Jackson invoked what historian Marvin Meyers has described as a "persuasion," in order to restore republican faith of the fathers among sons pursuing worldly goods in the society of the Market Revolution.[19]

In life and in legend, Jackson was, in many ways, the archetype of the self-made republican man. "He seems to have been an orphan from the plow to the Presidency," a eulogist exclaimed many years after Jackson's death. "He must, therefore, be regarded as the architect of his own fortunes." Actually, Jackson *had* been an orphan: His father died two months before he was born in the Carolina frontier, and his mother died when he was fourteen years old. But before she left him forever, she gave him some republican advice: "Never tell a lie, nor take what is not your own, nor sue anybody for slander or assault and battery. Always settle them cases yourself!" Self-reliant and self-governing, Jackson virtually had no childhood, or at least no adolescence. To his admirers and to Jackson himself, this assumption of responsibility at an early age prepared him to "rise rapidly with a rapidly rising people." Looking back at his own childhood, Jackson attributed his success to the challenges and difficulties he had to overcome early in his life. "I have been Tossed upon the waves of fortune from youthood," he wrote, "I have experienced prosperity and adversity. It was this that gave me knowledge of human nature, it was this that forced into action, all the energies of my mind, and ultimately caused me to progress through life as I have done. . . ." Even as he referred to the "blood" of the "fore fathers," Jackson knew he could claim responsibility for securing his rights: He had been captured by the British in 1781 and was slashed with a sword by a British officer for refusing to blacken the man's boots.[20] Thus, as it turned out, the "blood" shed had included his own.

The fortune Jackson made was also his own. He squandered his inheritance in gambling houses and brothels; as a young lawyer, he was a "roaring, rollicking, game-cocking, horse-racing, card-playing, mischievous fellow. . . ." His life at this time was hardly one of republican virtue; yet, in a way, this profligacy reinforced Jackson's republican origins. His inheritance, his last remaining family tie destroyed, as Michael Rogin has noted, Jackson would begin "a new life totally alone." Completely responsible for himself and determined to be self-made, he would have no king, no parents even, and certainly no inheritance. In 1787, Jackson moved to Nashville to make his fortune on the frontier. There he practiced law, speculated in land, and opened stores to sell goods from Philadelphia. He also married into one of the leading families of the Cumberland and became a wealthy Tennessee planter with more than one hundred slaves. The key to his success was his involvement in land speculation—land acquired from Indians. In 1796, for example, Jackson paid a speculator $100 for a half-interest in 5,000 acres at the Chickasaw bluffs on the Mississippi, and

immediately sold half of his share for $312. He held on to the remaining
share until 1818, when he negotiated the Chickasaw treaty and opened the
area to white settlement; then he sold it for $5,000.[21]

No shining republican himself, Jackson nevertheless offered republican
advice to his nephew and son. He sent Andrew J. Donelson instructions on
the need to guard against temptations. Many snares, the uncle warned,
would be laid for the "inexperienced youth" to lead him into "dissipation,
vice, and folly." While the young man should not deprive himself of
"proper relaxation" or "innocent amusement," he should seek out only
"virtuous" company and exercise care in his relationships with women.
"Among the virtuous females, you ought to cultivate an acquaintance, and
shun the intercourse of the others as you would the society of the viper . . .
it is intercourse with the latter discription [sic] that engenders corruption,
and contaminates the morals, and fits the young mind for any act of unguarded baseness. . . ." On another occasion, Jackson warned his son
against accumulating debt: "Be always certain, if you wish to be independent, to keep your wants within your means, always when you have money,
paying for them when bought."[22] In his own conduct as a ribald young
lawyer and a land speculator, Jackson could not claim authority to teach
republican lessons even to his nephew and son, much less to society in
general. The source of this authority had to be located elsewhere—in the
fierce self-discipline and control Jackson had imposed on himself as a soldier and Indian-fighter.

For Jackson, republican virtue was achieved in war. The War of 1812
and the Creek War of 1813-14 gave him the opportunity to overcome what
he called the "indolence" which threatened to destroy him, and to seek
republican purification and regeneration through violence. A "free born
son" of America, Jackson went to war against the British to defend the
"only republick now existing in the world," the "fabric cemented by the
blood of our fathers." A "brave son of Tennessee," Jackson led troops
against Creeks in Mississippi to conquer "the cream of the Creek country"
for the expansion of the "republick" and to avenge the deaths of more than
two hundred people killed by hostile Creeks at Fort Mims. A soldier, separated from his frivolous and bourgeois past, he could now view himself as
a worthy republican son. From the battlefield, he wrote to his wife: "I can
only say your good understanding, and reflection will reconcile you to our
separation, the situation of our country require it for who could brook a
British tyranny, who would not prefer dying free, struggling for our liberty
and religion, than live a British slave." Jackson believed Americans had to
have republican discipline and to exercise it in war in order to protect their
freedom. They must "never prefer an inglorious sloth, a supine inactivity to

the honorable toil of carrying the republican standard to the heights of Abraham," Commander Jackson told his troops. As a soldier, Jackson could lay claim to the republican virtue of respectable work, which he could not do as a land speculator.[23]

As Jackson marched against the Indians, he also waged a private battle against his own body. His "fore fathers" had had to discipline the physical self in order to deny pleasure; Jackson had to discipline his body in order to defy pain. His had been a life of illness and physical agony. He had contracted smallpox as a teenager, and suffered from recurrent malaria, fevers, and rheumatism. Chronically constipated, he was often in extreme discomfort in the field, especially during "a severe attacke of the Bowell complaint." He suffered from attacks of dysentery, which caused painful cramps and diarrhea. His body reflected his sickly condition: Over six feet tall, he weighed only 145 pounds. Jackson felt an almost constant pain in his chest, where a bullet received in a duel with Charles Dickinson in 1806 was still lodged close to his heart. Shortly before he departed for the Creek campaign, he had exchanged gunfire with Thomas Hart Benton, and a bullet had fractured his left shoulder. His body broken and feverish, Jackson marched into the field against the Creeks. Called "Old Hickory" by his troops, he was admired for his power to withstand hardship and pain. His victory over the British at New Orleans was interpreted as a personal triumph over his ailing body. There, as one observer described the battle, Jackson barely had the strength to stand erect without support. "His body was sustained alone by the spirit within," and "the disease contracted in the swamps of Alabama still clung to him." Jackson prevailed over both the British and the body. "Reduced to a mere skeleton, unable to digest his food, and unrefreshed by sleep, his life seemed to be preserved by some miraculous agency."[24]

His body disciplined, Jackson used violence to bring Indians under control. His struggle to dominate both his body and the Indians was integrated: Military campaigns in the Creek War enabled him to subordinate his physical self and to destroy Indians. Indians, for Jackson, personified the body. He believed they were impulsive and lacked "discipline." He also viewed Indian men as sexual threats to white women; few incidents aroused his wrath as much as the Indian capture of white women. Jackson made the case of Mrs. Crawly his "own." Angrily protesting her capture and confinement to "a mortar, naked, lascerated," he demanded that the "brave sons of Tennessee" wipe away this "blushing shame."[25]

During the campaign against the Creeks in 1813–14, Jackson denounced his Indian enemies as "savage bloodhounds" and "blood thirsty barbarians," and urged his troops to exterminate them. "I know," he told his men, "you will teach the cannibals who reveled in the carnage of our unoffending Citizens at Fort Meems that the thunder of our arms is more terrible than the Earth quakes of their Prophets, and that Heaven Dooms to inevitable destruction the wretch who Smiles at the torture he inflicts and who neither spares female innocence, declining age nor helpless infancy." Shortly before the battle of Horse Shoe Bend in March 1814, Jackson was in a state of rage. "I must distroy [sic] those deluded victims doomed to distruction by their own restless and savage conduct," he wrote to Major General Thomas Pinckney. The next day, he sent Pinckney another letter, and again he snarled at his enemies. Calling them "savage dogs," he wrote: "It is by the charge I distroy from eight to ten of them, for one they kill of my men, by charging them I have on all occasions preserved the scalps of my killed." At the battle of Horse Shoe Bend, Jackson and his troops surrounded some eight hundred Creeks at a bend in the river and killed almost all of them, including women and children. After the battle, he sent cloth worn by the slain warriors to the ladies of Tennessee. His soldiers cut long strips of skin from the bodies of the dead Indians and used them for bridle reins; they also cut the tip of each dead Indian's nose to count the number of enemy bodies.[26]

In the Creek War of 1813-14, Jackson had accomplished more than the conquest of Indian lands, or what he described, in a letter written to Thomas Pinckney after his victory at Horse Shoe Bend, as the "valuable country" west of the Cosee and north of the "allabama." He had also done more than punish Indians for exercising "lawless tyranny" over "helpless and unprotected" white women, for murdering white mothers and their "little prattling infants," and for capturing white women. Most importantly, in the war, Jackson had purified the republican self: He was no longer a high-living lawyer and shady land speculator. In the wilderness, he had disciplined and chastened himself, and triumphed over "indolence," "sloth," pain, and Indians. Jackson was ready to be the leader of a democracy in quest of the restoration of republican virtue; he was also ready to lead the nation in the removal of Indians.[27]

Fourteen years later, Jackson, still remembered as a heroic Indian fighter, was elected to the presidency. During the age of Jackson, some seventy thousand Indians were removed from their homes in the South and driven west of the Mississippi River. Due to violence, disease, starvation, dangerous travel conditions, and harsh winter weather, almost one-third of the southern Indians died. By 1844, the South was, as far as Indians were concerned, a "white man's country." Jackson had extended Jefferson's empire of liberty by removing Indians toward the "Stony mountains."[28]

As President, Jackson played a complex and decisive role in Indian removal. Shortly after his election, he supported the efforts of three southern states—Georgia, Alabama, and Mississippi—to abolish Indian tribal units and laws and to extend state authority over Indians. Georgia subjected them to militia duty, state taxes, and suits for debt, while it denied them the suffrage as well as the right to bring suits and to testify in court. All three states opened Indian territory to white settlement; they also encouraged intruders and allowed whites to take Indian lands, including "improved" or cultivated tracts. As the states imperialistically extended their authority over Indian territory, President Jackson told Congress: "If the states chose to extend their laws over them it would not be in the power of the federal government to prevent it." Actually, as Michael Rogin has pointed out, Jackson's assertions of federal impotence in this case made him "the passive spectator of a policy he had actively advocated." Jackson knew what his responsibility in this matter was as the chief executive of the United States. Treaties and federal laws had given Congress, not the states, authority over the Indians. The Indian Trade and Intercourse Act of 1802 had provided that no land cessions could be made except by treaty with a tribe, and that federal law, not state law, would operate in Indian territory. In 1832 the United States Supreme Court ruled against the extension of state law into Indian territory, but President Jackson refused to enforce the Court's decision.[29]

While claiming federal powerlessness, Jackson collaborated and conspired with state officials to usurp tribal lands and remove Indians. In a letter to Jackson, dated February 3, 1830, General John Coffee outlined the strategy for this collaboration:

> Deprive the chiefs of the power they now possess, take from them their own code of laws, and reduce them to plain citizenship . . . and they will soon determine to move, and then there will be no difficulty in getting the poor Indians to give their consent. All this will be done by the State of Georgia if the United States do not interfere with her law—. . . . This will of course silence those in our country who constantly seek for causes to complain—It may indeed turn them loose upon Georgia, but that matters not, it is Georgia who clamors for the Indian lands, and she alone is entitled to the blame if any there be.[30]

In this strategy to break up tribes, "reduce" Indians to citizenship, and force them to give up their lands and move away, all Jackson had to do, as President, was to make certain the federal government did not interfere with the law of the State of Georgia.

But Jackson did not limit himself to noninterference. He also met with Indians to inform them he had no power to help in their resistance against the states and to advise them to migrate to the West. Jackson even employed "confidential agents" to manipulate the chiefs and persuade them to accept removal. The secret mission of these "confidential agents," as stated in a letter from Secretary of War John Eaton to General William Carroll, was to use bribery to influence "the Chiefs and influential men." "It is believed," wrote Eaton, "that the more careful you are to secure from even the Chiefs the official character you carry with you, the better—Since no circumstance is too slight to excite their suspicion or awaken their jealousy; Presents in your discretion to the amount of not more than $2000 might be made with effect, by attaching to you the poorer Indians, as you pass through their Country, given as their friend; and the same to the Children of the Chiefs, and the Chiefs themselves, in clothes, or otherwise."[31] Jackson did not have to depend heavily on deception and bribery to remove Indians, however. He had available two "legal" methods—indirect removal through the land allotment program and direct removal through treaty.

Used to deprive Creeks, Choctaws, and Chickasaws of their territories, the land allotment program provided for granting land in fee simple title to individual Indians. As a landowner, an Indian could be "reduced" to citizenship, or he could sell and move west of the Mississippi River. In the Treaty of Dancing Rabbit Creek, for example, Choctaw families and individuals were instructed to register with an Indian agent within six months after the ratification of the treaty if they wished to remain in the state of Mississippi and receive a grant of land. Seemingly, the program gave Indians a choice as well as a fair chance to succeed in white society. Under this program, however, thousands of individual Indians were "given," sometimes forced to accept, land grants only to have land speculators take their fee simple titles. Everywhere federal certifying agents cooperated with speculators to defraud Indians of their lands. The Columbus Land Company, for instance, took a group of Creeks from one agent to another to sign contracts for grants. Speculators bribed certifying agents to approve fraudulent contracts; often the agents were the speculators themselves. After they had secured lands for individual Indians, speculators set up stores which extended credit to them in exchange for land titles as collateral, and then took over the deeds as they failed to pay off their debts. Under the program, Mary Young has calculated, speculators acquired eighty to ninety percent of the lands granted to southeastern Indians, or some 25 million acres of land.[32]

The land allotment program enabled white speculators, farmers, and planters to take Indian lands "legally" and to absolve themselves from responsibility for the Indians' poverty, removal, and destruction. Indians had been "given" land and responsibility for their own welfare; whites could not be blamed if they got into debt, lost their lands, and had to remove beyond the Mississippi. As Secretary of War Lewis Cass explained, "[O]ur citizens were disposed to buy and the Indians to sell. . . . The subsequent disposition which shall be made of these payments seems to be utterly beyond the reach of the Government. . . . The improvident habits of the Indians can not be controlled by regulations. . . . If they waste it, as waste it they too often will, it is deeply to be regretted yet still it is only exercising a right conferred upon them by the treaty."[33] A Lockean contractual framework had been imposed upon the Indian: He was no longer defined as a member of a community or tribe but as an individual. Entitled to own and sell private property, he was thrust into the market system. Thus, a victim of manipulation and fraud, the Indian was blamed for his own ruin.

In a letter to General John Coffee, April 7, 1832, President Jackson bluntly stated the real purpose of the land allotment program: "The object of the government now is, to have all their reservations surveyed and laid off as early as we can." Once Indians had been granted individual land allotments, they would "sell and move to the West." And then Jackson added: "When the reserves are surveyed it will require but a short time to compleat the ballance and have it into markett. . . ."[34] What Jackson wanted in the market was the Indian's land, not the Indian himself as a Lockean farmer.

Where Jackson was not able to buy out and remove Indians individually, he turned to the treaty method to remove the entire tribe directly. This was the strategy used against the Cherokees. In 1834, Jackson failed to secure a treaty for the cession of Cherokee lands and removal of the tribe to the West. The next year he sent the Reverend J. F. Schermerhorn to negotiate a treaty with the pro-removal faction of the Cherokees. The treaty provided that the Cherokees would cede their entire eastern territory and relocate beyond the Mississippi in exchange for $4.5 million from the federal government. Signed in Washington on March 14, the treaty had to be ratified by the tribe in full council to be effective. The council rejected the treaty, however, and Schermerhorn made arrangements for another meeting in December, to be held in New Echota, Georgia, to negotiate a new treaty. To Secretary Cass, he wrote: "We shall make a treaty with those who attend, and rely upon it." Meanwhile, the Georgia militia jailed the anti-removal leader, John Ross, and suppressed the Cherokee newspaper. With the opposition silenced, Schermerhorn proceeded to make a treaty with those in attendance, even though they constituted only a tiny fraction of the entire Cherokee tribe and though none of the principal officers of the tribe were present. The Treaty of New Echota was signed and sent to Washington for ratification by Congress.[35]

President Jackson "relied upon it," and successfully urged Congress to ratify the treaty. But the federal government's dishonesty could not be covered up; appointed to enroll the Cherokees for removal, Major W. M. Davis found out what had actually happened at New Echota and wrote a letter to Secretary Cass to expose Schermerhorn's shameful chicanery:

> Sir, that paper . . . called a treaty, is no treaty at all, because not sanctioned by the great body of the Cherokee and made without their participation or assent. I solemnly declare to you that upon its reference to the Cherokee people it would be instantly rejected by nine-tenths of them. . . . The most cunning and artful means were resorted to to conceal the paucity of numbers present at the treaty. . . . Mr. Schermerhorn's apparent design was to conceal the real number present and to impose on the public and the government on this point. The delegation taken to Washington by Mr. Schermerhorn had no more authority to make a treaty than any other dozen Cherokee accidentally picked up for the purpose.[36]

The Treaty of New Echota was a known fraud; still the President responded to it as if it were the voice of the Cherokee people.

Ratification triggered the movement of thousands of white intruders into Cherokee teritory. They seized Cherokee farms and cultivated lands, forcing out and often murdering the inhabitants. Still the Cherokees refused to recognize the treaty and leave their territory; finally, in 1838, the federal government ordered the army to round up 15,000 of them. Placed in detention camps and then marched west beyond the Mississippi in the dead of winter, more than 4,000 Cherokees died on the "Trail of Tears."

As the President responsible for Indian removal, Jackson was a philosopher as well as a policy-maker. While he negotiated fraudulent treaties and schemed with state leaders to acquire Indian lands, he offered solemn reflections on the destinies of whites and Indians. A leader of his people, he recognized the need to explain the nation's conduct toward Indians, to give it moral meaning. In his writings, messages to Congress, and personal letters, Jackson presented a philosophical justification for the extermination of native Americans.

Jackson's metaphysics began with a confession: White efforts to civilize the Indian had failed. Whites had purchased lands from Indians and thrust them farther into the wilderness, forcing them to remain in a "wandering state." Some Indians in the South had become civilized and learned the art of farming, Jackson noted; but they had set up an "independent government" within the state of Georgia. Such a "foreign government" could not be tolerated. Thus civilized Indians had to submit to the state. But, unlike Jefferson, Jackson did not believe the Indian could remain within the state, surrounded by whites in civilized society, and survive. "The fate of the Mohigan, the Narragansett, and the Delaware is fast overtaking the Choctaw, the Cherokee, and the Creek. That this fate surely awaits them if they remain within the limits of the State does not admit of a doubt." Like the tribes before them, they would disappear. "Humanity and national honor demand that every effort be made to avert so great a calamity." Driven by "feelings of justice," Jackson asked whether something could be done "to preserve this much-injured race." And he offered an answer: He proposed that a district west of the Mississippi be set aside—"to be guaranteed to the Indian tribes as long as they shall occupy it." There they would be free to live in peace and to have their own government "as long as the grass grows, or water runs."[37]

Urging Indians to seek new homes beyond the Mississippi, Jackson encouraged them to follow the example of whites, become a people in motion, restless and expansive. "Doubtless it will be painful [for Indians] to leave the graves of their fathers," Jackson told Congress. "But what do they more than our ancestors did or than our children are now doing? To better their condition in an unknown land our forefathers left all that was dear in earthly objects. Our children by thousands yearly leave the land of their birth to seek new homes in distant regions." Movement, geographical and social, represented progress and a Jacksonian way of life: It enabled white Americans to develop "power and faculties of man in their highest perfection."[38]

Time and again, President Jackson insisted he wanted to be "just" and "humane" toward the Indians. He wanted to protect them from the "mercenary influence of white men," and to exercise a "parental" control over them and perpetuate their race. He explained that he wanted them to be happy and that their happiness depended on removal. Jackson regarded himself as a "father," concerned about the welfare of his Indian "children." He instructed Major David Haley to transmit to the chiefs of the Choctaws his advice as their "father." "That the chiefs and warriors may fully understand this talk," wrote Jackson, "you will please go amongst, & read it to, and fully explain to them. Tell them it is from my own mouth you have rec'd it and that I never speak with a forked tongue." His advice to the Indians was to move beyond the Mississippi; and, if they refused to accept this advice, Jackson warned, they must then be responsible for whatever happened to them. "I feel conscious of having done my duty to my red children," he said, "and if any failure of my good intentions arises, it will be attributable to their want of duty to themselves, not to me."[39]

Ultimately, as Jackson revealed in his removal of the Seminoles, white paternalism drew its power from the barrel of a gun. In his letter to the Seminoles in 1835, the President offered paternal advice as he threatened paternal power. Addressing them as "My Children," he said he was sorry to learn that they had been listening to "bad counsel." "You know me," he assured, "and you know that I would not deceive, nor advise you to do anything that was unjust or injurious." As a "friend," Jackson claimed he offered them "the words of truth." White people were settling around them, and the game had disappeared from their country. "Your people are poor and hungry," he observed. "Even if you had a right to stay, how could you live where you now are?" Then he warned them about the market system as if it were an impersonal force and he were not a part of it. "You have sold all your country. . . . The tract you have ceded will soon be surveyed and sold, and immediately afterwards will be occupied by a white population." Thus, Seminoles should migrate to the West where game was yet abundant and where they would be far away from the market and whites. If they remained, they would starve and be forced to steal from whites. "You will be resisted, punished, perhaps killed," the white father predicted. Again, he urged them to leave, and then added: "But lest some of your rash young men should forcibly oppose your arrangements for removal, I have ordered a large military force to be sent among you."[40]

Seminoles, under the leadership of Osceola, refused to accept Jackson's fatherly advice and took up armed resistance. Enraged, Jackson sent enough troops to Florida "as might eat Powell [Osceola] and his few." But the Seminoles were not so easily crushed. After Jackson left office in 1837, he continued to focus his fury on the insubordinate tribe. In a memorandum on the Florida campaign, he recommended a strategy to bring Seminole defiance to a quick end. American commanders should conduct search and destroy missions, and order their troops to find Seminole villages and capture or destroy the women. Unless they knew "where the Indian women were," Jackson wrote, United States soldiers would never be effective: Their effort would be "like a combined operation to encompass a wolf in the hamocks without knowing first where her den and whelps were."[41]

Here was the propensity for violence which Jefferson had fearfully described as the "most boisterous passions," and which Jackson had disguised, giving it moral legitimacy. Many years before Indian removal, Commander Jackson had declared to his troops after the bloody victory at Horse Shoe Bend:

The fiends of the Tallapoosa will no longer murder our women and children, or disturb the quiet of our borders. Their midnight flambeaux will no more illumine their Council house or shine upon the victim of their infernal orgies. They have disappeared from the face of the Earth. In their places a new generation will arise who will know their duties better. The weapons of warfare will be exchanged for the utensils of husbandry; and the wilderness which now withers in sterility and seems to mourn the desolation which overspreads it, will blossom as the rose, and become the nursery of the arts. . . . How lamentable it is that the path to peace should lead through blood, and over the carcases of the slain!! But it is in the dispensation of that providence, which inflicts partial evil to produce general good.

There, on the dark and bloody ground of the West, General Jackson had developed a justification for violence against Indians and a metaphysics for genocide. White violence was a necessary partial evil for the realization of a general good—the extension of white civilization and the transformation of the wilderness into an agrarian society and a nursery of the arts. As President, Jackson took this rationale and incorporated it into the national consciousness. In his second annual message to Congress, he declared:

Humanity has often wept over the fate of the aborigines of this country, and Philanthropy has been long busily employed in devising means to avert it, but its progress has never for a moment been arrested, and one by one have many powerful tribes disappeared from the earth. To follow to the tomb the last of his race and tread on the graves of extinct nations excite melancholy reflections. But true philanthropy reconciles the mind to these vicissitudes as it does to the extinction of one generation to make room for another.

In all this, the President reassured the nation, as the general had earlier reassured his troops, that nothing was to be "regretted." "Philanthropy could not wish to see this continent restored to the condition in which it was found by our forefathers." And the metaphysician then asked: "What good man would prefer a country covered with forests and ranged by a few thousand savages to our extensive Republic, studded with cities, towns, and prosperous farms . . . filled with all the blessings of liberty, civilization, and religion?" As the President meditated on the disappearance of Indians and the "melancholy reflections" it excited, he claimed for white Americans their moral innocence. What had happened to the Indians was inevitable, even moral.[42]

The metaphysics of Indian-hating, for Jackson, had begun in the Creek War of 1813-14 and was completed in the Bank War of 1832-36. In his war against Indians, Jackson had used them to define savagery: Thus, he described them as "cannibals," "savage dogs," "bloodhounds," and "blood thirsty" slayers of innocent white women and children. His attack on Indians, however, did not enable him to formulate a clear and precise definition of civilization, especially a republican one. His references to the "free born sons" of the "republick" and the republican "fabric" of the Revolutionary forefathers were vague and inadequate. Victorious over "savages," Jackson still needed to identify the possessors of republican virtue—the "real people." This he did in his war against the Bank of the United States.

In Jackson's mind, the Bank War was similar to his military campaign against the Creeks: It was a struggle to preserve the virtues of the Old Republic. The privately controlled Second Bank of the United States, chartered in 1816 and the depository for federal funds, was "a system at war" with "the genius" of the institutions the republican fathers had established. Scheduled for a renewal of its charter during Jackson's presidency, the Bank encountered his republican wrath. "Our Fathers," he declared, had "perilled their lives" to arrest the "natural instinct to reach after new acquisitions." The "Revolutionary struggle" should not be weakened in "lavish public disbursements"; corporations with "exclusive privileges" should not be allowed to undermine the "original" checks and balances of the Constitution.[43]

The Bank represented, to Jackson, an even greater and more insidious threat to republicans than the Creeks. The red enemies were "stupid mortals," relying on "subterfuges" such as their "grim visages" and "hideous yells" rather than on their bravery. By contrast, the Bank constituted a consolidation of power: Through its "silent" and "secret" operation and through shrewd manipulation, a few corrupt men were able to acquire control over the "labor and earnings of the great body of the people." In his famous bank veto message, which resulted in the destruction of the Bank, Jackson declared:

> It is to be regretted that the rich and powerful too often bend the acts of government to their selfish purposes. Distinctions in society will always exist under every just government. Equality of talents, of education, or of wealth can not be produced by human institution. In the full enjoyment of the gifts of Heaven and the fruits of superior industry, economy, and virtue, every man is equally entitled to protection by law; but when the laws undertake to add to these just advantages artificial distinctions, to grant titles, gratuities, and exclusive privileges, to make the rich richer and the potent more powerful, the humble members of society—the farmers, mechanics, and laborers—who have neither the time nor the means of securing like favors to themselves—have a right to complain of the injustice of their Government.

The Bank and its system of paper money engendered a "spirit of speculation injurious to the habits and character of the people," an "eager desire to amass wealth without labor," a "craving desire for luxurious enjoyment," and a "sickly appetite for effeminate indulgence." The republican fathers had located the source of corruption in the king; Jackson located it in the Bank. The new "hydra of corruption" drained from the people their power to resist cupidity, idleness, temptation, and extravagance.[44]

Regardless of whether he was struggling against the "moneyed power" or the Indians, Jackson excluded both groups from the "real people"—the farmers, mechanics, and laborers. "The bone and sinew of the country," they depended on their own "honest industry" and economy for success. Self-governing and independent, they cultivated the soil, earned the fruits of their own labor, and possessed the "habits of economy and simplicity" so congenial to the "character of republicans." But the corrupt men of wealth and the Indians were antagonistic to honest labor. While the former exploited the privileges granted to them by the government in order to enrich themselves, the latter lacked the "intelligence, industry, the moral habits," "the desire of improvement," and the capacity for self-government. "Observation proves that the great body of the southern tribes of Indians," Jackson claimed, "are erratic in their habits, and wanting in those endowments which are suited to a people who would direct themselves. . . ." "Children of the forests," they did not cultivate the land. How could they, asked Jackson, make claims on tracts on which they had neither dwelt nor made "improvements," merely because they had "seen them from the mountain or passed them in the chase?" In Jackson's judgment, neither men of "artificial distinctions" nor Indians had a place in a republican society.[45]

The parallel between Jackson's military campaign against Indians and his war against the Bank was distressingly evident to Nicholas Biddle. "The worthy President," observed Bank Director Biddle, "thinks because he has scalped Indians . . . he is to have his way with the Bank." Biddle's was a most perspicacious remark. Indeed, in Jackson's fantasy, Indians were "those monsters," while the Bank was "the monster." Indians threatened to kill Jackson and other whites in the West and lay waste "the abodes of industry." The Bank, too, "waged war upon the people" of the "republick" and appeared to threaten Jackson personally. "The bank, Mr. Van Buren, is trying to kill me, *but* I will kill it," the President exclaimed in fury. "I've got my foot upon it and I'll crush it." A slayer of "monsters," Jackson destroyed the Creeks at Horse Shoe Bend and the Bank of the United States and swept both of them from "the face of the Earth."[46]

Confidence, as Melville suggested in his novel, was a political style which depended on role-playing, and which was widely used in Jacksonian society. Unlike Melville's confidence man, Jackson employed confidence as a technique to take himself and his society away from rather than toward exposure, critical awareness, and redemption. In Jackson's service, disguises enabled him to give events his own definitions, and to judge his and the nation's actions in a variety of ways and in accordance with their economic interests and psychological needs. His was a "persuasion" which not only allowed him to destroy the Bank as he nurtured a nostalgia for an old agrarian republic but also made it possible for him to advance the market as he articulated compassion and regret for the Indians.

In the removal and killing of Indians, the expansion of the market, and the formulation of a metaphysics of Indian-hating, Jackson was in effect the nation's confidence man. Undeniably, as President Jackson himself acknowledged, how whites conducted themselves in relations with Indians was "deeply interesting" to their "national character." They must not be guilty of capitalist corruption, moral absurdity, or mass murders. As President, Jackson told them they were not, and skillfully exercised confidence in his own conduct toward Indians. He excluded them from the "real people" and claimed they were hunters and wanderers as he encouraged intruders to seize cultivated and improved Indian lands. He called himself "father" and Indians "children" as he employed "confidential agents" to deceive and bribe Indians in order to remove them from their lands; he insisted that the government be kept pure and separated from the corruption of land speculators as he permitted the government to be used in their service. He assured the Indians that his advice to them was based on "feelings of justice" as he moved their lands into the "markett." Indeed, through the use of a multitude of disguises, Jackson protected the moral character of the American people as he served the class interests of the speculators, farmers, and planters seeking to appropriate Indian lands.

But what Jackson *"was"* and what he *"did"* involved more than the appropriation of millions of acres of Indian lands. As general and as President, Jackson had built a "pyramid of skulls": Indians lost their lives as well as their lands. A Jibbenainosay in reality, he accomplished what Bird fantasized—Indian deaths. He helped to bring about that "calamity" which he said he was seeking to avoid, and succeeded precisely where Nathan Quaker/Slaughter had failed. He was able to dissociate his acts of violence against Indians from his claims of compassion, and to integrate both into a metaphysics of civilization which allowed whites to destroy the Indian and assure themselves that the Indian's extinction was not to be "regretted." This was an integration Nathan Quaker/Slaughter could not achieve: Unable to engage in self-deception, despite all of his disguises, Nathan knew he was a killer—knew murder was murder and evil was evil.

He possessed a singular sanity Jackson did not have. Both Quaker and Slaughter, Jackson was seemingly able to be what Melville's confidence man thought was impossible for Colonel John Moredock—a man of love and also of hate, a good father and also an Indian-killer. Soon after the battle of Horse Shoe Bend, Jackson wrote to his wife: "The *carnage* was *dreadful* . . . . I hope shortly to put an end to the war and return to your arms, kiss my little andrew for me, tell him I have a warriors bow and quiver for him." "No cold husband or colder father," Jackson was at the same time like the Jibbenainosay, a "Leather-stocking Nemesis." "And Natty, what sort of a white man is he?" asked D. H. Lawrence. "Why, he is a man with a gun. He is a killer, a slayer. Patient and gentle as he is, he is a slayer. Self-effacing . . . still he is a killer."[47]

CHAPTER VI

THE METAPHYSICS OF CIVILIZATION: "THE BLACK RACE WITHIN OUR BOSOM"

Depravity in the oppressed is no apology for the oppressor; but rather an additional stigma to him, as being, in a large degree, the effect and not the cause of oppression.

—Herman Melville

Labour cannot emancipate itself in the white skin where in the black it is branded.

—Karl Marx

As Alexis de Tocqueville sadly reflected on the horrors of Indian removal, he contrasted the fate of Indians with the future of blacks in America. He remembered an incident which he thought contained the dynamic elements of the nature of triracial relations. The experience so impressed the French visitor that he recorded it in *Democracy in America:*

> While I was traveling through the forests which still cover the state of Alabama, I arrived one day at the log house of a pioneer. I did not wish to penetrate into the dwelling of the American, but retired to rest myself for a while on the margin of a spring, which was not far off, in the woods. While I was in this place (which was in the neighborhood of the Creek territory), an Indian woman appeared, followed by a Negress, and holding by the hand a little white girl of five

or six years, whom I took to be the daughter of the pioneer. A sort of barbarous luxury set off the costume of the Indian; rings of metal were hanging from her nostrils and ears, her hair, which was adorned with glass beads, fell loosely upon her shoulders; and I saw that she was not married, for she still wore that necklace of shells which the bride always deposits on the nuptial couch. The Negress was clad in squalid European garments. All three came and seated themselves upon the banks of the spring; and the young Indian, taking the child in her arms, lavished upon her such fond caresses as mothers give, while the Negress endeavored, by various little artifices, to attract the attention of the young Creole. The child displayed in her slightest gestures a consciousness of superiority that formed a strange contrast with her infantine weakness; as if she received the attentions of her companions with a sort of condescension. The Negress was seated on the ground before her mistress, watching her smallest desires and apparently divided between an almost maternal affection for the child and servile fear; while the savage, in the midst of her tenderness, displayed an air of freedom and pride which was almost ferocious. I had approached the group and was contemplating them in silence, but my curiosity was probably displeasing to the Indian woman, for she suddenly rose, pushed the child roughly from her, and, giving me an angry look, plunged into the thicket.

The scene for Tocqueville was emblematic of Indian independence and black dependence. Where Indians refused to conform to white civilization, less from "a hatred of it than from a dread of resembling the Europeans," blacks had been forcefully denied their African language, culture, and even the remembrance of their country. Describing the European or white character, Tocqueville commented on the consequences of this difference between the two races: "The European is to the other races of mankind what man himself is to the lower animals: he makes them subservient to his use, and when he cannot subdue he destroys them." Thus, Tocqueville predicted, the Indians would perish in the same isolated condition in which they lived, but blacks would continue to be "fastened" to whites "without intermingling."[1]

The Black Child/Savage: A Jacksonian Persuasion

During the age of Jackson, blacks were not regarded as "sons of nature" or the subjects of "melancholy reflections"; nor were they "obstacles" which had to be removed beyond the Mississippi River or destroyed. Rather, blacks lived in the settled areas of the United States, within white civilization, in physical proximity to whites. As workers, blacks possessed the labor slaveholders appropriated in order to cultivate the "vacant lands" they had taken from Indians and to produce surplus for the market. Thus, blacks had a unique future in America: Unlike Indians, they were not to be expelled but to be even more securely chained to white society and its political economy.

"Free" in the North and enslaved in the South, blacks had different regional relationships to the process of production. Constituting two percent of the northern and thirty-three percent of the southern population, they were peripheral to industrial production in the North and essential to agricultural production in the South. Still, everywhere, whites "branded" blacks as "children" and "savages." As the economy of the Market Revolution became dependent on black labor, as the southern planter class escalated its defense of slavery, and as industrial cities and a white proletariat developed in America, the racial ideology of the black "child/savage" served both caste and class functions in an increasingly complex way in the North as well as the South.

The North was not the promised land for blacks. Racism was both virulent and violent in the states above the Mason and Dixon Line during the years before the Civil War. Tocqueville even thought racial prejudice was greater in the free than in the slave states. Though they were no longer slaves, northern blacks were victims of racial discrimination and segregation. "The same schools do not receive the children of the black and the European," the French visitor observed. "In the theaters gold cannot procure a seat for the servile race beside their former masters; in the hospitals they lie apart; and although they are allowed to invoke the same God as the whites, it must be at a different altar and in their own churches, with their own clergy. The gates of heaven are not closed against them, but their inferiority is continued to the very confines of the other world. When the Negro dies, his bones are cast aside, and the distinction of condition prevails even in the equality of death."[2] What Tocqueville observed in the North raises a puzzling question: Why was anti-black racism ubiquitous in northern society, where blacks were comparatively few in number and where the exploitation of their labor was not a crucial basis for production?

Tocqueville's observations can be easily corroborated. As Leon Litwack has documented, blacks encountered racism everywhere in the North.[3] They were barred from most hotels and restaurants, and sat in separate sections in theaters and churches, invariably in the back. Black children usually attended separate and inferior schools which reinforced their caste status at an early age. Transportation facilities were often segregated. In Philadelphia, blacks were allowed to ride only on the front platforms of streetcars, and New York City had separate bus cars—one exclusively for blacks. Traveling on New York ferry boats, blacks were forced to stay on deck at all hours and in all conditions of weather. Crowded into dirty ghettos of northern cities, blacks found themselves trapped in squalid slums and were told their presence in white residential districts would depreciate property values.

In the North they were also denied the right to vote. Significantly the political proscription of blacks was often related to the constitutional extension of the suffrage for whites. New York is a case in point. In 1821 the state constitutional convention granted the vote to all free "white" male citizens of the state who possessed a freehold, paid taxes, had served in the state militia, or had worked on the highways. This amounted to universal manhood suffrage, but for whites only. The new constitution, moreover, not only retained the old property qualification for blacks but increased it from $100 to $250. Twenty-five years later another New York constitutional convention defeated, by a vote of 63 to 37, a motion to strike out the word *white,* removing the discriminatory provision. The question was then submitted to the voters of New York and defeated by an overwhelming margin of 223,834 to 85,306. Meanwhile, in Pennsylvania, the 1838 constitutional convention provided for universal white manhood suffrage, and thus disfranchised blacks completely. As the actions of these conventions reveal, the political coming of age of the common white man signified the political degradation of the black man.

Proscribed politically in a democracy for white men only, blacks were also repressed economically. The Market Revolution was an era of economic growth and expanded employment opportunities for thousands of workers in the cities. Yet blacks benefited little from the new demand for labor because white workers often demanded the exclusion of blacks from the job market. White mechanics in Cincinnati publicly condemned their union president for training a black youth; whites in a cabinet shop in Cincinnati forced their employer to fire a recently hired black worker. In New York, white workers regarded the docks as a white labor monopoly and used violence to keep away black workers. Thus greater economic opportunity for whites came to mean greater economic proscription for blacks. Unable to find employment in skilled jobs, most blacks were forced into menial labor. In the 1850s, eighty-seven percent of New York's gainfully employed blacks held menial jobs, and, in New Haven, nine out of ten blacks were menial workers. Thus the skilled/unskilled stratification of the labor market had a caste pattern: It located blacks at the bottom of the occupational scale.

While blacks struggled for economic survival, they also suffered from attacks by mobs generally composed of white workers and led by "gentlemen of property and standing." White working-class fears of black labor competition and professional and commercial class anxieties generated by the new industrial order often united in violent outbursts against urban blacks. Time and again in northern cities, white mobs invaded black ghettos, attacking and killing blacks and destroying the homes and churches of their victims. Philadelphia was the scene of several bloody anti-black riots: In 1834, a white mob, seeking to force blacks to leave the city and thereby remove them from economic competition, assaulted the black community. Seven years later, in Cincinnati, white workers used a cannon against blacks, who armed themselves to defend their families and homes. The mayor then persuaded about 300 black men to go to jail for their own security, assuring them protection for their wives and children. But the white rioters took advantage of the situation and again attacked the black community; finally the governor of Ohio intervened and forcefully imposed law and order.

During the 1840s and 1850s, northern white working-class antagonism toward blacks also helped generate strong opposition against the extension of slavery into the territories. The 1846 Wilmot Proviso, prohibiting slavery in territories acquired from Mexico, was both anti-black and anti-slavery. On the floor of Congress, the sponsor of the proviso, David Wilmot of Pennsylvania, declared: "I plead the cause and rights of white freemen. I would preserve to free white labor a fair country, a rich inheritance, where the sons of toil, of my own race and own color, can live without the disgrace which association with negro slavery brings upon free labor." Two years later, the Free Soil party was organized to check the expansion of slavery: Many of its supporters sought to reserve the territories for free labor and white men.

Painfully aware of their grim prospects for equality in the North, blacks were discouraged and bitter. "Why should I strive hard and acquire all the constituents of a man," a black youth complained, "if the prevailing genius of the land admit me not as such, or but in an inferior degree! Pardon me if I feel insignificant and weak. . . . What are my prospects? To what shall I turn my hand? Shall I be a mechanic? No one will employ me; white boys won't work with me. . . . Drudgery and servitude, then, are my prospective portion." Here was a recognition of one of the frightening realities of northern society: America was a white man's country. No wonder that, during the 1850s, while Frederick Douglass struggled for the abolition of slavery and the realization of freedom within American society, an increasing number of black abolitionists came to a separatist conclusion. Profoundly alienated from white America, militant black leaders like Martin Delany advocated black emigration to South America and Africa. Racism in the North, they argued, had compelled them to seek their identity and freedom in a black country.[4]

The social, political, and economic racial oppression blacks experienced in the North interacted dynamically with a powerful black child/savage ideology which contained a cluster of negative images of blacks. While these images helped to shape the repression of blacks, the patterns of discrimination, segregation, and mass violence degraded and reduced blacks to deplorable conditions of illiteracy, hopelessness, and poverty. The repression itself, in turn, reinforced the anti-black images widespread in northern white society. Once in motion, this cycle reproduced both the conditions and ideology of black debasement in a formidable process which affected caste as well as class structures in northern society.

For many northern whites, the black seemed unable to develop beyond childhood—the period before adult responsibilities and work. Freedom for the black in the North, it was claimed, only conferred on him the "privilege of being more idle." Viewed as "immature" and "irresponsible," he was denounced as "indolent" and "good-for-nothing." He was, a white Pennsylvanian charged, "simply unfit," "naturally lazy, childlike." A New York merchant argued that black laborers had to be treated as children, for they required adult white guardianship. Stereotypes of black childhood were linked to notions of black intellectual inferiority which leaders like Jefferson had advanced. Lacking the necessary intelligence, the black was said to be incapable of maturity. Whites believed his "understanding" was "weak," and were inclined to look upon him as "a being intermediate between man and the brutes." White parents warned their children to improve themselves or they would be as ignorant as a "nigger." A Philadelphia doctor, Samuel Morton, offered whites presumably scientific evidence of black intellectual inferiority: He had measured the cranial capacities of the skulls of whites and blacks, and discovered those of whites were larger. His findings, published in a book entitled *Crania Americana* in 1839, soon found their way into the public consciousness and political rhetoric. Since the black was mentally inferior, whites argued, he did not have an understanding of civil liberty and the capacity to take the first step toward civilization. In 1850, an Indiana senator declared: "The same power that has given him a black skin with less weight or volume of brain has given us a white skin, with greater volume of brain and intellect. . . ." The implication of this difference was clear to the senator: It meant the black, frozen in childhood and inferior in intelligence, lacked the potential for equality in American society.[5]

The blacks' alleged deficiencies in industriousness, maturity, and intelligence were often associated with what influential whites claimed were the blacks' criminal tendencies—their disrespect for law and their violent character. During the 1820s, the governor of Pennsylvania expressed apprehension about the increasing crime rate among blacks, and newspapers in that state reported many crimes as Negro burglaries, Negro robberies, and Negro assaults. In this way, politicians and editors helped to stereotype the black as a criminal. Influenced by this image, many white legislators sought to restrict black migration into their states. Ohio and Indiana, for example, required blacks entering to post a $500 bond as a guarantee against becoming a public charge and as a pledge of good behavior. Ohio politicians described the black as lazy and immoral, and insisted that the black population of the state should not be allowed to increase by migration. The editor of an Indiana newspaper complained how there was not a "nigger" in town who had given his bond, and demanded the enforcement of the law designed to discourage black migration and "drive away a gang of pilferers."[6]

Regarded as a savage, the black was fearfully thought to be a creature under the domination of his passions, especially his sexuality. He lived in the section of town called "New Liberia" or "New Guinea" or "Little Africa"—places which whites associated with vice, promiscuity, and immoral entertainment. Northern whites anxiously saw him as a sexual threat to white women and white racial purity. During an anti-Republican parade in New York in 1860, floats showed a thick-lipped black embracing a white woman and a black man leading a white woman into the White House. In 1821 white citizens of Pennsylvania petitioned the legislature to declare mixed marriages void and make it a penal action for a black to marry a "white man's daughter." Northern states such as Indiana and Illinois prohibited interracial marriages, and white social sentiments vigorously discouraged relationships between blacks and whites. In a petition to the legislature of the Indiana territory, whites sought to prevent the settlement of blacks because they believed white wives and daughters would be insulted and abused by "those Africans." At the Illinois constitutional convention of 1847, a delegate warned that the lack of a restriction on black migration was tantamount to allowing blacks "to make proposals to marry our daughters." School segregation was also influenced by fears of interracial unions: In 1842 whites petitioned the Indiana senate to establish separation of the races in public schools. The question was referred to the committee on education. In its report supporting racial exclusion, the committee argued that the black race was inferior and that the admission of black children into "our public schools would ultimately tend to bring about that feeling which favour their amalgamation with our own people." Some northern white politicians even demanded the disfranchisement of blacks, for they feared that black suffrage could lead to miscegenation. A delegate to the New York constitutional convention of 1821 favored such disfranchisement because he wanted to avoid the time "when the colours shall intermarry." In their effort to deny the suffrage to blacks in Wisconsin, Democrats argued that the extension of political rights to blacks would encourage them to marry "our sisters and daughters."[7]

Even northern white antislavery was based partly on an abhorrence of racial mixing. Many white abolitionists condemned the institution as one which promoted interracial sexual unions. Some Indiana abolitionists declared that they were "opposed to the amalgamation of the white and black inhabitants of our country, and . . . that the only means by which it can be prevented, is to abolish slavery, so that colored females, may be instructed in the moral and religious duties, and be placed under the protection of righteous laws." They also warned that the loose morals of slaves would "cause a compound of the human species." This concern for white racial purity contributed to the movement against the expansion of slavery into the western territories. One of the leaders of the Republican party, Abraham Lincoln, candidly stated that the separation of the races was the "only perfect prevention of amalgamation," that a very large proportion of the Republican party supported racial separation, and that the "chief plank in their platform—opposition to the spread of slavery"—was "most favorable to that separation."[8]

Significantly, blacks were not the only group characterized as "children" and "savages" in America. While they did not generate antimiscegenationist fears and could not be condemned because of color or African origin, the new urban white workers, particularly Irish immigrants, were also degraded in terms of the "child/savage" imagery. Newspaper editors, educators, ministers, and industrial capitalists called the white lower and working classes the "slaves" of their "passions." "Ignorant," "lazy," and "sensual," Irish immigrants and other industrial workers were interested in seeking the "lower" rather than the "higher" pleasures; they possessed a "love for vicious excitement" and satisfied a "gratification merely animal." Living in congested cities, these groups were swept by the "current of sensuality" and pulled into crime, poverty, and sin. Irish immigrant children were "undisciplined" and "uninstructed," "inheriting" the "stupidity of centuries of ignorant ancestors." Factory workers were dismissed for gambling, drinking, or committing "any other debaucheries" as well as for "levity" and "impudence." They were also scolded for their "idleness" and "brutal leprosy of blue Monday habits." Jersey City Irish workers demanding wages the Erie Railroad owed them were described by a newspaper editor as "a mongrel mass of ignorance and crime and superstition, as utterly unfit for its duties, as they are for the common courtesies and decencies of civilized life." Urban workers were condemned for their lack of habits of "regularity," "punctuality," and "industry." More importantly, they were denounced for their failure to develop self-restraint—the quality which separated adult from child: "Children act[ed] from the impulses of their natures quickened by the objects around them." Irish immigrants were blamed for their want of self-control, particularly in their sexual conduct. In a society in which restraint was the most widely used method of birth control, large Irish families were viewed as signs of this weakness: "Did wealth consist in children, it is well known, that the Irish would be rich people. . . ." The *New York Independent* characterized the Irish immigrant as "a creature with all the brutal passions and instincts of man in the first savage state. . . ." Worried about the bulging cities and the alarming presence of the new proletariat, Horace Mann saw his mission to educate the new masses as one which would save "a considerable portion" of the citizenry from "falling back into the conditions of half-barbarous or of savage life."[9]

This image of the "child/savage" not only helped maintain the racial structure of white over black but also served class interests within the structure of white social relations. As it functioned within the northern society of the Market Revolution, the ideology of the "child/savage" received considerable force from general white middle-class fears of the new urban industrial society; it also reflected the particular class concerns of industrial employers and reinforced the degradation and control of industrial workers. As Irish immigrants crowded into growing cities and as America acquired an industrial proletariat, racial and class imagery often blurred together into a caste/class ideology and intensified anti-black antagonism even in the virtually all-white society of the North.

While the image of the black "child/savage" was also widely held among whites in the South, it had a basis peculiar to a society where blacks were present in large numbers and where production depended on the exploitation of their labor. The image also had a unique regional function, for it serviced a southern paternalism which integrated racial and class hegemony and which described the slave as a Sambo—childlike, docile, irresponsible, given to lying and stealing, lazy, affectionate, and happy. What we need to analyze here is not how the slave was transformed into a Sambo—which was the question Stanley Elkins asked in his study of slavery[10]—but whether or not such a slave personality existed and why slaveholders as individuals and as a class needed a Sambo.

"Slaves never become men or women," a traveler in the South commented. Slavemasters frequently referred to adult blacks as "grown up children," or "boys" and "girls"; regarding themselves as guardians, they claimed their slaves had to be "governed as children." They also cherished the bonds of affection they believed existed between themselves and the dependent childlike slaves. In his *Black Diamonds Gathered in the Darkey Homes of the South,* published on the eve of the Civil War, proslavery writer Edward Pollard exclaimed: "I love to study his affectionate heart; I love to mark that peculiarity in him, which beneath all his buffoonery exhibits him as a creature of the tenderest sensibilities, mingling his joys and his sorrows with those of his master's home."[11]

Yet, while slavemasters fondly praised their bondsmen for their affection and dependency, they also complained about their laziness, and repeatedly noted how black laborers had to be supervised or they would not work. Blacks were like children in their inability to plan and to calculate: They would not "lay up in summer for the wants of winter" and "accumulate in youth for the exigencies of age." If slaves were freed, they would become "an insufferable burden to society." William Gilmore Simms gave this argument literary expression; in his novel *The Yemassee,* Simms had the slave Hector respond to a proposal for his freedom. "I d--n to h-ll, massa, if I gwine to be free!" Hector protested. "De ting aint right; and enty I know wha' kind of ting freedom is wid black man? Ha! You make Hector free, he turn wuss more nor poor buckra—he tief out of de shop—he git drunk and lie in de ditch. . . ." Obviously, slavemasters explained, the black must be kept in slavery; otherwise he would surely become an "indolent lazy thievish drunken individual, working only when he cannot steal. . . ."[12]

The slave's laziness was often associated with the land of his origin. In a review of J. Leighton Wilson's *Western Africa: Its History, Condition and Prospect,* the *Charleston Mercury* commented in 1856: "The prospects [of progress] for Africa, can only begin when her people shall be made, by a power and will superior to their own, to obey the first law of God—the foundation of all the laws of God—and be coerced to earn their bread in the sweat of the brow." And two years later, the *Mercury* argued that blacks must be forced to do "honest labor" without which a people must always remain worse than "slaves—savages and cannibals."[13] Slavemasters were quick to seize what they considered evidence suggesting blacks had been improvident in Africa before they became slaves in America.

What especially impressed slavemasters was the bondsman's content-ment. They profusely proclaimed to the North and to Europe that the slaves of the South were the happiest people in the world: They worked little and spent the rest of their time "singing, dancing, laughing, chatter-ing, and bringing up pigs and chickens. . . ." In terms of "general happiness," slavemasters stated, it would not be amiss to alter an old adage and say: "As merry as a negro slave." But such claims of happiness were not made only in public announcements; slavemasters also recorded them in their private journals. One of them scribbled into his diary on January 1, 1859: "The hands as usual came in to greet the New Year with their good wishes—the scene is well calculated to excite sympathies; notwithstanding bondage, affections find roots in the heart of the slave for the master."[14]

While these descriptions of slave behavior show that many slavemasters thought slaves were Sambos, they do not prove that bondsmen were indeed Sambos. To be sure, there was a Sambo-making machine, designed to break the slave's spirit and mold the perfect slave. Slavemasters, hopeful that contented slaves would be obedient, sometimes used kindness to control them. A Georgia planter explained: "Now, I contend that the surest and best method of managing negroes, is to love them. We know . . . that if we love our horse, we will treat him well, and if we treat him well, he will become gentle, docile and obedient . . . and if this treatment has this effect upon all the animal creation . . . why will it not have the same effect upon slaves?" But if slavemasters offered their slaves presents and holidays as incentives for good conduct, they also knew that strict discipline was essential and that their power must be based on the principle of fear. Senator James Hammond of South Carolina, who owned more than 300 slaves, fully understood the need for the absolute submission of the slave to his master. "We have to rely more and more on the power of fear," he declared. "We are determined to continue masters, and to do so we have to draw the reign tighter and tighter day by day to be assured that we hold them in complete check."[15] Whether they treated their slaves "well," as they did their horses, or drew the "reign tighter," slavemasters had the same objective in mind. To achieve it, they also made efforts to brainwash the bondsman into believing he was racially inferior and racially created to be a slave. They kept him illiterate and ignorant, and told him he was unfit to care for himself. Everything slavemasters did was intended to reduce the slave to dependency.

Slavemasters had designed an awesome system of slave management; yet the development of this Sambo-making machine raises doubts about Sambo's existence. This is not to say there were no docile, happy, even affectionate slaves in the South. Indeed, there were slaves who behaved like Sambos. And they might have truly been Sambos, their actions reflecting their inner selves. But slaves who behaved like Sambos might not have actually been Sambos, for they might have been playing the role of the loyal and congenial slave in order to survive, their inner selves hidden in their actions. Slavemasters themselves sometimes recognized how difficult it was to determine a slave's true personality. "So deceitful is the Negro," one explained, "that as far as my own experience extends I could never in a single instance decipher his character. . . . We planters could never get at the truth." Indeed, as ex-slave Frederick Douglass reported, slaves were fearful of punishment, and consequently when they were asked about their condition and the character of their masters, they would almost "invariably" say that they were "contented and their masters kind." Many wore smiling masks. "It is a blessed thing," Douglass commented, "that the tyrant may not always know the thoughts and purposes of his victim."[16] The reality may have been even more complex and subtle. Sambo-like behavior may have been not so much a veil to hide inner emotions of rage and discontent as an effective means of expressing them. Lying, stealing, laziness, immaturity, ignorance, and even affection all contained within them an aggressive quality: They constituted in effect resistance to efficiency, discipline, work, and productivity. Where the master perceived laziness, the slave saw refusal to be exploited. Thus the same action held different meanings, depending on whether one was master or slave.

Slavemasters had a particular need for their meaning during the nineteenth century, especially after 1830, as antislavery criticism from the North mounted. Forced to justify their "peculiar institution" as a "positive good," they bragged about the pleasant intercourse between master and slave, and the ties of affection binding them together. Southern planters proudly announced that theirs was a "patriarchal institution . . . founded in pity and protection on the one side, and dependence and gratitude on the other." "At present we have in South Carolina," one slavemaster boasted, "two hundred and fifty thousand civilized and peaceable slaves, happy and contented. . . ."[17] Under their paternal care and direction, slavemasters insisted, they had transformed the "savage" African into a Sambo—a loyal, dependent, affectionate, and happy slave.

Slavemasters needed a Sambo to convince themselves as well as the North that slavery was moral. They realized that the sectional conflict was one of ideas—between the idea in the North that slavery was morally wrong and the idea in the South that slavery was morally right. The struggle, proslavery southerners argued, must be waged on the battlefield of principles. But they knew there were contradictory principles warring within southern white society and within the minds of slavemasters themselves. In the past, especially before 1830, slavemasters had admitted that slavery was wrong. During the American Revolution, they had confessed that they could not justify slavery, an institution "repugnant to humanity" and "destructive of liberty." Even after the invention of the cotton gin and the expansion of cotton cultivation during the Market Revolution, both of which had given slavery a new profitability, slavemasters continued to apologize for their "peculiar institution." During the 1820s, the governor of Mississippi admitted slavery was "an evil at best," and other slavemasters described it as "an evil" whose "curse" was "felt and acknowledged by every enlightened man" in the slave-holding states. A South Carolina representative declared in Congress: "Slavery, in the abstract, I condemn and abhor. . . . However ameliorated by compassion—however corrected by religion—still slavery is a bitter draught, and the chalice which contains the nauseous potion, is, perhaps, more frequently pressed by the lips of the master than of the slave."[18] Here, then, was a master class in moral turmoil.

Even after proslavery polemicists like Thomas R. Dew and John C. Calhoun had proclaimed slavery a "positive good" and even after the South had supposedly become a closed society, many slavemasters were still deeply uneasy about the morality of their institution. "This, sir, is a Christian community," a white Virginian said in 1832. "Southerners read in their Bibles, 'Do unto all men as you would have them do unto you'; and this golden rule and slavery are hard to reconcile." Writing to his wife in 1837, a slavemaster expressed his troubled conscience: "I sometimes think my feelings unfit me for a slaveholder." While distressed slavemasters were reluctant and fearful to admit their feelings of guilt publicly, they sometimes recorded their anguish in diaries. "Oh what trouble," one wrote on December 21, 1858, "running sore, constant pressing weight, perpetual wearing, dripping, is this patriarchal institution! What miserable folly for men to cling to it as something heaven-descended. And here we and our children after us must groan under the burden—our hands tied from freeing ourselves." Ten days later he added: "I am more and more perplexed about my negroes. I cannot just take them up and sell them though that would be clearly the best I could do for myself. I cannot free them. I cannot keep them with comfort. . . . What would I not give to be freed from responsibility for these poor creatures. Oh, that I could know just what is right." No wonder, during the 1850s, proslavery men noticed that many slavemasters felt hesitant to defend their institution on moral grounds. "There was," they observed, "the feeling, that, in some sense, they [slaves] were plunder, which it was enough to get out of the way with."[19]

Proslavery advocates, worried about this moral anxiousness, felt they had to declare aggressively that slavery was right in order to help slavemasters themselves overcome their inner doubts. "We must satisfy the consciences," defenders of slavery argued, "we must allay the fears of our own people. We must satisfy them that slavery is of itself right—that it is not a sin against God. . . ." They described to slaveholders the perfect biracial society of the South: Here the black had an "enlightened," "humane," and

"Christian" master; here the slave was "submissive," "docile," "happy," "conscious of his own inferiority and proud of being owned & governed by a superior." The image of the slave as a Sambo helped to comfort the tortured consciences of many members of the ruling class. Few slaveholders, a European traveler in the South observed, could "openly and honestly look the thing [slavery] in the face. They wind and turn about in all sorts of ways, and make use of every argument . . . to convince me that the slaves are the happiest people in the world. . . ."[20]

But the slavemasters' need for a Sambo was more complex than the desire to defend the peculiar institution and to mitigate guilt: The image helped to assure them that the slave was contented and controlled. Surely a happy slave would not violently protest his bondage; surely he would not slit his master's throat at night. So slavemasters wanted to believe. Yet, while they were comforted by the happy Sambo, they were also terrified by the specter of the rebellious "savage." Aware of the successful and bloody slave revolts in the West Indies, they feared that blacks "only cease[d] to be *children* when they degenerate[d] into *savages.*" After the brutal suppression of the Denmark Vesey slave conspiracy of 1822, a worried South Carolina gentleman exclaimed: Our blacks were "barbarians who would, IF THEY COULD, become the DESTROYERS of our race." This southerner's fear was not wholly paranoid. Several years later in Southampton, Virginia, Nat Turner and his fellow slave rebels took up the knife against their oppressors and slew nearly sixty whites. Slavemasters, appalled by the violence, denounced the rebels as a "band of savages." "It will long be remembered in the annals of our country," wrote a Virginian, "and many a mother as she presses her infant darling to her bosom, will shudder at the recollection of Nat Turner. . . ." Slavemasters were deeply concerned about servile insurrection, and Southern newspapers frequently reported news of slave unrest and "evidences of a very unsettled state of mind among the servile population." The wife of a Georgia planter observed that the slaves were "a threatening source of constant insecurity, and every southern *woman* to whom I have spoken on the subject, has admitted to me that they live in terror of their slaves." A former Louisiana planter said he knew "times here, when there was not a single planter who had a calm night's rest; they then never lay down to sleep without a brace of pistols at their side."[21] Here was a society which was almost hysterically fearful of slave rebellions and which needed Sambos, even imagined ones.

If Sambo protected slavemasters from their nightmares of Nat Turner, he also promised order in a society apprehensive about white class divisions. Sambo was symptomatic of racial and white class tensions within southern society. As long as he existed and as long as he served his master, he offered security and comfort in a South which was in reality heterogeneous in terms of both race and class. The "world the slaveholders made" had masters and slaves: It also had white nonslaveholders and white workers. In fact the overwhelming majority of the white population in the South did not own slaves and had no direct economic interest in the "peculiar institution." In 1850, only 6.2 percent of the southern white population possessed slaves.

Due to increased slave prices in the 1850s, slaveholding became even more restricted. Throughout the 1840s, the South had been in a severe depression caused chiefly by the collapse of cotton prices, which hit a disastrous low of 5¾ cents per pound in 1845. Four years later, however, the price of cotton shot up to 11½ cents per pound, and boosted the price of slaves as the demand for slave labor increased. The cost of a prime field hand in the New Orleans market skyrocketed from $700 in 1845, to $1,000 in 1850, to $1,800 in 1860, and slave prices in the Virginia, Georgia, and South Carolina markets followed the same pattern. Due to the demand for slave labor, prices were ranging far above what slaveholders considered their "legitimate point": While cotton prices had doubled, slave prices had tripled. During this decade, with the cost of purchase so high, nonslaveholders found it increasingly difficult to buy slaves and enter the ranks of the slaveholding class. By 1860, slaveholders comprised only 5.5 percent of the white population, becoming an even more exclusive elite.[22]

This monopolization of slave labor, more and more in evidence shortly before the Civil War, sharpened the social divisions within southern white society. The era of sectional conflict which led to the disruption of the Union also witnessed white class tensions within the South. During the slavery debate in the Virginia legislature of 1831-32, the institution was condemned as antagonistic to white workers. Slavery, declared the Virginia critics, "banishes free white labor, exterminates the mechanic, the artisan, the manufacturer. It deprives them of occupation. It deprives them of bread. . . . Shall all interests be subservient to one—all rights subordinate to those of the slaveholder? Has not the mechanic . . . rights—rights incompatible with the existence of slavery?" A decade later, competition between white workers and slaves became even more intense as planters directed their slaves into the mechanic trades and hired them out to employers. White workers protested bitterly against this competition. In Mississippi white mechanics forced the enactment of municipal ordinances which prohibited slaves from hiring themselves to employers for wages; in Georgia white mechanics pressured the legislature to prohibit the hiring of slaves and free blacks as mechanics. White labor resentment was also expressed in South Carolina, where grand juries demanded the enforcement of a law against slave competition. During the 1850s, slaveholders continued to pit their slaves directly against white workers. In Texas slaveholders underbid white workers for the contract to construct the state capitol building, and in Savannah shipping merchants used slaves to break a white labor strike in 1856. In their struggle to defend their interests, white workers retaliated against both slaveholders and slaves. In Wilmington, North Carolina, white workers destroyed the framework of a new building erected by black carpenters; in New Orleans, white mechanics threatened to drive every black out of town. A slave told a northern reporter traveling in the South that he had been forced to leave San Antonio because "they made a law that no nigger shouldn't hire his time in San Antone, so I had to cl'ar out, and mass'r wanted me, so I come back to him."

White workers also responded politically to slave competition, and challenged the slaveholding class in municipal councils and state legislatures. In a petition presented to the Atlanta city council, 200 white mechanics and laborers complained that slave mechanics were underbidding them. The Mechanical Association of Jackson, Mississippi, resolved that the use of slaves as public mechanics should be suppressed, and the Mechanics Institute of Little Rock demanded legislation to outlaw slave mechanics. In 1859 a resolution to consider the enactment of a law prohibiting slave competition was introduced in the Alabama legislature, and a bill forbidding slaves to be public craftsmen came up before the legislature in Mississippi. Even South Carolina, the storm center for secession, was the scene of organizational and political reactions from white workers. Between 1854 and 1860, organizations like the Charleston Mechanics Association and the South Carolina Mechanics Association of Charleston sent the state legislature no fewer than ten petitions and memorials for the prohibition of slave hiring and the removal of slave competition. Worried about this escalating conflict between white classes in the South, the editor of a Mississippi newspaper issued a warning to the slaveholding class: "The [slaveholders'] policy of teaching negroes the various trades . . . tends to make the rich richer and the poor poorer, by bringing slave labor into competition with white labor, and thus arraying capital against labor, (for the negro is capital) and this will produce a spirit of antagonism between the rich and poor. Such a policy . . . tends to elevate the negro at the expense of the poor white man, and makes the poor mechanic [in] the South the enemy of the negro and of the institution of slavery." A unique pattern of class conflict was taking shape in the Old South—white labor versus the slaveholding class and their slave "capital."[23]

Conscious of this class antagonism, Hinton Rowan Helper of North Carolina hoped *The Impending Crisis and How to Meet It,* published in

1857, would give the nonslaveholding protest ideological focus and political direction. Driven by a hatred for blacks and a love for the South, Helper called for the abolition of slavery and the removal of all blacks from the country. In his vitriolic protest against the poverty and powerlessness of the southern nonslaveholding class, he exposed the relationship between racial hegemony and class rule of the planter elite. "The lords of the lash are not only absolute masters of the blacks, who are bought and sold, and driven about like so many cattle, but they are also the oracles and arbiters of all nonslaveholding whites, whose freedom is merely nominal, and whose unparalleled illiteracy and degradation is purposely and fiendishly perpetuated." For Helper, social revolution was the only way to meet the internal "impending crisis." White nonslaveholders of the South had to unite, overthrow the oppressive planter and slaveholding class, and destroy slavery, "the frightful tumor on the body politic."[24]

In their response to northern abolitionists' criticism of slavery and to southern nonslaveholders' threat to planter-class hegemony, southern defenders of slavery like John C. Calhoun, George Fitzhugh, Henry Hughes, and Leonidas W. Spratt formulated an argument which contained a critique of northern and European capitalism and which justified slavery as a system of caste labor. They criticized the ills of the free labor system and the exploitation of white workers, and predicted that free labor societies were doomed to a "continually recurring catastrophe." They also claimed slavery prevented the "conflict between labor and capital, which must ever exist in populous and crowded communities," where wages were the regulator between the classes. In societies where labor was white and free, workers had certain political rights and could not be effectively controlled or suppressed. But in the South, where labor was black and in bondage, "capitalists" could exercise total power over the working class. Black workers had no right to assemble, vote, or bear arms, and could be punished without restraint for acts of insubordination. As slaves, they were also "capital," and slaveholders had to be concerned with the welfare of their workers. Unlike northern capitalists, slaveholders had to keep their laborers in the "best possible working order" and could not afford to let valuable property "die by starvation." Unlike the exploited and miserable white workers of the free labor society, slave workers were "comfortable," "docile," "submissive," and "happy" Sambos. Thus, for southern capitalists, slavery was "intensely conservative of peace and order."[25]

During the 1850s, proslavery theoreticians like Hughes and Spratt took their caste/class ideology to its logical conclusion and proposed reopening the African slave trade. Their agitation for the proposal gathered considerable momentum as the Southern Commercial Conventions became engines for promoting the reopening of the trade, and as southern publications like the *Charleston Mercury,* the *Jackson Mississippian,* and *De Bow's Review* called for the repeal of the 1808 federal prohibition of the trade and demanded the importation of labor from Africa. In effect, African slave laborers would constitute what Marx called an "industrial reserve army," which the master class would wield in their struggle against white labor in the South. As white workers from the North and Europe moved into the South, in response to high wages and an increased demand for labor, African slave-trade advocates warned slaveholders of the class threat developing below the Mason and Dixon Line: "If we cannot supply the demand for slave labor, then we must expect to be supplied with a species of labor . . . which is . . . antagonistic to our institutions." Only the importation of Africans, they insisted, would enable the South to overcome this "internal peril." It would reduce soaring slave prices, make slaves more available to nonslaveholding whites, and broaden the base of the slaveholding class. It would also lower wages for white labor, discourage further migration of white laborers into the South, and help to eliminate the white workers struggling in competition with slave labor and "distinctly conscious" of the "difference between 'labor' and 'slave labor.' " What these "Marxes of the Master Class" hoped to achieve was more than a separate nation, more than a slaveholding Confederacy: They were determined to create a society where classes would constitute caste divisions, where white over black would signify capital over labor, and where the ruling class would have at their disposal an "industrial reserve army" of black labor drawn from Africa and would not have to worry about trade unions, strikes, and social revolution.[26]

The ideology of the black "child/savage" had both caste and class purposes, and must be viewed within the context of the age of Jackson and the Market Revolution—extension of the suffrage, cultivation of new farms, erection of factories, construction of canals and railroads, expansion of the market, and accumulation of money and material goods. All of these developments intersected and reinforced each other in a dynamic process.

Images of blacks as children and savages did far more than buttress segregation in the North and slavery in the South: Promoted by white culture-makers and policy-makers, these images also constituted a "persuasion" which gave whites direction and identity in Jacksonian society. What is significant is how whites defined blacks *vis-à-vis* themselves. In its report on "the negro problem," a special committee of the Ohio legislature declared that blacks had "no incentive to industry or the acquisition of an honorable reputation" and lacked the "intelligence and moral restraint

necessary to qualify them for the privileges and immunities of citizens."
And, in the South, a professor at William and Mary College explained: "In
the free black, the principle of idleness and dissipation triumphs over that
of *accumulation* and the desire to better our condition; the animal part of
the man gains the victory over the moral, and he, consequently, prefers
sinking down into the listless, inglorious repose of the brute creation, to
rising to that energetic activity which can only be generated amid the
multiplied, refined, and artificial wants of *civilized society.*"[27] Thus, whites
saw the black "child/savage" in counterpoint to their own self-image: The
antithesis of themselves and of what they valued, he lacked "incentive to
industry," "moral restraint," the principle of "accumulation," and control
over the "animal part" of man.

In the North and the South, the racial ideology of the black "child/
savage," in its emphasis on the need to develop self-restraint and accumulate goods, complemented the ideology of capitalism and gave specific support to Jacksonian individualism and enterprise. "Born equal," white male
Americans were encouraged to assert proudly how they had no king, no
traditions, and no past (even no parents, as Tocqueville noted). The American ideal was the "self-made man." Raised on McGuffey readers, they
were taught to be oriented toward work and achievement. *Harper's New
Monthly Magazine* reported in 1853: "The idea instilled into the minds of
most boys, from early life, is that of 'getting on.' The parents test themselves by their own success in this respect; and they impart the same notion
to their children."[28] White men in Jacksonian society were urged to exercise self-restraint and industry—virtues republican fathers like Rush and
Jefferson had promoted.

In the republican society of the Market Revolution, the black "child/
savage" represented what whites thought they were not, and more important—what they must not become. Their image of blacks enabled them to
delineate more precisely the qualities of republican man in Jacksonian
society. As psychologist Kai Erikson has explained, "deviant forms of behavior, by marking the outer edges of group life, give the inner structure its
special character and thus supply the framework within which the people
of the group develop an orderly sense of their own cultural identity. . . .
One of the surest ways to confirm an identity, for communities as well as
for individuals, is to find some way of measuring what one is *not.*"[29] The
black "child/savage" defined deviancy and served in effect to discipline
whites, especially working-class and immigrant groups, into republican
conduct.

This need to define the norms for white society had a specific relation to the age of the Market Revolution and capitalist class needs in an expanding wage-labor structure of social relations. Enormous material and social changes were occurring—the unprecedented growth of cities, the massive influx of immigrants, and the formation of an urban industrial proletariat. These changes generated fears of social disorder in the republic and nervous demands for greater cohesion and control in society. As a Jacksonian "persuasion," the ideology of the black "child/savage" reflected these fears and demands as it served important class functions. In the North, the ideology not only operated as a repressive racial mechanism; it also paralleled a class ideology that separated the poor, the immigrant, and even the factory worker at times from the "real people" as it characterized the lower orders, whether black or white, as "lazy," "ignorant," "sensual," "childish," and "savage." In the South, the racial ideology not only reinforced the system that controlled blacks and appropriated their labor; it also helped to maintain the hegemony of the planter class over white nonslaveholders and white workers in the South.

The existence of both racial and class anxieties during the Jacksonian era may well be why the ideology of the black "child/savage" and the "discovery of the asylum" occurred at the same time in American society. As blacks were degraded into children and savages and as they were subjected to greater institutional controls in Jacksonian America, institutions were developed for deviant and dependent members of the white community. In the society of the Market Revolution, to paraphrase Harry Braverman, whole new strata of the helpless and dependent were created, which could not secure care from an "atomized community" or from families geared to survive and "succeed" in a market society. Consequently the care of all these layers became institutionalized. Asylums for the insane, penitentiaries for the criminal, and almshouses for the poor were created to clear the marketplace of all but the "economically active" and "functioning" members of society. These institutions helped to discipline white indigent, delinquent, and lower working classes, and to inculcate Protestant and republican values. In short, institutions of social control and regimentation, which had class significance, were established—in the words of Michel Foucault—to impose, in a universal form, a morality which would prevail from "within" upon those who were "strangers" to it.[30]

In the total structure of American society, racial and class developments interpenetrated each other. White over black had an organic relationship to class divisions and conflicts forming within white society. Thus, as we shall see more specifically in our analyses of proslavery theoretician Henry Hughes and of the 1850 Harvard Medical School admissions controversy, the ideology of the black "child/savage" was part of larger social, political, and economic developments under way in Jacksonian America.

"Warranteeism": A Vision of a "Marx of the Master Class"

Critics of slavery in the South, northern abolitionists generally did not complain about the system of "wage slavery" in the North, where a growing class of laborers worked under strict discipline in factories and exchanged their labor for wages. Curiously, the most insistent and elaborate criticism of "wage slavery" came from the South, in the form of the proslavery argument. What southern defenders of slavery formulated in their counterattack against northern abolitionists was a unique class ideology— the integration of class and caste. One of the most systematic formulations of this analysis was Henry Hughes's concept of "warranteeism." Though Hughes himself was not a planter—the owner of twenty or more slaves— he was an agent of the planter class and a member of what Karl Mannheim would call their "intelligentsia." A state senator in Mississippi, an agitator for the reopening of the African slave trade, and the author of *Treatise on Sociology,* Hughes understood the class nature of social relations in the North and the South. In his vision of a society where white capitalists would have hegemonic institutional power and would exercise paternal care and control over the black "child/savage," Hughes was a "Marx of the Master Class."[31]

Born into the "master class" in 1829, Hughes was a member of a slaveholding family living in Port Gibson in Claiborne County, Mississippi. Early in his childhood, he developed close relationships with slaves, especially Uncle Aleck. "The very first anecdote of myself while I was almost a baby," Hughes later recalled in his diary, "was related to me by a lady; she saw me playing where some little boys were throwing stones, and on asking me whether I was afraid, I replied seriously, that if my eye was put out, I would get Uncle Aleck who was our teamster, to drive me in his waggon up to heaven; and God there would fix my eye for me." The fact that Aleck was called "Uncle" had added significance. As Bertram W. Doyle has pointed out, the title *uncle* was given to a slave who was "considered, more or less, as part of the family." Many years after his childhood days, Hughes continued to seek affection from loyal blacks. During the Civil War, he took his body servants with him to the battlefront. In a letter to his nephew, he wrote: "Frederic will soon come home to see his wife and child and Mistress. I want him to come. Nobody loves me so much as Frederic and Morgan do. Frederic takes care of me like I belonged to him."[32] If slaves were regarded as sources of affection, they were also valued for their labor.

During Hughes's childhood years, the Market Revolution was under way in Mississippi, as the Creeks were removed and their lands made available for white settlement. "This country was just setting up," reported the chronicler Joseph G. Baldwin. "Marvellous accounts had gone forth of the fertility of its virgin lands; and the productions of the soil were commanding a price remunerating to slave labor as it had never been remunerated before." In the 1830s, Mississippi's cotton production quadrupled and its slave population doubled. By 1840, blacks outnumbered whites in the state, and were heavily concentrated in the cotton-producing counties. In Hughes's home county, Claiborne, the slave population increased 222 percent during this decade, and the county's ratio of slaves to whites rose to four to one by 1840. These were "flush times" for Mississippi.[33] During this era of great development, slaveholders became dependent on blacks for labor and on slavery to control them.

No wonder Mississippi white society was extremely sensitive to the danger of slave insurrections. The master class was surrounded by the black working class, and was anxiously aware of its own vulnerability. The 1831 Nat Turner slave revolt in Virginia, far away on the eastern seaboard, sent ripples of fear through the Gulf states. The prospect of a "repetition" of the "scenes of Southampton" terrified whites in Mississippi, and slave patrols were instructed to be especially vigilant. Four years later a slave insurrection scare in that state drove whites into a panic. In certain counties, the fear of slave violence was so intense that white women and children were gathered into guarded places at night. Lynch mobs brutally whipped slaves to extort information about the alleged plot, and then hanged their victims. A Mississippi lawyer observed: "Never was there an instance of more extraordinary or even maddening excitement amid a refined, intelligent and virtue-loving people than that which I had the pain to witness in the counties of central Mississippi in the summer of 1835."[34] Claiborne County, where young Hughes lived, bordered this circle of hysteria.

Due to the tremendous influx of slaves into Mississippi, the dread of slave rebellions, and the emergence of northern abolitionism, the master class of Mississippi was driven into a feverish defense of slavery. Mississippi slavemasters realized they had to make an unequivocal commitment to the institution. In 1825 the governor had admitted that slavery was an evil; a year after the 1835 slave insurrection scare, a state legislative committee declared that the people of Mississippi looked upon slavery "not as a curse, but as a blessing."[35] As Hughes was growing up, the slaveholding class was transforming Mississippi into a fanatically proslavery society.

Too young to be preoccupied with the slavery question, Hughes was mainly interested in his education. Precocious as a child, he entered the local college at the age of sixteen. He was a hardworking student and did not "drink, chew, smoke or play cards."[36] Outstanding in mathematics, languages, history, and philosophy, he graduated with honors in 1847; he then studied and practiced law in New Orleans.

As a young lawyer, Hughes devoted much of his time to the reading of legal treatises. But his highly curious mind and his passion for books led him to read Gibbon, Shakespeare, Cicero, Macaulay, Bancroft, Kant, Locke, Carlyle, Fourier, and Mill. Like many southerners of his day, Hughes was an avid reader of Sir Walter Scott's romantic novels. He also had a keen interest in anatomy and geology, and found time to invent a cotton press, a steam engine, and a screw with a variable thread. He calculated and organized his time so systematically that even Rush would have been impressed. On June 16, 1850, for example, Hughes recorded in his diary the activities for the day.

> During the day: study 1 before breakfast—Gibbon's "Rome"—nearly finished, 2 and then extemporize; 3 after breakfast, study or rather investigate the nature of composition—perfection being the end—psychology—the noblest and best—beloved of my investigations—the supporter of all—vocalize 6 gesture & principles & practice, 7 compose study Milton's & Getty's oratory; dine; 8 of Civil Engineering, read ten pages, 9 investigate the nature of law with a view to a perfect society; 10 read aloud; study—investigate politics; 12 study Demosthenes translated—a little; 13 study words—synonyms chiefly—writing them; 14 read of law ten pages, walk—sup; 15 read of Civil Engineering ten pages; 16 miscellaneous reflection; 17 before retiring memorize from . . . Shakespeare . . . & for principles or classifications, look into law, zoology, ethics; extemporize, jesticulate; 18 retire, pray, thoughts on psychology, miscellaneous thoughts.[37]

An energetic and ambitious young man possessing a diversity of talents and interests, Hughes hated the tedium of his law practice, and felt a painful and profound emptiness. He "detested" the practice of law, finding it "too Mechanical," and developed a "growing aversion" to spending time in his work. His try at a career in law was a failure; his law business was slow and "quite limited." In his diary, he complained: "Life grows practical. And such practice. Law—I abhor it. Was I destined to squander precious hours in squeezing from it a scanty & unsatisfactory livelihood?" His work offered much boredom and little meaning. His crisis involved the -need to forge for himself what Erik Erikson has described as "some central perspective and direction, some working unity," out of the "effective remnants" of his childhood and the hopes of his "anticipated adulthood," and to resolve the crisis through participation in "ideological movements."[38]

The practice of law, Hughes could see, would never enable him to realize the hopes of his adulthood—his fantasies of "greatness, glory, power" which no "mortal man" had ever possessed. He wanted to place himself upon a throne from which he could look down on Alexander, Caesar, Cicero, Bonaparte, and Washington. Impatient to achieve recognition and success, he asked in his diary: "When Shall I accomplish Something which will confer visible tangible fame? . . . Am I impatient, Am I too young? . . . Cannot summer produce the fruits of autumn?" Hughes had already plotted his strategy for greatness. During the summer of 1847, he had joined a division of the Sons of Temperance in order to be given the opportunity to speak at one of its meetings. Excitedly, several months later he recorded in his diary how he had addressed the group and how his speech had been published in the *Port Gibson Herald.* Hughes hoped he could advance himself through speech-making and writing; on November 30, 1851, he decided he would begin "writing for publication" as the way to bring him "power, fame & subsistence."[39]

But illness and problems with women threatened his strategy. Hughes suffered frequently from failing eyesight, deafness, and severe chest pains; like Andrew Jackson, he had to war against his ailing body. "My eyes are still very bad. For the last few days I have been attacked with a slight deafness," he wrote in his diary. He also experienced what Jefferson called the "strongest of all human passions" and had relationships with women which he found unfulfilling. He "purposely tried" "experiments" with them to "learn the vanity of sensual & forbidden enjoyments" and "reaped a little of the whirlwind of experience." Time and again he recorded his sexual adventures in his diary: "Have I ever had a pleasure in which woman was not an element. Since my eighteenth year, I have not been unloved. And so again and—still—clasped hands, embracing arms, kissed lips, and pillowing bosoms, Ambition and Love, these are my life." Regarding his body as vulnerable to both disease and women, Hughes feared they would distract him and dissipate his energy. "Would that the flesh had no weakness," he pleaded. "Disease has been preying upon me. . . . Beneath its noiseless influence I feel my nerves relax, strength decrease, energy slacken. . . . But what I most lament is a disposition which is so naturally convivial that in the gentle but unguarded excitement of a Society in which are many gay female friends;—I descend from the grave seriousness which should characterize my demeanor, and participate in their levities." To achieve the success he yearned for, Hughes knew he could not live "at random" and had to make everything "a matter of calculation."[40]

During this time, frustrated in his law career and worried about the "weaknesses" of his "flesh," young Hughes often considered suicide. Shortly after he had begun practicing law in New Orleans, he admitted that only his quest for "power & fame" kept him away from "a yearning after annihilation." He felt "gloomy, Oh so gloomy," and cried out: "If Oh my Soul, there is for me no Father, no caressing God; let then all Earth yawn its chops and gorge with men & blood its gut of fire; let all stars suns and comets shoot short into solid coal and flickers into ashy nothing." On September 15, 1850, Hughes scribbled into his diary the crossroad before him: "Thought on suicide, often have the wish, but something seems to detain me. . . . If I, in Mississippi, lived; I could, I think, enter Congress, immediately after my twenty-fifth year."[41]

Two years later, Hughes returned to Port Gibson to live. He had decided he did not want to be "a money-catcher" in New Orleans, where death had "the slow victory" and where all "hateful" and "loathsome" things existed—sickness, adulteries, seductions, hypocrisies, and selfishness. He had to get away from "gay female friends," the "dust & glare of Streets & houses" which irritated his eyes, and the "regular confinement" which created pains in his chest. He had to make a break from the career he "abhorred" and found enervating. In Port Gibson, where he was born and had grown up, Hughes knew he would find "shadier walks" and "purer air." There, in his "native place," he was confident he would regain his health, and work out "by literature, politics, law, philosophy, science" what he thought God had sent him to do.[42]

During this time of personal crisis, Hughes had also begun to focus his attention on the slavery issue, which was at the center of the growing sectional conflict. His views on slavery were profoundly ambivalent. Though he had grown up in a proslavery society and was a slaveholder himself, he shared with many white Mississippians moral misgivings about the institution. On April 13, 1851, he admitted in his diary that he thought slavery was "sinful" and should be "abolished."[43] But five months later, shortly before his return to Port Gibson, Hughes wrote in his diary: "Examined the morality of slavery. Thoughts of becoming a candidate for the legislature." The juxtaposition of his interest in the morality of slavery and his political ambitions could hardly have been coincidental. His hopes for a political career were identified with the defense of slavery; he undoubtedly knew there was no other way in Mississippi during the 1850s. If he could work out a theory for a moral master-slave relationship, then he could possibly come to terms with his own qualms about slavery as well as "enter

Congress." Soon he was investigating the question of the right of secession and reading proslavery novels and treatises; he avidly read Calhoun's writings on nullification and slavery and considered the senator's *Disquisition on Government* "an able work." He also "looked through" Harriet Beecher Stowe's *Uncle Tom's Cabin* and criticized it as "womanish" and "absurdly unprincipled." As he immersed himself in his study he felt a powerful stirring within and found himself drawn toward participation in the most fervent "ideological movement" in the South. On August 15, 1852, after he had commented on Calhoun and Stowe, he exclaimed in his diary: "I feel like I am the man for times coming." Two months later, still exhilarated, he called himself "the devotee" of "Slavery Perfect Society."[44] By then Hughes had already begun writing his own wordy analytical justification of southern slavery.

In 1854, at the age of twenty-five, Hughes published his *Treatise on Sociology.* His book immediately received favorable recognition in the South. The southern writer William Gilmore Simms described it as a profound and conclusive defense of slavery. Another reviewer praised the book as a worthy effort to overcome the southern "habit" of admitting that slavery was "an evil in the abstract." Sociologist George Fitzhugh thought Hughes's book, which departed from the old southern inclination to apologize for the institution, was helping to revolutionize southern public opinion on slavery. Literary recognition had political implications for the youthful author. Reprinting Simms's review, the editor of the *Port Gibson Reveille* declared that Hughes was "well qualified by natural talents and astute learning for any position that the people of his native State might assign him. We know of no man who would represent the views of the Southern people in Congress with more ability and fidelity than Mr. Hughes."[45] Two years later the editor would be able to announce the election of Hughes to the Mississippi state senate.

In formulating the concepts for his *Treatise,* Hughes had been influenced by the writings of Charles Fourier and by the sociological theories of Auguste Comte. Fourier, the theoretician of utopian socialism who advocated the reorganization of society into communities called phalanxes, had an enormous impact on Hughes's thinking. "Finished the first volume of Fourier's 'Passions of the Human Soul.' That book's influence on me!" Hughes continued his reading. "I do not think that this book will mislead, nor make me visionary. It will generate conceptions; it will supply elements." The following year he went to Paris, where he studied the ideas of Comte. The French philosopher's influence was apparent in Hughes's use of such terms as *sociology* and his belief that social phenomena could be reduced to science and laws. But Hughes was interested in these European thinkers only because he wanted to use their ideas and methods to refute the charges that slavery was "morally evil, and civilly inexpedient."[46]

In his sociological defense of southern slavery, Hughes noted the institution's critical caste function: It maintained the social subordination of blacks and racial purity in southern society. White southerners, Hughes wrote, had a "moral duty" to continue the preservation and progress of their race. "Degeneration is evil. . . . Impurity of races is against the law of nature. Mulattoes are monsters." Society must be divided between white and black. And economic divisions must parallel racial lines: Whites must "mentalize" and blacks must "manualize." Otherwise "economic amalgamation" would lead to "sexual amalgamation." Blacks must also be kept out of the political structure, for "political amalgamation" was "sexual amalgamation": "Power to rule" was "power to marry"—the power to repeal or annul discriminating laws. In the caste system of the South, "the purity of the females of one race" was systematically preserved, and interracial marriages between black women and white men were prohibited. Such a prohibition was necessary, for otherwise black women would choose white men from "natural preference" or ignorant white men would choose black women. "These motives are certain; and certainty of motive, is certainty of movement," Hughes explained. "The law must therefore forbid amalgamation." While Hughes undoubtedly knew about the sexual relations between white men and black women already taking place under slavery, he feared that the repeal of legal prohibitions against interracial marriage would mean the dangerous loss of controls and the unrestrained rise of a population of mulatto "monsters."[47]

But, in his *Treatise,* Hughes advanced more than a mere polemic against miscegenation, more than a mere reaffirmation of the caste system. What the southern proslavery theoretician offered was a vision of class rule. In his analysis of labor and social relations in America, he asserted that there were two forms of "societary organization"—the "free sovereign" society of the North and the "ordered sovereign" society of the South. The labor system of the North was based on a private relationship between the capitalist and the free laborer. Their interests were antagonistic, for the wealth of the capitalist was derived from the want of the laborer. The "rich and poor" are in constant "conflict," and "strikes and riots are not eliminated," Hughes observed. Thus class conflict and social anarchy threatened the "free sovereign" society of the North. The South, on the other hand, had an "ordered sovereign" society. Its labor system, which Hughes called "warranteeism" rather than slavery, involved an institutional relationship between the white master and the black servant, between the "warrantor" and the "warrantee." Blacks in the South were not slaves; they were not property. "Property in man," Hughes explained, "is absurd. Man cannot be owned. In warranteeism, what is owned is the labor-obligation, not the obligee. The obligee is a man." Both the "warrantor" and the "warrantee" shared common interests. As a valuable "material product," the black laborer was appreciated and given sufficient food and necessities. Hence poverty and strikes were absent in the "ordered sovereign" society of the South. Under "warranteeism" black workers in the South were "manageable": They had no military organizations and no power to meet in "riotous assemblies" without fear of punishment. Slavemasters had military might and organization and thus "a white regiment" could keep the peace of a "black nation."[48]

Thus, "warranteeism" provided order—social, economic, and political order—in the biracial society of the South. In a great burst of poetic flurry, Hughes ended his *Treatise* with a description of the harmony and happiness which allegedly existed in the "warrantee" society of southern plantation phalanxes.

Then, in the plump flush of full-feeding health, the happy warrantees shall banquet in PLANTATION-REFECTORIES; worship in PLANTATION-CHAPELS; learn in PLANTATION-SCHOOLS; or in PLANTATION-SALOONS, at the cool of evening, or the green and bloomy gloom of cold catalpas and magnolias, chant old songs, tell tales; or to the metred rattle of chattering castanets, or flutes, or rumbling tamborines, dance down the moon and evening star, and after slumbers in PLANTATION-DORMITORIES, over whose gates Health and Rest sit smiling at the feet of Wealth and Labor, rise at the music-crowing of the morning-conchs, to begin again welcome days of jocund toil, in reeling fields. . . . When these and more than these, shall be the fulfilment of Warranteeism; then shall this Federation and the World, praise the power, wisdom, and goodness of a system, which may well be deemed divine; then shall Experience aid Philosophy, and VINDICATE THE WAYS OF GOD, TO MAN.[49]

Here was the ultimate vision of total institutional governance. Slavery was an asylum for everyone—whites and blacks as well as men and women.

What Hughes had formulated in this defense of the peculiar institution was a class ideology which protected him against his own moral doubts about slavery, helped him realize his social and political ambitions, and advanced a justification for the world the slaveholders had made. His was a formidable critique of the free labor system, or "wage slavery": Wherever workers, regardless of color, had to exchange their labor for wages, there would be injustice, poverty, riots, strikes, and class conflicts. The future of American society under the capitalist system of wage labor appeared evident to Hughes in the social and class tensions present in the cities of the

North during the Market Revolution. For Hughes, "warranteeism," controlling a "black nation," offered an alternative to the class disorder rampant in northern society. Unlike the North, the South had a biracial population; its working class was black and denied rights which had to be granted to the white working class of the North—the rights to assemble, vote, and bear arms. Based on institutional control and class/caste hegemony, "warranteeism" guaranteed order in relations between whites and blacks, capital and labor.

Aesculapius Was a White Man: Race and the Cult of True Womanhood

During his travels in America, Tocqueville observed how blacks were degraded and assigned animal or brutish qualities, and how white women were elevated and praised for their morality. While blacks were segregated and enslaved, white women were placed within a narrow circle of domestic life and in a condition of dependency. Had Tocqueville reflected more deeply on these two developments, he would have noticed how the subordination of blacks in the ideology of the black "child/savage" and the confinement of white women in the cult of "true womanhood" were interdependent, and how both of them interacted dynamically in a process of mutual reinforcement. During the age of Jackson, America became more virulently than ever before a "white man's country" as institutional and ideological patterns of white over black and male over female were strengthened.

Recently, due to the social ferment of our times, scholars have begun to give unprecedented attention to the racial and sexual patterns that Tocqueville noted. But one of the effects of these studies has been evasive: They have tended to focus on the outgroups rather than those responsible for the plight of the oppressed. While studies by scholars like C. Wright Mills and G. William Domhoff have demonstrated that power in America has been almost exclusively a monopoly of white men, they have neither analyzed the relationship of the oppressions of different outgroups nor explored adequately the motivations of white men in power in America. While studies by historians like Eugene Genovese and Eleanor Flexnor have advanced our understanding of the subordination of blacks and women respectively, they have tended to analyze the two groups separately. Such a fragmented approach has precluded a comparative analysis of the stereotypes applied to blacks and women, and fails to recognize how the oppression of different groups served common needs of white men. Thus a fascinating and disturbing question still remains largely unanswered: Why have white men historically relegated people unlike themselves to specially defined "places"? This relationship between racial and sexual domination has been apparent at times. One such moment occurred in 1850 at Harvard Medical School where Oliver Wendell Holmes was dean and where faculty were seeking to professionalize medicine.[50]

Traditionally Harvard Medical School had been an institution for white men only. But in November 1850, the faculty admitted three black men— Martin Delany, Daniel Laing, and Isaac Snowden—and a white woman— Harriot K. Hunt. Actually the admissions were hardly expressions of enlightened views on race and sex. The faculty understood that the black students would emigrate and practice medicine in Africa after graduation. Their application for admission probably would have been denied had they wished to remain in America. The conditionality of their admission was suggested in the correspondence between Dean Holmes and Dr. H. H. Childs of the Pittsfield Medical School. Asked for advice on the admission of black students, Dr. Childs told Dean Holmes that he was willing to train blacks sponsored by the American Colonization Society. "We have had applications," he added, "to educate colored students to practice medicine in this country which have been uniformly refused." Hunt's admission was also conditional: Allowed to attend lectures, she would not be permitted to take the examination for the degree.[51]

The admission of the four students provoked a storm of protest. At a meeting held on December 10, Harvard medical students demanded the dismissal of the blacks and Hunt. The faculty quickly capitulated. "Leading members of the faculty" met privately with Hunt and persuaded her to withdraw her application. Meeting at the home of Dean Holmes, the faculty deemed it "inexpedient" to allow blacks to attend medical lectures. The professors argued that their commitment to teaching and academic excellence required the exclusion of blacks from the school. The "intermixing of the white and black races in the lecture rooms," they pointed out, was "distasteful to a large portion of the class, & injurious to the interests of the school." The presence of blacks was a "source of irritation and distraction" and interfered with "the success of their teaching."[52]

In the judgment of these worried Harvard students and professors, the honorable calling of Aesculapius, the ancient physician consecrated to holy mysteries, should be reserved for white men only. The exclusion of blacks and white women from Harvard Medical School helped students as well as faculty identify themselves as white and male.[53] What is important here is the way in which Harvard white men defined Delany and Hunt as people unlike themselves—how they imaged those who should not be admitted to one of the foremost educational institutions in America. Their images of blacks and white women not only told them who they were but also what kind of society America was and should be.

In their protest, Harvard students denounced blacks as intellectual inferiors. Here they were reflecting notions of black inferiority in intelligence which were ubiquitous in mid-nineteenth century American society and which their own professors promoted. Dr. Morton's *Crania Americana,* which contained the Philadelphia physician's findings on the differential cranial capacities of whites and blacks, was in the private libraries of Harvard medical professors. Dean Holmes had such a high regard for the writings of Dr. Morton that he considered Morton's research "permanent data for all future students of Ethnology. . . ."[54] Thus, for Harvard students, black men might have had strong bodies, but mind or intelligence was a monopoly of the white race, especially the males of that race.

The presence of Delany and the other black students in the lecture room was a disturbing contradiction to the belief in white intellectual superiority. Delany, as the letters of recommendation from his private instructors Dr. Joseph Gazzam and Dr. Julius Le Moyne indicated, had shown impressive competence in the study of medicine. As editor of the *Pittsburgh Mystery* and then as coeditor of the *Rochester North Star* during the 1840s, Delany had attacked segregated education in his struggle to topple oppressive notions of white over black. But Harvard students could not or did not want to admit that black men like Delany could compete with them intellectually. To have done so would have been disastrous for their own self-image. Instead they complained that the admission of blacks would lower academic standards. "For the reputation of the school," they argued, ". . . it is to be hoped that the professors will not graduate their instructions according to their estimation of the intellectual abilities of the negro race; at least, not until the number of blacks preponderate!" And the protesters anxiously warned that the admission of blacks was "but the beginning of an Evil, which, if not checked will increase, and that the number of *white* students will, in future, be in inverse ratio, to that of *blacks.*" The angry students also claimed the admission of blacks jeopardized caste lines in society, and refused "to be identified as fellow-students, with blacks, whose company we would not keep in the streets, and whose society as associates we would not tolerate in our houses."[55] In their demand for the exclusion of blacks and in their defense of academic standards, Harvard men were reinforcing the caste lines of northern Jacksonian society and reaffirming their claims to membership in a race of superior intelligence.

Significantly Harvard men viewed intelligence as a matter of sex as well as race. For them, mind was masculine. This belief was an important underpinning of the ethos of American white male society. Early nineteenth-century white male claims of female intellectual inferiority often bore a curious resemblance to the racist theory of Dr. Morton: It was "almost universally believed that a woman's brain was smaller in capacity and therefore inferior in quality to that of a man." In his book *Females and Their Diseases* (1848), Dr. Charles Meigs noted that a woman had "a head almost too small for intellect but just big enough for love." But the idea of masculine intelligence required vigilant defense in an age when women like Margaret Fuller were demanding greater educational opportunities and threatening to prove to white male America that women were intellectually equal, even superior, to men. The relationship between Fuller and Holmes has some relevance to our analysis here. Arrogantly brilliant, Fuller had made Holmes feel uncomfortable. As a boy, Oliver had tried to compete with "smart" Margaret in school. "Some themes were brought home from the school for examination by my father," he recalled, "among them one of hers. I took it up with a certain emulous interest . . . and read the first words. 'It is a trite remark,' she began. I stopped. Alas! I did not know what *trite* meant. How could I ever judge Margaret fully after such a crushing discovery of her superiority?"[56]

Like Margaret Fuller, Harriot Hunt threatened masculine white America. Deeply involved in the women's rights movement, Hunt complained that the American Revolution had given freedom to the "white man only," and called for "another revolution" to realize "freedom for all." Already a practicing physician (defiantly "undegreed") in Boston for more than twelve years, she was refusing to be what men like Holmes thought women should be—nurses rather than doctors. Hunt's admission to the medical school distressed Harvard men because she was repudiating their images of women as "modest" and "delicate" beings. She was "unsexing" herself. She was impudently violating their cherished dichotomy between the world of men and that of women. She was revolting against the confining role men had assigned to her, and insisting that "mind was not sexual." In her letter requesting admission, she bluntly challenged: "Shall mind or sex, be recognized in admission to medical lectures?"[57] Obviously she threatened what white men at Harvard thought was their "self-respect" and "dignity."

The Harvard student protest against Hunt's admission reflected some of the significant developments in male-female relationships which occurred during the Market Revolution. The tremendous economic changes of this era transformed patterns of work and relations between the two sexes. In an agrarian society, work was to a large extent non-sexual: It belonged to both men and women. The factory system and urbanization, however, tended to undermine this pattern. Women were employed in factories, but at this time, at least, on a temporary basis, their employment taking place during a brief period before marriage. Increasingly industrial and urban work became largely male, and men's work was located away from home. As the *Monthly Religious Magazine* observed in 1860, the need for business and professional men to travel long distances to their places of "duty," produced "little short of an absolute separation from their families."[58]

As middle-class men were separated from home and family, they increasingly worshipped the "cult of true womanhood." No doubt for ages men had been claiming that woman's place was in the home, but during the 1840s and 1850s, this claim became a cult. In books, magazines, speeches, and sermons, men sang praises to woman and her sacred place—the home. Women were told to be "feminine," "domestic," "modest," and "delicate"; they were exalted as moral guardians of the hearth and radiant sources of purity in a moneymaking and enterprising society.[59] Given a "lofty" place, white women were confined to the home, segregated from the marketplace and from the professions, including medicine.

The relationship between Dr. Holmes and his wife, Amelia, illustrates this "cult of true womanhood." One of Mr. Holmes's biographers described Mrs. Holmes as the "kindest, gentlest, and tenderest of women," "a *helpmate* the most useful, whose abilities seemed to have been arranged by happy foresight for the express purpose of supplying *his* wants." Mrs. Holmes "took care of him and gave him every day the fullest and freest chance to be always at his best, always able to do his work amid cheerful surroundings. She contributed immensely to *his* success. . . . She eschewed the idea of having wit or literary and critical capacities. . . ." Indeed, Mrs. Holmes was "an ideal wife." She was what Mr. Holmes wanted a wife to be. In a letter to Harriet Beecher Stowe (whose prolificness as a writer made Holmes feel "ashamed") written long after the admissions controversy, Mr. Holmes remarked: "Men are out-of-door and office animals; women are indoor creatures essentially. . . ."[60]

The dichotomy between the marketplace and the home which developed during the Market Revolution served an important psychological function for enterprising and career-oriented men: It enabled them to make raids into the anarchistic business world of men, then retreat into what they thought or wished to think was the calm and moral world of women. This need to dichotomize life was especially intense in a society where the pressure upon "a multitude of business and professional men" was "really frightful," and where Americans thought it was not "uncommon for the same man in the course of his life to rise and sink again through all the grades that lead from opulence to poverty."[61]

Harvard medical men had a particular reason for insisting on a separation between the office and the home. Research on cadavers, Professor John Ware warned in his introductory lecture in 1850, could make young men forget that "the object" before them was "anything but a mere subject of our art." Thus the pursuit of scientific knowledge could make them callous. A woman was particularly vulnerable in this regard. Convinced that the practice of medicine would be found unsuitable to woman's "physical, intellectual, and moral constitution," Professor Ware declared that it was "difficult to conceive that she should go through all that we have to encounter in the various departments of the study of medicine, without tarnishing that *delicate* surface of the female mind, which can hardly be imagined even to reflect what is gross without somewhat defilement."[62]

But men, too, were susceptible to this danger. Thus white men of enterprise needed white women to be moral and delicate custodians of the home, which became a counterpoint to the market and a safety valve for its pressures. Leading and respected ministers, like the Reverend Horace Bushnell, advised women to stay in the home: "Let us have a place of quiet, and some quiet minds which the din of our public war never embroils. Let a little of the sweetness and purity, and, if we can have it, of simple religion of life remain. God made woman to be a help for man, not to be a wrestler with him." In his novel, *Elsie Venner,* published nine years after the admissions controversy, Dr. Holmes also located the woman's place in the home for similar reasons. He noted how the education of the community to "beauty" flowed mainly through its women, and how female educational institutions served an important function in the inculcation of "higher tastes" among them. Surrounded by "practical and every-day working youth," women had a particular responsibility for the preservation of culture. "Our young men come into active life so early," Holmes warned, "that, if our girls were not educated to something beyond mere practical duties, our material prosperity would outstrip our culture; as it often does in large places where money is made too rapidly."[63] Thus, in a market society, the home was to be the domain of "true women," the sanctuary of "sweetness," "purity," and "beauty," where busy and weary businessmen could rest from the pressurized labor of the office and where insensitive doctors could restore their humanity away from the "defiling" laboratories.

The racial and sexual divisions which prevailed in Jacksonian society and which surfaced at Harvard Medical School in 1850 were dialectically involved in a powerful cultural and psychological process. A clue to the understanding of this process may be found in a letter published in the *Boston Journal* during the admissions controversy. This letter, signed "Common Sense," attempted to justify the exclusion of the blacks and the white woman from Harvard Medical School. The presence of the three black men in the lecture room, he explained, "occasioned a good deal of feeling in the school . . . and, anon, the report was circulated that a *woman* had taken tickets for the lectures! The pent up indignation now broke forth, and two series of resolutions were passed, remonstrating against this *amalgamation of sexes and races.*"[64] Thus the admission of nonmale and nonwhite students meant not only the "unsexing" of women (and implicitly also of men), but also the mixing of white women and black men.

Such "amalgamation" also constituted a symbolic mixing of the "savagery" and "culture" which blacks and white women respectively represented in the minds of white men. Like the old black servant Sophy in Holmes's *Elsie Venner,* blacks were viewed as "cannibals," "terrible wild savages," or their descendants, while white women represented the force of culture; they were preservers of all that was "beautiful" in society. Living in the highly competitive and constantly changing conditions of the Market Revolution, white men like the students of Harvard felt compelled to bifurcate society on the basis of race and sex. The image of the black "child/savage" and the image of the "true woman" served as reference points for these nervous white men. Together, racial and sexual imagery enabled them to delineate their own white male identity—to affirm, through the degradation of blacks, the virtues of self-control and industry, and to protect, through the elevation of white women, the culture and beauty which white men feared were in danger in a society where blacks were present and where science and the rapid making of money could "defile" white men themselves.[65]

Thus, in the eyes of uneasy Harvard students, Delany and his black colleagues and Hunt threatened the social and cultural divisions which supported white male supremacy, and had to be excluded from the temples of knowledge and power. This need to separate themselves from black men and white women, however, did not preclude the possibility or even the desire for integration, if integration could be achieved on a hierarchical basis—white over black, male over female. White Harvard students were upset because Delany and Hunt had been permitted to attend lectures as fellow students. They would not have objected to the presence of black janitors or female nurses. Frederick Douglass, an astute analyst of the white male psychology, painfully understood the reality of this hierarchical integration. "While we are servants," he explained, "we are never offensive to the whites. . . . On the very day we were brutally assaulted in New York for riding down Broadway in company with ladies, we saw several white ladies riding with *black servants.*"[66] This kind of hierarchical integration, involving physical proximity but in a definite superior-inferior relationship, helped to reinforce the identity of white men.

But more than white male identity was at stake in the Harvard Medical School admissions controversy. The exclusion of Delany and Hunt was related to the professionalization of medicine in America. During the 1840s, medicine in this country became increasingly professionalized: The American Medical Association was founded in 1847 and medical schools emphasized the importance of formal training and degrees. One of the leaders of this effort, Dr. Holmes called for greater recognition for scholarly and professionally trained doctors, and denounced the "self-taught genius" and the "fancy practitioner." While this professionalization indicated a desire to provide scientific, skilled, and responsible medical services, it developed from a concern for the intense competition which existed in the medical business. Doctors thought their numbers were already excessive; in 1848, a committee of the American Medical Association reported that the ratio of physicians to the population in the United States was five times as high as in France. Two years later, in his introductory lecture, Professor Ware told Harvard medical students that the medical field was "always filled by eager and aspiring competitors," and that young men were anxious about their chances for "success"—a "large practice" and "large income." Resentful toward competition from "ignorant novices," the graduates of "*inferior medical schools,*" Harvard medical men feared black admissions would "lessen" the "value" of their diplomas. Thrust into the nervous struggle for "success," they were also apprehensive about competition from women, especially in the areas of gynecology and obstetrics, where women had traditionally provided services as midwives. After Hunt had been forced to withdraw from Harvard, she bitterly remarked: "If we could follow those young men [Harvard medical students] into life, and see them subjecting woman to examinations *too often unnecessary*—could we penetrate their secret feelings, should we not find in some, that female practitioners *are needed* . . . ?"[67]

Professionalized, medicine in America would become the monopoly of university-trained white men: It would maintain the exclusion of blacks and remove the competition of white women from medical practice. Given the responsibility and power to train and credential a professional elite, universities would institutionalize the reproduction of a stratified class structure in American society based on both race and sex. But what Harvard students and professors did not fully realize was how the professionalization of medicine was part of the development of a "culture of professionalism,"[68] and how the hegemony of experts based on their exclusive control of specialized knowledge was penetrating all the professions in America. Neither did they foresee how professional elites would become integrated into bureaucratic corporate structures and their needs in a technological society, or how their republican "iron cages" which demanded strenuous competitive activity and the domination of the black "child/ savage" and the "true woman" would give way to the corporate "iron cage" in America.

PART THREE

TECHNOLOGY

An organised system of machines, to which motion is communicated by the transmitting mechanism from a central automaton, is the most developed form of production by machinery. Here we have, in the place of the isolated machine, a mechanical monster whose body fills whole factories, and whose demon power, at first veiled under the slow and measured motions of his giant limbs, at length breaks out into the fast and furious whirl of his countless working organs.

—Karl Marx

CHAPTER VII

AN AMERICAN PROSPERO
IN KING ARTHUR'S
COURT

Never was the average man, his soul, more energetic,
*   more like a God,*
Lo, how he urges and urges, leaving the masses no rest!
His daring foot is on land and sea everywhere, he colonizes
*   the Pacific, the archipelagoes,*
With the steamship, the electric telegraph, the newspaper,
*   the wholesale engines of war,*
With these and the world-spreading factories he interlinks
*   all geography, all lands. . . .*

                                    —Walt Whitman

In 1829 Professor Jacob Bigelow, one of the Harvard Medical School faculty opposed to the admission of blacks and women, published a book
which heralded a Promethean era of technology in America. Entitled *Ele-*
ments of Technology, it was a prodigious work: Its 507 pages dealt with a
wide range of topics, such as gunpowder, machinery, steam power, and the
steam engine. Bigelow's primary interest was the practical application of
scientific knowledge in man's effort to "convert" nature and natural materials to "usefulness." Science offered man an opportunity to use his mind to
control nature, and to rely on machines and instruments as "a substitute
for human strength." The invention of gunpowder had given the "mind"
advantage over the "body" in the arts of war, and the invention of certain
machines had enabled a few men to perform the labor of a hundred work-

ers. Significantly, Bigelow regarded technology, the use of the machine to replace the human body in production, as an "American inventive genius." Identifying technology with America, he compared steam power with the power of kings. In his judgment, America represented a new concept of power in the world.[1]

Bigelow's identification of technology with mind reflected a growing tendency in Western culture to dissociate mind from body and raise rationality to authority over the instinctual life. This movement toward the triumph of mind in America had been under way long before the nineteenth century, as the Protestant ethic and capitalism transformed Western civilization. The development of technology gave additional impetus to the elevation of rationality and self-renunciation. As Hans Sachs has suggested in his seminal essay on "The Delay of the Machine Age," the increasing presence of negative feelings toward the body seemed to coincide with the invention and use of machines which substituted mechanical for human labor. Both Johan Huizinga and Harvey Cox have noted that as Western capitalist society became more and more industrialized in the nineteenth century, it became more and more repressive: It left little room for play, and work schedules squeezed to a minimum time and energy for festivity. Karl Marx observed how self-renunciation had set boundaries around life, and how men had to deny themselves the pleasures of "the theatre, the dance hall, and the public house" in order to accumulate capital.[2]

What was happening generally in the nineteenth century throughout Western society had particular force and significance in the United States. Transformed from an agricultural-commercial economy to a complex industrialized economy, this country became the most highly developed technological society in the world. Technology, both as ideology and as economic development, had an enormous impact on culture and race in America: It served as metaphor and materialist basis for the domination of mind over body, capital over labor, and whites over Indians, blacks, Mexicans, and Asians.

The New Body

The publication of Bigelow's book was timely: After 1830 America entered into a celebration of technology as an expression of its nationalism and progress. In his third annual message, President Jackson praised science for expanding man's power over nature, improving the mail system, moving cities closer to each other in travel time, and opening lines of communication and trade to settlers isolated by the obstacles of nature. Joseph Ingersoll claimed that two inventions—the steam engine and the magnetic telegraph—had been designed mainly for American society, where people were in constant motion, socially and geographically. Both of them enabled a population "spread over an immense extent" and "migratory in habit and tendency" to "hold immediate intercourse in one shape from the remotest distances, and personally to visit and become familiarly acquainted through the length and breadth of the land without loss of time, material expense or fatigue."[3] Indeed, Americans could point with pride to their achievements in transportation and communication. While the American railroad system had only 73 miles of tracks in 1830, it quickly leaped beyond the total miles of tracks in all of Europe as it stretched to 3,328 miles in 1840, to 8,879 in 1850, and to 30,636 in 1860. Thirteen years after Samuel Morse had patented the telegraph in 1837, all the important towns and cities east of the Mississippi River were connected with telegraph lines.

In their celebration of technology, many Americans viewed the machine as a replacement for the human body. For them, steam power especially possessed amazing abilities and could do far more than human labor. In his discussion on the railroad, a writer for *Hunt's Merchants Magazine* described the versatility and power of steam: "We see it stamping with exquisite forms the fabric which is to enrobe the bosom of the bride . . . or thundering on . . . across the plains . . . leaping forward like some black monster, upon its iron path, by the light of the fire and smoke which it vomits forth. . . . This powerful agent is ever found [everywhere] ready to do the bidding of men. . . ." In 1853 a newspaper editorial, entitled "The Spirit of the Times," predicted that "the human race very soon need not *toil,* but merely direct: hard work will be done by steam. Horses themselves are rapidly becoming obsolete. In a few years, like Indians, they will be merely traditional. Steam itself, with its seventy miles an hour, is voted *too slow;* and electricity is fast superseding the iron horse. . . ." New England abolitionist Theodore Parker compared the employment of technology in New England with the exploitation of black bodies in the South. "While South Carolina has taken men from Africa, and made them slaves," he said, "New England has taken possession of the Merrimack, the Connecticut, the Androscoggin, the Kennebeck, the Penobscot, and a hundred smaller streams."[4] Man no longer had to depend on the horse, or even the human body; slavemasters no longer had to rely on black labor. Technology would enable Americans to free themselves from toil, make steam do their bidding, and enslave the rivers.

The language Americans used to express their enthusiasm and hopes for steam power was suggestive: Steam power was described in terms of the new body. As Perry Miller has noted, in the celebration of steam—"the pure white jet that fecundates America"—the "imagery frequently becomes, probably unconsciously, sexual, and so betrays how in this mechanistic orgasm modern America was conceived." Terms such as marriage and birth were employed to describe steam. "With consummate skill the marriage of water and heat was effected," declared J. A. Meigs in 1854. "The child of that marriage has grown to be a herculean aid to onward moving humanity. Certainly steam is a benefactor to the race. The printing press and the electric telegraph have become the handmaids of thought." In his speech at the Chicago Railroad Convention in 1847, William M. Hall described the emergent railroad as a virile masculine force, plucking out the forests, tearing up and flinging aside the seated hills, and making his way into the "body of the continent" with the step of a "bridegroom" going to his chamber. With its locomotive ejecting the "pure white jet," the railroad was penetrating what Henry Nash Smith has called the "virgin land."[5]

The use of steam and the elevation of mind in this new era held great promise to many Americans. With steam to toil for man, Charles Fraser wrote in *Hunt's Merchants Magazine* in 1846, he would have time and energy to cultivate his mind and realize "the perfection of his nature." In his speech to the Boston Mechanics Institute in 1828, Daniel Webster eloquently expressed this hope for human perfection in a technological America.

> Steam . . . [is] on the rivers, and the boatman may repose on his oars; it is on the highways . . . it is in the mill, and in the workshops. . . . It rows, it pumps, it excavates, it carries, it draws, it lifts, it hammers, it spins, it weaves. . . . It seems to say to men . . . "Leave off your manual labor, give over your bodily toil; bestow your skill and reason to the directing of my power, and I will bear the toil,—with no muscle to grow weary, no nerve to relax, no breast to feel faintness."

And what would be man's new role? He would use science to stretch "the dominion of mind farther and farther over the elements of nature," Webster declared, and make those elements "submit to human rule, follow human bidding, and work together for human happiness."[6] Steam would become his new body, one which would never become tired and one which would make it possible for the first time in history for man to become mind.

The new technology, as it was welcomed by certain reformers, would also have "moral" influences on the American character. In a speech on the greatness of the railroad, Charles Caldwell said the railroad would increase industriousness and suppress idleness. It would bring everyone into the market; in the new technological order, people would be employed in "useful business" and would not have the time or inclination for "vicious practices." The market itself, extended as a result of the railroad, would become a mechanism to control passion: It would engage the "feelings" of Americans and "better direct" their thoughts, and would "reclaim" the "irregular and licentious." Thus, the railroad would be a civilizing force, promoting knowledge and morality, helping to restrain man from "the inordinate indulgence of his animal propensities" and to divert his mind from "sensual pursuits."[7]

Thus the new technology was viewed as a way for men to use machines and steam power to replace their bodies as sources of labor, and as a way to keep men busy and controlled in a market society. It promised a future of great wealth and population for America: Steam would "fecundate" the land. In its address to the people of the United States, the Memphis Commercial Convention of 1850 described the procreative potency of this new power. Noting the relationship between the introduction of the steamboat to the Mississippi River and the rise of the valley's population, the convention called the valley the "creation of the *steam engine*," which had used its "magic power" to transport people there, bring "the progress of the arts and enterprise," and sweep away "the traces of savage life." Since the dominion of steam had been established upon the Mississippi, the convention pointed out, the great West had increased from a population of 2,217,-463 in 1820, to 3,672,509 in 1830, to 5,302,918 in 1840, and to nearly 10,000,000 in 1850. In this vision, it appeared almost as if steam were literally giving birth to an American people.[8]

Technology did more than destroy "the traces of savage life"; it also transformed production and labor in America. Production became mechanized, and mechanized production quickly outdistanced craft and domestic production. Between 1815 and 1860, the value of American manufactured goods increased eightfold and their volume approximately twelvefold. The impact of the machine on woolen manufacturing illustrates the dominance of the machine in production: While household production of wool exceeded factory production in 1830, it fell far behind after 1840. Federal census reports showed that the average per capita value of household manufacturing for the country declined from $1.70 in 1840, to $1.18 in 1850, to $.78 in 1860. By 1894, the value of American manufactured goods exceeded the value of goods manufactured by any European nation, and was not far from equaling the total combined value of the manufactures of England, France, and Germany. Labor patterns in the United States reflected these changes in production. In 1840, agricultural workers consti-tuted 68.6 percent of all gainfully employed workers, while workers in manufacturing, hand trades, and construction represented only 14.5 per-cent. Sixty years later, workers in agriculture had decreased to 36.8 percent, while workers in manufacturing and related areas, including trans-portation and public utilities, had increased to 34.7 percent of the total gainfully employed work force.[9]

This transformation from domestic to factory production radically al-tered the relationship between laborers and their work. Many artisans like Smithfield, Rhode Island, shoemaker Stafford Benchley were drawn into the labor force of local textile mills. In this process, technology actually did not eliminate bodily labor; rather it degraded labor, separating the intellec-tual power of production from manual labor. Transformed from craftsman to factory laborer, the worker could find little creativity in the productive activity. Even the "lightening" of labor, as Marx noted, became a "sort of torture," for the machine did not free the laborer from work but rather deprived work of interest. The laborer had entered a system of manifold machines where the motion of the whole system proceeded not from the workman but from the machinery. Surrounded by clattering engines, whir-ring gears, humming belts, and pumping levers, workmen found them-selves and also their families—their wives and children—pressed into the service of factory production. In the cotton mills of Pawtucket in 1831, for example, children constituted approximately 40 percent of the total work force, while women represented another 30 percent.[10]

The factory imposed a new definition of time and subjected workers to the discipline of factory bells. Time was no longer determined by the "natural" rhythms of the sun and the tides, observed E. P. Thompson. The industrial revolution required a "synchronization of labour" and the clock became the regulator for the "new rhythms of industrial life." This demand for "a greater exactitude in time-routines" and synchronized labor devel-oped in societies of nascent industrial capitalism which used time measure-ment as a means of labor exploitation. One American worker captured in rhyme the experience of this new dimension:

> The Clock in the workshop,—it rests not a moment;
> It points on, and ticks on: eternity—time;
> Once someone told me the clock had a meaning,—
> In pointing and ticking had reason and rhyme. . . .
> At times, when I listen, I hear the clock plainly;—
> The reason of old—the old meaning—is gone!
> The maddening pendulum urges me forward

> To labor and still labor on.
> The tick of the clock is the boss in his anger.
> The face of the clock has the eyes of the foe.
> The clock—I shudder—Dost hear how it draws me?
> It calls me "Machine" and it cries [to] me "Sew"!

Thus the clock became an instrument of labor control and exploitation. The hands of the factory clock, itself an instrument of gears and wheels, now moved inexorably to determine the beginning and end of each work day as factory owners and foremen pressed buttons or pulled levers to start and stop the activity of machinery and workers.[11]

More than ever before, as the mode of production became mechanical, workers became appendages to the machines. A worker in a shoe factory felt he had become a "mere machine" in the modern system of shoe production. "Take the proposition of a man operating a machine to nail on forty to sixty pairs cases of heels in a day," he complained. "That is 2,400 pairs, 4,800 shoes, in a day." Driven to see how many shoes he could handle and surrounded by "noisy machinery," the factory operative did "one thing over and over and over again" and suffered from "nervous strain." Life in the textile factory was, according to a contemporary description,

> with the exception of prison life, the most monotonous life a human being can live. . . . [A weaver] has got at least six looms to tend. They are arranged in a double row and his position is between them. He passes from one to the other. He must keep his eyes on them all and be ready to "change the shuttle" when the "filling runs out." He tramps thus back and forth up and down his "alley" for five hours, with no time to sit down and rest for a moment. After dinner he resumes his position at the looms and repeats the story and this goes on day after day, week after week, for months and years, the same round of toil. . . .

The reference to "prison life" contained in the above description of work in a textile factory was appropriate. As historian David Rothman noted, both the prison and the factory were "among the first [organizations] to try to take people from casual routines to rigid ones." Prison reformers sometimes even used the factory as a model for designing methods to inculcate regularity, punctuality, and routine. The prison itself was constructed along factory lines: "a long and low building, symmetrically arranged with closely spaced windows, all very regular and methodical."[12]

In the brave new world of machinery, the very celebration of steam as the new body shrouded the degradation of labor that was occurring in America. Supposedly intended to liberate people from bodily toil and allow them to realize their "perfection," technology in capitalist America had class ramifications. Workers were not only "alienated" from control over the process of production and the ownership of their products but also relegated to repetitious and noncreative activity. Actually only the elite—the factory owners and the managers—became mind, while the masses of laborers, enclosed inside factories that resembled "prisons," were reduced to body workers.

White Technology: Anglo Over Mexican

As white Americans identified themselves with technology and increased in their minds the distance between "civilization" and "savagery," they also viewed westward expansion in terms of technological progress. As a writer for the *Southern Quarterly Review* declared in 1828, they could "perceive neither justice, nor wisdom, nor humanity in arresting the progress of order and science, that unproductive and barren wastes may be reserved for the roaming barbarian." And they confidently removed Indians as President Jackson welcomed the new power which technology had given them: "Science is steadily penetrating the recesses of nature and disclosing her secrets, while the ingenuity of free minds is subjecting the elements to the power of man and making each new conquest auxiliary to his comfort."[13] This imperial vision, which integrated science and expansion, captured the imagination of Thomas Hart Benton.

United States Senator from Missouri, Benton personified the West and its expansionist spirit. He grew up in Tennessee, serving in the militia under Jackson in 1812, and represented Missouri in the Senate for more than two decades. A quote from Benton, inscribed on his statue in St. Louis, expresses the focus of his life ambition: "There is the East [Asia]; there lies the road to India." The quote was from his 1825 Senate speech favoring the military occupation of Oregon. A philosopher of expansionism, Benton was proud of his son-in-law, John C. Frémont, western explorer and conqueror of Monterey.

As early as 1818, Benton envisioned Americans migrating beyond the Rocky Mountains, and the "children of Adam" completing the "circumambulation of the globe" by marching to the West until they arrived at the Pacific Ocean "in sight of the eastern shore of that Asia in which their first parents were originally planted." Benton regarded himself not as a new prophet of American destiny but as a disciple of Columbus and Jefferson. "Columbus, going west to Asia," he said, "was arrested by the intervention of the two Americas. . . . Mr. Jefferson . . . this rare man, following up the grand idea of Columbus . . . early projected the discovery of an inland route to the Pacific Ocean." The "grand idea," for Benton, had great significance for America. If the passage to India were realized, he promised, America would dominate the trade route to Asia, and all commerce between the East and the West would flow through America. Civilization in America would be given new life. Under the "touch" of the "American road to India," the western wilderness would "start" into life, a long line of cities would grow up, and existing cities would be revitalized. Commerce with Asia would make America independent from Europe and enable her to establish her own national identity. "The nations of Europe hold us in contempt," he complained, "because we are their servile copyists and imitators; because too many among us can see no merit in anything American but as it approaches the perfection of something European." Americans must nationalize their character and their institutions, and establish a commerce based upon the resources of their country and geographical position, free from the interruptions and intrigues of European nations. To accomplish this, Benton insisted, the commerce of Asia was "indispensable."[14]

Shortly after the declaration of war against Mexico in 1846, Benton explained to Congress the racial significance of "the grand idea of Columbus." The arrival of the "White" race on the western coast, "opposite the eastern coast of Asia," he declared, would benefit humankind. On the other side of the ocean was the "Yellow" race, once the "foremost of the human family in the arts of civilization, but torpid and stationary for thousands of years." While the "Yellow" race was far above the "Black" and "Red" races, it was still far below the "White" and like all the rest "must receive an impression from the superior race whenever they come in contact." Benton claimed the "White" race alone had received the "divine command, to subdue and replenish the earth," for it was the only race which searched for new and distant lands. As whites made their restless movement from "western Asia," they developed religion, art, and science, destroying "savagery" and "savages" in America as they advanced civilization. Commenting on the disappearance of Indians from the Atlantic Coast, Benton said he could not murmur against what appeared to be the effect of "divine law." He could not repine that the "Capitol" had replaced the "wigwam," "Christian" people had replaced "savages," and "white matrons" had replaced "red squaws." Now crossing the Rocky Mountains and reaching the Pacific Ocean, the "White" race had finally circumnavigated the earth to bring new life and civilization to the "Yellow" race. "The sun of civilization must shine across the sea: Socially and commercially, the van of the Caucasians and the rear of the Mongolians must intermix. They must talk together, and trade together, and marry together." In this relationship, the "White" race would take the ascendant, elevating and improving the inferior race, waking up and reanimating "the torpid body of old Asia."[15]

In Benton's vision, America's identity was located in the movement westward, toward Asia and away from Europe. What made the realization of this identity possible was the development of technology. Benton gave "thanks to the progress of the mechanic arts! Which are going on continually, converting into facilities what stood as obstacles in the way of national communications. To the savage, the sea was an obstacle: mechanical genius, in the invention of the ship, made it a facility. The firm land was what the barbarian wanted: the land became an obstacle to the civilized man, and remained so until the steam car was invented." The railroad, Benton predicted, would stretch from Missouri to California, "debouching at each end into the midst of business populations" and opening up a "new channel to the commerce of Asia."[16] In the progress of technology, the domination of civilization over nature, American expansion westward, and the destruction of Indians and Mexicans, the destiny of white America seemed manifest.

In his bifurcation of savagery and civilization, peoples of color and white Americans, and torpidity and technological progress, Benton was able to reaffirm the values of enterprise and republican society. Yet, the very process leading toward reaffirmation could, in rare moments of reflection, recoil and open the way toward a criticism of American civilization. This happened to Richard Henry Dana. A member of the New England aristocracy, or Brahmin class, Dana was forced to leave his studies at Harvard due to trouble with his eyes. To help restore his health, he decided to go to sea as a common sailor and sail to California on a trading vessel. He kept a diary which he published in 1840, six years before America's war against Mexico. As it turned out, Dana's *Two Years Before the Mast* was no mere sea story: Rich in its descriptions of California and its inhabitants, the book popularized many Anglo-American images of Mexicans and promoted American economic interest in California. Moreover, it was a narrative of his mind's voyage toward a painful reassessment of himself and his republican civilization.[17]

As Dana sailed out of Boston harbor, he could not have realized how far the voyage would take him within his inner world; and yet he must have suspected much would be in store for him as his ship "floated into the vast solitude of the Bay of San Francisco." The land's beauty and innocence overwhelmed him. "All around was the stillness of nature," he observed. "There were no settlements on these bays or rivers, and the few ranchos and missions were remote and widely separated. . . . On the whole coast of

California there was not a lighthouse, a beacon, or a buoy. . . . Birds of prey and passage swooped and dived about us, wild beasts ranged through the oak groves, and as we slowly floated out of the harbour with the tide, herds of deer came to the water's edge . . . to gaze at the strange spectacle."[18] Dana felt he had entered a primeval world whose natural rhythms and idyllicness stood in sharp contrast to the frenetic activity he had left behind in New England. In the midst of this land of edenic solitude, the young sailor noticed the presence of people, living in the few ranchos and missions.

Even before he had reached the shores of California, Dana had felt negative emotions toward Spanish-speaking people of the Americas. While visiting the island of Juan Fernandez, where his ship had stopped briefly, Dana had noted: "The men appeared to be the laziest of mortals; and indeed, as far as my observation goes, there are no people to whom the newly invented Yankee word of 'loafer' is more applicable than to the Spanish Americans." They have, he added, the "habitual occupation of doing nothing." Thus, the Spanish-American was stereotyped as a contrast to the Yankee.[19]

In California, Dana elaborated on these differences in his descriptions of Mexicans. He was struck by the wide range of complexions the Californians had. Some of them had "clear brunette complexions" and were "sometimes even as fair" as the English; but there were few who were of "pure Spanish blood" and they formed the upper class. From this class, Dana observed, the people "go down by regular shades, growing more and more dark and muddy, until you come to the pure Indian, who runs about with nothing upon him but a small piece of cloth, kept up by a wide leather strap drawn around his waist." Racially mixed and mostly "dark and muddy" in complexion, Californians were described as "an idle, thriftless people." They lacked the enterprise and calculating mentality which characterized Yankees. Thus, although they grew an abundance of grapes, they bought "at a great price, bad wine made in Boston"; they also bartered their hides, valued at two dollars, for something which cost only seventy-five cents in Boston.[20] Inefficient in enterprise, they spent themselves in pleasure-giving activities such as festive parties called fandangos. What distinguished the Anglo-Americans from the inhabitants of California, in Dana's observations, were their white racial purity and their Yankeeness—their industry, frugality, sobriety, and enterprise.

Dana saw that the Yankees living in California were successful in business, but he worried about what would happen to them in the future. Yankee businessmen were not allowed to remain in California unless they conformed to the Roman Catholic Church. Furthermore, they were marrying "natives" and bringing up their children as Catholics and Mexicans. Impressed with the natural resources of California—its forests, its grazing land, and its harbors, Dana regretfully exclaimed:

> In the hands of an enterprising people, what a country this might be! . . . Yet how long would a people remain so, in such a country? The Americans . . . who are fast filling up the principal towns, and getting trade into their hands, are indeed more industrious and effective than the Mexicans; yet their children are brought up Mexican in most respects, and if the "California fever" [laziness] spares the first generation, it is likely to attack the second.[21]

Thus, Dana feared that Anglo-Americans, while they could come to California and advance themselves, would ultimately fail to bring progress.

Yet, while Dana was committed to the Anglo-American values of work and progress, he also felt a dissatisfaction with, an alienation from, Yankee American culture. Thus, at a profound level, he experienced an agonizing ambivalence. Although he was a part of his past and his culture, he nevertheless began to recognize the repressiveness of that culture—what we have called the republican "iron cage" which elevated the rational self and subordinated the human spirit in its emphasis on self-control and material development. An interior rebellion against the confinement of republican culture may already have been under way before Dana left Harvard: His illness may have been symptomatic of resistance. But his experiences at sea and in California, raising his critical consciousness, pitted him even more sharply against his culture.

Working before the mast, Dana witnessed the degradation of the maritime working class. Sailors were like slaves: They had no rights, were whipped and overworked. While reflecting on the Mexicans' seeming indifference toward work, Dana realized how much Anglo-Americans were "a time and money saving people," and how much American shipmasters cruelly exploited their crews in order to get the most for their money. Indeed the values of American culture made shipmasters efficient, hard, calculating, and exploitative. The American emphasis on productivity and profits, moreover, had a stifling effect on the quality of human life in the work situation. Dana graphically described the perniciousness of this emphasis in his comparison between an Italian ship and his American ship. The Italian ship was much smaller than Dana's; yet there were three times as many sailors. While the American ship was run more efficiently, its crew worked harder, silently and with "discontented looks." While less efficient, the crew on the Italian ship had more men to share the work, and they were doing something which deeply impressed Dana: They were singing.[22]

This critical understanding of American culture was reinforced as Dana interacted with the people of California and began to recognize their sense of pride and their concern for the quality of life. In this process of reevaluation, Dana discovered that they had admirable qualities which Anglo-Americans did not and could not have. He noticed, for example, that Mexicans had and appreciated fine voices with beautiful intonations. "A common bullock-driver, on horseback, delivering a message, seemed to speak like an ambassador at a royal audience. In fact, they sometimes appeared to me to be a people on whom a curse had fallen, and stripped them of everything but their pride, their manners, and their voices."[23] Somehow Anglo-Americans lacked this sensitivity for the simple beauty of voice. But why? Republican culture, Dana could see, had reduced Anglo-Americans to a materialistic and austere people.

The process which turned Dana toward a critical understanding of American civilization reached a high point when he observed on board his ship two passengers who seemed to epitomize some of the differences between the Mexican and the Yankee. As Dana described him, Don Juan Bandini was a "gentleman." He was from a family of great wealth but no longer possessed the pecuniary basis for his high position because of misfortune, extravagance, and "the want of any manner of getting interest on money." Yet he still possessed much pride and maintained the dignity as well as the manners of a gentleman. "He had a slight and elegant figure, moved gracefully, danced and waltzed beautifully, spoke good Castilian, with a pleasant and refined voice and accent, and had, throughout, the bearing of a man of birth and figure." Representing a sharp contrast to Don Bandini was a "yankee trader." He was, according to Dana, a "fat, coarse, vulgar, pretentious fellow." He had made money in San Diego, and was profiting at the expense of the Mexicans, "eating out the vitals of the Bandinis, fattening upon their extravagance, grinding them in their poverty; having mortgages on their lands, forestalling their cattle, and already making an inroad upon their jewels, which were their last hope." Clearly, Dana found his fellow Yankee ugly and repulsive. But he knew, too, that the trader represented the values of enterprise and progress which Dana himself believed in and which could make possible the realization of California's great economic potential. Thus, Dana could condemn the Yankee degradation and exploitation of Mexicans, and yet he could exclaim: "What a country this might be in the hands of an enterprising people!"

Dana's confusion and ambivalence became even more painful as he worked with the "Kanakas," or brown people from the Hawaiian Islands, laboring in Santa Barbara and San Pedro. Dana saw the Hawaiians as generous, proud, warm, humane, and happy; they were spontaneous and enjoyed singing. They worked hard but had no interest in making money to get ahead. Once the captain asked some of them to do extra work for him, and they replied that they already had enough money. He then asked whether they wanted to make more money, and they said they did not. One of the men from Hawaii, Hope, and Dana became good friends. "Intelligent," "kind-hearted," and "always civil," Hope felt much affection for Dana, whom he called his "aikane"—his "particular friend."

But a great tragedy awaited both Dana and Hope. The Kanaka was cut down by a dreadful disease, syphilis. The hideous appearance of the sick Hope stunned Dana. "My friend and aikane, Hope, was the most dreadful object I had ever seen in my life," Dana cried out, "his eyes sunken and dead, his cheeks fallen in against his teeth, his hands looking like claws, a dreadful cough, which seemed to rack his whole shattered system; a hollow, whispering voice. . . ." Dana was witnessing what he thought was the ultimate horror whites had brought upon a brown race as they advanced technology and civilization westward. "The white men with their vices," he protested, "have brought in diseases before unknown to the islanders, which are now sweeping off the native population of the Sandwich Islands. . . . They seem to be a doomed people. The curse of a people calling themselves Christians seems to follow them everywhere. . . ." Dana's lament was bitter, overflowing with self-guilt and self-condemnation. His fellow Christian Americans—an "enterprising people"—had entered California, opening the way for progress; and his aikane Hope was close to death, stricken by a disease carried by white men.[24]

Dana had sailed to California on the *Alert,* owned by the Boston firm of Bryant & Sturgis; the cargo, Dana reported, included goods from the manufacturing centers of the United States—"boots and shoes from Lynn" and "cotton from Lowell." Lynn and Lowell represented the advance of American technology and the expansiveness of American capitalism. Even before the American war against Mexico and even before the United States annexed California, the Market Revolution had developed an important economic relationship between the United States and Mexico. Shortly after Mexican independence in 1822, Boston mercantile houses began importing hides from California in huge quantities to supply the raw material needs of the New England boot and shoe industry; during the next twenty years, Bryant & Sturgis alone transported about half a million hides. During this period, Mexico became one of the chief foreign markets of American cotton manufacturers; it also took more American reexports, or European goods exported from the United States, than any other country. Thus the interregional specialization of the United States economy became increasingly complex as Mexico, particularly California, became a virtual economy colony where the United States marketed its goods in exchange for raw material. As sperm oil, extracted from the whale, became an important fuel and lubricant in the society of the Market Revolution, the American whaling industry sent its ships to the North Pacific and Asia and increasingly depended on the harbors of California for repairs and provisions. The first whaling vessels had entered the Pacific Ocean in 1791, and more than 30 vessels cruised along the Japanese coast in 1823. In 1846 the fleet numbered 736 vessels, about 600 of which were whaling in Pacific waters. In his 1846 Senate speech on Oregon, Thomas Hart Benton stressed the importance of the Pacific Ocean for the American whaling industry: "The sea which washes their shores is every way a better sea than the Atlantic— richer in its whale and other fisheries. . . ." Related to these economic developments was the strategy to seize the harbors of San Francisco and San Diego and develop them into entrepôts for American trade with Asia. In his message of December 1847, President James K. Polk declared that the California harbors "would afford shelter for our navy, for our numerous whale ships, and other merchant vessels employed in the Pacific ocean, and would in a short period become the marts of an extensive and profitable commerce with China, and other countries of the East."[25] Clearly, in the minds of expansionists like Polk, California had a special role in America's manifest destiny.

Shortly after the signing of the Treaty of Guadalupe Hidalgo, which ended the war between the United States and Mexico and placed California in the "hands of an enterprising people," the editor of the *Southern Quarterly Review* discussed the significance of the "Conquest of California." He first noted that the American Revolution had given this country a "national existence" and that the War of 1812 had provided "security." The Mexican-American War had clarified the national purpose, he declared. By their violence, United States troops had chastised arrogant and "fraudulent" Mexicans; they had "punished the insolence of her sons in the sight of her daughters." They had demonstrated their "superior courage" and the reason why the "señoritas of California" "invariably preferred" the men of the Anglo-Saxon race. Jackson-like, the editor then invoked a metaphysics of Mexican-hating: "There are some nations that have a doom upon them. . . . The nation that makes no onward progress . . . that wastes its treasures wantonly—that cherishes not its resources— such a nation will burn out . . . will become the easy prey of the more adventurous enemy." White Americans had wasted no time. Their enterprise had already "penetrated" the remote territory of California, developing her vast and hidden riches, and would soon make her resources "useful," opening her "swollen veins" of precious metals.[26]

During the war, the editor of the *Scientific American* also viewed the conflict as a manifestation of the national future. "Every nation now distinguished for greatness and power," he asserted, "has encouraged . . . Scientific and Mechanical attainments, and we can confidently say that just in proportion as a nation or people progress in true knowledge so do they become great and powerful." Thus, American expansion into Mexico represented a triumph of "mechanical genius." "We hold the keys of the Atlantic on the east and the Pacific on the far distant west," the editor exclaimed. "Our navies sweep the Gulf of Mexico and our armies occupy the land of the ancient Aztecs. . . . Every American must feel a glow of enthusiasm in his heart as he thinks of his country's greatness, her might and her power." Indeed, like Bigelow and Benton, the editor of the *Scientific American* was certain America's special destiny was bound to her genius in technology.

The war against Mexico not only affirmed in Anglo minds their technological superiority; it also opened the way for the extension of American technology and the market into the Southwest, and the appropriation of Mexican labor in these newly acquired territories. Unlike Indians who were removed beyond the Mississippi River or relegated to reservations after they had lost their land, Mexicans had their land annexed and then were incorporated into a "labor-repressive system." What emerged after the Mexican-American War was the integration of the Southwest into the American economy and the development of a caste/class structure of social relations.[27]

As American capitalism expanded into the Southwest, it depended heavily on Mexican labor. Mexicans were used extensively as laborers in agriculture and ranching in Arizona and New Mexico, and served as a critical labor force for the development of Anglo industries in the Southwest. Railroad construction, particularly after the exclusion of Chinese workers, relied increasingly on Mexican labor. By 1900, for example, the Southern Pacific Railroad had 4,500 Mexican employees in California. Mexicans were also recruited to work in the mining industries, especially the copper-mining industry of Arizona which developed in the 1880s. Copper production was directly related to the emergence of technology in nineteenth-century America, for the "red metal" was used for the manufacture of electrical wires. "One might say," observed historian Carey McWilliams, " . . . that Mexican miners in the copper mines of Arizona, Utah, and Nevada, have played an important role in making possible the illumination of America by electricity."[28]

Seeking "cheap labor," the mining industries developed a caste labor system. During the 1870s they recruited Chinese workers released by the Central Pacific Railroad after the completion of the transcontinental railroad. Then, after the enactment of the Chinese Exclusion Law of 1882, they increased their reliance on "cheap" Mexican labor. Mining companies instituted a dual wage system in which Mexican workers received less pay than Anglo workers for performing the same work. In the silver mining industry in the 1870s, Mexican miners received between $12 and $30 a month plus a weekly ration of flour, while "American" miners were paid between $30 to $70 a month and given their board as well. In the copper industry, companies listed their Mexican employees on their payrolls under a special heading of "Mexican labor," paying them at lower rates than Anglo laborers in the same job classifications. An analysis of pay scales for Anglo and Mexican miners between 1860 and 1890 reveals an enormous wage differentiation.

Table 5. Pay Scales for Anglo and Mexican Miners, 1860–1890

	1860	1870	1880	1890
ANGLO WAGES PER DIEM*	$1.25	$1.75	$2.75	$3.25
MEXICAN WAGES PER DIEM†	$ .37	$1.00	$1.50	$1.75

*Until about 1880, pay usually included board.
†Until about 1880, pay included a ration of flour.

Anglo capitalists offered a philosophy to explain this wage inequity and the structure of social relations in the mining industry. One mine owner, Sylvester Mowry, spelled out the advantages of "cheap" Mexican labor:

> The question of labor is one which commends itself to the attention of the capitalist: cheap, and under proper management, efficient and permanent. My own experience has taught me that the lower class of Mexicans, with the Opata and Yaqui Indians, are docile, faithful, good servants, capable of strong attachments when firmly and kindly treated. They have been "peons" [servants] for generations. They will always remain so, as it is their natural condition.[29]

Thus, "in the hands of an enterprising people," the Southwest was being modernized under the leadership of men like Mowry. The process reinforced Anglo class control and Mexican caste subordination as the values of progress and images of Mexican inferiority were dynamically counterpointed in the development of industrial capitalism. The "genius" of white technology was reaffirmed as the mode of production became mechanized and as the stratification of the labor force in the Arizona copper mines emblematized the superiority of Anglo over Mexican.

The Triumph of Mind in America

Still, nineteenth-century middle-class Americans were asked whether technology could truly be regarded as progress. They could see that technological progress involved the destruction of nature, and were they not "Nature's nation"? This anxiety was present in a review of J. F. Cropsey's landscapes published in *The Literary World* in 1847. "The axe of civilization is busy with our old forests," the reviewer observed. "What were once the wild and picturesque haunts of the Red Man, and where the wild deer roamed in freedom, are becoming the abodes of commerce and the seats of manufactures. . . . Yankee enterprise has little sympathy with the picturesque, and it behooves our artists to rescue from its grasp the little that is left, before it is too late." Destroyed by civilization and Yankee enterprise, nature would be preserved in America's art. Even as Charles Fraser celebrated the glory of steam, he feared that the new force might be converted into "an engine of destruction"—"a weapon to enforce the *law of violence.*" And he questioned: "If that beautiful moral fabric which is rising in grandeur before an admiring world, would be assailed by its own architect, its ornaments mutilated . . . where, ever, can be found the master-hand to restore it?"[30] America's future, Fraser sensed, would not be without irony: Technology would threaten not only nature but civilization as well.

Few Americans in the nineteenth century pondered over the meaning of the triumph of technology more profoundly or more personally than Henry Adams. As a boy, he had visited industrial Birmingham, England; frightened, he had run away from the "darkness lurid with flames," the "unknown horror in this weird gloom," and the "dense smoky, impenetrable darkness." His encounter with the factories had evoked in him images of hell. Years later, at the Great Exposition of 1900, he gazed upon the dynamo, silently producing power, and allowed his imagination to wander far back in time to the Virgin Mary, the power of the Middle Ages. Symbol of technology, the dynamo lacked those qualities of softness and beauty which the Virgin had possessed and which had inspired men to discover in themselves a creativity and joy beyond the ability of modern man to experience. In Chartres, Adams had seen what he regarded as "the highest energy known to man, the creator of four-fifths of his noblest art, exercising vastly more attraction over the human mind than all the steam-engines and dynamos ever dreamed of. . . ." And he regretted that this kind of energy was unknown to the American mind. "An American Virgin would never dare exist." Then he asked himself whether he knew of any American artist who had ever insisted on "the power of sex," and he could only think of Walt Whitman. "All the rest had used sex for sentiment, never for force; to them Eve was a tender flower. . . . American art, like the American language and American education, was as far as possible sexless. Society regarded this victory over sex as its greatest triumph. . . ."[31] To Adams, this repression of emotion and love accompanied technological progress in America.

This relationship between technology and repression which Adams observed also received attention from doctors concerned with what appeared to be a widespread presence of an illness called "neurasthenia." One of them, Dr. George Beard, addressed himself directly to this illness in *American Nervousness,* published in 1881. In his diagnosis, this New York City neurologist delineated several causes of this affliction: (1) competition and social mobility—"the stimulus given to Americans to rise out of the position in which they were born," resulting in constant friction and unrest and painful striving to get ahead of everyone else; (2) a time orientation— attention to clocks, to the future; (3) the rapidity of the pace of change; (4) technology. The development of a technological society, Dr. Beard observed, involved the loss of a relationship with nature. No longer did Americans hear "natural rhythms" like the roar of the sea, the singing of birds, and the swaying of branches, which "savages" heard. Now Americans were subjected to new sounds—the harsh, dissonant noises of factories, steamboats, and railroads. Under the impulse of steam power and inventions, manufacturing and business had expanded and become enormously complex; the market had become more than ever before a "source of anxiety." To illustrate his diagnosis, Dr. Beard used an "electric machine" as a metaphor for the human body.

The force supplied by any central machine is limited, and cannot be pushed beyond a certain point. . . . The nervous system of man is the centre of the nerve-force supplying all the organs of the body. . . . The force in the nervous system can, therefore be increased or diminished by good or evil influences, medical or hygiene . . . but nonetheless it is limited; and when new functions are interposed in the circuit, as modern civilization is constantly requiring us to do, there comes a period . . . when the amount of force is insufficient to keep all the lamps actively burning; those that are weakest go out entirely or, as more frequently happens, burn faint and feebly—they do not expire, but give an insufficient and unstable light—this is the philosophy of modern nervousness.

Nervousness was a condition of modern civilization, Dr. Beard explained, increasing with the advance of culture and refinement, and the reliance on "brain" over "muscle" labor. The distance between savagery and civilization could be measured by the degree of nervousness. In savagery, life was mostly "sensual," emotional, and unrestrained; while in civilization, the intellect dominated and "inhibited" the emotions. The rational control which civilized men imposed upon themselves was a major cause of the increase of nervous diseases. Anticipating Sigmund Freud's *Civilization and Its Discontents,* Dr. Beard concluded: "Constant inhibition, restraining normal feelings, keeping back, covering, holding in check atomic forces of the mind and body, is an exhausting process, and to this process all civilization is constantly subjected."[32] Thus, as Dr. Beard diagnosed it, the problem of nervousness in American society was civilization itself, especially civilization in a technological era.

But what happens when "atomic forces," especially those of the body, are held in check? This was a question Mark Twain probed in his novel *A Connecticut Yankee in King Arthur's Court,* which appeared midway between the publication of Beard's study of *American Nervousness* and Adams's encounter with the dynamo at the Great Exposition of 1900. Like Adams, Twain traveled back in time to assess his own age and its Yankee enterprise and technology; like Beard, he offered a diagnosis of American civilization and its nervousness.

Twain's novel about a Yankee mechanic in Arthurian England reflected an American fantasy pervasive in nineteenth-century society. Decades before Twain spun out his tale, Massachusetts Governor Edward Everett had told Yankee mechanics: "Mind, acting through the useful arts, is the vital principle of modern civilized society. The mechanician, not the magician, is now the master of life." The *Mechanic's Register* had proudly noted that American mechanics were working in Europe, and that the "kings think well of them and honor them with their friendship. . . ." In an essay entitled "American Genius and Enterprise," the editor of the *Scientific American* had also reported the presence of American mechanics in Russia, directing the construction of railroads. "Who knows but in a few years the now Russian serf," the editor exclaimed, "may stand a freeman at his own cottage door, and as he beholds the locomotive fleeting past, will take off his cap, kneel and bless God that the Mechanics of Washington's land were permitted to scatter the seeds of social freedom in benighted Russia."[33] Twain's novel contained all of the components of this American fantasy: His "Connecticut Yankee" is a "mechanician" rather than a "magician"; honored by a king, he, too, is the modernizer of a feudal society. What he scatters, however, are the seeds of destruction.

The Connecticut Yankee—Hank Morgan—reminds us of Nathan Quaker/Slaughter and Andrew Jackson: He is an idealist who turns out to be a killer, a philanthrope who is actually a misanthrope. The Yankee is also representative of Tocqueville's nervous American—active, restless, and on the make. A modern Prospero, he is determined to control not only himself but the people around him; but while Prospero has Ariel, a spirit, to assist him in his effort to dominate Miranda and Caliban, Hank Morgan has technology. Morgan is very much a nineteenth-century American: He works in a "great arms factory" in Connecticut, and knows how to make "everything: guns, revolvers, cannon, boilers, engines, all sorts of labor-saving machinery."

In the story, Hank Morgan is mysteriously transported back in time to Arthurian England, a medieval and pre-industrial era. The land seems innocent and pure, like America at the time when it was inhabited only by Indians. The Yankee notices the air full of the smell of flowers, the buzzing of insects, the twittering of birds, and other natural rhythms. Quickly he decides to take over this backward land; he civilizes and modernizes Arthurian society, introducing technology and setting up railroads, steamboats, telegraph systems, and smoking factories. He also puts everyone to work, for there is to be no idleness in this new technological order. Even the religious hermit, standing on a pillar and bowing his body to his feet in prayer, is not allowed to pray without being productive. The Yankee reports:

> His stand was a pillar sixty feet high, with a broad platform on top of it. He was now doing what he had been doing every day for twenty years up there—bowing his body ceaselessly and rapidly almost to his feet. It was his way of praying. I timed him with a stopwatch, and he made twelve hundred and forty-four revolutions in twenty-four minutes and forty-six seconds. It seemed a pity to have all this power going to waste. It was one of the most useful motions in mechanics, the pedal movement; so I made a note in my memorandum book, purposing some day to apply a system of elastic cords to him and run a sewing machine with it. I afterwards carried out that scheme, and got five years' good service out of him; in which time he turned out upwards of eighteen thousand first-rate tow-linen suits. . . .

Here, man becomes literally an appendage of the machine. The Yankee takes pride in his imaginative achievements, and views himself as "just another Robinson Crusoe cast away on an uninhabited island, with no society but some more or less tame animals, and if I wanted to make life bearable I must do as he did—invent, contrive, create, reorganize things; set brain and hand to work, and keep them busy."[34]

A busy scientific manager, Hank Morgan introduces soap and imposes cleanliness on the Arthurian people. His obsession with cleanliness reflects his negative attitude toward the physical self and contrasts strongly with the people's acceptance of their bodies. Shortly after he arrives in King Arthur's court, Morgan notices that small boys and girls run around naked and that no one is aware of their nudity. Interested in the Yankee's strange clothes, the Arthurians proceed to strip him, and he finds himself "as naked as a pair of tongs!" But he is the only person there who seems to be concerned at all. "Dear, dear, to think of it: I was the only embarrassed person there. Everybody discussed me; and did it as unconcernedly as if I had been a cabbage." In another incident, the Yankee, wearing a suit of armor, develops an itch and wants to take off his armor so he can scratch and relieve himself. But Sandy, a young lady, is with him, and he is too embarrassed to remove the armor in her presence; yet he is fully clothed underneath.

Holding in check his "atomic forces," Morgan builds a modern cosmos. In a fashion Dr. Bigelow of Harvard would have admired, the Connecticut Yankee pits the power of American technology against traditional European power, the monarchy and the church, and triumphantly transforms this pastoral country into a land of factories and modern cities. As he surveys the new industrial order, he proudly exclaims: "The telegraph, the telephone, the phonograph, the typewriter, the sewing machine, and all the thousand willing and handy servants of steam and electricity were working their way into favor. We had a steamboat or two on the Thames, we had steam warships, and the beginnings of a steam commercial marine; I was getting ready to send out an expedition to discover America." But before he can dispatch this expedition, the Yankee encounters a rebellion against his rule. Under his command, steam and electricity are turned into servants of death. As the story ends, Morgan is at war with an army of knights; during the Battle of the Sand Belt, he retreats to his fortress and uses technology to destroy the entire civilization he has built. With the press of a button, he dynamites his factories and cities.

Where Jackson philosophized about Indian deaths, Morgan trivializes the mass murder of Arthurians. "As to the destruction of life," he excitedly comments, "it was amazing. Moreover, it was beyond estimate. Of course we could not *count* the dead, because they did not exist as individuals, but merely as homogeneous protoplasm with alloys of iron and buttons." As armored knights attack his technological fortress, the Yankee pulls a switch and electrocutes thousands of them. His dynamo produces electricity, which is used to kill, and, like Henry Adams, Morgan observes how the dynamo does its work "silently." To finish off the remaining knights, the

Yankee trains on them a Gatling gun—another of the achievements of nineteenth-century American technology.[35]

Hank Morgan, as it turns out, is not so much a self-taught mechanic as an expert: Like the white men of Harvard, he is a professional. Exploiting his technological knowledge, he reduces Arthurian Englishmen to incompetence, as he creates a complex system which only he can understand and direct. A scientific manager, he establishes a centralized bureaucracy to increase efficiency and productivity. Ultimately, however, his aim is not production or profits but control for the sake of control. And in the end, as his hegemony is challenged, he chooses to destroy society rather than to relinquish control over it.

Significantly, administrator Morgan views the Arthurian people in terms of "savages" and "Indians." He describes them as "merely modified savages," and thinks they are like Indians, for they lack cleanliness and a civilized orientation toward time and work. He notices that Sandy shows no impatience to get breakfast, and remarks: "That smacks of the savage. . . ." He calls the English practice of fasting on journeys "the style of the Indian." King Arthur's court is "a sort of polished up court of Comanches," and the ladies of the court are "squaws" ready "to desert to the buck with the biggest string of scalps at his belt." A man of "science," the Yankee possesses modern knowledge which he uses against the "savage" Englishmen. "It came into my mind, in the nick of time," he reports, "how Columbus, or Cortez, or one of those people, played an eclipse as a saving trump once, on some savages, and I saw my chance." And, after the battle of the Sand Belt, surrounded by the corpses of 25,000 knights, the Yankee could regard his victory as the triumph of civilization, of "mind" over "savagery" and "white Indians."[36]

Here, then, in Twain's novel, we have a condemnation of arrogant Yankee misuse of technology, and a frightening fable which exposed what was actually happening in nineteenth-century American society. The "enterprising" men of white America—the farmers, merchants, manfacturers, and engineers— were making an errand into the wilderness; they were "improving" the land as they cleared the forests, erected factories, and expanded the market. They were creating a modern world of corporate capitalism in which horses were becoming "obsolete" and Indians "merely traditional." They were populating the West as steam—"the pure white jet"—fecundated America in a "mechanistic orgasm." Determined to destroy "savagery" in America, they were training Gatling and Hotchkiss guns on Indians at places like Wounded Knee where Big Foot and three hundred followers fell in a hail of bullets. In their westward expansion, men of enterprise and technology were importing hides from California for the New England shoe factories and sending their ships into Asiatic seas in search of whales and a "new channel to the commerce of Asia." They were entering and modernizing the Southwest as they transformed Mexicans from peasants into industrial workers to produce the copper for the electrical wiring of America. They were, like Bigelow and Webster, praising mind and calling technology American genius. As they built their "America by design," they were employing technology as a mode of production as well as an instrument for the domination and reinforcement of social relations in a capitalist society. Like Hank Morgan, they were creating centralized bureaucracies and placing society under the direction of professionals and scientific managers. They were substituting technology for the body and also channeling men, women, and children into factories and reducing them to machine attendants. The most civilized people in the world, men of progress were dissociating themselves even further from their bodies as they sought to become "mind" and thus achieve "perfection," and were increasingly becoming afflicted with what Dr. Beard diagnosed as "American nervousness." Restraining their "atomic forces," they were turning them into demonic forces of destruction. As they sharpened in their minds the conflict between civilization and nature and as they set themselves further and further apart from peoples of color, they were directing toward nature and toward Indians, Mexicans, and Asians the violence and "boisterous passions" that the domination of ascetic rationality had been stoking.

CHAPTER VIII

THE IRON HORSE IN
THE WEST

The building of railroads, and the access thereby given to all the agricultural and mineral regions of the country, is rapidly bringing civilized settlements into contact with all the tribes of Indians. No matter what ought to be the relations between such settlements and the aborigines, the fact is they do not harmonize well, and one or the other has to give way in the end. A system which looks to the extinction of a race is too horrible for a nation to adopt without entailing upon itself the wrath of all Christendom and engendering in the citizen a disregard for human life and the rights of others, dangerous to society.
—President Ulysses S. Grant,
First Annual Message, 1869

We do not want you here. You are scaring away the buffalo.
—Red Cloud,
to engineers surveying
for the railroad in Wyoming

In 1873, four years after the completion of the transcontinental railroad, a chromolithograph entitled *American Progress* dramatically depicted the tension between technology and the Indian, which both President Grant and Red Cloud had noted from their different perspectives. Twelve by sixteen inches in size, this work of art was intended to decorate the homes of white America—"from the miner's humble cabin to the stately marble mansion of the capitalist." At the center of this painting is a beautiful white woman, floating through the air and bearing on her forehead the "Star of Empire." Pure and innocent, she symbolizes the advance of civilization: In her right hand, she carries a book, emblem of education and

American Progress, *1873, chromolithograph published by George A. Crofutt,*
reproduced from the collection of the Library of Congress

knowledge, and holds in her left hand telegraph wires which she is string-
ing across the plains. Behind her, in a clear lighted sky, are cities, factories,
steamboats, and railroad trains. Three locomotives follow her; the ends of
her long white gown, blowing in the wind, fade off into the tracks of the
railroad, signifying the union of womanhood and technology. Beneath her,
Jefferson's yeoman farmers plow their fields, while pathfinders—the Natty
Bumppos and Nathan Quaker/Slaughters of America—explore the "vacant lands." The course of empire is westward. Before the ethereal white
woman, in a dark stormy sky, are buffalo, a bear, and Indians, in flight
toward the "Stony mountains," yielding to her and the dynamic material,
cultural, and racial forces she represents. What *American Progress* offered
was a panoramic self-portrait of American civilization—its cult of true
womanhood, its faith in technology, and its expansionist thrust toward the
Pacific Ocean.[1]

American Progress depicted one of the most significant themes of American history—the westward advance of the frontier, the line between white
settlement and the wilderness. Historically, the West offered whites the
promise of property ownership and a stable republican future, and provided Indians an area where they could farm, hunt, and live apart from
whites. As long as the frontier existed, there would be places for both
whites and Indians. In the West, beyond the Mississippi River and beyond
the line of white settlement, President Jackson had promised, Indians
would be free to live in peace "as long as the grass grows, or water runs."
After the Civil War, however, the railroad penetrated the plains and
stretched toward the West Coast. Soon there would be no frontier in America.[2]

In 1869, the year of the completion of the transcontinental line, the
editor of the *Cheyenne Leader* described the train as "the advance guard of
empire." "The iron horse in his resistless 'march to the sea,' " he wrote,
"surprises the aborigines upon their distant hunting grounds and frightens
the buffalo from the plains where, for untold ages, his race has gazed in the
eternal solitudes. The march of empire no longer proceeds with stately,
measured strides, but has the wings of morning, and flies with the speed of
lightning." Similarly, in the same year, Secretary of Interior J. D. Cox
reported how the railroad had "totally changed" the nature of westward
migration. Previously settlement had taken place gradually; but the railroad had "pierced" the "very center of the desert" and every station had
become a "nucleus for a civilized settlement." A turning point had been
reached: The "iron horse" had entered the history of the American West.[3]

The railroad was more than a metaphor: It was, in reality, a corporate
interest aggressively involved in the white settlement of the West and the

destruction of Indians. Behind this "resistless 'march to the sea'" were deliberate corporate efforts to usurp Indian lands for railroad construction. Right-of-way through Indian territory had to be secured, and railroad companies regarded the tribe as one of the chief obstacles to the progress of the railroad in the West. To remove this "obstacle," they subsidized newspapers to support their interests and employed lobbyists to influence legislation granting them right-of-way through Indian territory. Railroad companies gave strong support to the passage of the 1871 Indian Appropriation Act, which declared that "hereafter no Indian nation or tribe within the territory of the United States shall be acknowledged or recognized as an independent nation, tribe, or power, with whom the United States may contract by treaty." The Act did more than abolish treaty-making with Indian tribes. Shortly after it became law, an attorney for the Atlantic and Pacific Railroad stressed its significance: "It is not a mere prohibition of the making of future treaties with these tribes. It goes beyond this, and destroys the political existence of the tribes." Free from tribal political opposition, railroad companies hoped to obtain title to Indian lands more easily; they knew the value of their stocks depended on the land titles they could secure. When the Commissioner of the General Land Office decided the Atlantic and Pacific Railroad did not have title to lands in Indian territory, its bonds fell sharply to five cents each. Speaking before the House Committee on Territories in 1876, the attorney for the Missouri, Kansas and Texas Railroad explained bluntly: "You, then, gentlemen, representing the United States, must hold the scales fairly and equally between the parties before you—the railroad on the one hand, and the Indians on the other." The bondholders, he added, had been informed that the federal government had granted a vast tract of land to the corporation, and they had loaned funding on this basis.[4] Thus railroad progress required the destruction of Indian tribal power and the appropriation of Indian property.

The railroad made the West more accessible than ever before to white settlement. The entry of railroad lines into Indian territory often had dramatic and visible effects in terms of the white population: The Indian territory between Kansas and Texas had a white population of only 7,000 in 1880; by 1889, five years after the completion of the railroad in this area, the white population had exploded to 110,000. Symbolically, when President Benjamin Harrison announced the opening of the Oklahoma District to white settlement, sixteen trains of the Santa Fe Railroad carried thousands of white homesteaders over the line on the day of the great "run." The railroad also gave the United States military strategic advantages over Indians, enabling it to move troops rapidly and respond effectively to Indian resistance. In his 1883 report on the elimination of the Indian threat in the West, General William Sherman called the railroad instrumental in the "great battle of civilization" against "barbarism."[5] As it disgorged thousands and thousands of white settlers in Indian territory and as it provided critical logistical support to United States troops, the railroad also made possible the destruction of the buffalo: It opened the plains to buffalo hunters and transported the hides back to eastern markets. Soon the buffalo would become extinct and a new future for the Indian in the West would have to be defined.

"What shall we do with the Indians?" asked a writer for *The Nation* in 1867, as the Irish crews of the Union Pacific and the Chinese crews of the Central Pacific raced to make the momentous connection. "It is plain something must be done with the Indians, and that it must be something different from anything yet done." The "highways to the Pacific" must not be obstructed, and the United States must have peace with the Indians. There were two possible solutions: The Indians must either be "exterminated," or subjected to the "law and habits of industry." In the writer's judgment, civilizing the Indians was "the easiest and cheapest as well as only honorable way of securing peace." This required the integration of the Indians into white society, their transformation into republican citizens. "We need only treat Indians like men, treat them as we do ourselves, putting on them the same responsibilities, letting them sue and be sued, and taxing them as fast as they settle down and have anything to tax."[6] The question on the future of the Indian demanded urgent attention in the new era ushered in by the railroad.

Aware of the presence of the "iron horse" in the West, white culture-makers and policy-makers shared *The Nation*'s concern for the need to do "something different from anything yet done." But they had diverse views on what should be done, as may be seen in the ways two men responded to the "Indian Question"—Lieutenant Colonel George Armstrong Custer and Commissioner of Indian Affairs Francis Amasa Walker. Each man responded to the question from very different perspectives: Custer from the West, where he encountered Indians while sitting in his saddle, and Walker from Washington, where he made plans for Indians while sitting behind his desk.

"Red Gifts" and "White Gifts": The World Custer Lost

More than any other individual of his era, Custer personified the masculine advance guard of civilization: He was the counterpart of the feminine white woman portrayed in *American Progress*. Like Jackson, he was a "Leather-stocking Nemesis," as he demonstrated in his "victory" at the Washita River in the winter of 1868. There he had tracked Black Kettle's band of Cheyennes, and knew he had them trapped as he quietly surveyed the Indian encampment in the darkness and heard the cry of an infant. Custer divided his 800 men into four groups and ordered them to surround the village and its sleeping inhabitants. Then, at dawn, with his band playing "Garry Owen," Custer and his troops mounted a four-pronged attack, destroying the lodges, killing 103 Cheyennes, and capturing 53 women and children. As they marched into Camp Supply triumphantly, Custer's troops waved the scalps of Black Kettle and other slain Cheyennes.

Eight years later, Custer met his own violent death at the Little Big Horn. News of his death provoked shrill cries for revenge. Buffalo Bill was so angry he closed his wild west show and pledged to go west and take the "first scalp for Custer." Demanding the federal government avenge Custer's defeat, the editor of the *Bismarck Weekly Tribune* called for the establishment of "Indian posts" where all the peacefully inclined would have to go "or die of war and famine." In their loud clamor for retaliation, both Buffalo Bill and the editor failed to discern the special irony that Custer's death contained, for they did not know what Custer had found in the West, among Indians.[7]

The Indian, as Custer viewed him, was a counterpoint to civilization. Like James Fenimore Cooper, whose novels he had read as a child, Custer believed in what Cooper had called "red gifts" and "white gifts." According to this view, Indians and whites had different racial attributes—distinctive and peculiar natural characteristics. "I have always known," Cooper's Natty Bumppo declared, ". . . that men have their gifts." For Natty Bumppo, the "gifts" of each of the two races were unique: Indians were heathen and savage, while whites were Christian and civilized. Custer shared this perspective, claiming that "Nature" intended the Indian to be in a "savage state." "Every instinct, every impulse of his soul inclines him to it . . . . He cannot be himself and be civilized; he fades away and dies." Thus, the Indian was a "savage," in constant tension with civilization.[8] As a "savage," the Indian drew from Custer two sets of responses: repulsion and identification, hate and admiration, violence and sorrow.

In his prolific writings on the West and the Indian character, Custer insisted that the Indian was not the "*noble* red man" portrayed in Cooper's Leatherstocking Tales. Under the domination of the passions and vices that accompanied a "savage nature," Indians "infested" the Plains, their "cruel and ferocious nature" far exceeding that of any "wild beast." Their savagery evoked in Custer a fear of Indian men as threats to white women, including his wife, Libbie, whom he took west with him in an ambulance fixed up with curtains. One incident revealed the depth of his anxiety. During a visit to an Indian camp, Custer was sitting in a tent among the chiefs until late at night in order "to study the Indian character a little." "No other officers or soldiers were present," he wrote to Libbie. The Indians were preparing supper and boiling meat over an open fire. "When it was cooked, they of course ate in quite a primitive style—with their fingers—each gnawing at his bone. . . ." Sitting between two chiefs, Custer noted that the chiefs were in full-dress costume, with all the Indian paraphernalia, paint, and ornaments. "While sitting, or, rather, lying, on the buffalo robe, surrounded as I was by this strange and picturesque looking group, I could not but wonder what your sensations would be, if you could peer through the smoke of the Indian fire and see me, dressed as at home, surrounded by a dozen or more of these dusky and certainly savage-looking chiefs." Suddenly a "shudder" ran through Custer as a frightening thought "darted" into his mind: "What if Libbie should ever fall into the hands of such savages!" Custer believed such a capture would be "a fate worse than death" for Libbie, and instructed his officers to shoot his wife rather than allow her to be captured by "savage" Indians.[9]

But, while Custer viewed Indians as "wild savages" and threats to white women, he also felt a certain empathy for them. In an essay written at West Point in 1858, he described Indians as a "noble race." When Europeans arrived in America, he wrote, they found the natives in their homes of "peace and plenty," the "favored sons of nature." They stood in their "native strength and beauty, stamped with the proud majesty of free born men." But what were they now, these "monarchs of the west"? Their homes and their forests had been swept away by the ax of the woodsman; they had been driven to the "verge of extinction," resolved to die amidst the "horrors of slaughter." Even after Custer encountered them in the West, he continued to find much to be admired in the Indian character— his "remarkable taciturnity," his "perseverance" for revenge and conquest, his "stoical courage," and his senses with their "wonderful power and subtlety." No simple Indian-hater, Custer felt deep ambivalence: In his warfare against Indians, he was killing both what he found "disgusting" and what he "admired."[10]

Still, for Custer, the ambivalence only sharpened the nagging question: What would happen to the Indian in a technological society? He believed that the Indian had a grim future. Even to locate the Indian on a reservation would serve only to degrade him, make him "grovel in beggary, bereft of many of the qualities which in his wild state tended to render him noble. . . ." To civilize the Indian would be to require him to abandon the only mode of life in which he could be a warrior, and to sacrifice his manhood in working for a living. Custer thought that "if" he were an Indian, he would choose the "free open plains" rather than submit to the "confined limits of a reservation, there to be the recipient of the blessed benefits of civilization with its vices thrown in without stint or measure." The Indian, as Custer viewed him, could not become a republican or self-governing individual guided by "appeals to his ideas of moral right and wrong, independent of threatening or final compulsion." The solution to the "Indian Question," Custer declared, was to let the Indian hunt and roam, provided he did not interrupt the advance of civilization. "When the soil which he has claimed and hunted over so long a time is demanded by this to him insatiable monster," Custer reflected, "there is no appeal; he must yield, or, like the car of Juggernaut, it will roll mercilessly over him, destroying as it advances. . . . At best the history of our Indian tribes . . . affords a melancholy picture of loss of life."[11]

Ironically, even as Custer accompanied a "scientific detachment" to explore the Black Hills, even as he protected the building of the Pacific railroad against Indian interference, and even as he waged war against the Indian, he identified with him. Deep within Custer was a rage against civilization, the very modern society which he was helping to extend into the West. The East and civilization were to Custer what the reservation was to the Indian. He wanted to be free from the restraints of settled society, its commercialism, "luxuries," and "easy comforts." Indeed, after the Civil War, he had turned down several offers of vice-presidencies in companies; he did not want a career in business. The settled society of the East, in his judgment, threatened Protestant and republican virtues. His parents had, he said, instilled into him the principles of industry, self-reliance, and honesty; but where could young men realize such principles in an urban and industrial world? "How I wish," Custer wrote to his wife, Libbie, from the Yellowstone River, "that some of our home boys, who possess talent and education, but lack means and opportunity would cast themselves loose from home and try their fortunes in this great enterprising western country, where the virtues of real manhood come quickly to the surface. . . ." Custer also resented the strictly drawn social lines of Monroe, Michigan. The son of a blacksmith, he had found it embarrassing to court Libbie Bacon, the daughter of a judge. Ladies were not supposed to be acquainted with men outside of their restricted class circles. "I know your family by sight," Libbie confessed to Custer. "I stood near them at the Lilliputian Bazaar. I think they knew me." Even as a cadet at West Point, while attending a ball and mingling for the first time with the social elect,

Custer could not feel completely comfortable. After graduation from the academy, Custer found military life competitive and anxious, and tended to bifurcate his life into the office and the home. He kept the "perplexities" of his work away from his wife as much as possible. "He wished to spare me anxiety," Libbie said, "and the romp or the gallop over the fragrant field, which he asked for as soon as office-hours were over, was probably much more enjoyable with a woman with uncorrugated brow."[12]

The nervousness of civilization, reflecting as well as reinforcing dichotomies between Indians and whites, men and women, wilderness and settlement, drove Custer to seek "forgetfulness in a wild unfettered existence" in the plains. There, beyond the railroad and beyond the telegraph, Custer could still "indulge in the wild Western life with all its pleasures and excitements," and recover the "virtues of real manhood." There, like the Indian, he could roam the plains and hunt buffalo; he could experience in the buffalo chase an "excitement" which "nearly approached a cavalry charge."[13]

In the wilderness Custer had entered a "new world, a Wonderland." The beauty of the Wichita Mountains overwhelmed him: "The air is pure and fragrant, and as exhilarating as the purest of wine; the climate entrancingly mild; the sky clear, and blue as the most beautiful sapphire, with here and there clouds of rarest loveliness, presenting to the eye the richest commingling of bright and varied colors; delightful odors are constantly being wafted by. . . ." And everywhere were sounds—the singing of the mockingbird, the colibri, hummingbird, and thrush. Custer's body and its senses were intensely aware of the vibrant colors, shapes, smells, and sounds all around him. Swept away by the magnificence of nature, he felt an intoxication which he had not experienced in the effete and commercialized East and which even his poetic language could not fully express. Riding across the plains—with horizon after horizon of grass, Custer felt hypnotized, drawn irresistibly into its awesome vastness. Its undulations reminded him of the ocean: They were like "gigantic waves," "standing silent and immovable." The initial encounter with the plains, Custer warned, could be quite puzzling. The inexperienced traveler

imagines, and very naturally too, judging from appearance, that when he ascends to the crest he can overlook all the surrounding country. After a weary walk or ride of perhaps several miles, which appeared at starting not more than one or two, he finds himself at the desired point, but discovers that directly beyond, in the direction he desires to go, rises a second wave, but slightly higher than the first, and from the crest of which he must certainly be able to scan the country as far as the eye can reach. Thither he pursues his course, and after a ride of from five to ten miles, although the distance did not seem half so great before starting, he finds himself on the crest . . . but again only to discover that another and apparently a higher divide rises in his front, and about the same distance. Hundreds, yes, thousands of miles may be journeyed over, and this same effect witnessed every few hours.

Here was the ultimate and final expanse of "vacant lands." The West offered Custer an "escape" (to use Libbie Custer's term)—a world still beyond the noises of the machine and the constraints of modern civilization.[14]

The West also offered Custer a place where he could seek regeneration through violence, where he could lead his troops into battle against red warriors and experience in the moment and act of violence an almost mystical union. On one of these occasions, according to his own account, Custer watched the cavalry come into line on a gallop, and gave the command to "draw sabre." As the "bright blades flashed from their scabbards into the morning sunlight" and as the infantry brought their muskets to a carry, Custer witnessed a "most beautiful and wonderfully interesting sight" spread out before him. "Here in battle array, facing each other, were the representatives of civilized and barbarous warfare. The one . . . stood clothed in the same rude style of dress, bearing the same patterned shield and weapon that his ancestors had borne centuries before; the other confronted him in the dress and supplied with the implements of war which the most advanced stage of civilization had pronounced the most perfect." For Custer, the totality of the scene—the battlefield, the men, the movements, the sunlight—was breathtaking. He did not think a "more beautiful battle-ground" could have been chosen: "Not even a bush or even the slightest irregularity of ground intervened between the two lines which now stood frowning and facing each other."[15] Everything seemed pure, simple, and beautiful to him as the military representatives of both cultures prepared to meet each other in a ritual—romantic and violent.

Seeking refuge from modern American society, Custer had found in the oceanic plains, among the people with "red gifts," a freedom and a solitude which he himself was destroying even as he was experiencing them. He was a Natty Bumppo who would soon be without another river to cross or another mountain range to climb, leaving behind the sounds and smells of civilization. As he hunted buffalo on the grassy plains, he could watch, as did the Indian, the "iron horse" throwing off fire and smoke, hurtling itself toward the Pacific Ocean. The material forces of settlement and the market which Custer advanced and from which he fled would, he could see, soon turn against him. Technological and commercial society would, like the "car of Juggernaut," "roll mercilessly" over him and his "Wonderland." Already he felt out of place in American society, where individualism and heroism had been rendered obsolete and where planning, rationalized methods, and centralized bureaucracies were rapidly dominating every area of life, including the military.[16] Custer had to view his own future with "melancholy." Perhaps he understood only too clearly and profoundly as he stood on the grassy hillside of the Little Big Horn in that final moment of union, how much he and the Indian shared a common fate in a technological society.

The Scientific Management of Indians

Perhaps no one represented the world of technology in nineteenth-century America as consummately as Francis Amasa Walker. Like Twain's Hank Morgan, Walker was a Yankee and a man of many interests and achievements: He was the chief of the Federal Bureau of Statistics, the superintendent of the United States Census, professor of political economy at Yale, author of *Political Economy* (regarded as "the most widely used work in the introductory course in college economics from 1883 to the turn of the century"), the president of the Massachusetts Institute of Technology, and the commissioner for Indian affairs. A formidable reformer, Walker believed in "scientific" management—the employment of technology and science to control nature and direct society.[17]

The son of Amasa Walker, one of the active enterprisers of the age, Francis recognized the relationship between technology and the Market Revolution early in life. An enthusiastic promoter of the railroad, Amasa Walker was the director of the Western Railroad in Massachusetts; as early as 1838, he predicted men would be able to travel by rail from Boston to the Mississippi River in five days, sleeping and eating on the train. He was also the co-owner of a Boston shoe manufacturing and wholesale company which had extended its operations beyond the Mississippi. He had done more to open the trade of Boston with the South and Southwest, Francis later wrote, than any other merchant of his generation. The son of an industrial businessman, growing up during the "take-off stage" of American economic development, Francis Walker viewed the machine and the market as great forces of civilization in America.

Like Jacob Bigelow and Hank Morgan, Walker equated technology with progress. He believed the "onward march of invention" and the "increasing power of machinery" would reduce the hours of labor for the working classes and enable them to live in reasonable comfort. "How greatly has farm-labor been diminished by the introduction of machines for plowing, planting, mowing, reaping, etc!" he exclaimed. "To what a minimum has the strength expended in the production of textile fabrics been reduced by the power-loom and spinning jenny!" To Walker the increase in production signified "illimitable progress." Indeed, technology had made possible the elevation of mankind from primitive conditions to civilization. "The labor that is made free by discoveries and inventions," he wrote in *Political Economy,*

> is applied to overcome the difficulties which withstand the gratification of new-ly-felt desires. The hut is pulled down to make room for the cottage; the cottage gives way to the mansion, the mansion to the palace. The rude covering of skins is replaced by the comely garment of woven stuffs; and these, in the progress of luxury, by the most splendid fabrics of human skill. In a thousand forms wealth is created by the whole energy of the community, quickened by a zeal greater than that which animated the exertions of their rude forefathers to obtain a scanty and squalid subsistence.[18]

The drama of progress, for Walker, was inspiring and reassuring.

What made it especially so was his view of technology as American genius—a theme which he forcefully advanced in his history of *The Making of the Nation, 1783-1817.* As Walker described the new nation, he could have been Mark Twain writing about England during the age of King Arthur. "As we begin this story of the life of the American nation during the first years of its accomplished and recognized independence," he observed, "it is appropriate . . . to call the reader's attention to the fact that he is contemplating the experience of a people born, bred, and living under conditions, many of them now gone forever . . . a time when . . . electricity was recognized only through its terrific and destructive agency as lightning; when biology . . . was still deeply buried under ignorance, prejudice, and superstition. . . . In agriculture the implements were hardly a whit improved from those in use twenty-five hundred years before." Yet, the people of the new nation possessed a "mechanical genius," which would enable them to transform the United States from an agricultural to an industrial society.[19]

From where did this genius spring? Walker traced its origins to the racial superiority and to the frontier experience of the white settlers. The early settlers belonged to the "great inventive Teutonic race"; they constituted "a picked population." Virtually echoing Jefferson's remark on the "improvement" of animals, Walker wrote: "The possibilities of improvement which reside in breeding from the higher, stronger, more alert, and aggressive individuals of a species are well recognized in the case of domestic animals; but there have been few opportunities for obtaining a measure of the effect that could be produced upon the human race, by excluding from propagation the weak, the vicious, the cowardly, the effeminate, persons of dwarfed stature, of tainted blood, or of imperfect organization." America offered one of those few opportunities. The inhabitants of the English colonies were a select group representing "mental vigor, intellectual inquisitiveness, enterprise, and self-reliance." From their experience of living in the wilderness, they had developed a "calculating faculty." They had learned how "to make shifts; to save time; to shorten labor; to search out substitutes for what was inaccessible or costly; to cut corners and break through barriers in reaching an object. . . ." They had extended settlement and fenced the wilderness, covering the land with roads and crossing the streams with bridges; they had dotted the plains and hills with houses, barns, schools, and churches. Life in America was "no routine," as it was in Europe. Here, in Walker's vision, a "picked" people, constituting what Benjamin Franklin had earlier called the "lovely White," had developed under frontier conditions a particular character and perfection.[20]

For Walker, American "engineering genius," the product of racial characteristics and the frontier experience, could be used to direct the development of industrial society. As the working population entered the factory, Walker observed, labor in an industrial order could be "engineered." As early as 1868, he explained how this could be done. In an article on "Legal Interference with the Hours of Labor," he questioned the assumption that the effectiveness of workers diminished after eight hours of continuous labor. Due to technology, he argued, a great part of labor was performed in "connection" with machinery. Thus, workers were made to "conform" to the movements of the machinery, which was "always worked up to its highest available speed." Unable to hasten or retard the work in which they were engaged, workers could "earn but little if any more in proportion in eight hours than ten." The use of technology to regulate the pace and amount of labor also had moral significance. In the republican tradition of founding fathers like Rush and Jefferson, Walker added: "Men were not made to be idle. The most industrious people are the most progressive, enlightened and powerful."[21] The factory would be for Walker what the asylum had been for Rush: In the factory where workers were organized in relation to machinery, men would be disciplined and reformed.

The concept of control in the factory was part of Walker's larger concern for the control of social development and change. As George Frederickson has noted, Walker belonged to a group of "social scientists" who believed social planning could give them power to control the development of society. "Armed with the knowledge of how to deal 'scientifically' with national problems, they could lay claims to new positions of power and influence." A "scientific reformer," Walker was one of the early critics of the philosophy of laissez-faire. "I believe in general that that government is best which governs least, and that interference with trade or manufactures is very undesirable," he told a Senate committee. "Yet I recognize the fact that evils may and do exist which require correction by the force of law." Walker believed that the key to improving society was social planning. Even poverty could be scientifically eliminated in American society. To accomplish this task, there must be a systematic effort to "strain out of the blood of the race more of the taint inherited from a bad and vicious pool." Here was a late-nineteenth-century version of the earlier republican notion of a "homogeneous" society. "The scientific treatment which is applied to physical disease must be extended to mental and moral disease," Walker recommended in a language used earlier by Dr. Rush, "and a wholesome surgery and cautery must be enforced by the whole power of the state for the good of all." This involved the use of state power to restrict immigration and to promote Teutonic purity in America. Population statistics, as he had analyzed them, revealed that the native white population was declining in terms of the rate of national increase. He feared that the "tumultuous access of vast throngs of ignorant and brutalized peasantry from the countries of eastern and southern Europe" would "degrade" American citizenship and the standard of living. The new immigrants lacked the "inherited instincts of self-government" and "self-restraint" upon their passions. The solution to this problem, Walker insisted, was to restrict immigration and to make certain population increase came "wholly out of the loins of our own people."[22] Thus, to Walker, the possibility of perfection seemed within men's grasp: The state under the direction of social engineers like himself could reform society.

Three years after the publication of "Legal Interference with the Hours of Labor," Walker was appointed the commissioner of Indian Affairs. In his 1872 *Annual Report,* which was also published as *The Indian Question,* Walker recommended a way to manage and reform Indians scientifically: The reservation would be for Indians what the factory would be for workers.

As an "expert" on Indian affairs, Walker had only limited contact with Indians. He had made one visit of inquiry and inspection to the agencies of the Sioux in the Wyoming and Nebraska territories. During this tour, he had an unforgettable experience:

The day and the hour of the feast came. We met in a great tepee; and I sat, as was proper, on the right of Swift Bear. The chiefs and braves, with the agent and the interpreter, sat around in a circle. Soon some young men entered, bearing the steaming food. . . . Under my eyes, under my nose, was set down one of those bowls, which contained a quarter of puppy, with leg lifting itself towards me in a very tempting way. I think I could have stood even that, had it not been for the little velvet mats, where the claws were, or should have been. The Indian cook had been too realistic in his desire to give the fullest possible effect to nature. I looked down and felt myself growing white.

Except for this visit, Walker learned about Indians from government reports and books, including *Sheridan's Troopers on the Border* by De B. R. Keim and *The Last of the Mohicans* by James Fenimore Cooper.[23]

For Commissioner Walker, the "Indian Question" had two parts: "What shall be done with the Indian as an obstacle to national progress?" and "What shall be done with him when, and so far as, he ceases to oppose or obstruct the extension of railways and settlements?"[24] The answer Walker offered reflected his zeal for social planning: Promote the "Peace Policy" and locate Indians on reservations where they could be systematically educated and civilized.

In the formulation of his response to the "Indian Question," Walker calculated that the "savages"—the Sioux, Kiowas, Cheyennes, and Comanches—could bring 8,000 warriors into the field and precipitate a contest which would involve "untold misery to our border population." Thus, the most sensible approach would be to pursue the "Peace Policy"—to buy off and feed Indians in order to avoid a "desolating war." Implicitly criticizing Custer's attack on the Cheyennes at the Washita, Walker contended it was "cheaper and more humane" to give a few chiefs free rides on railroad trains and Broadway omnibuses in order to impress them with white power than to surprise "their camps on winter nights" and shoot down "men, women, and children together in the snow." In defense of the "Peace Policy," the commissioner arrogantly commented:

> In the first place, it should be remarked that there can be no question of national dignity involved in the treatment of savages by a civilized power. The proudest Anglo-Saxon will climb a tree with a bear behind him, and deem not his honor, but his safety, compromised by the situation. With wild men, as with wild beasts, the question whether to fight, coax, or run, is a question merely of what is easiest or safest in the situation given. Points of dignity only arise between those who are, or assume to be, equals.[25]

Thus, whites did not have to worry about points of dignity in their relations with Indians. Indeed, their choice of what was "easiest or safest" only underscored white racial superiority.

The "Indian Question," for Walker, had particular urgency in the age of the "iron horse." The completion of the transcontinental line, he noted, signified the end of the Indian way of life. The railroad—"the great plough of industrial civilization"—had drawn its "deep furrow" across the continent and had accelerated the movement of white settlers into the West: Whites now penetrated the new territory in every direction, "creeping along the course of every stream, seeking out every habitable valley, following up every indication of gold among the ravines and mountains . . . and even making lodgement at a hundred points on lands secured by treaty to the Indians." The railroad and civilization would soon lead to the extinction of the buffalo, and the hundred thousand Indians who had found on the great central plains an apparently inexhaustible supply of food and clothing must now face "the great food question."[26] Progress was reducing Indians to hunger and poverty.

A scientific planner, Walker insisted that the response to the Indian problem be farsighted and systematic. Since the "progress of our industrial enterprise" had cut Indians off from their traditional modes of livelihood and left them without resources, they had a claim to temporary support and assistance necessary to develop a means of livelihood "compatible with civilization." The most effective way to accomplish this transition, Walker recommended, was to make the reservation system the "general and permanent policy" of the federal government. The system would control Indians effectively through planning: Warlike tribes would be located on extensive tracts, and all Indian bands outside the reservation would be "liable to be struck by the military at any time, without warning, and without any implied hostility to those members of the tribe" living within the reservation. Such areas outside the reservation would be in effect "free fire zones." The reservation system would also "consolidate" Indian tribes onto one or two "grand reservations" with railroads cutting through them here and there, and leave all the remaining territory open for white settlement, free from Indian "obstruction or molestation." Thus the settlement of Indians and whites would take place in a planned and peaceful way.[27]

More importantly, the reservation system which Walker proposed would enable the federal government to extend over Indians "a rigid reformatory discipline." The crucial term is *reformatory*. The "discovery of the asylum" in white society had its counterpart in the invention of the reservation for Indian society. Based on "the principle of separation and seclusion," the reservation would do more than merely maintain Indians: It would train and reform them. Indians, Walker reported, were "unused to manual labor, and physically unqualified for it by the habits of the chase, unprovided with tools and implements, without forethought and without self-control

. . . with strong animal appetites and no intellectual tastes or aspirations to hold those appetites in check." Unless the government planned their education, the "now roving Indians" would in the future become "vagabonds" and "festering sores" in the midst of civilization. On the reservation, Indians would not be allowed to "escape work": They would be "required" to learn and practice the arts of industry until at least one generation had been placed on a course of "self-improvement."

Segregated in reservations, Indians would not be permitted to leave, except upon express authority of law. "We mean by this," Walker explained, "something more than that a 'pass system' should be created for every tribe under the control of the government, to prevent individual Indians from straying away for an occasional debauch at the settlements." Authorities should have power to keep Indians on the reservations assigned to them and to "arrest" and return those who wandered away. Otherwise, Walker warned, whenever they became "restive under compulsion to labor," they would break away and resume their "old roving spirit." Seclusion was also necessary because Indians were disposed toward the "lower and baser elements of civilization" and the acquisition of the vices rather than the virtues of whites. Walker's reservation resembled Benjamin Rush's "colonies" designed to educate and "cure" blacks: It was to be a reformatory, a place where the government could prepare Indians for citizenship and inculcate in them republican and Protestant habits of self-control and domination over the "strong animal appetites."[28]

All he hoped to do, Walker said, was to help the Indians over the rough places on "the white man's road." He believed he knew, from his own experiences, what was required for them. He once told a friend that the Indians were like "children" who disliked school and would not attend if they could "play truant at pleasure." Then he added: "I used to have to be whipped myself to get me to school and keep me there, yet I always liked to study when once within the school-room walls." On another occasion, Walker recalled: "I was born with an unfortunate disposition, which, in my early years, gave a great deal of trouble and anxiety to my parents. During my years at college, I was able to bring myself increasingly under control, so that I left college with a pretty steady temper, which has got away with me during my whole subsequent life fewer times than I can count upon the fingers of one hand." Grateful for the "whipping" he had received as a child and proud of the great self-discipline he had developed, Walker was certain "wild Indians" would not become "industrious" and "frugal" except through "a severe course of industrial instruction and exercise under restraint."[29]

In his effort to reform Indians, Commissioner Walker, like Jackson before him, expressed a compassion for them and a reverence for the ways of Providence. The "only hope of salvation for the aborigines of the continent," he piously declared, was the reduction of all Indians to the "condition of suppliants for charity." Indeed, if they stood up against the progress of civilization and industry, they must be "relentlessly crushed." The westward course of population was neither to be denied nor delayed for the sake of all the Indians who ever called America their home. Indians must "yield or perish." There was even something "savoring" "providential mercy" in the rapidity with which their fate was advancing upon them, leaving them scarcely the chance to resist before they would be surrounded and disarmed. "It is not feebly and futilely to attempt to stay this tide . . . but to snatch the remnants of the Indian race from destruction from before it, that the friends of humanity should exert themselves in this juncture, and lose no time." A "friend of humanity," Walker was determined to "lose no time" in his work to redeem the Indians. The only way to "snatch the remnants of the Indian race from destruction" was to teach them self-control and industry and to prepare them for civilization. In Indian affairs (as in white affairs), Commissioner Walker was convinced, there must be social planning: Indians should not be left alone, "letting such as will, go to the dogs, letting such as can, find a place for themselves in the social and industrial order."[30]

The use of scientific management to "reform" the Indian in a technological society came to a culmination in the Dawes Act of 1887. Also known as the Indian Allotment Act, it proposed to break up the reservations in order to accelerate the transformation of the Indian into a property owner and a citizen of the United States. White reformers hailed it as the "Indian Emancipation Act" and claimed it closed a "century of dishonor." It promised to be the final solution to the "Indian Question."[31]

The Dawes Act was based on the concept of allotment of lands in severalty, an idea which had been discussed throughout the nineteenth century. In the Choctaw Treaty of 1805, the federal government had reserved certain tracts of lands for individual Choctaws and issued patents to many of them. President Jefferson told a delegation of chiefs three years later: "Let me entreat you . . . on the land now given you, to begin to give every man a farm; let him enclose it, cultivate it, build a warm house on it, and when he dies, let it belong to his wife and children after him." Time and again allotment had been recommended—by Secretary of War William Crawford in 1816, President James Monroe in 1819, Secretary of War John C. Calhoun in 1822, Indian Commissioner George Manypenny in 1854, Secretary of Interior Carl Schurz in 1877, reformer Helen Hunt Jackson in *A*

Century of Dishonor, published in 1881, and President Grover Cleveland in his annual messages of 1885 and 1886. Commissioner of Indian Affairs T. Hartley Crawford summed up a sentiment widespread among allotment advocates when he stated in 1838: "Unless some system is marked out by which there shall be a separate allotment of land to each individual . . . you will look in vain for any general casting off of savagism. Common property and civilization cannot co-exist."[32] The allotment movement accelerated after 1850, as the white population reached the Pacific Coast and as the transcontinental railroad threatened the very existence of the frontier.

But the Dawes Act went far beyond allotment. It gave the President power, at his discretion and without the Indians' consent, to allot reservation lands to individual Indians in the amount of 160 acres to each family head. It also conferred citizenship upon the allottees and any other Indians who would abandon their tribes and adopt the "habits of civilized life." In addition, the law permitted the federal government to secure tribal consent to sell "surplus" reservation land—land which remained after allotment had taken place—to white settlers in 160-acre tracts, and to hold money derived from such sales in trust for the Indians, to be used for their "education and civilization." Significantly, the act also stated that none of its provisions affected the right of Congress to grant right-of-way through any Indian lands for telegraph lines or railroads. For whites, the Dawes Act promised much: the destruction of Indian tribes, the availability of lands for white settlement, and the "assimilation" of the Indian into American civilization.[33] Thus, it appealed at once to the land-hungry white westerners and the railroad interests as well as to the white humanitarians and reformers.

White farmers and business interests were well aware of the economic advantages the allotment program offered them. In 1880, Secretary Schurz predicted that allotment would "eventually open to settlement by white men the large tracts of land now belonging to the reservations, but not used by the Indians." In his recommendation for the removal of the Chippewas from their lands in Dakota and Minnesota and the allotment of lands in severalty to them after their consolidation on the White Earth Reservation, the commissioner of Indian affairs pointed out how the present Chippewa lands were "valuable for the pine timber growing thereon, for which, if the Indian title should be extinguished, a ready sale could be found." The transfer of lands from Indians to whites did not take a long time. By 1900, only thirteen years after the passage of the Dawes Act, Indians held only 77,865,373 of the 138,000,000 acres they possessed in 1887. Between 1887 and 1934, when the allotment policy was terminated, sixty percent of the Indian land base had been transferred to whites: 60,000,000 acres had been sold as "surplus" to whites by the federal government, and 27,000,000 acres or two-thirds of the land allotted to individual Indians had been transferred to whites through private transactions. Legislation which granted railroad interests right-of-way through Indian lands coincided with the adoption of the Dawes Act: In 1886–87, Congress passed the allotment act as well as six laws for railroad grants. "The past year," the Indian commissioner observed in September 1887, "has been one of unusual activity in the projection and building of numerous additional railroads through Indian lands." During its next two sessions, Congress enacted twenty-three laws granting railroads right-of-way through Indian territories.[34]

From the perspective of the white humanitarians and reformers, the Dawes Act would undermine the tribal system, which was perpetuating the "savagery" of the Indian. Doubting whether "any high degree of civilization" would be possible without individual ownership of land, they called the Allotment Act "one of the most effective civilizing agencies." The "habits of nomadic barbarism" had to be destroyed in order for the Indian to learn the ways of civilization. As long as Indians lived in tribes, an agent for the Yankton Sioux insisted, they would not change; they would continue to live in idleness, frivolity, and debauchery. And as long as Indians owned their land in common, Senator Henry Dawes contended, they would lack "selfishness," which was "at the bottom of civilization." Indians had to divide the land among themselves as individuals, or they would not make much progress toward civilization. John Wesley Powell, director of the Bureau of American Ethnology, was convinced "no measure could be devised more efficient for the ultimate civilization of the Indians of this country than one by which they could successfully and rapidly obtain lands in severalty." In her eloquent protest against "a century of dishonor," Helen Hunt Jackson advocated the parceling out of tribal lands to individual Indians. "Instead of a liberal and far-sighted policy looking to the education and civilization and possible citizenship of the Indian tribes," she complained, "we have suffered these people to remain as savages. . . ." They should not be allowed to continue so, she argued; they should be "entirely changed." To accomplish this, they should be made to "feel both the incentives and the restraints which an individual ownership of property is fitted to excite." Here, revived, was essentially Jefferson's vision of red Lockeans, promoted even more actively as the "vacant lands" began to disappear and as white civilization itself stretched beyond the "Stony mountains."[35]

The concerns of the humanitarians were voiced repeatedly during the debate on the Dawes Bill in Congress. Allotment advocates declared that the act was intended to give the individual Indian a title to the land in order to "stimulate him to work and improve his land and accumulate property, to make him feel more independent and self-reliant." With the breakup of reservations and the sale of "surplus" lands to whites, the Indian would learn the "habits of thrift and industry" from his white neighbor. This process, allotment supporters promised, would surely civilize the Indian:

> Give to our people, under such discretion as the President may exercise, the right to go upon the Indian lands and make, side by side of the Indian farm, a farm tilled by the aggressive and enterprising Anglo-Saxon, and in a little while contact alone will compel these people to accept the civilization that surrounds them on every side. . . . With white settlers on every alternative section of Indian lands, there will be a school-house built, with Indian children and white chidren together; there will be churches at which there will be an attendance of Indian and white people alike. They will readily learn the tongue of the white race. They will for a while speak their own language, but they will readily learn the ways of civilization.

In this "assimilationist" process, Indians would eventually enter capitalist and technological society: Beginning as herders, they would become farmers and eventually "be prepared to go into mechanical pursuits." Thus, the Dawes Act would transform Indians from "savages" to citizens, even workers in an industrial society.[36]

The civilization and "assimilation" of the Indian, allotment supporters predicted, would be accelerated in the era of technology and the railroad. They saw the railroad as a blessing to the Indian, and promoted its extension in their efforts to civilize him. At the 1885 meeting of the Lake Mohonk Conference, the Reverend Lyman Abbott described the railroad as the great civilizer of the Indians. The railroad, he declared, would bring Indians into the marketplace: A "Christianizing power," it would educate them and do even more to teach them "punctuality" than a "schoolmaster or preacher." Two years later, the agent of the Fort Peek office in Montana reported on the social effects the railroad would have on Indians: "The Montana division of the St. Paul, Minneapolis & Manitoba Railway, now being constructed east and west, through this reservation, will, in my opinion, have a greater tendency to civilize these Indians than any other one thing, for the reason that it will bring them in contact with the whites, the most of whom in this country are energetic, pushing people." This point was raised again in the Senate of the United States during the debate on the Dawes Bill. "The railroads that are being constructed in every section of the country by the side of reservations and across reservations," a senator declared, "will bring these people in contact with the white settlement."

Across the Continent, Westward the Course of Empire Takes Its Way, *reproduced from the collection of the Library of Congress*

Indeed, like the Currier and Ives print *Across the Continent,* the mighty steam locomotive would be the carrier of civilization—its engine blowing black smoke into the faces of Indians, its cars debouching white settlers, and its tracks pointing westward and creating new towns.[37]

As the railroad advanced technological society to the Pacific, it was transforming Indians into "vanishing Americans." Shortly after the Congress had passed his bill, Senator Dawes spoke before a gathering of reformers at the Lake Mohonk Conference, and recounted a trip he had taken recently on the railroad. "I went . . . four hundred and eighty miles on a railroad every foot of which was built since last April, all over an Indian reservation, where the Indians had been set apart on the British border, so far away from civilization that the game was forever to furnish him food and support; and yet the game had disappeared years ago. . . . The land I passed through was as fine a wheat-growing country as it could be. The railroad has gone through there, and it was black with emigrants ready to take advantage of it." The railroad and the forces it represented—the expansion of white settlement, civilization, and the market—made it apparent, Senator Dawes concluded, that the Indian of the "past" had no place in technological America.[38]

CHAPTER IX

CIVILIZATION IN THE "NEW SOUTH"

To work at a machine, the workman should be taught from childhood, in order that he may learn to adapt his own movements to the uniform and unceasing motion of an automaton. . . . The technical subordination of the workman to the uniform motion of the instruments of labour . . . give[s] rise to a barrack discipline, which is elaborated into a complex system in the factory. . . .

—Karl Marx

Present in the West where Indians were being destroyed, re-formed in reservations, or forced to become individual property owners, "progress" also penetrated the states below the Mason-Dixon Line where it was known as the "New South." This enthusiastic southern quest for the building of a new industrial order in the 1870s and 1880s had more than racial and sectional significance, for it contained a class appeal to industrial capitalists in the North as well as the South. But, while the promoters of the "New South" offered ideological weaponry to capitalists fearful of class conflicts, they worried about the corrosive effects southern industrialization would have on the paternalism that had developed in the Old South.

Paternalism had very different meanings for masters and slaves. According to historian Eugene Genovese,

for the slaveholders paternalism represented an attempt to overcome the fundamental contradiction in slavery; the impossibility of the slaves' ever becoming the things they were supposed to be. Paternalism defined the involuntary labor of the slaves as a legitimate return to their masters for protection and direction. But, the masters' need to see their slaves as acquiescent human beings constituted a moral victory for the slaves themselves. Paternalism's insistence upon mutual obligations—duties, responsibilities, and ultimately even rights—implicitly recognized the slave's humanity.

Thus, paternalism had provided both masters and slaves a "fragile bridge across the intolerable contradictions inherent in a society based on racism, slavery, and class exploitation."[1] After the Civil War and the abolition of slavery, however, southern white leaders had to determine whether such a "fragile bridge" could exist in an industrializing society based on wage labor, and be used to legitimatize racism and class rule.

Machines and Magnolias: Black Labor in an Industrial Order

Actually, the "New South" had roots in the Old South. Antebellum dependency on agriculture, particularly cotton cultivation, did not preclude an interest in the development of industry. During the 1850s the editor of the *New Orleans Picayune* anticipated both the language and spirit of newspaper editor Henry W. Grady and the "New South" of the 1880s. "The South can manufacture for the world," the editor proclaimed. "Manufactures contiguous to the cotton fields have already proved more profitable than cotton culture itself. . . . The smoke of the steam engine should begin to float over the cotton fields, and the hum of spindles and the click of looms make music on all our mountain streams."[2] This celebration of southern industrialization was not an isolated expression: It could also be found in the essays and speeches of southern industrialist William Gregg, the widely read *De Bow's Review,* the excited southern newspaper announcements of the establishment of new factories, the messages of governors, legislative reports, and the Southern Commercial Conventions.

A political response to northern abolitionism, this zeal for southern industrialism in the 1850s was not motivated simply by a love of progress but also by a deep hatred of southern economic dependence upon the North. The resentment of southerners toward their inferior economic status was bitter and was often directed against themselves. An Alabama editor noted one of the ironies involved in the defense of slavery:

> At present, the North fattens and grows rich upon the South. We purchase all our luxuries and necessaries from the North. . . . With us, every branch and pursuit in life . . . is dependent upon the North. . . . The slaveholder dresses in

Northern goods, rides in a Northern saddle . . . sports his Northern carriage, patronizes Northern newspapers, drinks Northern liquors. . . . The aggressive acts upon his rights and his property arouse his resentment—and on Northern-made paper, with a Northern pen, with Northern ink, he resolves and resolves in regard to his rights!

Unless southern slaveholders overthrew this despised economic dependence, they could not expect to "counteract the incessant and vexatious attacks of the North." Thus, slavery defenders like W. Sykes and George Fitzhugh advocated the construction of railroads and factories as "the Best Guaranty for the Protection of Southern Rights."[3]

The key to southern industrial development, proslavery men argued, would be the introduction of the slave into the factory. But they were questioned whether the black slave was suitable for industrial labor. Had he not "limited mental capacities," and was he not "unfit for anything save the plantation and menial services"? In their responses, proslavery advocates of southern industrialism claimed the black was uniquely qualified to operate machines: "The negro, in his common absence from reflection, is, perhaps, the best manipulist in the world." Some proslavery southerners even demanded the reopening of the African slave trade, which had been prohibited by Congress in 1808. "What hinders the South from manufacturing her own cotton? Want of labor," they contended. What the South needed was black labor to fill the factories. "Give us, then, more and cheap operatives, and we would not only have the will, but be enabled to diversify our labor, and improve our country. We would build our own vessels and steamboats, railroads . . . erect manufactories and foundries. . . ."[4]

While most slaveholders were not willing to support the reopening of the African slave trade, they knew blacks could be effectively used in industrial production. Indeed, in the 1850s, thousand of slaves were already working in the iron and tobacco industries of Virginia, the hemp factories of Kentucky, the cotton textile mills of South Carolina and Tennessee, the sawmills of Alabama, the distilleries of Louisiana, and the flour mills of Georgia. Between 160,000 and 200,000 slaves, or about five percent of the total slave population, worked in industry. In 1859 the *Jackson Semi-Weekly Mississippian* reported: "Ten Africans were sold in Vicksburg varying in price from four hundred to one thousand dollars each. . . . These gentlemen wish to establish a manufactory and place their Mississippi-born negroes under an overseer, who will learn them to spin, weave and attend the machinery, while they make the Africans cultivate their crops, help to build levees and construct railroads." During the Civil War, more than half of the labor force of the Tredegar Iron Works, the Virginia "ironmaker to the Confederacy," was black. The expansion of slavery, the master class could see, had no "natural limits," and an industrial society could be based on black labor.[5]

After the Civil War, a renewed commitment to industrial progress appeared in the South which acknowledged the need for adjustment and reconciliation but which had the emotions and language of the old sectionalism. As early as 1870, former Confederate propagandist Edwin De Leon called for the rise of a "New South." Charting the future direction of the South, he wrote: "The Northerner will carry South his thrift, his caution, his restless activity, his love of new things: the Southerner will temper these with his reckless liberality, his careless confidence, his fiery energy, and his old-time conservatism; and both will be benefited by the admixture." Eleven years later, the editor of the *New Orleans Times-Democrat* reported that a "magic transformation" had occurred in the South. The "stagnation of despair" had given way to the "buoyance" of hope and courage, the "silence of inertia" to the "thrilling uproar of action." Southerners were a "new people" and their land was experiencing a "new birth." The thrust of the movement for a "New South" was to transform the old Cotton Kingdom into an industrial society, compete with the North, and even out-Yankee the Yankee. The depth of the southern determination to succeed in this effort was demonstrated dramatically in 1886. In order to eliminate the bottleneck which tied railroad traffic at the sectional border, the southern railroad companies decided to "adjust" the gauge of their tracks by three inches to conform to the "standard" gauge of the northern tracks. Thus, on May 30, 1886, the Louisville and Nashville Railroad Company, employing an army of 8,000 men, adjusted 2,000 miles of track—all in one day![6]

The signs of "progress" were evident elsewhere in the South, especially in the rise of cities and the proliferation of factories. Atlanta, which had only 14,000 people when General William Sherman marched his army to the sea, had a population of 21,789 in 1870, 37,409 in 1880, and 89,872 in 1900. The growth of Birmingham, Alabama, was even more startling— from 3,086 in 1880 to 38,415 in 1900, or a tenfold increase in two decades. The pride of the "New South's" manufacturing was located in textile and iron production. The number of spindles jumped from 600,000 in 1860 to nearly 175,000,000 in 1890; the number of mills increased from 161 in 1880 to 400 in 1900. By the late 1880s southern pig-iron production surpassed the total output of the entire country in 1860. Jefferson County, in which Birmingham was located, had only 22 manufacturing establishments in 1870; thirty years later, it had almost 500 plants with 14,000 workers. Southern readers of *A Connecticut Yankee in King Arthur's Court* could look around them and see resemblances between Twain's fantasy and the industrial transformation under way in the land of Dixie.[7]

During this period, blacks were drawn into the factories and mills of the "New South." Although they were systematically excluded from certain industries such as textiles, and although they continued to be employed primarily in agriculture, blacks constituted an important source of industrial labor. Southern industrial capitalists revealed strong interest in and support for the use of black labor. Richard H. Edmunds, editor of the *Manufacturers' Record,* regarded blacks as "the most important working factor in the development of the great and varied resources of our country." The superintendent of the Saluda Cotton Factory, whose labor force was one-fourth black, praised his black workers, saying they performed as effectively as whites, were less expensive, and could be "easily controlled." The manager of the Shelby Iron Works insisted he would not exchange black workers "for any other people on earth." After white workers struck the Chattanooga and Knoxville iron companies in 1883, black workers were put into every phase of the iron industry. The companies found black labor to be "fully as good as" white labor, and reported that they had never had a more successful working of the mills than during the period when they had used black labor almost exclusively. In 1891 *The Tradesman* sent a circular to every important manufacturing company in the South to determine the extent they employed blacks, in what capacity, and the degree of their satisfaction with them. In their replies, Southern businessmen indicated that they satisfactorily employed blacks in both unskilled and skilled capacities, and that they "unanimously" intended to continue the employment of blacks and to advance them to more skilled positions. The extent of black labor in Southern manufacturing was not insignificant. In 1890, 6 percent of the total black work force was employed in manufacturing compared with 19 percent of the total native white work force. Between 1890 and 1910, the number of black male workers in nonagricultural occupations increased by two-thirds, or to 400,000, due mainly to expansion in saw mills, coal mining and railroad construction and maintenance. In 1880, 41 percent of Birmingham's industrial workers were black; the Immigration Commission reported in 1907 that blacks made up 39.1 percent of all steelworkers in the South.[8]

As they developed the "New South," many southern industrialists held in "tenderest reverence" the "memory" of the Old South, and the factories they erected often resembled antebellum plantations. The old paternalism reemerged as welfare capitalism as industries like the Tennessee Coal and Iron Company (United States Steel) and the De Bardeleben Coal Company placed former bondsmen under their care and control. In order to transform illiterate blacks into efficient skilled workers and to keep out the unions, these companies provided schools, hospitals, recreational facilities, and housing for their workers. They even offered the children of their employees scholarships to Booker T. Washington's Tuskegee Institute, and hired graduates of Tuskegee to direct their programs of welfare capitalism.[9] Here, in effect, was Henry Hughes' "warranteeism" resurrected in the industrial order of the "New South."

Still, for the promoters of modernization, industrialization created new racial problems. Wherever industries developed, they tended to undermine the rural plantation ambience which helped to sustain white notions of paternalism. The new order needed black factory workers who had been taught to adapt their own movement to the "uniform and unceasing motion" of "automatons" rather than affectionate, loyal, and dependent Sambos. The "bonds of affection" that Hughes had cherished were being broken as new patterns of industrial social relations widened the distance between the races and transformed planters into corporation managers and executives and former slaves into a factory proletariat. Located in cities where anonymity and population concentration had already rendered white surveillance and control difficult in antebellum times, many black workers were now better able to shield themselves from the intimacy and control of white paternalism.[10] Thus, the "New South" contained a vexatious contradiction within its creed and the conditions it was developing.

No one illustrated the problems of this contradiction as sharply as the theoretician of the "New South" ideology—Henry W. Grady. Born into a class that benefited from the Market Revolution and the appropriation of Indian land and black labor, Grady was the son of a Georgia merchant, an aggressive businessman who had moved into the territory opened to white settlement after Cherokee removal in the 1830s. Only eleven years old when the South seceded from the Union, Grady grew up to become a peacemaker between the sections, and called for reconciliation based on southern independence and industrial development. As editor of the *Atlanta Constitution,* he commanded great influence in the South; in the late 1880s, his paper had one of the largest subscription lists below the Mason and Dixon Line. Moreover, Grady was viewed in the North, especially in circles of business and political power, as a spokesman of the South and its postbellum commitment to progress. In this role, he delivered speeches at banquets in establishments like the Hotel Vendome in Boston and Delmonico's in New York, before packed audiences which included such men as J. P. Morgan, John H. Inman, Andrew Carnegie, Oliver Ames, Leverett Saltonstall, and Grover Cleveland. Grady's death in 1889 evoked eulogies from both sections. Carnegie had a wreath placed on "the grave of the eloquent peacemaker between the North and South," and fondly noted Grady's singular contribution to reconciliation: "Only those who stood at his side and heard him at Boston can estimate the extent of the nation's loss in his death. It seemed reserved for him to perform a service to his country which no other could perform so well." The press, North and South, eulogized Grady as the "embodiment of the spirit of the New South." One editor summed up the sentiments of the press when he wrote: "Mr. Grady was a warm and confident advocate of industrial advancement in the land of his birth. He wanted to see the South interlaced with railroads, her rich mineral deposits opened to development, her cities teeming with factories, her people busy, contented and prosperous." The apostle of the "New South," Grady offered a vision of sectional and class salvation.[11]

"What shall the South do to be saved?" asked Grady in an 1887 Dallas speech, "The South and Her Problems." The South, he explained, had a twofold problem—its "race problem" and its "no less unique and important industrial problem."[12] In Grady's judgment, to solve the first problem the South must have home rule, and to have home rule the South must have industrial progress and economic development.

To Grady, home rule had a racial purpose: It would enable the South to settle "the social relations of the races" according to white southerners' own views of what was "right and best," and to "fix" the "social status" of citizens in the South without interference from "an outside power." White southerners did not want the restoration of slavery, Grady claimed; indeed, they even "rejoiced" that the institution had been "swept forever from American soil." But they were determined to maintain white supremacy—the rule of the race of intelligence and self-control over the race of ignorance and impulsiveness. The "truth" of the superiority of the white race, Grady said, would "run forever" in the "blood" of "Anglo-Saxon hearts." Whites, North and South, must not allow "Negro rights" to splinter white racial solidarity; they should never be divided on the issue of "the rights of an alien race." They must show the same spirit of racial unity which had led them to "cut down" the Indian as a "weed" because he hindered the way of white Americans, and which had inspired them to enact the 1882 Chinese Exclusion Law. Urging whites everywhere to acknowledge their feeling of racial superiority, Grady declared: "There is not a white man North or South who does not feel it stir in the grey matter of his brain and throb in his heart. . . . It speaks in Ohio, and in Georgia. . . . It has just spoken in universally approved legislation in excluding the Chinaman from our gates. . . ." Thus, whites in the South should be allowed to exercise at home, below the Mason-Dixon Line, the white superiority and power which could be found in national actions and legislation.[13]

In an editorial written a year after the passage of the Chinese Exclusion Act, Grady advocated racial segregation in the South. "The line has been drawn just where it should be," he argued. "Just where nature drew it and where justice commends. The negro is entitled to his freedom, his franchise, to full and equal legal rights. . . . Social equality he can never have. He does not have it in the north, or in the east, or in the west. On one pretext or another, he is kept out of hotels, theatres, schools and restaurants, north as well as south." Whites in the South, in segregating the races, were merely conducting themselves in the same way as whites everywhere. But white southerners, Grady noted, had a unique need for racial control. Removal and exclusion, which had been applied to Indians and Chinese respectively, were not possibilities available as solutions to the "Negro Problem" in the South. Carrying within her "body politic" two races nearly equal in numbers, the South had to know "where to draw the line," and to have regional autonomy and self-determination in racial matters.[14]

In his speeches and writings, Grady specified the "new conditions" requisite for southern home rule. The problem was economic dependency on the North. "The old South rested everything on slavery and agriculture," he said, "unconscious that these could neither give nor maintain healthy growth." Consequently, the South had become a virtual economic colony of the North. Grady realized this dramatically during a funeral service in Pickens County, Georgia—a "particularly sad" experience for him. What made it so was the conspicuous presence of the North, and the irony reflected in almost every aspect of the burial. As Grady told the story:

> They buried him in the midst of a marble quarry: They cut through solid marble to make his grave; and yet a little tombstone they put above him was from Vermont. They buried him in the heart of a pine forest, and yet the pine coffin was imported from Cincinnati. They buried him within touch of an iron mine, and yet the nails in his coffin and the iron in the shovel that dug his grave were imported from Pittsburgh. . . . The South didn't furnish a thing on earth for that funeral but the corpse and the hole in the ground. . . . [They] buried him in a New York coat and a Boston pair of shoes and a pair of breeches from Chicago and a shirt from Cincinnati, leaving him nothing to carry into the next world with him to remind him of the country in which he lived, and for which he fought for four years. . . .[15]

Something of a "reminder," at the very least, was needed for Grady. The war for southern independence, in which the buried man had fought, was not over; Grady had not surrendered. The South had to open a new battle-front: The new army would be composed of factory workers, the new generals would be business leaders, and the new weapons would be woolen mills, iron furnaces, and iron factories. "We are coming to meet you," Grady declared in Boston in 1889. "We are going to take a noble revenge . . . by invading every inch of your territory with iron, as you invaded ours twenty-nine years ago."[16] Here were the language of war, the emotions of the Confederacy.

But the conditions would be "new." Like Jacob Bigelow and Twain's Connecticut Yankee, Grady welcomed the new age of science and technology. Impressed with the miraculous powers of machinery and mind, he exclaimed: "A button is pressed by a child's finger, and the work of a million men is done. The hand is nothing—the brain is everything." The very process of production had been altered: "Before the war, when the Southern planter had a little surplus money he bought a slave. Since the war, he buys a piece of machinery." The shift from slave to machine labor could be heard in the sounds of production: "The spinning wheel of the past that filled all the country-side with its drowsy music, as the dusky spinner advanced and retreated, with not ungrateful courtesy and a swing-ing sidewise shuffle, will find its sweet voice lost in the hum of modern spindles." The "most wonderful machines" were replacing human labor, and machinery would soon be employed to pick cotton. The new source of power and production was electricity—the "viewless bondsmen." The South had the resources—the cotton and the ore—to industrialize and achieve independence from the North. All she needed to do, Grady in-sisted, was to construct factories in her fields, and to spin and weave the cotton she cultivated. In his essay "Cotton and Its Kingdom," published in 1881, Grady proudly reported that the number of looms in the South had increased from 11,602 in 1870 to 15,222 in 1880, and the number of spin-dles had nearly doubled during this decade. The greatest symbol of south-ern industrial pride, however, was the postbellum development of her iron industry. Grady was certain the South would dominate the world's iron production. In his Dallas speech, he announced that southern iron produc-tion had leaped from 212,000 tons in 1880 to 845,000 tons in 1887, and predicted that Birmingham alone would manufacture more iron in 1889 than the entire southern production for 1887. Little wonder he called Bir-mingham one of the "magic cities" of the South, and aggressively an-nounced that iron was becoming "King."[17]

Many years after he had attended that funeral in Pickens County, Grady returned to the gravesite and described the wonders the "New South" had wrought.

There are now more than $3,000,000 invested in marble quarries and machinery around that grave. Its pitiful loneliness is broken with the rumble of ponderous machines, and a strange tumult pervades the wilderness. Twenty miles away, the largest marble-cutting works in the world put to shame in a thousand shapes its modest headstone. Forty miles away four coffin factories, with their exquisite work, tempt the world to die. The iron hills are gashed and swarm with workmen. Forty cotton mills in a near radius weave infinite cloth that neighboring shops make into countless shirts. There are shoe factories, nail factories, shovel and pick factories, and carriage factories, to supply the other wants. And that country can now get up as nice a funeral, native and home-made, as you would wish to have.[18]

Here was a new South with its air filled with the smoke of factories, its quiet countryside broken by the rumble of monstrous machines, and its hills torn open as swarms of workers extracted the minerals.

To Grady the "New South" offered more than industrial progress and a "home-made" funeral: It also buttressed racial order. In the new industrial society, blacks were carpenters, masons, shoemakers, and mechanics; integrated into the economic sector, they worked with whites in the fields and factories. But socially, in schools, churches, theaters, and trains, the two races were segregated. Thus, Grady noted, bricklayers or carpenters, black and white were working "side by side," but when the trowel or the hammer was laid aside, the laborers parted, each going his own way.[19]

Yet, the "New South" which Grady was promoting also threatened the old order he loved and its agricultural way of life. An apostle of a vision of factories and cities, he was nostalgic for the antebellum rural and agrarian ways. He lamented the movement of the rural population to the new urban centers: "In the diminution of this rural population, virtuous and competent, patriotic and honest, living beneath its own roof-tree, building its altars by its own hearthstone and shining in its own heart its liberty and its conscience, there is abiding cause for regret."[20] Thus, progress, for Grady, involved a profound loss and the realization of Jefferson's fears of an urbanized society. The tension between means and ends—the development of southern industrialization in order to achieve southern independence—was one Grady was never able to resolve.

More importantly, the industrial and segregationist order of the "New South" posed a racial dilemma for Grady. Both the proletarization of blacks in the production process and the establishment of rigid lines of segregation which he was advocating undermined the relationship of intimacy and paternalism which he believed had existed between masters and slaves. Thus, even as Grady crusaded for a "New South," he fondly recalled the past. He wanted no better friend than the "black boy" who had been raised by his side, and "no sweeter music" than the "crooning" of his "old mammy," bending her "old black face" over him and leading him smiling into peaceful sleep. He wanted to exercise paternal care for blacks: As an eight-year-old child, he had had the habit of waking up in the night when the weather was cold and saying: "Dear mother, do you think the servants have enough cover? It's so cold, and I want them to be warm." Grateful for slave loyalty during the Civil War, he remarked: "It is doubtful if the world has seen a peasantry so happy and so well-to-do as the negro slaves in America. The world was amazed at the fidelity with which these slaves guarded, from 1861 to 1865, the homes and families of the masters who were fighting with the army that barred their way to freedom." After the Civil War, Grady wanted to continue to have near him docile and happy old-time Negroes, especially Cuffee, the "steadfast figure," "good-natured" and "undisturbed by change of relation or condition." Ironically, as Grady praised electricity as the "viewless bondsmen," as he replaced the "drowsy music" of the "dusky spinner" with the "hum of modern spindles," and as he called for both the transformation of the black "peasantry" into factory workers and for the social segregation of the races, he felt even more intensely the need to depend on blacks as a source of rootedness, a point of stability and reference in the midst of the changes and industrial progress of the "New South."[21] He knew only too well how the "new conditions," which he promised would make possible the preservation of antebellum southern ways, were advancing further the social disintegration he was desperately struggling to reverse.

Still, Grady tried to ignore this dilemma as he inducted antebellum paternalism into the service of the gospel of the "New South" and as he carried into the North an ideology of racial and class order. Virtual class warfare, Grady saw, had broken out in American society, especially in the northern industrial cities, which had become "center spots of danger," places of corruption, and spawning grounds for "clubs and societies of anarchy and socialism." In his class appeal to northern businessmen, Grady described the peaceful social relations between labor and capital in the South: "Nowhere on earth is there kindlier feeling, closer sympathy, or less friction between the two classes of society than between the whites and blacks of the South today." Economic class relations as well as race relations under home rule were harmonious. In an article published in the *Century Magazine* a year before the 1886 Haymarket Riot, Grady made his point even more explicit in a comparison between southern order and northern disorder: "The races meet in exchange of labor in perfect amity and understanding. Together they carry on the concerns of the day, knowing little or nothing of the fierce hostility that divides labor and capital in other sections." And a few months after the violent confrontation between labor and capital in Chicago, Grady told business leaders in New York: "No section shows a more prosperous laboring population than the negroes of the South, none in fuller sympathy with the employing and land-owning class." Clearly, Grady was not only proclaiming a "New South" but also promoting a new industrial order based on black labor and class control. His message contained a class criticism of labor unions, and an implied invitation to northern capitalists to utilize the reserve army of black labor in the South. No wonder northern businessmen like Carnegie who were locked in combat against white labor applauded Grady, and even began transporting black workers into East St. Louis, Detroit, Chicago, and other northern cities within two decades after Grady had given his speech in New York. A "peacemaker between the North and South," to borrow from Carnegie's eulogy, Grady was even more effective than John C. Calhoun or Henry Hughes of the Old South as a "Marx of the Master Class," for he helped capitalists of both sections become conscious of their common class identity and interests.[22]

The "Negro Question": "Higher Life" in the South

Grady's most outspoken critic was a fellow white southerner, George Washington Cable.[23] The conflict between Grady and Cable over the issue of rights for blacks must be regarded as one of the intriguing ironies of the postbellum South. While he differed from Grady over the questions of integration, civil rights, and southern home rule, Cable actually shared with the apostle of the "New South" a basic commitment to white civilization. Cable's thinking on race was so subtle Grady did not realize he was castigating a man whose seemingly heretical views and activities were intended to be the means to achieve white southern goals.

But Grady should not be judged too harshly for his lack of discernment, for Cable certainly appeared to be a white southern heretic. Author of the antislavery novel The Grandissimes and the antisegregation essays "The Freedman's Case in Equity" and "The Negro Question," Cable called for a "New South" which included not only the rapid multiplication of mills, furnaces, and railways but also a new "civil order" for blacks. "The New South of Coal, Iron and Spindles . . . must be kept well to the fore," he argued, "but with the constant application" of the "fundamental principles of justice." In a reference to impoverished blacks, he warned: "The South can never take rank in the great march of progress until she has lifted this lower class—the lowest lower class in Christendom—out of the mire."

Cable also spoke out courageously against the denial of civil rights for blacks during an era of intense and violent racial repression. While white southerners legislated the segregation of blacks, Cable advocated integrated schools in New Orleans, and fought against separate sections for blacks in theaters, trains, and public facilities. He also criticized the entire southern penal system for its exploitation and cruel treatment of black inmates. His most defiant breach of southern white principles was his support for the Lodge Bill which provided for the federal supervision of local Congressional elections. "It is only a 'Force Bill' to those who cannot be kept from fraud except by force," Cable remarked. "There is at least one Cotton State whose Electoral System is confessedly calculated to outwit the weakest and most defenseless classes of its lawful voters." For Cable, local injustice against black citizens was "the nation's business."[24]

Cable's forthright stand on the race question drew ire from the South and praise from the North. White southerners denounced Cable as a "nigger-lover," and Grady singled him out as a traitor to the white race. Cable experienced so much hate and hostility from white southerners that he decided to move his family to New England. Northern white abolitionists and blacks admired Cable as a courageous advocate of racial justice. Harriet Beecher Stowe told him that she took "much delight" in his writings, and William Lloyd Garrison, Jr., praised him for his "brave stand for a downtrodden people at the cost of Southern popularity." W. E. B. Du Bois welcomed Cable's "clear utterance and moral heroism," and William B. Edwards, black president of Connecticut's Sumner Union League, called him "another Sumner, the founder of all our civil rights."[25]

Actually, both Cable's detractors and his admirers misunderstood the New Orleans novelist: They thought they saw white racial heresy or progressive racial views, respectively, in matters where Cable was orthodox, a believer in white supremacy. Cable's racial thinking needs to be unraveled, for it reflected the complex ways a major white southern writer responded to the racial and class dilemmas confronting the industrializing biracial society of the "New South."

At the center of Cable's racial ideology was his concern for what he called the "higher life," which he identified as "civilization," or the "subordination of instinct to reason." The South, in his judgment, was hardly civilized; the worst example of this backwardness among southern whites was the Louisiana Creole, who knew "nothing and care[d] nothing but for meat, drink, and pleasure." The region which commanded Cable's respect was New England, "the intellectual treasury of the United States," where cultivation, refinement, and taste could be found. Certain women, especially his New England mother, possessed the qualities of the "higher idea"—

intellectual ambition, moral austerity, intolerance toward indolence and pleasure, and an "intense love of the beautiful." A man of "order, system, diligence," Cable cultivated in himself the "self-denying frugality" and the genteelness he believed a civilized society required. Still, he doubted whether he would always be able to govern his instincts, to keep himself from "pure savagery." On one occasion, he recorded in his diary: "Yesterday great temptation out of which providence, as it seems to me, rather than grace brought me. If I didn't keep going, going, I should go to pieces. I am like a top that will fall if it stops spinning. Nothing but utmost diligence in God's service keeps me out of the devil's."[26]

To Cable, the primary threat to the "higher life" in the South had been slavery. The southern defense of slavery had isolated white southerners from western culture morally and intellectually. Speaking through Frowenfield, one of the characters in *The Grandissimes,* Cable criticized the closed society of the proslavery South: "Human rights is, of all subjects, the one upon which this community is most violently determined to hear no discussion. It has pronounced that slavery and caste are right, and sealed up the whole subject. What, then, will they do with the world's literature? They will coldly decline to look at it, and will become, more and more as the world moves on, a comparatively illiterate people." If the defense of slavery had reduced whites in the South to comparative illiteracy, the exploitation of black labor had corrupted them, making them idle and indolent. As Frowenfield complained, "industry is not only despised, but has been degraded and disgraced, handed over into the hands of African savages." Like Jefferson who feared the "boisterous passions," Cable believed that slavery had an even more "maiming" effect: It had destroyed the white Southerner's self-control. The completeness of power the master exercised over the bondsmen made him the slave to his own passions. Without restraints, the slavemaster yielded to his urge for violence; one of the slaves portrayed in *The Grandissimes*—Bras Coupé—had his ears shorn and his tendons severed behind his knees as punishment for running away. Sexual passions, uncontrolled, drove slavemasters to use slave women to satisfy their animal lusts. Thus slavery had inculcated in white Southerners "an attitude of arrogant superiority over all constraint."[27]

But the abolition of slavery, Cable thought, had opened the way for white southerners to achieve the "higher life." The only obstacle which remained was the black population. Constituting a "lower class," blacks threatened to drag down all of society. In Nashville in 1887, Cable wandered into the streets after supper and witnessed the "Saturday night outpour of the town's black squalor." "I came to a market house," he wrote to his wife. "I cannot describe its offensiveness & squalor. I moved through the throng trying constantly to avoid being touched by the vile rags that hung upon the larger part of the noisy crowd." Black poverty and debasement, for Cable, seemed due to racial inferiority as well as class degradation. In his fictional writings and his essays, Cable repeatedly portrayed blacks as a race under the domination of the instinctual life, antagonistic to civilization and its self-control, refinement, and high intelligence. Thus he described the black of colonial Louisiana as a "most grotesque figure," "nearly naked," his neck, arms, thighs, shanks, and "splay feet" "shrunken, tough, sinewy like a monkey's." One of Bras Coupé's most striking qualities was his "magnificent, half-nude form," his flesh quivering. The "bestialized savagery" of the black was expressed in his wild singing, his "barbaric love-making," and his "sensual" and "devilish" dances. Almost echoing Jefferson's claims of black inferiority, Cable observed: "His songs were not often contemplative. They voiced not outward nature, but the inner emotions and passions of a nearly naked serpent-worshipper. Sleep was his balm, food his reinforcement, the dance his pleasure, rum his longed-for nepenthe. . . ." Under the domination of the "dark inspiration of African drums," blacks danced frenziedly in places like Congo Square in New Orleans, their seminaked bodies turning and bowing in "saturnalian" movements. To Cable, blacks epitomized the "frightful triumph of body over mind."[28]

Fearfully aware of the presence of this body-dominated group within southern society, Cable insisted that the South should offer blacks "justice" and try to reform them, not oppress them and perpetuate their "barbarity." Thus Cable arrived at a simple solution to the "Negro Question." White southerners should let nature take its course. "Inequality" was a "principle in nature," Cable assured them, and social equality of the races was a "fool's dream." They should not work so hard and enact so many laws to "hold apart two races" which really had "no social affinity at all." Such legislation was unnecessary, for the two races had "natural preferences of like for like." In his protest against segregation in the schools, published in the New Orleans Bulletin in 1875, Cable urged white southerners to leave alone natural social affinities:

Our children will do as we did when we were in school. They will select and confer free companionship upon certain playmates, according to their own and their parents' ideas of mental caliber, moral worth, and social position, and the rest of the school may go its way. This fact, then, is rather an argument against our hostility. The schoolroom neither requires nor induces social equality. Social equality is a matter of personal preference, which preference must be mental before the social equality can begin to exist.

Essentially Cable was calling for laissez-faire in race relations: Free from government interference and regulation, the "instinctive antagonism" between the two races would prevail and the "Caucasian race" would preserve its "high purity" without the aid of "onerous civil distinctions."[29]

For Cable, whites had a special responsibility to preserve their racial purity: They were the custodians of mind and civilization. He repeatedly stated his opposition to social integration and racial amalgamation. Grady revealed how much he misunderstood Cable when he argued that "the South will never adopt Cable's suggestion of the social intermingling of the races." After the publication of Grady's attack, Cable insisted: "I have never in so much as a sentence, whether spoken or written, advocated any private social commingling of the two races. I heartily deprecate any rash experiments in that direction." In "The Silent South," published in 1885, Cable wrote: "Now, 'The Freedman's Case in Equity' pleads for not one thing belonging to the domain of social relations. Much less family relation; it does not hint the faintest approval of any sort of admixture of the two bloods. . . . Nationalization by fusion of bloods is the maxim of barbarous times and peoples." Such "times" had occurred under slavery. Cable argued that slavery, undermining the self-control of white men—the masters of black slave women—had been responsible for the "pollution" of the races.[30]

Cable's hope was the development of national unity without "hybridity." Since the two races were not inclined to "mix spontaneously," this could be achieved "naturally." The common enjoyment of equal civil rights had never mixed the two races, he claimed, but "oppressive distinctions" between the races held out "temptations to vice" and led to the "fusion of bloods." Made forbidden and illicit, interracial sex became powerfully appealing to both races. In this respect, segregation threatened rather than preserved racial order, tempting "superior Caucasians" to mix promiscuously with blacks, causing their biracial offspring to desire desperately to be white. Cable made this point repeatedly through his fictional characters. Laws for segregation were "crezzie," snaps Madame Delphine in one of Cable's stories in Old Creole Days as she ridicules the law prohibiting interracial marriage. Then insightfully, she adds that whites did not make that law to keep the two races apart: "Separate! No-o-o! They do not want to keep us separated; no, no! But they do want to keep us despised." But to make blacks feel despised, Cable apprehensively noted, was also to force mulattoes to hide their racial identity and become an elusive and anxious threat to white racial purity. In another story, " 'Tite Poulette," a mother instructs her daughter: "If any gentleman should ever love you and ask you to marry—not knowing, you know,—promise me you will not tell him you are not white." Cable's warning was clear: Better to abolish segregation and give blacks "public equality" than for whites not to know who was "not white."[31]

Cable's plea for "justice" for blacks sprang not only from a concern for white racial purity but also from a desire to raise blacks as individuals to the "higher life." He urged whites to feel "magnanimity not scorn" for the "inferior" blacks; they should give blacks the opportunity to uplift themselves, make themselves as much as possible intelligent and "genteel." Whites should treat blacks as individuals: "The core of the colored man's grievance is that the individual in matters of right that do not justly go by race is treated . . . without regard to person, dress, behavior, character, or aspirations, in public and by law, as though the African tincture, much or little, were itself stupidity, squalor, and vice." In this way, the individual black would be encouraged to become civilized. No longer shut out from aspirations, he would work to overcome temptations and turn with "new hope and desire toward the prizes of industry, frugality, and a higher cultivation." He would refine his tastes so that the "rank energies to his present nature" would not, as they presently did, "run entirely to that animal fecundity characteristic of all thriftless, reckless, unaspiring populations. . . ." Thus the solution to the "Negro Problem," for Cable, was to grant blacks "public rights" so that individually they would be free to improve themselves and develop republican qualities or "decline and disappear."[32]

His "animal fecundity" repressed, the black as a "genteel" individual was particularly attractive to Cable. As a writer, Cable sought out the company and friendship of refined and cultivated black intellectuals. He was fond of Booker T. Washington, the educator who had assisted him in his research on southern blacks. He also enjoyed his conversations with the black historian George Washington Williams, whom he regarded as "a scholar, a man of affairs, polished, graceful." Cable developed an even deeper and more pleasurable relationship with the black novelist Charles W. Chesnutt. He took a special interest in Chesnutt, wanting to help the aspiring writer get started. He sent one of Chesnutt's short stories to the editor of the *Century Magazine,* and the young writer was most appreciative. "I trust your kind word in its favor, coupled with such merits as the story itself may possess," Chesnutt wrote to his literary sponsor, "will help 'Rena Walden' to run the gauntlet of editorial criticism and break into the charmed pages of the 'Century.' " Cable saw in Chesnutt what he hoped blacks as individuals would be. After visiting Chesnutt's home, he wrote to his wife with great pleasure: "I went & found a very bright little home & four goodlooking, well behaved children. . . . I was heartily pleased. He had me look at some of his ms and I got to making suggestions until tea was ready & I staid to tea. The quiet ease & dignity with which they managed their humble but admirable hospitality was worth seeing." Cable, in fact, was so pleased he soon afterward asked Chesnutt to become his personal secretary.[33]

Here were examples of blacks who had achieved the "higher life." What made the relationship with black writers like Chesnutt so enormously satisfying was the assurance it offered: Blacks could, individually, cultivate the restraint and gentility he admired. In the midst of the "New South," where urban "black squalor" and a "noisy" and "vile" black "lower class" threatened civilization, and where blacks were increasingly drawn into an industrial working class, Cable desperately needed such assurance. Shortly before Cable met Chesnutt, he had visited the smelting furnaces of Birmingham, Alabama—the southern counterpart of the industrial inferno that Henry Adams had encountered in England. There Cable witnessed a scene that terrified him and that had racial significance. As he walked among the burning blast furnaces, he saw "dark, brawny men standing or moving here and there with the wild glare of molten cinder and liquid metal falling upon their black faces and reeking forms." Black men were working the smelting furnaces and transforming the crude ore of the earth into "one of the prime factors of the world's wealth." Clearly, Cable could see, blacks were already supplying the labor for the massive industrialization of the "New South." This industrial proletarization of blacks alarmed Cable. He believed that the dulling toils of the coal pit and the furnaces and "huddled life" of factory work would create a "thirst for ferocious excitements" and transform these blacks into "dangerous and intractable animals." And he feared that blacks as industrial workers would be drawn toward "the evil charms of unions, secret orders, strikes and bread riots," and look upon the "capitalist" as a "natural enemy." Amid the iron and steel mills of Birmingham, Cable apprehensively viewed the technology of the "New South" and the modern life of industrial conditions and class conflicts it was ushering in as threats to "higher life" in the South.[34]

Despite their differences on the question of segregation, both Grady and Cable shared a need for reassurance from blacks. Grady wanted to have around him old-time blacks, good-natured and steadfast in their loyalty, while Cable sought relationships with the "genteel" and refined. Both men feared that the employment of blacks in the industries of the "New South" would undermine southern paternalism and the racial intimacies they longed to have. Thus, for both Grady and Cable as well as for many white southern businessmen, a tension existed between the hope for industrial "progress" and the desire for racial dependency and order. If they could only have it both ways, wealthy white southerners could feel secure; no wonder they cheered so excitedly and even wept when they heard Booker T. Washington deliver his startling message at the 1895 Atlanta Exposition.

The exposition itself was a symbol of the "New South," and everywhere in the exhibits was Grady's presence. "The man whose genius inspired the enterprise has passed away," a newspaper reporter observed, "but everywhere the dead hand of Henry W. Grady moves and controls this new thing which has come to life." Twenty-five to fifty thousand out-of-town visitors crowded into Atlanta to witness the achievements of the "New South" in industry, commerce, and the arts. Included among the exhibits were the latest advances in technology, such as a battery of eight boilers and fourteen engines with a capacity of 2,250 horsepower, and also a "Negro Building" designed and erected wholly by black mechanics and devoted to "showing the progress of the Negro since freedom." The main entrance of this building had relief work which represented the "slave mammy" and the face of Frederick Douglass; inside, a steam engine built by students was on display at the Tuskegee Institute's exhibit. In contrast to the technological progress the event wished to celebrate, the exposition included reproductions of a "Mexican village," a "Chinese village," an "Indian camp," and a "Dahomey village," in front of which a white man urged visitors not to miss seeing the "wild cannibals" from Africa.[35]

The most noted speaker at the opening of the exposition was Booker T. Washington, principal of the Tuskegee Normal and Industrial Institute of Alabama. The invitation to be one of the speakers had greatly moved him. From slave to honored guest, he was pleased to be given the opportunity to speak to an "audience composed of the wealth and culture of the white South," the representatives of his former masters. The event was momentous: It was the first time in southern history that a black man had been asked to speak at such an important occasion. Actually Washington was not widely known in the South or the nation; it was only after his address, called the "Atlanta Compromise," that he was elevated by white men in power to be the leader of his race.[36]

The reasons why Washington was suddenly catapulted into prominence and leadership were based on both racial and class developments which occurred in the 1890s. Throughout much of the nineteenth century, Frederick Douglass had personified militancy in the struggle for racial equality, and his death in February of 1895 created a vacuum in black leadership. The southern movement to disfranchise and segregate blacks as well as the increase in antiblack lynchings in the South forced them to seek their rights more cautiously and deliberately. Both developments—Douglass's death and the intensification of southern racial repression—encouraged the rise of an accommodationist black leadership. More importantly, at this time industrial capitalists were extremely worried about class strife and disorder, and Washington offered them a vision of a prosperous industrial South where racial and class order and harmony prevailed. A black man, he was preaching the gospel of the "New South."

As Washington stood on the platform, acknowledging "the flower and culture and beauty of the South" on either side of him, he told his black and white listeners sitting in the segregated auditorium, to "cast down their buckets" where they were. To blacks, he declared: "It is at the bottom of life we must begin, and not at the top." Blacks must cultivate friendly relations with the southern white man, their next-door neighbor. The brightest future for the black man was in the South, where he was given a "man's chance in the commercial world." The agitation for "social equality" was the "extremest folly": "The opportunity to earn a dollar in a factory just now is worth infinitely more than the opportunity to spend a dollar in an opera-house." To whites, Washington recommended: Cast down your bucket "among the eight millions of Negroes whose habits you know, whose fidelity and love you have tested in days when to have proved treacherous meant the ruin of your firesides. Cast down your bucket among these people who have, without strikes and labour wars, tilled your fields, cleared your forests, builded your railroads and cities. . . ." Washington assured whites that they would in the future, as they had in the past, be surrounded by "the most patient, faithful, law-abiding, and unresentful people" the world had seen. To both races, Washington dramatically announced: "In all things that are purely social we can be as separate as the fingers, yet one as the hand in all things essential to mutual progress."[37]

Washington's speech "electrified" whites in the audience, drawing from them a "delirium of applause." The "multitude was in an uproar of enthusiasm, handkerchiefs were waved, canes were flourished, hats were tossed in the air," the *New York World* reported. "The fairest women of Georgia stood up and cheered. It was as if the orator had bewitched them." Washington himself was swept up in the wave of excitement. "As I saw these Southern men and these black men and beautiful and cultured Southern women wave their hats and handkerchiefs and clap their hands and shout in approval of what I said, I seem to have been carried away in a vision. . . ." At the close of the speech, former Georgia Governor Rufus B. Bullock rushed across the platform, and for a few moments, the two men stood facing each other, hand in hand. Whites showered Washington with congratulations, saying, "God bless you" and "I am with you." Clark Howell, editor of Grady's *Atlanta Constitution,* burst out: "That man's speech is the beginning of a moral revolution in America."[38]

In his Atlanta address, Washington had in effect offered white men in power a "compromise." The black educator could see anti-black repression everywhere around him in the South: There was an average of about 188 lynchings a year in the country during the 1890s, and recently enacted "Jim Crow" laws were defining the "Negro's place" in trains, streetcars, schools, parks, theaters, hotels, and hospitals. The disfranchisement of blacks was under way as southern states established the poll tax and the literacy requirement for suffrage. In his response to this hardening of racial repression, Washington veiled his rage and publicly promised black accommodation and black support to capitalists in their struggle with labor, in exchange for racial peace and white upper-class paternal care and protection. Within the context of his discussion on race, Washington had given assurances of racial and class order to both the Gradys and Cables of the South, concerned about the "societies of socialism" in the cities and the "evil charms of unions, secret orders, strikes and bread riots." He also made a pledge to businessmen everywhere in the United States that the black, true to his antebellum self, would remain close and loyal to white capitalists and work hard to earn a "dollar" in a "factory."

No wonder upper-class whites in the great hall cheered wildly as the new black "leader" depicted the industrial progress and interracial dependency that awaited them in the "New South," and told them that his people would work patiently and faithfully in its fields and factories without "strikes" and "labour wars." Apprehensive of the social disorders and class tensions which threatened their hegemony in the early 1890s—the Homestead Strike, the New Orleans General Strike, the miners' armed rebellion against the Tennessee Coal and Iron Company, and the Pullman Strike—white businessmen were pleased and anxious to have a black leader tell them they could look forward to the cooperation of black workers in the conflict between capital and labor.

Shortly after Washington had given his opening speech, President Grover Cleveland telegraphed a message of good wishes to the Atlanta Exposition. Then, in Gray Cables, Massachusetts, the President pulled a switch, turning on the Exposition's great fountain and thousands of lights. As they witnessed the dramatic dispatch of an electric spark from Massachusetts to Georgia, white men of power and progress could feel confidence in their technology; and, as they looked at the interracial scene around them, they could affirm their superiority over peoples of color. In the electric incandescence could be seen whites intermingling with what one visitor described as "horn-blowing Dahomeyans," "sombre-eyed Mexicans," "American Indians," and "old-time Negroes in old-time costumes." And, here and there in the crowds could also be seen "gorgeous pig-tailed Chinamen."[39]

CHAPTER X

THE "HEATHEN CHINEE" AND AMERICAN TECHNOLOGY

A surplus labouring population . . . forms a disposable industrial reserve army, that belongs to capital as absolutely as if the latter had bred it at its own cost. . . . [I]t creates, for the changing needs of the self-expansion of capital, a mass of human material always ready for exploitation. . . . The industrial reserve army, during periods of stagnation and average prosperity, weighs down the active labour-army; during the periods of over-production and paroxysm, it holds its pretensions in check.

—*Karl Marx*

In 1851, six years before Hinton Helper would issue his inflammatory appeal for the overthrow of the planter class and the forced removal of all blacks from America, he traveled to California where he was appalled to see so many Chinese living and working in the recently conquered territory. Like Jefferson, Helper believed society should be homogeneous. "Certain it is," he wrote in his book *The Land of Gold,* "that the greater the diversity of colors and qualities of men, the greater will be the strife and conflict of feeling." He had left North Carolina to get away from blacks and to find vacant lands and freedom from the "diversity of color" that existed in the settled parts of the country. His hope that the West would offer sanctuary to white America was shattered when he encountered the Chinese in California. "Our population was already too heterogeneous before the Chinese came," he protested. "I should not wonder at all, if the copper of the Pacific yet becomes as great a subject of discord and dissension as the ebony of the Atlantic."[1]

Eighteen years later, the Reverend John Todd of Massachusetts visited California where he found the Chinese in even greater numbers. But Todd did not feel racial anxiety. In his account of his trip, *The Sunset Land,* he gave reassurance to the Helpers of America:

> If, then, I am told, as I am almost every day, that this conglomerate mass, made up of Anglo-Saxons, Europeans, Africans, Chinamen, and a sprinkling of all nations, is hereafter to cement into a sort of puddingstone race, I reply, it may be so, but I do not believe it. God has given this continent to the strongest race on earth, and to the freest and best educated part of that race, and I do not believe he is going to let it drop out of hands that can handle the globe, and put it into hands that are hands without educated brains.

Reverend Todd was confident such a divine plan existed, for he believed he had seen it manifested at Promontory Point, Utah. There he had offered official prayers at the celebration for the completion of the transcontinental railroad.[2]

Ah Sin in America

What Helper and Todd were witnessing was the influx of thousands and thousands of immigrants from the Far East. Between 1850 and 1880, the Chinese population in the United States shot up from 7,520 to 105,465, a fifteenfold increase; in 1870 the Chinese constituted 8.6 percent of the total population of California and an impressive 25 percent of the wage-earning force.[3] Significantly, in their descriptions of these new immigrants, whites tended to identify them with groups they had historically set apart from themselves—blacks and Indians.

During the years of first encounters and impressions, the Chinese were subjected to what historian Dan Caldwell has described as a process of "Negroization." Time and again the Chinese immigrants were likened to blacks. Shortly after the Civil War, *The New York Times* issued a warning which depicted both the newly freed blacks and the newly imported Chinese as threats to republicanism: "We have four millions of degraded negroes in the South . . . and if there were to be a flood-tide of Chinese population—a population befouled with all the social vices, with no knowledge or appreciation of free institutions or constitutional liberty, with heathenish souls and heathenish propensities, whose character, and habits, and modes of thought are firmly fixed by the consolidating influences of ages upon ages—we should be prepared to bid farewell to republicanism. . . ." The *San Francisco Chronicle* compared the Chinese "coolie" to the black slave, and condemned both as antagonistic to free labor: "When the coolie arrives here he is as rigidly under the control of the contractor who brought him as ever an African slave was under his master in South Carolina or Louisiana." Invoking Jefferson's idea of colonization, Senator John T. Morgan of Alabama regretted the impossibility of black removal and warned: "After you have got the Chinese here, and they become incorporated in one way or another with your social, industrial, and political institutions, the power will be found wanting to expel them." Governor Henry Haight echoed the free soil argument in his 1868 "Inaugural Remarks" when he declared: "No man is worthy of the name of patriot or statesman who countenances a policy which is opposed to the interests of the free white laboring and industrial classes. . . . What we desire for the permanent benefit of California is a population of white men who will make this State their home, bring up families here and meet the responsibilities and discharge the duties of freemen. We ought not to desire an effete population of Asiatics. . . ." Thus, the Chinese, like blacks, were stereotyped as enemies to republican and free-labor society.[4]

The language used to describe the Chinese had been employed before: Racial qualities that had been assigned to blacks became Chinese characteristics. Calling for Chinese exclusion, the editor of the *San Francisco Alta* claimed the Chinese had most of the vices of the African: "Every reason that exists against the toleration of free blacks in Illinois may be argued against that of the Chinese here." Heathen, morally inferior, savage, and childlike, the Chinese were also viewed as lustful and sensual. Chinese women were condemned as "a depraved class," and their depravity was associated with their almost Africanlike physical appearance. While their complexions in some instances approached "fair," one writer observed, their whole physiognomy indicated "but a slight removal from the African race." Chinese men were denounced as sexual threats to white women. White parents were advised not to send their daughters on errands to the Chinese laundry where horrible things happened to white girls in the back rooms. On one occasion in 1876, a *New York Times* reporter inquired about "a handsome but squalidly dressed young white girl" he found in an opium den. The owner replied: "Oh, hard time in New York. Young girl hungry. Plenty come here. Chinaman always have something to eat, and he like young white girl, He! He!" Writing for *Scribner's Monthly,* Sarah E. Henshaw instructed American mothers: "No matter how good a Chinaman may be, ladies never leave their children with them, especially little girls." White workers were told that Chinese competition drove wages down and forced wives of poor white men into prostitution. Compelled to sell their bodies to "Chinamen," white women were infected with the

THE QUESTION OF THE HOUR: *Uncle Sam:*—Gosh! I've got this critter lassoed right enough but how in thunder am I going to git him over thar to China?

From The Wasp Magazine, *January–June 1893, Vol. 30, pp. 10–11. I am grateful to the California State Library, Sacramento, and to Roberto Haro for helping me locate this cartoon.*

"leprosy of the Chinese curse." Concerned over what he thought was the syphilitic threat of the Chinese, Dr. Arthur B. Stout warned that the introduction of Chinese and blacks into American society was like "a cancer" in the "biological, social, religious and political systems." The "Negroization" of the Chinese reached a high point when a magazine cartoon depicted them as a bloodsucking vampire with slanted eyes, a pigtail, dark skin, and thick lips. White workers made the identification even more explicit when they referred to the Chinese as "nagurs."[5]

While the Chinese were "Negroized," they were also assigned qualities which distinguished them from blacks in important ways. They were viewed as "intelligent," not "ignorant and brutish" like blacks; they would make "dexterous cotton-pickers, never bungling ones." "Quiet" and "peaceful," they were not given to "excessive hilarity"; they made "excellent houseservants," occasionally "sullen but never stupid." "Emancipation has spoiled the negro and carried him away from the fields of agriculture," the editor of the *Vicksburg Times* wrote in 1869. "Our prosperity depends entirely upon the recovery of lost ground, and we therefore say let the Coolies come. . . ." That same year a southern planters' convention in Memphis announced that it was "desirable and necessary to look to the teeming population of Asia for assistance in the cultivation of our soil and the development of our industrial interests." In his address to the convention, labor contractor Cornelius Koopmanshoop said that his company had imported 30,000 Chinese workers into California, and that many of them were working as mechanics and railroad laborers. Other supporters of Chinese labor suggested that the Chinese need not replace the blacks as workers. Rather the Chinese could be used as models to help discipline and reform blacks. Hard-working, economical, and frugal, the Chinese would be the "educators" of the blacks. In terms of industrial labor, the Chinese were thought to have more ability than blacks. The introduction of machinery was rendering black labor obsolete, it was claimed, for what was required in an industrial mode of production was "a much higher standard of intelligence." When placed in charge of labor-saving machines, the Chinese were found to be quick learners and competent operators. Even the qualities that were thought to distinguish the Chinese from blacks served as a basis for racial and class domination: They justified the use of Chinese as servants and a factory proletariat.[6]

The Chinese in America were compared not only with blacks but also with Indians. The winning of the West from the "Red Man" would be in vain, the editor of California's *Marin Journal* declared, if whites were now to surrender the conquered land to a "horde of Chinese." Indeed, for many whites, the Chinese were the "new barbarians." The association between Indians and Chinese suggested one way to handle the "Chinese Problem." "We do not let the Indian stand in the way of civilization," stated former Governor Horatio Seymour of New York, "so why let the Chinese barbarian?" In his letter published in *The New York Times,* Seymour continued: "Today we are dividing the lands of the native Indians into states, counties and townships. We are driving off from their property the game upon which they live, by railroads. We tell them plainly, they must give up their homes and property, and live upon corners of their own territories, because they are in the way of our civilization. If we can do this, then we can keep away another form of barbarism which has no right here." Senator Morgan of Alabama said he "likened" the Chinese to the Indians, "inferior" socially and politically and subject to the control of the federal government. If the Congress could locate Indians on reservations, he asked, why could it not do it also to the Chinese?[7]

Occasionally all three groups—blacks, Indians, and Chinese—were lumped together. What they all had in common was made clear in the 1854 California Supreme Court decision in the case of *People v. Hall.* "No black, or mulatto person, or Indian shall be allowed to give evidence in favor of, or against a white man," the court declared. "Held, that the words, Indian, Negro, Black, and White are generic terms, designating races. That, therefore, Chinese and all other people not white, are included in the prohibition from being witnesses against whites." Thus, like blacks and Indians, the Chinese were "not white." The California superintendent of education applied the same color line to public schools. In 1859 he insisted the schools be racially segregated. "If this attempt to force Africans, Chinese, and Diggers [a term applied to a group of California Indians] into one school is persisted in it must result in the ruin of the schools," he warned. "The great mass of our citizens will not associate on terms of equality with these inferior races; nor will they consent that their children should do so." A year later, the California legislature authorized him to withhold public funds from any school which admitted the proscribed groups, and set up provisions for separate schools. This tendency to group together blacks, Indians, and Chinese was not peculiar to California. President Rutherford Hayes viewed the "Chinese Problem" within the broad context of race in America. The "present Chinese labor invasion," he wrote in 1879, was "pernicious and should be discouraged. Our experience in dealing with the weaker races—the Negroes and Indians, for example,—is not encouraging. . . . I would consider with favor any suitable measures to discourage the Chinese from coming to our shores."[8]

In the imagination of anti-Chinese exclusionists, however, the "race" from the Far East posed a greater threat to white America than did blacks and Indians. Intelligent and competitive, Chinese men could easily eliminate the need for white labor and force white workers into poverty and idleness. Moreover, since they were coming only to make money and return to China, they could drain America of her wealth and energies.

All of these fears were acted out in 1879 in the play *The Chinese Must Go*, by Henry Grimm of San Francisco. In this fantasy, the Chinese conspire to destroy white labor, as the audience learns from a conversation between Ah Coy and Sam Gin.

> AH COY.   By and by white man catchee no money; Chinaman catchee heap money; Chinaman workee cheap, plenty work; white man workee dear, no work—sabee?
>
> SAM GIN.   Me heep sabee.
>
> . . .
>
> AH COY.   White man damn fools; keep wifee and children—cost plenty money; Chinaman no wifee, no children, save plenty money. By and by, no more white workingman in California; all Chinaman—sabee?

In the play, the Chinese danger is depicted in terms of a vivid metaphor—Chinese "parasites" attacking the body of "Uncle Sam." Thus Frank B., a white man, says to a friend:

> You wasted your dimes in a candy store, I see. Let me tell you, if I take a four-bit piece, buy meat and flour with it, digest it, it turns into blood; therefore, money is blood. Now, what would you think of a man who would allow a lot of parasites to suck every day a certain quantity of blood out of his body, when he knows that his whole constitution is endangered by this sucking process; mustn't he be either an idiot or intend self-destruction? And suppose those Chinese parasites should suck as much blood out of every State in the Union, destroying Uncle Sam's sinews and muscles, how many years do you think it would take to put him in his grave?

Here, indeed, was a most ominous future for the republic. Men without families here to support, the Chinese could work for low wages. Unless the Chinese were excluded from America, they would continue to render white men impotent in the job market, and "suck" the blood from "Uncle Sam."[9]

Three years later, Congress prohibited the immigration of Chinese laborers. The 1882 Chinese Exclusion Act made it unlawful for Chinese laborers to enter the country, and declared the Chinese already here ineligible for United States citizenship. The law was a candid expression of racism; as Massachusetts Senator George F. Hoar put it in his criticism of the bill, the law discriminated against the Chinese because of "the color of their skin." Support for the legislation was overwhelming and geographically wide-spread: The House vote, for example, was 201 yeas, 37 nays, and 51 absent. While congressmen from the West and South gave it unanimous support, a large majority from the East (53 out of 77) and the Midwest (59 out of 72) also voted for the prohibition. Once more, as they had in their encounters with blacks and Indians, white Americans had to ask themselves who were the "real people ," to use President Jackson's phrase. Once more, as they had in the enactment of the 1790 Naturalization Law which required the prospective citizen to be "white," they had to define their national purpose and to determine the relationship between race and nationality. The discussion this time, however, had a different emphasis. In the white imagination, the Chinese were located in the future. Unlike blacks and Indians, they were "coming" to America; moreover, they were directly identified with America as a modern industrial society, and their presence as an "industrial army of Asiatic laborers" was exacerbating the conflict between white labor and capital. Exclusionist supporters feared this conflict would lead to social revolution and chaos. They anxiously asked whether the American mechanic and worker, "forced to the wall" and degraded by Chinese labor, would continue to place his own labor in the market with the "faith" that he could receive a "civilized price" for it. They worried about the struggle between labor unions and the industrial "nabobs" and "grandees," the employers of Chinese labor; and they apprehensively viewed the "disorder, strikes, riot, and bloodshed" sweeping through the industrial cities of America. "The gate," exclusionists in Congress declared, "must be closed." Thus, one of the most critical concerns which led to the Chinese Exclusion Act was the fearful prospect that American society would be destroyed between the millstones of a hungry and violent white working class and a yellow proletariat under the control of an American industrial elite.[10]

During the congressional discussion on the exclusion bill, the editor of *The Nation* remarked that the prohibition of Chinese immigration would appeal to white workers, particularly the "hard-working" "Bill Nyes" of the Pacific Coast. Ironically the man who had created Bill Nye and who played a crucial role in the development of anti-Chinese attitudes in America regarded himself as a friend of the Chinese. This was Bret Harte, editor of the *Overland Monthly* and author of the poem "Plain Language from Truthful James," also known as "The Heathen Chinee." Published in Harte's magazine in 1870, the poem became very popular as newspaper after newspaper across the country reprinted it and imprinted the phrase *Heathen Chinee* in the mind of white America.[11]

The poem gave Harte instant and gratifying attention. Noticing Harte's sudden rise to fame, Mark Twain observed that the poem had brought "reverberations of delight which reached the last confines of Christendom," and that Harte's name "from being obscure to invisible" in one week had become "as notorious and as visible in the next as if it had been painted on the sky in letters of astronomical magnitude." On January 7, 1871, the editors of the *New York Globe* announced that they had been obliged to publish the poem twice to answer the demands of the public, and claimed that every newspaper in the country had printed the poem. "Certainly nothing has been printed of late, if ever, which has run through the newspapers of this country as this has," the editor of the *Springfield Republican* declared in his review of the poem. "Part of this effect is owing to the temporary excitement of the public about the Chinese question,— but the combination of delicate humor, and force of expression, both plain and grotesque, seen in these verses would have made them famous at any time."[12]

The timing of the poem's publication was the most important factor contributing to its immense and sudden popularity. The transcontinental railroad had been completed in 1869, and thousands of Chinese, released from employment in railroad construction, were moving into the cities and becoming more visible than ever before. White workers in California increasingly saw the Chinese as competitors in the job market, working for low wages and depressing the standard of living. Furthermore, fear of the Chinese was no longer confined to the West. Until 1870, the Chinese had been mainly a "California problem"; three months before the appearance of Harte's poem, however, the first Chinese workers had arrived in North Adams, Massachusetts, setting off hysterical reactions in the East. Thus the "Chinese problem" had become national.[13]

Harte's poem on the "heathen Chinee" helped to crystallize and focus anti-Chinese anxieties and paranoia. White workers used the poem for their slogans and politicians quoted from it as they argued for the exclusion of the Chinese, while cartoonists illustrated and playwrights dramatized the poem. Intended to be humorous, Harte's rhymes evoked from white America a nervous chuckle.

The poem describes a card game between Ah Sin and William Nye. Determined to beat his opponent, Nye has cards stuffed up his sleeves; yet, even with his extra cards, he loses time and again. Ah Sin has a "childlike" smile, but the reader learns

> That for ways that are dark
> And for tricks that are vain
> The heathen Chinee is peculiar

Suddenly, Nye catches Ah Sin cheating, and shouts: "We are ruined by Chinese cheap labour." As Nye attacks the "heathen Chinee," he discovers that Ah Sin, too, has cards stuffed up his sleeves.[14]

Clearly, the poem is ambiguous: While it negatively stereotypes the Chinese, it also portrays Nye as a cheat and a man of violence. Yet, what most impressed Harte's readers, feeling amused and anxious at once, was the "heathen Chinee's" "peculiar" ways, his deceptiveness and slyness, his "sin"-fulness, and his threat to white labor. Harte himself quickly realized what was happening: He saw that the poem was appealing to the racism of American society and to the class resentment of white workers worried about "Chinese cheap labour." The success of the poem plunged him into painful ambivalence. He enjoyed the fame and wealth the poem's popularity gave him; yet he also hated himself for writing a poem which helped to galvanize hostility against the Chinese. Unable to contain his feelings of guilt, he once privately remarked: "Perhaps you can have little respect for a poet who wrote such trash as the *Heathen Chinee.*" Harte reportedly also called it "the worst poem I ever wrote, possibly the worst poem anyone ever wrote."[15]

Yet, as a young writer on the make, Harte was extremely anxious about success, hungering for literary recognition and worrying constantly about financial problems. After the publication of the poem, Harte's magazine, the *Overland Monthly,* increased its circulation substantially. The poem also boosted Harte's success as a writer of sentimental local-color short stories such as "The Outcasts of Poker Flat." A year after the poem had rippled eastward across the country, Harte made a pilgrimage to Boston, the heartland of culture, where he met and had dinner with the important literary men of the age—Richard Henry Dana and William Dean Howells. The *Atlantic Monthly* offered him a generous contract, and he lectured to large audiences filled with distinguished people. Harte had, it seemed, made it.[16]

But then Harte had to worry about whether he would be able to maintain his reputation. The attention as well as the fortune he received disappeared almost as suddenly as they had appeared, and for the rest of his life Harte struggled desperately to recapture his success. Leaving his wife and children in America, he went to Europe to take a government position in order to give himself more time to write, producing a prodigious amount of mediocre literature. In letters to his wife, Harte left behind a sad record of his obsession to rework the tailing of his literary materials and strike again the vein of success. "I grind out the old tunes on the old organ," he wrote to her on September 13, 1879, "and gather up the coppers, but I never know whether my audience behind the window blinds are wishing me to 'move on' or not." But he kept writing, forcing himself to the "grim routine" of his work, only to be told, as he reported to her on August 17, 1885, that the United States minister to Germany had remarked that Harte was completely "played out" in America. Two years later he admitted to her that he had placed his work "above *everything else*" and had gone into exile in order to give his publishers the impression he was "independent" and "a distinguished foreigner" and to keep up the "prices" of his writings in America. "These are the selfish considerations that are keeping me here, in spite of estranging years, apart from each other, and adding an unnatural loneliness to our lives."[17] Unable to regain the literary laurels which had slipped away, Harte never did return to America.

After the publication of "The Heathen Chinee," he continued to write about the Chinese in America. While he felt sorry for them and may have felt a special sympathy for them because of his partly Jewish heritage, he also created in his writings negative images which helped to perpetuate the injustice and violence committed against them. Thus, like his popular poem, his short stories, such as "Wan Lee, the Pagan" and "See Yup," protested against yet reinforced anti-Chinese racism in America.

In "Wan Lee, the Pagan," the narrator visits merchant Hop Sing who is described as a "grave, decorous, handsome gentleman" with a pigtail and a complexion "like a very nice piece of glazed brown paper-muslin." He has an "urbane, although quite serious" manner, and speaks French and English fluently. In the merchant's warehouse, which has a "deliciously commingled mysterious foreign odor," they have a snack, drinking tea and tasting sweetmeats from a "mysterious jar" that looks as if it might contain "a preserved mouse."

The principal character in the story is Wan Lee, a twelve-year-old youth who lives with Hop Sing in San Francisco. Harte finds Wan Lee very likable: He is also quite impish, good at "imitation," and "superstitious," carrying around his neck "a hideous little porcelain god." Wan Lee "knows but little of Confucius, and absolutely nothing of Mencius," reports Hop Sing. "Owing to the negligence of his father, he associated, perhaps too much with American children." Thus Wan Lee seems to be partly acculturated, and as the story develops, his acculturation becomes crucial to the plot: He meets and falls in love with a white girl.

Wan Lee and the girl have much affection for each other. "Bright," "cheery," and "innocent," she "touches" and reaches "a depth in the boy's nature that hitherto had been unsuspected." As she goes to school, he walks behind her, carrying her books—an act of affection which provokes attacks from "Caucasian Christian" boys. He also makes beautiful presents for her, and she reciprocates. She reads and sings to him. Representing the mainstay of beauty and culture, she is delicate and feminine, epitomizing the qualities of true womanhood. She teaches him "a thousand little prettinesses and refinements only known to girls"; gives him a "yellow" ribbon for his pigtail, as best suiting his "complexion"; shows him wherein he is "original and valuable"; takes him to Sunday school with her, against the "precedents" of the school. "Small-womanlike," she triumphs. "So they got along very well together—this little Christian girl, with her shining cross hanging around her plump, white, little neck, and this dark little Pagan, with his hideous porcelain god hidden away in his blouse." But a tragedy awaits them. At the end of the story, Wan Lee is killed during two days of anti-Chinese mob violence in San Francisco—"two days when a mob of her citizens set upon and killed unarmed, defenseless foreigners, because they were foreigners and of another race, religion, and color, and worked for what wages they could get." Enraged at the atrocities of the mob, Harte fires a blast at the "Christian" murderers of Wan Lee.

As it is in his poem on "The Heathen Chinee," the message of "Wan Lee, the Pagan," is ambiguous. The Chinese, in the character of Wan Lee, are depicted as the unfortunate victims of white working-class hatred and cruel and barbaric racism; yet they are also portrayed as a threat to white workers and to racial purity in America. Like Ah Sin, the Chinese who are attacked in San Francisco are described as "cheap labor," working "for what wages they could get." An economic threat, they also endanger racial homogeneity: Wan Lee has a relationship with a white girl, his "dark" and "yellow" skin contrasting with her "white" complexion. Thus Harte's protest against the violence perpetrated by white workers is at odds with the racial images in the story—the images of the Chinese as mice-eaters, "pagan," "dark," "impish," "superstitious," "yellow," and subversive to white labor and to white racial purity—which formed important bases for the victimization of the Wan Lees of America.[18]

Like "Wan Lee, the Pagan," the story of See Yup was intended to condemn the abuse and violence whites inflicted upon the Chinese in California. Yet, again the negative stereotypes were presented: See Yup, a laundryman in a small mining town, is a "heathen," "superstitious," and has a "peculiar odor"—half ginger, half opium—called the "Chinese smell."

In this story, See Yup is the target of racist attacks from the town's white miners. "Subject to the persecutions of the more ignorant and brutal," he is "always" a "source of amusement" to whites. White boys tie his pigtails to a window, and white miners take their dirty clothes to his laundry and then pick up their cleaned clothes without paying him. One of these miners arrogantly exclaims that his "finer religious feelings" revolt against paying money to a "heathen." The victim of racial scorn and exploitation, See Yup knows he can find no justice or recourse in the courts.

Narrator Harte notices that the miners, who degrade See Yup, are suffering from indigestion. This surprises him. Why should healthy young men, living outdoors, have heartburn? And he comments:

> Whether it was the result of the nervous, excitable temperament which had brought them together in this feverish hunt for gold; whether it was the quality of the tinned meats or half-cooked provisions they hastily bolted, begrudging the time it took to prepare and consume them; whether they too often supplanted their meals by tobacco or whiskey, the singular physiological truth remained that these young, finely selected adventurers . . . actually suffered more from indigestion than the pampered dwellers of the cities.

Thus, in the gold fields of California, the qualities of nervousness and acquisitiveness which Tocqueville thought were pervasive in American society during the Jacksonian era seem to have been extracted from the East and concentrated in the West. The white miners are so anxious to strike it rich they hastily wolf down "tinned" and "half-cooked" food. They also live in a virtually all-male society, far away from the genteel society of women and family in the East. The dichotomization between men (the world of business) and women (the world of the home) seems to have become regionalized, located respectively in the West and the East. And in the male society of the mining camp, white men turn to the Chinese—to See Yup—to do their laundry.

This relationship provides Harte with the framework for his plot. See Yup, the victim of exploitation and assaults, enters the Wells Fargo office one Saturday, and sends to San Francisco a bag of gold dust valued at $500 which he appears to have gathered while working the tailings of an abandoned mine. He sends gold to San Francisco three Saturdays in a row; the clerk at the Wells Fargo office notices See Yup's good fortune and quickly spreads the news that See Yup has made a strike. The white miners organize themselves into a committee and visit See Yup's mine. In two short hours, they witness See Yup and his fellow Chinese miners take out $20 worth of gold from the sand and gravel. The work is being performed in the "stupidest, clumsiest, yet *patient* Chinese way." And the white miners exclaim: "What might not white men do with better appointed machinery!" The miners form a syndicate and force See Yup to sell his mine, offering him a meager $20,000. Aware he has no choice, he yields to the miners' demand and leaves town. The miners take over operations, bringing in "new machinery" to assist them. Some gold is taken in the first week, but nothing is found the next week. Suspicious, the miners soon learn what had happened. See Yup had secretly borrowed $500 worth of gold dust from a friend, openly sent the gold to San Francisco, and had Chinese runners return it to him. After he had been compelled to sell his mine at a "loss," he had salted the mine with some gold dust and left town, taking with him the money his oppressors had forced him to accept.

Harte's point is clear: The white miners deserve what they got. Significantly, See Yup used deception, intelligence, and Chinese runners to triumph over the miners and their technology—their "new machinery" and their telegraph. The references to technology help to delineate the difference between Chinese and whites. During one of their conversations, Harte asks See Yup: "Don't you think the electric telegraph wonderful?" And the laundryman replies: "Velly good for Mellican man; plenty makee him jump." Harte could not tell whether See Yup had confounded the telegraph with electrogalvanism, or was only satirizing "our American haste and feverishness." The Chinese have something mysterious which makes up for their lack of technology. "We knew that the Chinese themselves possessed some means of secretly and quickly communicating with one another," Harte remarks. "Any news of good or ill import to their race was quickly disseminated through the settlement before *we* knew anything about it. An innocent basket of clothes from the wash, sent up from the river-bend, became in some way a library of information; a single slip of rice-paper, aimlessly fluttering in the dust of the road, had the mysterious effect of diverging a whole gang of coolie tramps away from our settlement."[19] Thus, See Yup represents Merlin-like an ominous threat to nervous American men: He is able to render impotent white superiority in technology.

In his poem and stories about the "heathen Chinee," Harte was criticizing American society—its pressure on everyone to strive for material success, its arrogant pride in technological progress, and its racism, particularly the anti-Chinese antagonism and violence of the white working class. Yet his life and his writing, reflecting some of the achievement-oriented anxieties and the very racist values he satirized and condemned, contained within them an irony Harte himself could not have missed. Moreover, in these writings, Harte was portraying the Chinese not only as merchants and laundrymen but also as laborers. Unlike Hop Sing and See Yup, Ah Sin represented "Chinese cheap labour" and participated in the advancement of American technology as a worker. Like Bill Nye and other white workers, he was a part of the working class which American capitalists inducted into their service and exploited; involved in the construction of the transcontinental railroad and the industrial development of the West, Ah Sin was the persona of a yellow proletariat.

A Yellow Proletariat: Caste and Class in Industrial America

Many years before the widespread presence of the Chinese in the West and before Harte's poem on "The Heathen Chinee," Aaron H. Palmer, a "Counsellor of the Supreme Court of the United States," had formulated a plan for the future use of Chinese labor in America. Shortly after the end of the war against Mexico, which enabled the United States to acquire California, Palmer submitted to Congress a recommendation for the expansion of American markets into Asia and the importation of Chinese workers to develop American industries. Calling attention to the "increasing importance" of American trade with China, he urged Congress to strengthen steam communication in the Pacific and transform San Francisco into the entrepôt of the West Coast. "The commodious port of *San Francisco*," he declared, "is destined to become the great emporium of our commerce on the Pacific; and so soon as it is connected by a railroad with the Atlantic States, will become the most eligible point of departure for steamers to . . . China." To build the transcontinental railroad as well as to bring the "fertile lands of California" under cultivation, Palmer advocated the immigration of Chinese laborers. "No people in all the East are so well adapted for clearing wild lands and raising every species of agricultural product . . . as the Chinese."[20] Here, in this remarkable report, Palmer had presented a blueprint which explicitly integrated American expansion into Asia and the importation of Chinese laborers.

Twenty-one years later, a writer for the *Overland Monthly* remarked: "If Chinese labor could be used to develop the industries of California," it would be "the height of folly to forbid its entrance to the Golden Gate." The industrial potential of California was enormous: It had every variety of climate and soil for the production of raw material, a nearly completed railroad, an abundance of fuel and water power, markets in Asia and the Pacific, and an "unlimited" supply of "cheap" labor from China.[21] Actually, what this supporter of Chinese immigration was urging was already well under way. The Chinese were already present everywhere in the industrial development of the West.

Nowhere could the importance of Chinese labor be more clearly seen than in the construction of the transcontinental railroad. Due to the short supply of white workers, the Central Pacific Railroad depended almost entirely on Chinese labor. Approximately ninety percent of its 10,000 workers were Chinese. The use of Chinese labor enabled the Central Pacific to accelerate construction. Time was critical to the company's interests, for the amount of money it received in land and subsidy was based on the miles of track it built. The savings derived from the employment of Chinese rather than white workers for the years 1866-69 totaled approximately $5.5 million. The company paid the Chinese workers $31 a month; had it used white workers it would have had to pay them the same wages plus board and lodging, which would have increased labor costs by one-third.[22]

The construction of the railroad, especially through the Sierras, was a Chinese achievement. Not only did they endure the sheer drudgery required to clear woods and lay tracks; they also performed important technical work which involved the use of power drills and explosives to bore tunnels through the Donner Summit. The Chinese workers were, in one observer's description, "a great army laying siege to Nature in her strongest citadel. The rugged mountains looked like stupendous ant-hills. They swarmed with Celestials, shoveling, wheeling, carting, drilling and blasting rocks and earth. . . ." Since time was money for the Central Pacific, the company forced its laborers to work through the winter of 1866. The snow drifts covered men and mountains; the Chinese lived and worked under the snow, with shafts to give them air and lanterns to light the way. Snow slides occasionally buried camps and crews, and frozen corpses, still upright, with tools in their hands, were found in the spring. "The snow slides carried away our camps and we lost a good many men in those slides," a company official reported; "many of them we did not find until the next season when the snow melted."[23]

The Chinese workers went on strike in the spring. Demanding higher wages and an eight-hour day, three to five thousand laborers refused to work; on June 24, 1867, after a strike demand printed in Chinese had been circulated, the Chinese workers walked out "as one man." The company offered to raise their wages from $31 to $35 a month, but the strikers spurned the offer and insisted on $45 a month and a two-hour reduction in the work day. The *San Francisco Alta* condemned the strike as a conspiracy: "The foundation of this strike appears to have been a circular, printed in the Chinese language, sent among them by designing persons for the purpose of destroying their efficiency as laborers." The insinuation was transparent: The strikers' demands had been merely drummed up, and agents of the Union Pacific were behind the Chinese protest. Meanwhile, the Central Pacific management wired New York to inquire about the feasibility of transporting 10,000 blacks to replace the striking Chinese workers. Central Pacific Superintendent Charles Crocker isolated the strikers and cut off their food supply. "I stopped the provisions on them," he reported, "stopped the butchers from butchering, and used such coercive measures." The strike was broken within a week. Called "Crocker's pets," the laborers were praised only as long as they were, in the words of company president Leland Stanford, "quiet, peaceable, industrious, economical—ready and apt to learn all the different kinds of work required in railroad building."[24]

Beaten, the laborers returned to work and completed the railroad, the "new highway to the commerce of Asia." The crucial role of the Chinese workers was widely admitted. In an essay on "Manifest Destiny in the West," a writer for the *Overland Monthly* exclaimed: "The dream of Thomas Jefferson, and the desires of Thomas H. Benton's heart, have been wonderfully fulfilled, so far as the Pacific Railroad and the trade with the old world of the East is concerned. But even they did not prophesy that Chinamen should build the Pacificward end of the road." After the famous meeting of the Central Pacific and the Union Pacific at Promontory Point in 1869, a writer for *Scribner's Magazine* observed: "The Central Pacific would be today a thing of the future had it not been for the labors of the Chinese." And Stanford himself testified: "Without them it would be impossible to complete the western portion of this great national highway within the time required by the acts of Congress."[25] But, in their assessments, Stanford and others failed to mention the cost in terms of Chinese agony and lives required to realize Aaron Palmer's recommendation.

The ceremony at Promontory Point had symbolic significance for white America. Fifteen hundred people, including prominent individuals from across the country, gathered at the historic meeting place. As he watched the celebration, a witness caught the racial and class meaning of the great event:

> One fact . . . forcibly impressed me at the laying of the last nail. Two lengths of rails, fifty-six feet, had been omitted. The Union Pacific people brought up their pair of rails, and the work of placing them was done by Europeans. The Central Pacific people then laid their pair of rails, the labor being performed by Mongolians. The foremen, in both cases, were Americans. Here, near the center of the American Continent, were the united efforts of representatives of the continents of Europe, Asia, and America—America directing and controlling.[26]

The event was the message: The American foremen, in command, transmitted to the watching audience and the nation the superiority of America over Europe and Asia. Morever, the drama of the great connection portrayed symbolically the class and caste social relations in America. Seated in the stands, the class representatives of property watched the representatives of the working class, white and yellow, drive the last nails into the line.

As a labor force, the Chinese were not used exclusively in railroad construction: In fact, they were ubiquitous in the industries of California. By 1870, twenty-six percent of California's Chinese population lived in San Francisco, which was already, by Internal Revenue returns, the ninth leading manufacturing city in the United States. Chinese workers represented forty-six percent of the labor force in the city's four key industries—boot and shoe, woolens, cigar and tobacco, and sewing. The *San Francisco Morning Call* in 1872 reported that nearly half the workingmen employed in the city's factories were Chinese. Four years later, 14,000 Chinese were working in San Francisco industries. In terms of the entire state in 1880, Chinese workers constituted 52 percent of all boot and shoe makers, 44 percent of all brick makers, 84.4 percent of all cigar makers, and 32.7 percent of all woolen mill operators. The significant role of their labor in the industrial development of California was widely recognized. A. W. Loomis, in his article "How Our Chinamen Are Employed," noted the presence of thousands of Chinese factory operatives in woolen mills, knitting mills, paper mills, powder mills, tanneries, shoe factories, and garment industries. In his essay *Chinaman or White Man, Which?* the Reverend O. Gibson argued in 1873: "At the rates of labor which existed in the early days of California, or at the rates which would instantly prevail were the Chinese removed from our midst, not one of the few manufacturing interests which have lately sprung up on these shores, could be maintained a single day." And three years later, R. G. McClellan wrote in his book *The Golden State:* "In mining, farming, in factories and in the labor generally of California the employment of the Chinese has been found most desirable; and much of the labor done by these people if performed by white men at higher wages could not be continued nor made possible."[27]

The question of Chinese labor was not confined to California and the West. In 1870 the discussion suddenly focused on a small New England town: After a long ride on the recently completed transcontinental railroad, seventy-five Chinese workers arrived in North Adams, Massachusetts, to man one of its shoe factories.[28] A relatively unknown little town hidden in the mountains of western Massachusetts, North Adams immediately became the subject of national attention.

North Adams could have been one of Hank Morgan's creations. Between 1840 and 1870, the community had been transformed from an isolated rural village into an industrialized town. According to *Harper's New Monthly Magazine,* it was "one of the busiest little towns, humming and smoking with various industry, and nestled in the most picturesque and mountainous part of the valley of the Housatonic. . . ." The "take-off" for this town occurred after the railroad connected North Adams with Pittsfield in 1846 and opened new market possibilities. The impact of the market was dramatic. Within thirty years, dwellings had increased from 100 to more than 400, and the number of cotton looms had multiplied ten times, from 22 to more than 200. In 1868, the town's 4,000 workers produced $7 million worth of goods. Between 1860 and 1870, the population nearly doubled as it jumped from 6,924 to 12,090; almost one-third of the population were immigrants, particularly Irish. North Adams, in short, had become a concentration of manufacturing, the locus of thirty-eight factories—cotton mills, woolen mills, carriage manufactories, paper mills, and shoe factories.[29]

The owner of one of these busy factories, Calvin T. Sampson, personified the new manufacturing era of North Adams. A descendant of the original settlers of Plymouth Colony, he had begun "life as a farmer at eighteen, with only his father's debts as a legacy. These he assumed, though not legally or morally bound to do so, paying all off to the last penny, and finally establishing himself as a manufacturer of shoes." Washington Gladden, a Congregational minister in North Adams, described businessmen like Sampson as paragons of republican and Yankee virtues: "There is wealth here,—but all of it has been earned; none of it was inherited. All the leading business men began life with no stock in trade but brains and courage. Out of this capital they have created fortunes for themselves, and have built up a flourishing town." Known as "A Model Shoe Factory," Sampson's company produced more than 300,000 pairs annually; and the local press praised it as a successful business, "built up from small beginnings, by persistent energy, industry, economy, and judgment." Actually, Sampson's success depended more on the use of machinery and the exploitation of labor. Three years after he had established his factory in 1858, Sampson introduced the first of Well's pegging machines into shoe manufacturing. The use of heeling machines in his factory, a newspaper reported, increased both efficiency and profits: "Each machine performs the labor of six men, and effects a saving of two cents on every pair of shoes made." The machine also reduced workers to low-paid, unskilled laborers; it transformed craftsmen into tenderers of the machine. Sampson's workers opposed the new machinery and went on strike; Sampson defied the strike and broke it. The mechanization of the boot and shoe industry in Massachusetts enabled factory owners to reduce their labor force and increase their production: Thus, in 1875, they employed one-third fewer workers than in 1855 and produced 15 million more pairs of shoes.[30]

To protect themselves against labor-eliminating machines and low wages, in 1867 workers founded the Secret Order of the Knights of St. Crispin. Within three years, the Crispins became the largest labor organization in the United States; 50,000 strong in membership, the union was especially active in the shoemaking industries of Massachusetts. In 1870 the Crispins at Sampson's shoe factory struck. They demanded higher wages, end of the ten-hour day, access to the company's books in order to fix wages in accordance with profits, and the discharge of workers delinquent in their dues to the Crispin organization. Sampson fired the striking workers. Unsuccessful in his effort to hire scabs from a nearby town, he decided to declare total war against the Crispins and drive a "wedge" into the conflict.[31]

The "wedge" was a contingent of Chinese workers from San Francisco. A year before the Crispin strike against Sampson's factory, the official organ of shoe manufacturers, Hide and Leather Interest, had condemned the Crispins and urged employers to import Chinese workers as strikebreakers. Meanwhile, Sampson had read a newspaper article on the effective use of Chinese labor in a San Francisco shoe factory, and sent his superintendent there to sign a contract with a Chinese contract-labor company. Sampson's superintendent completed his mission successfully. According to the terms of the agreement, Sampson would pay the company a commission for the Chinese workers and transport them to Massachusetts; he would pay each worker $23 a month for the first year and $26 a month for the next two years plus room and fuel. The workers would labor for three years and pay for their own clothing and food.[32]

The arrival of the seventy-five Chinese workers in North Adams on June 13 was a moment of great interest in the East. "A large and hostile crowd met them at the depot," The Nation reported, "hooted them, hustled them somewhat, and threw stones at them. . . ." Thirty plainclothes policemen marched them to their dormitories at Sampson's factory, where they were placed behind locked and guarded gates. A few days later, the Boston Commonwealth exclaimed: "They are with us! the 'Celestials'—with almond eyes, pigtails, rare industry, quick adaptation, high morality, and all—seventy-five of them—hard at work in the town of North Adams." The Springfield Republican predicted the "van of the invading army of Celestials" would free Sampson from "the cramping tyranny of that worst of American trades-unions, the 'Knights of St. Crispin.' "[33] The Chinese, employed everywhere in the industries of California, had been brought to the East. Everyone—white workers as well as employers—watched as Sampson opened his factory again and began production.

They did not have to wait long for results. Within three months, the Chinese workers were producing more shoes than the same number of white workers would have made. The success of Sampson's experiment was reported in the press. "The Chinese, and this especially annoys the Crispins," the editor of *The Nation* announced even before the end of the three-month period, "show the usual quickness of their race in learning the process of their new business, and already do creditable hand and machine work. . . ." The editor of *Harper's New Monthly Magazine* visited Sampson's factory and described the new workers in the December issue: "They are generally small. . . . [A]bout sixty of the Chinese workmen [are] in the room, and there can be nowhere . . . a busier, more orderly group of workmen." Writing for *Scribner's Monthly,* William Shanks agreed. The Chinese "labored regularly and constantly, losing no blue Mondays on account of Sunday's dissipations; nor wasting hours in idle holidays," he reported. "The quality of the work was found to be fully equal to that of the Crispins." Through the use of Chinese labor, Sampson had widened the margin of his profits: The saving in the cost of production for a week's work was $840, which added up to $40,000 a year. These figures inspired Shanks to calculate: "There are 115 establishments in the State, employing 5,415 men . . . capable of producing 7,942 cases of shoes per week. Under the Chinese system of Mr. Sampson, a saving of $69,594 per week, or say $3,500,000 a year, would be effected, thus revolutionizing the trade."[34]

Sampson's success also impressed capitalists in the East. Three months after the Chinese had arrived, James B. Hervey brought sixty-eight Chinese to Belleville, New Jersey, to work in his Passaic Steam Laundry. Like Sampson, with whom he had consulted, Hervey had secured them through a labor contractor in San Francisco. Used to counter strikes by Irish workers and to meet the need for labor, 300 Chinese workers were eventually employed in Hervey's laundry. Meanwhile, the Beaver Falls Cutlery Company in Beaver Falls, Pennsylvania, had transported Chinese laborers east to work in its factory and help eliminate disruptions due to strikes by whites. Within a year, the cutlery company increased the number of its Chinese workers from 70 to 190.[35] The message of North Adams, Belleville, and Beaver Falls was clear: The Chinese constituted an enormous potential and useful source of labor in the development of American capitalism in the East.

The promise of Chinese labor had been proven in the West and its potential had been demonstrated in the East. But the use of Chinese labor and its success raised two crucial questions for white America. "What we shall do with them is not quite clear yet," remarked Samuel Bowles in 1869, in his book *Our New West*. "How they are to rank, socially, civilly, and politically, among us is one of the nuts for our social science students to crack,—if they can. . . ."[36] And what would be the future of white workers in this country as its industrial development depended more and more on Chinese labor?

One answer to both questions was a proposal for the development of a yellow proletariat in America. According to this view, the Chinese would constitute a permanently degraded caste labor force: They would be in effect a unique "industrial reserve army" of migrant laborers forced to be foreigners forever, aliens ineligible for citizenship. Neither "white" (a requirement of the 1790 Naturalization Law) nor "African" by nativity or descent (the naturalization right extended to blacks in 1870), the Chinese were ineligible for naturalized citizenship. They were what Benjamin Franklin had described as "Tawney"; they were not "lovely White." Unlike white ethnic immigrants such as Italians, Poles, and Irish, the Chinese would be a politically proscribed labor force. Thus they would be a part of America's production process but not her body politic. Serving the needs of American capitalism, they would be here only on a temporary basis. "I do not believe they are going to remain here long enough to become good citizens," Central Pacific employer Charles Crocker told a legislative committee, "and I would not admit them to citizenship." Businessmen like Crocker recognized that advances in technology had created new sources of labor for American capitalism: Steam transportation had brought Asia to America's "door" and given American industries access to the "surplus" labor of "unnumbered millions" in Asia. American capitalists would "avail" themselves of this "unlimited" supply of "cheap" Chinese labor to build their railroads and operate their factories; then, after they had completed their service, the Chinese migrant workers would return individually to the "homes" and the "land they loved," while others would come to replace them. The employers of Chinese labor did not want these workers to remain in the country and to become "thick" (to use Crocker's term) in American society.[37]

As an "industrial reserve army" composed of migrant and caste labor, the Chinese would be used to service the industrial needs of American capitalism without threatening the racial homogeneity of America's citizenry. They would be drawn into a labor-supply process which would move labor between China and the United States in a circular pattern. Repressive laws, economic exploitation, harsh working conditions, and racial hatred and violence would assist this process and compel the Chinese to leave the country after a limited period of employment. In this "labor-repressive system," whether the laborers themselves wished to return to China would matter little. Chinese laborers recognized this reality. Ginn Wall, for example, came to America in the 1870s to work on the railroad and brought his wife here. Many years later he told his son repeatedly: "Let's just fold up here. You come with me and we'll go back home. This is a white man's country. You go back to China when you make your money, that is where you belong. If you stay here, the white man will kill you." Other Chinese laborers, regardless of whether they viewed themselves as sojourners or settlers, must have shared Wall's apprehension and terror. The record of Chinese departing from the San Francisco Custom House indicated large numbers were returning to China. As the chart on Chinese arrivals and departures shows (Table 6), the number returning even exceeded the number arriving during the years 1864, 1866, and 1867, and remained constantly high proportionately for the fifteen-year period selected. The number of arrivals suddenly skyrocketed in 1868, 1869, and 1870 primarily in response to the railroad's needs for Chinese labor. This migrant-labor pattern was also reflected in the virtually all-male Chinese population in America. In 1870, for example, there were only 4,574 Chinese women out of a population of 63,199.[38] As a yellow proletariat, Chinese migrant workers would not have families in America, and America would not have a Chinese population granted citizenship by birth.

Table 6. Chinese Arrivals and Departures, 1860–1875: San Francisco Custom House*

Year	Chinese Arrivals	Chinese Departures
1860	7,343	2,088
1861	8,434	3,594
1862	8,188	2,795
1863	6,435	2,947
1864	2,696	3,911
1865	3,097	2,298
1866	2,242	3,113
1867	4,794	4,999
1868	11,085	4,209
1869	14,994	4,896
1870	10,869	4,232
1871	5,542	3,264
1872	9,773	4,887
1873	17,075	6,805
1874	16,085	7,710
1875	18,021	6,305

*Based on information from Mary Coolidge, *Chinese Immigration* (New York, 1969, originally published in 1909), p. 498.

Here, then, from the perspective of American capitalism, was a peculiarly ideal labor force.

As advocates of Chinese labor, capitalists like Sampson and Crocker and their supporters in the press offered a new caste/class ideology. They pointed out the benefits Chinese labor would have for white workers. They said Chinese "cheap" labor would reduce production costs, and the resulting reduction of prices for goods would be equivalent to an increase of wages for white workers. They also argued that Chinese labor would upgrade white workers, for whites would be elevated into foremen and directors. Whites would be the mind and the Chinese the body; the "inventive genius of Americans" would utilize "Asiatic skill and muscle." "If society must have 'mudsills,' it is certainly better to take them from a race which would be benefited by even that position in a civilized community, than subject a portion of our own race to a position which they have outgrown."[39] Thus the Chinese would work the machines, and whites would be the directors of both "Asiatic muscle" and American machinery.

The possibility for advancement which Chinese labor offered white workers would involve far more than mere promotion into foremenship. If they were diligent and thrifty, white workers were told, they could even become capitalists themselves—owners of factories and employers of Chinese labor. They were urged to find "employment for twenty Mongolians to labor, under their supervision, in ditches where they labored themselves before," and to "become employers instead of continuing common laborers." In his testimony before a special legislative committee on Chinese immigration, Charles Crocker explained how this elevation of white workers and the expansion of a white bourgeoisie could occur.

> I believe that the effect of Chinese labor upon white labor has an elevating instead of degrading tendency. I think that every white man who is intelligent and able to work, who is more than a digger in a ditch . . . who has the capacity of being something else, can get to be something else by the presence of Chinese labor easier than he could without it. . . . There is proof of that in the fact that after we got Chinamen to work, we took the more intelligent of the white laborers and made foremen of them. I know of several of them now who never expected, never had a dream that they were going to be anything but shovelers of dirt, hewers of wood and drawers of water, and they are now respectable farmers, owning farms. They got a start by controlling Chinese labor on our railroad.

Meanwhile, in the East, E. L. Godkin of *The Nation* urged white workers to raise themselves into the capitalist class. In an editorial on the employment of Chinese workers in North Adams, Godkin predicted that the importation of Chinese labor would become a favorite mode of resisting strikes all over the country. "Between India and China it is safe to say that capital now has within its reach . . . the labor of three or four hundred millions of very cunning hands, ready to work for small wages, and for as many hours as they can support." Thus it would be "ludicrous" for white workers to struggle against capital. What then should they do? The editor advised the striking Crispins to set up their own cooperative factories and become "capitalists" themselves.[40]

Thus, through Chinese labor, republican virtues of industry and thrift could be promoted and the work ethic could enable men to be "something else." Even the wives of such men could become "something else," for they could depend upon Chinese house servants to lighten their domestic duties. In "A Plea for Chinese Labor," published in *Scribner's Monthly,* Abby Richardson offered the housewives of America the promise of Chinese help in the home. "This is the age when much is expected of woman. She must be the ornament of society as well as the mistress of a well-ordered household." The introduction of Chinese domestics could free her from cooking dinners and nursing children, and give her time for literature, art, and music. Indeed, Richardson predicted, Chinese labor could become a feature of both the factory and the home. In this way tensions of class conflict in white society could be resolved, as Chinese migrant laborers became the "mudsills" of society and as Crispins became "capitalists" and their wives "ornaments of society."[41]

As a yellow proletariat, it was argued, the Chinese would not only provide opportunities for whites to enter the ranks of the bourgeoisie; they would also be used to suppress white workers and their unions. Chinese workers were viewed as "well-behaved" and "obedient"; they belonged to "no striking organizations." As an industrial reserve army, transported to and from America, they could be used to weigh down the "active labour-army" during periods of average prosperity, and hold the "pretensions" of white labor in check during periods of over-production and "paroxysm." Their value to capital in the war against the labor movement in America was widely recognized. In the West, a traveler noted the importance of Chinese workers as strikebreakers: "In the factories of San Francisco they had none but Irish, paying them three dollars a day in gold. They struck, and demanded four dollars. Immediately their places, numbering three hundred, were supplied by Chinamen at one dollar a day. . . ." In the East, Sampson's daring action had sobering effects on workers in the other shoe factories of North Adams. Ten days after the arrival of Sampson's "Mongolian battery," Parker Brothers, Cady Brothers, Millard and Whitman, and E. R. and N. L. Millard forced laborers to return to work with a wage reduction of ten percent. Commenting frankly on the significance of the experiment at North Adams, a contributor to *Scribner's Monthly* wrote: "If for no other purpose than the breaking up of the incipient steps towards labor combinations and 'Trade Unions' . . . the advent of Chinese labor should be hailed with warm welcome. . . ." The "heathen Chinee," he concluded, could be the "final solution" to the labor problem in America.[42]

A Vision of Catastrophe: Henry George and the American Tower of Babel

In their struggle against Sampson in North Adams, the striking Crispins tried to promote working-class solidarity by organizing a Chinese lodge of St. Crispin. Although little is known about this interesting Crispin response to the Chinese strikebreakers, it was probably conditioned by pragmatic concerns: The transformation of Sampson's "Mongolian battery" into Chinese Crispins would have given the union power to destroy Sampson's "wedge." Watching the Crispin drive to recruit the Chinese workers, the editor of *The Nation* remarked: "Chinese lodges and strikes will come in time when enough Chinamen are collected together in any given place; but the prospect appears not immediately flattering at North Adams." Based on practical self-interests rather than an ideological commitment to class solidarity, the Crispin attempt to unionize the Chinese quickly folded. At a meeting in Boston in July 1870 white workers turned against the Chinese workers, angrily condemning Sampson and his fellow capitalists for reducing "American labor" to "the Chinese standard of rice and rats." White labor was moving rapidly toward an exclusionist and racist response to the "Chinese Question." One of the leading theoreticians of this movement was Henry George.

Shortly after the arrival of the Chinese at North Adams, George spoke on the "Chinese Question" before 500 members of the Knights of St. Crispin in San Francisco. The use of Chinese labor, he insisted, must be viewed within the context of the great contradiction of the age: the enormous increase of wealth due to the technological advances in steam, electricity, and machinery, and the decrease in the workers' share of that wealth. This was the problem, and Chinese labor was aggravating it. "Chinese immigration really meant the reduction of wages, still greater inequality in the distribution of wealth, and . . . the substitution of Mongolians for Caucasians."[43] Nine years later, George presented a fully developed analysis of the problem in his book, aptly titled *Progress and Poverty*.

Remembered today as a reformer and as the author of one of the seminal books of the nineteenth century, George was also one of the key architects of the anti-Chinese ideology and the author of many widely read essays which contributed directly to the exclusion of Chinese from America. His ideas on reform and race complemented rather than contradicted each other: Both were responses to what he anxiously viewed as America's movement toward a catastrophe—a terrible and bloody class conflict in American technological society.

Born in Philadelphia in 1839, Henry George grew up in a Jacksonian society, which emphasized enterprise, activity, and the accumulation of goods in order to confirm one's worth. As a child, he was told he would be successful and rewarded if he were honest and industrious. In the 1850s, like so many young and ambitious men of his time, he went to California to look for gold and make his fortune. His parents, however, thought their son should not try to become rich too quickly: Wealth was, or should be, the result of earnest and long effort. "This making haste to grow rich is attended with snares and temptations and a great weariness of the flesh," his mother warned after he had started for the Fraser River gold rush in 1858. Time and again his father sent him advice: "Fortunes are not to be made in a hurry; it takes time and application." "Be careful and nurse your means; lay up what you can and owe no man anything and you will be safe." Here was what his parents considered sound republican wisdom.[44]

George's desire to strike it rich also evoked feelings of ambivalence and guilt, which were revealed in a letter to his sister Jennie:

> I had a dream last night—such a pleasant, vivid dream, that I must tell you of it. I thought I was scooping treasure out of the earth by handfuls, almost delirious with the thoughts of what I would now be able to do, and how happy we would all be—and so clear and distinct that I involuntarily examined my pockets when I got up in the morning, but alas! with the usual result. Is it an indication of future luck? or do dreams always go by contraries, and instead of finding, am I to lose? . . . "Lust for Gold!" Is it any wonder that men lust for gold, and are willing to give almost anything for it, when it covers everything—the purest and holiest desires of their hearts. . . . Sometimes I feel sick of the fierce struggle of our high civilized life, and think I would like to get away from cities and business, with their jostlings and strainings and cares altogether, and find some place on one of the hillsides . . . where I could gather those I love, and live content with what Nature and our own resources would furnish; but, alas, money, money, is wanted even for that.[45]

George woke up; discouraged, he went to work as a printer and also began to write as a newspaper reporter.

Yet, he still had hopes he would get ahead in life, and like Benjamin Rush before him, he decided to calculate his time and energy. To help him order his life and organize his activity, he began keeping a diary. "I have commenced this little book," he wrote in it on February 17, 1865, "as an experiment—to aid me [in] acquiring habits of regularity, punctuality and purpose." He would enter into the diary the experiences of the day as well as plans for the future. Admitting that he owed over $200 and that he had been unsuccessful financially, he resolved to practice a "rigid economy" until he had some money saved. And he developed a list of rules, which required him:

1st. To make every cent I can.
2nd. To spend nothing unnecessarily.
3rd. To put something by each week, if it is only a five cent piece borrowed for the purpose.
4th. Not to run in debt if it can be avoided.[46]

Thus, George consciously imposed self-controls in order to advance himself toward economic success.

Yet, his ascetic and "rigid economy" did not bring him any closer to success than did the dream of himself "scooping" treasure from the earth. Marriage and family, furthermore, were plunging him into greater debt and financial anxiety. In 1869, during this time of personal distress, George visited New York City, where he had what he called a "vision." In the city, he witnessed the disturbing contrast between poverty and wealth, and made a "vow" to seek out and remedy its cause. George posed the question: Why was there a deepening of poverty in the midst of advancing wealth? In his struggle to find an answer, he brought together a wide range of concerns: technology, corporate hegemony, the plight of white labor, and the presence of the Chinese in industrial America.[47]

George's question was directly related to his analysis of the meaning of technology. As a young man trying to get ahead in California, he had a moving experience which forced him to reflect on the significance of the railroad to the working class. He had been sitting in the gallery of the American Theatre in San Francisco on New Year's Eve; suddenly the curtain fell and the people in the audience sprang to their feet. On the curtain they saw depicted "what was then a dream of the far future— the overland train coming into San Francisco." After everyone had become hoarse from shouting in celebration of the magnificent machine, George began to wonder whether the railroad would benefit men like himself, who had nothing but their labor. He had great hope for the development of

California, "proud of her future greatness, looking forward to the time when San Francisco would be one of the great capitals of the world, looking forward to the time when this great empire of the west would count her population by millions." Yet, beneath the excitement electrifying the audience, George recalled what a miner had said to him during a discussion on the presence of the Chinese in the gold fields of California. What harm were the Chinese doing here, George had asked, if they were only working the cheap diggings? And the old miner had replied: "No harm now, but wages will not always be as high as they are today in California. As the country grows, as people come in, wages will go down, and some day or other white men will be glad to get those diggings that the Chinamen are now working." George had come away from the discussion worried about the country's future. "As the country grew . . ." he feared, "the condition of those who had to work for their living must become, not better, but worse."[48] As George watched the curtain fall and as he cheered in the American Theatre, he had a sudden, sobering insight: The Chinese were involved in the development of progress and poverty in America—in the building of the overland train which was becoming the symbol of both.

As George struggled to get ahead and as he pondered over the warning of the old miner, he encountered the Chinese personally. His diary contains several references to the "Chinaman" and his visits to the "Chinese quarter." On February 21, 1865, he recorded in his diary: "Worked for Ike. Did two cards for $1. . . . In evening had row with Chinaman. Foolish." The next day, he wrote: "Hand very sore. Did not go down till late. Went to work in 'Bulletin' at 12. Got $3. Went to library in evening. Thinking of economy." Here was George, working hard as a printer, worrying about making ends meet, studying and thinking about political economy, his hand sore from a fight he had had with a "Chinaman."[49]

Three years later, George wrote an essay on "What the Railroad Will Bring Us," which revealed the direction of his study of political economy and the concerns which he would analyze and articulate for the rest of his life. Calling the transcontinental railroad "the greatest work of the age," he predicted that it would convert the "wilderness" into a "populous empire." But, he quickly added, it would also bring problems. As population flowed into the West, land values would rise, benefiting only those few who were rich and owned land. Workers, on the other hand, would be forced into greater competition for employment, and thus would not be able to obtain the capital needed to buy land. Before the penetration of the railroad, California had been a Jacksonian Eden—a country "where all had started from the same level—where the banker had been a year or two before a journeyman carpenter, the merchant a foremast hand . . . and the laborer once counted his 'pile,' and where the wheel of fortune had been constantly revolving with a rapidity in other places unknown. . . ." But steam was ushering in a new era, in which wealth tended to be concentrated. The locomotive was "a great centralizer," killing little towns and little businesses and building up great cities and great businesses. This process made possible the rise of the "very rich," corrupted by "luxury," and undermined "personal independence"—"the basis of all virtues" in a "republican state." Much of this transformation, George argued, could already be seen in the mining business, where the "honest miner" had passed away, succeeded by the "millowner" with his "Chinaman."[50]

In his widely read essay "The Chinese on the Pacific Coast," published in the *New York Tribune* in 1869 George gave an elaborate explanation of what he thought was the relationship between American technology and the "Chinese Problem." He observed that the Chinese had possessed much knowledge of technology at one time, and had been able to realize such technological achievements as the compass, gunpowder, and printing. But then a "strange petrifaction" fell upon the Chinese. Consequently, they did not utilize technology; gunpowder, for example, was used merely as a toy. Turning to the nineteenth century, George noted how the steamship was breaking down the geographical isolation between the East and the West and making possible mass Chinese immigration to California. Here was a new peril. The 100,000 Chinese on the West Coast represented the thin end of the wedge which had for its base the 500 million people of eastern Asia.

Not only were the Chinese crowding into California and rapidly monopolizing employment; they also seemed to be ideal workers for technological production.

> The great characteristics of the Chinese as laborers are patience and economy— the first makes them efficient laborers, the second cheap laborers. . . . This patient steadiness peculiarly adapts the Chinese for tending machinery and for manufacturing. The tendency of modern production is to a greater and greater subdivision of labor—to confine the operative to one part of the process, and to require of him close attention, patience, and manual dexterity, rather than knowledge, judgment, and skill. The superintendents of the cotton and woolen mills on the Pacific prefer the Chinese to other operatives, and in the same terms the railroad people speak of their Chinese graders, saying they are steadier, work longer, require less watching, and do not get up strikes or go on drunks.

Thus, in George's view, the Chinese had certain qualities which made them "peculiarly" adaptable for use in machine-based production: They were patient, economical, manually dexterous, and controllable. As a controlled working class in industrial America, they represented the "peons" of the "captains of industry"—yellow labor pitted against white.

In assessing these "peons" as a threat to the white working class, George compared antebellum southern slave society with the new order emerging in technological America. While the ruling class of the Old South was white and the workers black, the ruling class of modern industrial America would again be white but the workers would be yellow. This posed a serious problem for the maintenance of a "homogeneous" society. While the Chinese differed from "our own race" by as strongly marked characteristics as did blacks, George warned, they did not so readily fall into "our ways." The black, when brought to this country, was "a simple barbarian with nothing to unlearn." The Chinese, on the other hand, had a civilization, a vanity which caused them to look down on all other races, and "habits of thought rendered permanent by being stamped upon countless generations." The yellow working class constituted "a population born in China, reared in China, expecting to return to China, living while here in a little China of its own, and without the slightest attachment to the country—utter heathens, treacherous, sensual, cowardly and cruel." Thus, they were a more serious problem than blacks: Unlike blacks, who were "docile" and capable of accepting white ways, the Chinese could not be "assimilated." Here, George declared, were "dragon's teeth enough for the sowing of our new soil—to germinate and bear ere long their bitter fruit of social disease, political weakness, agitation and bloodshed; to spring up armed men, marshalled for civil war. Shall we prohibit their sowing while there is yet time, or shall we wait till they are firmly imbedded, and then try to pluck them up?" His conclusion, advanced years before the appearance of Denis Kearney—fiery anti-Chinese orator and leader of the Workingman's Party of California—was clear: The Chinese must go![51]

Seeking a response on the "Chinese Question" from John Stuart Mill, George sent the English philosopher a copy of his essay. In his letter to George on October 23, 1869, Mill made a distinction between the moral issue and the economic issue. Chinese immigration to the United States raised "two of the most difficult and embarrassing questions of political morality—the extent and limits of the rights of those who have first taken possession of the unoccupied portion of the earth's surface to exclude the remainder of mankind from inhabiting it, and the means which can be legitimately used by the more improved branches of the human species to protect themselves from being hurtfully encroached upon by those of a lower grade in civilization." Concerning "the purely economic view of the subject," Mill stated he "entirely agreed" with George. He had no doubt that Chinese immigration, if it attained great dimensions, must be "economically injurious to the mass of the present population," diminishing their wages and lowering their standard of living. On this basis, exclusion would be justifiable. Yet, Mill held back from this conclusion. "Is it justifiable," he asked, "to assume that the character and habits of the Chinese are insusceptible of improvement?" In his comment on Mill's letter, George dealt specifically with this question. He claimed Mill's opinion justified the restriction of Chinese immigration, for there was little, if any, possibility for the improvement of the Chinese population in America. The Chinese did not settle here permanently; thus the Chinese population here would be composed continuously of "fresh barbarians, with everything to forget and everything to learn." Even American education would not provide much hope for Chinese children, for the traditions and influences surrounding them would render the majority of educated Chinese children still "essentially Chinese."[52]

George's essay on "The Chinese on the Pacific Coast" immediately became the center of excited commentary. In his endorsement of George's call for the restriction of Chinese immigration, the editor of the *San Francisco Daily Herald* estimated that it would be logistically possible to transport four million Chinese laborers to America within eighteen months if the demand for their importation were made. Thus the Chinese population in the United States could be increased within two years to equal the total black population in the country. "The question of Chinese settlement and labor in this country," the editor declared, "is one of great present concern. . . . Establish the Radical doctrines of political and social equality for all races, and then induce the Mandarins to 'supply the labor demand of the country' . . . and the day of the downfall of the Republic is not far distant."[53] Reprinted in journals and pamphlets of workingmen's organizations, George's essay helped to crystallize anti-Chinese racism, sharpened white working-class hatred of the Chinese, and contributed to the movement which culminated in the enactment of the Chinese Exclusion Act of 1882.

Many of the concerns which agitated George in his analysis of the "Chinese Question"—land, labor, industrialization—led directly to the writing of his most important book, *Progress and Poverty: An Inquiry into the Cause of Industrial Depressions and of Increase of Want with Increase of Wealth. The Remedy.* Published three years before the passage of the Chinese Exclusion Act, the book had an undeniable political relation to the question of Chinese immigration restriction which was a focus of national political discussion. George's publisher was aware of the controversy and recognized the opportunity to promote the book. In a letter to W. H.

Appleton, A. J. Steers of the editorial department recommended the publication of a "cheap edition" and predicted the book would have an "Enormous" sale. "It treats of a question of live interest at the present moment when the extraordinary influx of Chinese laborers now going causes fear of a labor Émente of the [Denis] Kearney Stamp to spread in the community and the book is so attractive that it would need but little advertising to make its own way."[54]

Progress and Poverty represented the culmination of ten years of research and reflection. George had finally developed an understanding of the problem of poverty in America and had also formulated a remedy. Opening his analysis with a litany on the utilization of steam and electricity and the introduction of labor-saving machinery, he pointed out the paradox of the existence of poverty amid material progress. Why was there poverty? George had an answer: Wages constantly tended to be minimal and to give but a bare living in spite of the increase of productive power because of the tendency of rents to increase faster than productive power and thus force down wages. The problem was the monopolization of the land. In order to "extirpate" poverty and make wages what justice demanded they should be, George argued, "common" ownership would have to be substituted for the individual ownership of land. This could be accomplished through a "single tax" on all "unearned increment"—the increased value of land generated from the increase of population and productivity. Unless the unjust and unequal distribution of wealth were remedied, American society would face an overwhelming crisis. The public domain and the availability of land in America had been in the past the "transmuting force," which had turned the "thriftless, unambitious European peasant into the self-reliant Western farmer." Foreshadowing Frederick Jackson Turner, George declared: "All that we are proud of in the American character; all that makes our conditions and institutions better than those of older countries, we may trace to the fact that land has been cheap in the United States, because new soil has been open to the emigrant." But, he observed ominously, the American advance had reached the Pacific. As George drew his book to a close, he referred specifically to the Chinese in his reaffirmation of American progress and civilization. While whites had progressed from a savage state to nineteenth-century civilization, the Chinese had stood still. The transformation of the European peasant into the American farmer did not apply to the Chinese immigrant: Due to the "Chinese environment," the immigrants from the East remained "Chinese."[55]

Thus, in George's view, the Chinese were "unassimilable," and shortly after the publication of *Progress and Poverty,* he spelled out the particular threat they constituted in industrial America. In his essay "Chinese Immigration," he identified technology with American civilization, and warned that the use of "Chinamen" in American industries would erode the progress of technology. The low wages and low standard of living in China, he argued, hindered the development of technology there, for machinery was unnecessary in a society where labor was cheap. The same thing could happen in America. Chinese cheap labor in this country could destroy the "spirit of invention," and "stagnation" could take the place of "progress."[56] The Chinese were a most awesome threat: Bodies—yellow ones—could undermine the ascendency of machinery and mind. The Chinese could not only retard but also subvert the very genius of the age—American technology.

Like Henry Adams and Mark Twain, George perceived catastrophe within the context of technology; but George related it directly to what he called the "Mongolization of America." Not only would the Chinese "barbarians," carried here by the magic of steam, throw America backward to an earlier age when society depended on the labor of men's bodies, they would also help to harden class divisions within the United States. The Chinese would accelerate the prevailing tendency of the concentration of wealth—"to make the rich richer and the poor poorer; to make nabobs and princes of our capitalists, and crush our working classes into the dust. . . ." As American industry developed and as the Chinese became the main supply of labor for the "captains of industry," there would be intense competition and conflict between white workers and "Chinese coolies." Thus there would be both progress and poverty, and in the midst of both, there would be bloody conflict.[57]

Such conflict was already evident. The fear and rage of white workers were expressed repeatedly in the frenzy of anti-Chinese violence. The victims of white working-class racist attacks, the Chinese were frequently beaten in the streets of San Francisco and driven out of Eureka, Truckee, and other towns. In 1871 a white mob in Los Angeles killed twenty-one Chinese and looted the Chinese quarters. An even more violent mob action occurred in 1885 at Rock Springs, Wyoming, where whites refused to work in the same mine with Chinese laborers; armed with rifles and revolvers, they invaded the Chinese section of town, shot Chinese workers as they fled, and burned the buildings. Fifteen Chinese were wounded and twenty-eight murdered during the massacre.[58] George could see that white working-class violence against Chinese laborers was only part of a larger conflict.

What horrified George was the possibility that the conflict could unleash the "savagery" latent in whites which their civilization had to restrain in order to maintain itself. "Nor should we forget," he cautioned, "that in civilized man still lurks the savage." Men of the nineteenth century, living in an era of progress, were still essentially the same as the men of the past, who "fought to death in petty quarrels," "drunk fury with blood," and burned cities and destroyed empires. While "social progress" had "softened manners," yet man was still capable of as "blind a rage as when, clothed in skins, he fought wild beasts with a flint." And present tendencies of class conflict threatened to rekindle passions which had so often before "flamed in destructive fury." Relating social tensions in America to the class strife already intense in Europe, George saw the "terrible struggle of the Paris commune" as a fiery example of the social conflicts which seemed to be punctuating Western civilization. "And in the light of burning Paris," he fearfully suggested, "we may see how it may be that this very civilization of ours, this second Tower of Babel . . . may yet crumble and perish."[59]

This vision which haunted George was depicted vividly in Ignatius Donnelly's novel *Caesar's Column.* In this story, published in 1890, an industrial elite, with the help of Chinese "coolies" as workers, take power and suppress the white workers and farmers of America. "Nabobs" and "a few great loan associations" own the land, driving the once independent farmers into labor competition with "vile hordes of Mongolian coolies." A bloody revolution is in the making. "When the Great Day comes, and the nation sends forth its call for volunteers . . . that cry will echo in desolate places; or it will ring through the triumphant hearts of savage and desperate men who are hastening to the banquet of blood and destruction. And the wretched, yellow, under-fed coolies, with women's garments over their effeminate limbs, will not have the courage or the desire or the capacity to make soldiers and defend their oppressors." During the revolution, a "banquet of blood and destruction" takes place; the bodies of the dead are stacked up in a huge pile and concrete is poured over them, forming a column rising toward the heavens like a skyscraper and symbolizing what George regarded as the "savagery" still lurking within "civilized man."[60]

PART FOUR

EMPIRE

Passage O Soul to India!

The earth to be spann'd, connected by network,
The races, neighbors, to marry and be given in marriage,
The oceans to be cross'd, the distant brought near,
The lands to be welded together.

I see ranks, colors, barbarisms, civilizations, I go among them, I mix
*   indiscriminately,*
I salute all the inhabitants of the earth.

*   —Walt Whitman*
*   "Passage to India"*

CHAPTER XI

THE MASCULINE THRUST
TOWARD ASIA

No one knows who will live in this [iron] cage in the future, or whether at the end of this tremendous development entirely new prophets will arise, or there will be a great rebirth of old ideas and ideals, or, if neither, mechanized petrifaction, embellished with a sort of convulsive self-importance. For the last stage of this cultural development, it might well be truly said: "Specialists without spirit, sensualists without heart; this nullity imagines that it has attained a level of civilization never before achieved."

—Max Weber

At the end of the Mexican-American War, Aaron Palmer had recommended the use of Chinese labor to construct the transcontinental railroad in order to open to American capitalism a "new world" in Asia. During the next half century, not only were Chinese workers drawn from an "industrial reserve army" to help build a Promethean industrial order in the West and serve as a "wedge" against white labor unions in the Northeast, but also Indians were forcefully relocated on reservations to make way for *American Progress* or were allotted land individually and were prepared to enter "mechanical pursuits" in a technological society, blacks were emancipated and made available for industrial labor in the "New South" as well as the manufacturing centers of the North, and Mexicans were directed into the mines of the Southwest to extract the "red metal" used for the electrical wiring of modern America. During the 1890s, these racial developments culminated in American expansionism as the United States fought a war against Spain, annexed the Philippines, and extended its markets into Asia. Symptomatic of a society in crisis—economic, social, and psychic—American imperialism reinforced the hegemony of corporate power over republican men and swept the nation into a jingoistic frenzy of international violence. Victorious in Cuba and the Philippines, civilization in the United States was reaching a new level of nullity as the purveyors of American aggression and destructiveness preached the gospel of the "strenuous life."

The "Iron Cage" in a Corporate Civilization

During the nineteenth century, political and business leaders built a modern industrial order which turned against the individualism and work ethic men like Rush, Jackson, Walker, and George believed were essential in a republican society. In this new system, bureaucratic state and industrial control subverted self-control and individual freedom; centralized corporate lines of force challenged Protestant and republican lines of will. The transformation of American society from self-regulated "republican machines" to corporate-regulated men involved a profound irony. As Max Weber described this process,

> the Puritan wanted to work in a calling; we are forced to do so. For when asceticism was carried out of monastic cells into everyday life, and began to dominate world morality, it did its part in building the tremendous cosmos of the modern economic order. This order is now bound to the technical and economic conditions of machine production which to-day determine the lives of all the individuals who are born into this mechanism, not only those directly concerned with economic acquisition, with irresistible force. Perhaps it will so determine them until the last ton of fossilized coal is burnt. In [Richard] Baxter's view the care for external goods should only lie on the shoulders of the "saint like a light cloak, which can be thrown aside at any moment." But fate decreed that the cloak should become an iron cage.

In this new order, large modern capitalist enterprises became the "unequalled models of strict bureaucratic organization." Precision, speed, knowledge of the files, strict subordination, and specialized functions that were emphasized as business operations were based on "calculable rules" which had no "regard for persons." "Chained" to their activity, bureaucratic functionaries became "cogs" in an "ever-moving mechanism." "More and more the material fate of the masses," Weber noted, depended on the "steady and correct functioning of the increasingly bureaucratic organizations of private capitalism." Thus Americans seeking to build within themselves republican "iron cages" became imprisoned in the corporate "iron cage" of the modern economic cosmos. As republican individuals, they lacked the collective identity and power required to enable them to resist the corporate leviathan of modern business, with its technology and "scientific planning" as well as its modern princes and pundits—its executives and experts.[1]

Large-scale bureaucracies, in government and in business, increasingly integrated people into impersonal and rationalized structures based on functions, rules, and regulations. Jacksonian democracy, with its egalitarian ethic and its specific application—"rotation in office"—helped to construct this new order of administrative efficiency which was dependent on the interchangeability of human "parts." "In this system individuals could be placed or replaced without upsetting the integrity of the whole," historian Lynn Marshall has observed. "Men were fitted into this system, not it to men. It was the administrative counterpart of the interchangeability of machine parts." As the machine became the model for the organization of human beings, formal bureaucratic structures operated impersonally, dependent on bookkeeping entries rather than personalities. Organizational functions were explicitly defined; official duties for all employees were given formal specifications. Impersonal information systems laid a new basis for the supervision of employees, as executives relied on staffs to provide information on and analyses of the performance and productivity of the agency or business. In large science-based corporations, engineer-managers applied scientific methods to business management. According to David F. Noble,

> they pioneered in formulating rationalized procedures in engineering, manufacturing, finance, and marketing; they quantified and systematized corporate operations, developing methods of cost accounting, statistical controls, forecasting techniques, and the procedures for gathering and processing huge amounts of detailed, accurate data to be used in appraising, planning, and coordinating the operations of extended plant and personnel. Equally important, they created the formal administrative structures for the giant corporations, with carefully defined lines of authority and channels of communication through which to control the process of production.

Rationality and calculation, values republican fathers had promoted for individuals, became the methods and goals of centralized structures that imposed regularity and uniformity everywhere they reached. "We do not ride on the railroad," remarked Henry David Thoreau; "it rides upon us."[2]

In this process of modernization, a new economic cosmos was constructed. Before 1850, historian Alfred D. Chandler observed, industrial enterprises were small, usually family owned and controlled operations. Few businesses required a clearly defined administrative structure, and even a large firm had only two or three men to direct all its functions. During the next fifty years, however, corporate bureaucratic capitalism came to dominate transportation as well as the production of oil, steel, machinery, and power. The key to their domination was the advance in business administration.

During the 1850s, railroad corporations pioneered in the development of systematic organizational structures. To meet the administrative needs that existed in the governance of extensive railroad lines, railroad managers established lines of authority and communication to coordinate activities between a central office and field divisions. These developments in railroad administration had ramifications for American business. The modern organizational structures of the railroads served as models for industrial enterprises; more importantly, the railroads made possible the great industrial growth that occurred in the late nineteenth century and created an extensive and nationwide market that encouraged the expansion and subdivision of manufacturing and marketing activities. By 1900, modern multi-functional structures characterized American industrial enterprises. Electrical manufacturing industries like General Electric and Westinghouse had departments for manufacturing, engineering, sales, and finance. Business leviathans like Standard Oil and United States Steel integrated their national structures vertically, owning virtually every phase of production and distribution for their products and controlling specific areas of the economy.

Administrators of modern business structures like Charles R. Flint of United States Rubber Company eagerly pointed to the advantages of consolidated management:

> Raw material, bought in large quantities, is secured at a lower price; the specialization of manufacture on a large scale, in separate plants, permits the fullest utilization of special machinery and processes, thus decreasing costs; the standard of quality is raised and fixed; the number of styles reduced, and the best standards are adopted; those plants which are best equipped and most advantageously situated are run continuously in preference to those less favored; in case of local strikes or fires, the work goes on elsewhere, thus preventing serious loss; there is no multiplication of the means of distribution—a better force of salesmen takes the place of a larger number; the same is true of branch stores; terms and conditions of sales become more uniform, and credits through comparisons are more safely granted; the aggregate of stocks carried is greatly reduced, thus saving interest, insurance, storage and shop-wear; greater skill in management

accrues to the benefit of the whole, instead of the part; and large advantages are realized from comparative accounting and comparative administration.

And business leaders like Union Pacific President Charles Francis Adams, Jr., even pontificated a new metaphysics of capitalist consolidation: "The principle of consolidation . . . is a necessity—a natural law of growth. You may not like it: You will have to reconcile yourselves to it." And to explain the existence of the new corporate order, Adams even enlisted a phrase that had been used earlier to justify American expansion into Mexico. "The modern world does its work through vast aggregations of men and capital," he declared. "This is a sort of latter-day manifest destiny."[3]

Actually, corporate consolidation was not the development of a "natural law" or the manifestation of an American destiny. Through mergers, trusts, and holding companies, business leaders made conscious decisions to consolidate their empires in order to earn profits from the promotion of stock sales, eliminate competition, and rationalize the production process. Moreover, as they emerged, trusts and monopoly capitalism—"a power distant from men's lives"—exercised enormous power to determine prices for the transportation of farm products, set interest rates, regulate wages, raise tariffs, control the press, influence educational institutions, and promote their interests in state legislatures and Congress. The integration of the corporation and the state in a bureaucratic network enabled businessmen to utilize centralized state power to handle problems they could not solve themselves in the marketplace. Bureaucracy itself, as it developed in an American capitalist economy, became an instrument of class power; in short, as Gabriel Kolko pointed out, "bureaucratic functions" became "class functions."[4]

During the late nineteenth century, American corporate capitalism was in crisis. Severe depressions kept punctuating the American economy—in 1877-78, 1882-85, and 1893-97. Capitalists had built a system which generated periods of economic instability, massive unemployment, and gluts in the market. Captains of industry said they had invested so much capital in machinery for giant integrated industries that they had to keep their plants in continual operation, regardless of market needs, in order to cover overhead expenses. Andrew Carnegie, in his "Law of Surplus," claimed that it cost "less to keep the machines running, even when no market was in sight, than it did to shut down the factories." Capitalists were expanding as well as maintaining the operation of their plants. "It is incontrovertible," reported Carroll Wright, the chief of the National Bureau of Labor, "that the present manufacturing and mechanical plant of the United States is greater—far greater—than is needed to supply the demand; yet it is constantly being enlarged, and there is no way of preventing the enlargement." Enlargement did not signify an increase in employment, however. In 1894, during the depression, 18.4 percent of the labor force was unemployed, and Secretary of State Walter Gresham noted: "We cannot afford constant employment for our labor. . . . Our mills and factories can supply the demand by running seven or eight months out of twelve." Then he added anxiously: "It is surprising to me that thoughtful men do not see the danger in the present conditions." Historian Brooks Adams, a thoughtful man, did see the danger. Aware that the United States had been "irresistibly impelled" to produce a large industrial "surplus" and the future of the country "hinged" on this "surplus," Adams warned: "The United States must provide sure and adequate outlets for her products, or be in danger of gluts more dangerous to her society than many panics such as 1873 and 1893."[5]

But certain American capitalists also recognized the "danger" and the need to find "outlets" for their "surplus." Indeed, many companies had already begun to open Asia to American enterprise, and one business journal, the *American Protectionist,* was predicting that China and Japan would soon offer American corporations "one of the largest outlets" for their products. In the 1890s, American capitalists directed "surplus" products as well as capital to Asia. American exports to Japan tripled from $3.9 million in 1894 to $13 million in 1897; in 1895 the government secured for American businessmen the concession to the Un-san mines in Korea and received nearly $15 million in profits from the gold extracted from them. The focus of American imperial expansion was China. During the depression of 1895-96, the State Department's Bureau of Foreign Commerce encouraged the "American invasion of the markets of the world," and described China as "one of the most promising" of those markets. A State Department official announced: "The opening up of China to the commerce of the world . . . cannot fail to be of special value to the United States." Brooks Adams justified America's war against Spain in terms of the China market: "The expansion of any country must depend on the market for its surplus product; and China is the only region which now promises almost boundless possibilities of absorption, especially in the way of iron for its railroads." American companies did increase their exports to China in the last decade of the century. Cotton-goods industries, for example, exported to China at least 22 percent of their products sold abroad between 1891 and 1905; the increase was dramatic between 1895 and 1897, skyrocketing from $1,741,942 to $7,489,141. Total United States exports to China likewise rose from $4,000,000 in 1890 to $6,900,000 in 1896 and to $11,900,000 in 1897. American businesses such as the Cramp Shipbuilding Company, Union Iron Company, American China Development Company, Bethlehem Iron Company, and American Trading Company actively sought to secure concessions from China. In April 1898, the American China Development Company was granted the right to build a railway between Hankow and Canton. Shortly before the outbreak of the Spanish-American War, as Germany, Russia, and Japan threatened American economic interests in China, the *New York Commercial Advertiser* declared that it was "supremely important that we should retain the free entry into the Chinese market. . . ."[6]

The danger which alarmed Secretary of State Gresham and Brooks Adams was the social unrest and violent class conflict which had become increasingly prevalent in industrial society. During the late nineteenth century, industrial capitalists and workers were engaged in class warfare as labor disputes erupted into strikes and violence—the Railroad Strike of 1877, the Haymarket Riot of 1886, the Homestead Strike of 1892, the Pullman Strike of 1894, and many others. Demanding higher wages, improved working conditions, greater control over the process of production, and the right to organize, workers were challenging the corporate domination of George M. Pullman, Andrew Carnegie, Henry Clay Frick, and other industrial captains. Workers tied up the railroad lines from Pennsylvania to California in 1877 and again in 1894. They demonstrated at mass meetings—10,000 workers in San Francisco and 20,000 in New York in 1877. They went out on mass strikes: On May 1, 1886, 350,000 workers in 11,562 establishments struck for the eight-hour day. In 1894, more than 150,000 workers throughout the country went on strike to protest the exploitation of Pullman workers in Chicago. Labor leaders were arrested, imprisoned, and in several cases hanged on questionable murder charges. Dozens of protesting workers were killed and hundreds wounded in the streets by police, militia, and Pinkerton detectives in confrontations between labor and capital at Pittsburgh, Chicago, New York, and other cities. Facing the power which came out of the barrel of a gun, workers engaged in armed resistance: Determined to defend themselves against Carnegie's war to destroy the Amalgamated Association of Iron and Steel Workers, strikers at the Homestead plant armed themselves with rifles and even a cannon, and successfully forced an army of 300 Pinkertons to surrender as "prisoners of war."[7]

The problems of industrial America—the domination of the corporate bureaucracy over the individual and the class conflicts or rebellions against corporate rule within urban civilization—worried many Americans, especially one of the country's leading Protestant ministers—the Reverend Josiah Strong. A Congregationalist pastor, active in the Home Missionary Society and later the Social Gospel Movement, Strong wrote one of the most widely read books of his time, *Our Country: Its Possible Future and Its Present Crisis.* Published in 1885, the book sold 175,000 copies within ten years, offering readers an almost hysterical assessment of modern industrial American society and a passionate plea for its reformation.

Like Henry Adams and Mark Twain, Strong saw that both civilization and progress were not without ambiguity. In *Our Country,* he expressed concern for the nervousness which he believed was prevalent in late-nineteenth-century society. Technology, Strong said, had created conditions which were severely affecting the "nervous organizations" of Americans. The steam engine had "annihilated" nine-tenths of space; vast regions had been settled but "never before under the mighty whip and spur of electricity and steam." Due to advances in technology, the "excitements of life" had been increased and the "rate of living" had been quickened. Referring to Dr. George Beard, Strong viewed "neurasthenia" as a "disease" of modern American civilization: Its symptoms—stress, restlessness, emotional disorder, intense activity, alcoholism—were afflicting Americans in growing numbers. Thus they were rapidly becoming the "most highly organized" and the "most nervous" people in the world.[8]

As he surveyed society in the 1880s, Reverend Strong feared the country was in grave peril. "Class" conflict was hardening; the cities were becoming huge festering sores of social ills; southern European immigrants were crowding into the land and threatening to outnumber the Anglo-Saxon population; and Roman Catholicism was entrenching itself in Protestant America. An illiterate, ignorant, immoral, and "criminal" population, dominated by their "appetites," prejudices, and liquor, was growing and swelling the ranks of the working class. Factory workers labored in "unsanitary" conditions, in "confined" situations where they did "one thing over and over again." Living in congested cities, these workers constituted a "tenement population," a class attracted to "socialism," claimed Strong. Meanwhile, men of great wealth were rising, worshipping material success. These "millionaires" possessed "oppressive" and "despotic" power to raise prices, close factories, and control production. As members of an elite "hereditary" class of capitalists and monopolists, they represented a "modern and republican feudalism."

This clash between "the dangerously poor" and "the dangerously rich," Strong warned, threatened the republican society of "individual liberty." More than ever before, the old republican and Protestant virtues had to be restored; both "socialism" and "modern feudalism" of monopoly capitalism had to be resisted. The future of America as a republican society depended on whether or not the individuals who composed it were capable of "self-government" and "self-control." "We deem ourselves a chosen people," Strong declared, "and incline to the belief that the Almighty stands pledged to our prosperity. Probably not one in a hundred of our population has ever questioned the security of our future. Such optimism is as senseless as pessimism is faithless." The faith of the republican fathers had to be renewed for "our country" to be saved from catastrophe. But how?

Thirteen years before the Spanish-American War, Reverend Strong advocated expansionism as a response to the crisis. The West, which had historically provided an "abundance of cheap land" and which had made possible the "general welfare and contentment" of the people, was being rapidly settled. "When the supply [of land] is exhausted," Strong predicted, "we shall enter upon a new era, and shall more rapidly approximate European conditions of life." Still, Strong was not pessimistic, for now there was a vista which had not existed in Jefferson's time. The very technology that was accelerating the settlement of the West, Strong saw, was also "compressing" the earth and creating new opportunities for the expansion of American markets. Through technology, the United States would add Africa and Asia to "our market" and become the "mighty workshop of the world."[9] Thus America would not let her workshops remain in Europe, as Jefferson had recommended; rather she would become the manufacturing center of a world capitalist system.

Shortly after the Spanish-American War, Strong offered an enthusiastic justification of American imperialism in his book *Expansion Under New World Conditions*. What he had suggested in *Our Country* was made explicit and emphasized in *Expansion:* the need for national aggression in Asia in order to reduce psychological and class tensions in America.[10]

What impressed Strong most as he reviewed the century which had just come to a close was the dramatic transformation of America from an agricultural to an industrial society. Since 1800, he observed, more than 4.5 million farms had been brought under cultivation; more importantly, 500 cities had been built and countless mills and factories had been erected. "With the railways which have been built," he boasted, "we could parallel every track in all Europe and then have enough left over, if we could use the equator as a road-bed, to girdle the earth. . . . It has taken thousands of years to make Europe, but on this continent as vast an area has been brought under the yoke of civilization in one century." For Strong, the magic of the age was technology—a power which he identified with the Anglo-Saxon race. "Only those races," he claimed, "which have produced machinery seem capable of using it with the best results. It is the most advanced races which are its masters. Those races which, like the African and the Malay, are many centuries behind the Anglo-Saxon in development seem as incapable of operating complicated machinery as they are of adopting and successfully administering representative government."[11] Like Francis Amasa Walker, Strong believed Anglo-Saxon Americans possessed a genius for both technology and republicanism.

But Strong also worried about the new problems which technology had created. Production in America was increasing at a faster rate than population. "During the last half-century our population increased three-fold," he noted, "while our manufactures increased eighteen-fold. And our present manufacturing plant is decidedly larger than is necessary to supply the home market." Unless American capitalism found foreign markets, the economy would continue to suffer from dislocations and depressions. Unemployment, Strong feared, would have grave consequences for the national character. "Men who are long idle, whether that idleness is voluntary or enforced, usually degenerate both physically and morally. And if to idleness is added want, mischief is doubly sure to follow. Want when it is wide enough and desperate enough becomes revolutionary." A member of the "army of the unemployed and discontented," the worker could become a *"revolutionist."* Strong reminded his readers that in 1877, "after a period of long industrial depression, we had railway riots in ten American cities; and ball and bayonet did their work amid incendiary fires."[12] To Strong, the choice was clear: America had to expand into foreign markets, or experience social revolution.

As the solution to the crisis of "our country," expansionism reflected, for Strong, a quest for moral perfection. In *The Times and Young Men* and *The New Era; or The Coming Kingdom,* published in 1901 and 1893 respectively, Strong linked the concern for individual moral perfection which had engaged the attention of Benjamin Rush and the commitment to social moral perfection which had inspired John Winthrop's vision of America as a City upon a Hill. Addressing himself to the young men of America, Strong defined what he believed to be the crucial "problem": "Evidently, getting the most good out of life, which is getting the most service into it, raises the problem of

The Body."*

The importance of the body was obvious to Strong: "Everything we value in life is more or less conditioned by it." Thus it had to be governed—to be

---

* The emphasis is Strong's—both the italics and indentation.

given sleep, food, and exercise—in order "to get the largest possible amount of service out of it." Young men should strive to achieve "the most perfect body." What would determine success in "the fierce competition of modern life" was "vitality or nervous force," and "the most perfect body" would furnish "the largest and best-sustained supply of nervous energy." The perfection of the body had social and spiritual significance. "We now know that the race cannot be perfected without perfecting the body," he contended. "Society cannot be entirely saved until man has been saved physically." An instrument of the "higher nature," the physical self would be "subservient to the soul" and serve "the intelligence." Perfected, the body would help to usher in the "New Era" or the "Coming Kingdom."[13]

In Strong's vision of the "Kingdom," Protestant perfectionism, republican ideology, racial dominance, and expansionism were all integrated into a world view: Mind and soul were separated from body, "civilization" from "savagery," and Anglo-Saxon Americans from Africans and Asians. The quest for the "Kingdom" required not only an inner control of the self but also an imperial involvement in the world and the affairs of other races. "In the world-life which is being organized," Strong reverently declared, "different classes, nations, and races are becoming so dependent on each other that it will be impossible to perfect in character or condition any one class or people until all are perfected. So that as citizens of the Kingdom we are bound to be interested in mankind." For Strong, no one in the "New Era" could be left alone, outside of the "Kingdom."[14]

During the 1890s, many businessmen, reformers, and intellectuals shared with Strong a fear of internal social disorder as they became increasingly conscious of a tremendous loss. Suddenly they saw around them what Jefferson had abhorred—a civilization of towns and large cities, without "vacant lands" and a frontier. People were getting "piled upon one another" in urban centers, "as in Europe"; indeed, the United States Census superintendent announced in 1891 that the frontier had come to an end. And two years later, addressing the American Historical Association meeting in Chicago, Frederick Jackson Turner assessed the meaning of this recent development.

In his paper, "The Significance of the Frontier in American History," Turner pointed out the most crucial force in the country's past: Offering "free land," the frontier had created the American character, with its "inventive turn of mind," "restless nervous energy," individualism, and democratic quality. In their history, Americans were continually beginning over again on the frontier—the "meeting point between savagery and civilization." They experienced "perennial rebirth" as they moved west, with its new opportunities, its continuous touch with the "simplicity of primitive society." Europeans originally, they had been "Americanized" by the wilderness. The process was powerful, effervescent, mystical.

> The frontier is the line of most rapid and effective Americanization. The wilderness masters the colonist. It finds him a European in dress, industries, tools, modes of travel, and thought. It takes him from the railroad car and puts him in the birch canoe. It strips off the garments of civilization, and arrays him in the hunting shirt and the moccasin. It puts him in the log cabin of the Cherokee and the Iroquois. . . . Before long he has gone to planting Indian corn and plowing with a sharp stick; he shouts the war cry and takes the scalp in orthodox Indian fashion. In short, at the frontier the environment is at first too strong for the man. He must accept the conditions which it furnishes, or perish, and so he fits himself into the Indian clearings and follows the Indian trails. Little by little he transforms the wilderness, but the outcome is not the Old Europe. . . . The fact is that here is a new product that is American.

Not only did the white man yield to the wilderness and thereby overcome it, he also advanced the frontier continually in wars against Indians. Each frontier—the fall line, the Alleghenies, the Mississippi River, and the Rocky Mountains—was "won by a series of Indian wars." Here, then, was a process which could be found in the fantasy of Robert Montgomery Bird and in the lives of men like Andrew Jackson and George Armstrong Custer. The European settler in America incorporated the land and its inhabitants and their cultures as he transformed himself into an American. White "rebirth" involved Indian death.[15]

As Turner analyzed the significance of the frontier in America's past, he confronted the industrial reality, apparent everywhere around him in Chicago. A bold historian, he did not hesitate to link the past to the present. Out of the frontier experience had evolved technological "progress," "the complexity of city life," and "the manufacturing organization with city and factory system," he said. The disappearance of the frontier marked the close of a great historic movement. The expansion of the industrial order had extended civilization, eliminating free land; it had also concentrated people in cities and transformed them from farmers into factory workers. But what, then, would the future hold for a frontierless America? "He would be a rash prophet," challenged Turner, "who should assert that the expansive character of American life has now entirely ceased." "Movement has been its dominant fact, and, unless this training has no effect upon a people, the American intellect will continually demand a wider field for its exercise."[16]

Turner was no rash prophet. The frontier had been a significant influ-ence on white American thought since Englishmen had encountered the new world. Puritans of the seventeenth century had viewed their mission to America as an errand into the wilderness; they would fail in their errand unless they tamed the land. Before they set foot on the new land, these Englishmen had declared: "The whole earth is the Lord's garden, and he hath given it to the sons of Adam to be tilled and improved by them. Why then should we stand starving here for the places of habitation . . . and in the mean time suffer whole countries, as profitable for the use of man, to lie wasted without any improvement." Piety demanded that America not be allowed to "lie wasted"; cultivated lands were signs of the errand's success. Yet, as they improved the land, these Englishmen had located their identity as Americans in nature and in the experience which took place on the frontier; it was this wilderness which had set America and themselves apart from Europe and their feudal past. The United States was "Nature's na-tion," and as long as there were vacant lands in America, thought Jeffer-son, Americans would be virtuous. The entire history of white America had been one of penetration into the "virgin land." The West had been the arena where white men could test the limits of their republican asceticism and experience regeneration through violence against Indians, where they could find raw material and expand the market for goods manufactured in the East, and where they could take possession of Indian lands and ad-vance themselves through land speculation and agricultural production.[17]

But as the machine increasingly dominated the American landscape, as the frontier disappeared, and as the market reached the physical limits of the continent, where could white men turn to perpetuate their national identity, expand the market, and find a safety valve against the depres-sions, strikes, and riots already tearing apart American society? Would the "age of machinery" and the "factory system" also be what Turner called the "age of socialistic inquiry"? American expansionists, now imprisoned in the corporate "iron cage" which Turner described as the "complex mazes of modern commercial lines," demanded a "wider field" as they rebelled against the confinement of the industrial bureaucracy and as they searched for a new market to sustain "the tremendous cosmos of the mod-ern economic order."[18] What was required, they believed, was the restora-tion of republican self-control and virtue through the pursuit of a new frontier in Asia where American white men could once again regenerate themselves. But what resulted was the ascendancy of the demonic "iron cage."

The New Empire: American Asceticism and the "New Navy"

No one did more to advance the American thrust toward Asia than Admiral Alfred Thayer Mahan. His influence on the making of American foreign policy was based not on his career as a naval officer but on his scholarship, his quiet work in archives, and his writings as an historian. His most important book, *The Influence of Sea Power upon History,* published in 1890, went through fifteen editions in eight years and was read all over the world. Assistant Secretary of the Navy Theodore Roosevelt found the study so engaging he read it "straight through and finished it." In a letter to Mahan dated May 12, 1890, Roosevelt praised the work as "the clearest and most instructive general work of the kind. . . . It is a *very* good book—admirable. . . . I wish . . . that the whole book could be placed where it could be read by the navy's foes, especially in Congress." Intended to boost the movement to build a "New Navy," Mahan's book immediately received considerable attention in the press. "We need a large navy," one reviewer concluded, "composed not merely of cruisers, but containing also a full proportion of powerful battleships, able to meet those of any nation." In the same year Congress authorized the construction of three battleships and began the work of rebuilding the Navy. Eight years later, on the eve of the Spanish-American War, from which the United States emerged as a power in Asia, a writer for *Blackwood's Magazine* noted Mahan's role in the rise of an expansionist spirit: "Mahan's teaching was as oil to the flame of 'colonial expansion' everywhere leaping into life. Everywhere a new-sprung ambition to go forth and possess and enjoy read its sanction in the philosophy ennobled by the glory of conquest." After Mahan died in 1914, the American Historical Association acknowledged that he had affected the course of world politics more than any American scholar of his day.[19]

This was an honor Mahan could hardly have imagined in 1886 as he began teaching a course on the history of naval strategy and tactics at the Naval War College in Rhode Island. While preparing his lectures, he hoped the study of history would provide "lessons"—"instructive material for the future." He was searching for a usable past, determined "to wrest something out of the old wooden sides and 24 pounders that will throw some light on the combinations to be used with ironclads . . . and torpedoes." The success of his lectures surprised him and encouraged him to rework them into a book.[20]

From his study of *The Influence of Sea Power upon History,* Mahan drew a "lesson": America should develop "colonies" to serve as coaling stations for the Navy and to increase the country's commerce. The key to the colonial strategy would be the development of America as a sea power. History as Mahan understood it indicated the future direction of the nation. The history of sea power, he explained, was largely a narrative of conflicts and wars between nations seeking to increase their wealth and power on the basis of their sea commerce. In his discussion of America's commercial development, he offered an interpretation of American history which anticipated Turner's frontier thesis. The energies of the nation, he observed, had been directed inward, toward the frontier. Internal activity, the settlement of the West and the cultivation of the wilderness, had turned the "eyes of the country" away from the sea. The time had arrived, however, for America to turn outward, beyond the continental borders. "The instinct for commerce, bold enterprise in the pursuit of gain, and a keen scent for the trails that lead to it, all exist; and if there be in the future any fields calling for colonization, it cannot be doubted that Americans will carry to them all their inherited aptitude for self-government and independent growth." But the country's commercial expansion would be severely limited, he warned, unless the United States became a sea power. "Internal development" and "great production" represented only the "first link in the chain" in the development of sea power. Factories, battleships, and markets were all linked together in the "chain." History had shown, Mahan argued, that the clashes of nations striving to gain commercial advantages and control of "distant unsettled commercial regions" eventually led to wars. Thus it was critical for the United States to build and maintain "an armed navy, of a size commensurate with the growth of its shipping." This "warlike preparation," Mahan concluded, would require the establishment of "naval stations" and "colonies attached to the mother-country" in those "distant parts of the world to which the armed shipping must follow the peaceful vessels of commerce."[21]

From his "lessons," Mahan developed a strategy for the building of an American empire; the architect of a theory for American colonialism, he was also a practitioner. In his letters to Assistant Secretary Roosevelt, his testimony before congressional committees, and his many articles and books, Mahan promoted American expansion into Asia, pointing out specifically those "distant parts of the world" destined for American colonization. Mahan, as his correspondence with Roosevelt reveals, exercised considerable influence in making expansionist policies and decisions. Repeatedly he advised the assistant secretary. "I would suggest as bearing upon the general policy of the Administration," he wrote to Roosevelt on May 1, 1897, "that the real significance of the Nicaragua Canal now is that it advances our Atlantic frontier by so much to the Pacific, and that in

Asia, not in Europe, is now the greatest danger to our proximate interests."
He also urged Roosevelt to place the "best admiral" in the Pacific, for
"much more initiative *may* be thrown on him than *can* be on the Atlantic
man." Roosevelt, in turn, respected Mahan's advice, disseminating it in
circles of power. On March 14, 1898, he wrote to Mahan: "I fear the
President does not intend that we shall have war if we can possibly avoid it.
I read to him your typewritten letter, dwelling upon the first page, saying
that the one important thing to my mind would be to disregard minor
punishment, and devote our attention to smashing Spain in Cuba." A week
later, Roosevelt thanked Mahan for his helpful guidance. "There is no
question that you stand head and shoulders above the rest of us! You have
given us just the suggestions we want. I am going to show your letter to the
Secretary first, and then get some members of the board to go over it. . . .
You probably don't know how much your letter has really helped me
clearly to formulate certain things which I had only vaguely in mind. I
think I have studied your books to pretty good purpose."[22]

In Mahan's vision, the future of American sea power and commercial
empire was located in Asia. Thus, while William Randolph Hearst and his
sensational and jingoistic journalism riveted the public's attention on
Cuba, Mahan and policy-makers in Washington were planning for actions
in Asia. Mahan saw this American thrust toward the Far East as a destiny
manifested in the history of the development of sea power in the nineteenth
century, particularly in the technological advances of the age. He interpreted the "opening" of Japan and China as "an incident of the general
industrial development which followed upon the improvement of mechanical processes and the multiplication of communications." The revolutionary effect of steam power on sea travel and transportation had created the
need for overseas colonies to serve as coaling stations. "The necessity of
renewing coal makes the cruiser of the present day even more dependent
than of old on his port," he noted. After the Spanish-American War, Mahan pointed out the significance of the annexation of the Philippines: It
had given the United States strategic naval bases in the East for coaling
stations and access to the "seas of China and to the valley of the
Yangtze."[23]

In his justification of American imperialism in Asia, Mahan brought
together Social Darwinism and the Protestant ethic. The American "possession" or "control" of territory in the Far East, he argued, would result
from decadent conditions there and the lack of Asian power to resist en-
croachments from a more "virile" nation. "Civilized" men required more
territory, and like all natural forces, the impulse to expand would take the
direction of least resistance. When the impulse came upon some "region

rich in possibilities, but unfruitful through the incapacity or negligence" of its inhabitants, the "incompetent race" would be destroyed, for the "inferior race" had always "fallen back and disappeared before the persistent impact of the superior." Thus, no one had a "natural right" to land; the right to own and control territory depended on "political fitness." Those who utilized the land, made certain its resources were not left "idle," were entitled to it. Here Mahan echoed John Winthrop's solemn pledge not to allow lands inhabited by Indians to lie in "waste." What had happened to the American Indian was, in Mahan's judgment, a result of a civilized and highly organized people trespassing upon the "technical" rights of possession of the previous occupants. Like President Jackson, the metaphysician of Indian removal, Mahan asked: "Will any one seriously contend that the North American continent should have been left forever in the hands of tribes whose sole use of their territory was to contravene the purposes of human life?" Thus, the experience in America provided, for whites, a basis for expansion into Asia; the Indian past manifested the Asian future. Aware American civilization had reached its continental limits, Mahan extended his view of "political fitness" to American overseas expansion: "Civilized" men would control the areas of the world which still remained in the possession of "savages," and "use" the land and its resources for the general good of the world.[24]

For Mahan, American expansion into Asia was an expression of what he called "Race Patriotism." Shortly after the United States had seized the Philippines, he identified the qualities embodied in the "race loosely called Anglo-Saxon"—a "particular type of political freedom," a "tenacious adherence to recognized law," and an "aptitude for self-government." As a "race patriot," Mahan saw the United States as the cutting edge of the West vis-à-vis the East. "Considering the American states as members of the European family, as they are by traditions, institutions, and languages, it is in the Pacific, where the westward course of empire again meets the East, that their relations to the future of the world become most apparent." As the advance guard of the West, America had a special role to play in Asia. To carry out her responsibility to regenerate the "stationary" and "barbarous" Chinese, "still in race-childhood," the United States must keep China open to American influence and be prepared to use force to assert her dominance in the East.[25]

Mahan's ideology of American colonialism—its masculinity, its Protestant temperament, and its "race patriotism"—was directly related to his personal needs: External aggressiveness signified inner torment. It is doubtful whether Mahan had, as historian Walter La Feber claims, "rifled the history books more than his soul or his past in order to construct what he believed to be the necessary world of the coming twentieth century." It is also questionable whether Mahan's "writings can be understood when separated from the personality of the author."[26] Mahan's view of American expansionism was derived from specific social and psychological circumstances which interacted with the economic conditions and culture of late-nineteenth-century America. The "New Navy" which was designed to serve expansionism also helped Mahan overcome a status anxiety and offered him a means of maintaining control over the emotions which his culture insisted he dominate.

Mahan's scholarship and his strategy of imperialism represented a rage against what he considered the degradation of the Navy. Only eight years before the publication of his book on sea power, the Navy had only one first-rate ship, fourteen second-raters, and twenty-two third-raters. Given such a small operation, the service had an oversupply of officers. In 1882, there were 937 officers on sea duty, 664 on shore duty, and 236 awaiting orders. Several years earlier, as a result of a budget cut, a number of officers, including Mahan, had been relieved from duty and placed on waiting orders with half pay. Pressed financially, Mahan had to ask a friend to return a $500 loan. The change in status (and income) outraged and distressed him. "It is very many years," he complained, "since the needs of the country in the way of a Naval Establishment have been dispassionately considered, in fact it may be doubted if it has ever been done." Mahan's demoralization deepened as he suffered in a personal way the neglect and indignity he saw the Navy experiencing. It seemed he could do nothing about the humiliation, except to protest bitterly and privately in his letters to a friend. On November 13, 1880, he wrote: "In a healthy condition of naval affairs, I should by this [time] be going to sea but the low ebb to which the navy is now reduced . . . gives me no hope of even such commands as we have for some time to come. I fear this state of things will have an injurious effect upon the spirit of naval officers." Two years later he estimated that the United States did not have six ships which could be kept at sea in war. "Immersed as our people are in peaceful and material pursuits," Mahan complained, "the military establishment is necessarily one of our lesser interests. . . . Practically we have nothing. Never before has the navy sunk so low." His discontent was sharpened by the contrast between the Navy's poverty and the "concentration of wealth and power in the hands of a protected few."[27]

During this period of dissatisfaction, Mahan began to develop a strategy to restore the support and importance he felt the Navy should have. First he abandoned any "anti-imperialist" notions he once had. "I was up to

1885 traditionally an anti-imperialist," he recalled in 1902, "but by 1890 the study of the influence of sea power . . . had converted me." Thus he became, he said in his autobiography, "frankly an imperialist." Mahan had at one time been critical of the use of American troops in foreign countries. "The very suspicion of an imperial policy is hateful; the mixing of our politics with those of Latin republics especially," he had written in 1884. "Though identified, unluckily, with a military profession I dread outlying colonies, or interests, to maintain which large military establishments are necessary." But this awareness of the link between colonies and the military converted Mahan to imperialism. Four years earlier, commenting on naval budgetary reductions, he had pointed out that the reason the country lacked concern for the Navy's development was the seemingly remote prospect of foreign entanglement. "Now the Canal at the Isthmus," he added, "*may* bring our interests and those of foreign nations in collision—and in that case . . . we must without delay begin to build a navy which will at least equal that of England. . . ." As he became an advocate for naval expansion, Mahan became increasingly conscious of the relationship between the restoration of self-respect and vitality for the Navy, and the development of American overseas interests. In a private letter written on March 11, 1885, he described the embarrassment United States naval officers felt. "If we are made to go from port to port in ships which are a laughing stock . . . you cannot expect that our pride and self-respect will escape unimpaired." But, he predicted, the United States would have a first-class ironclad navy if it had "interests out of our own border" and "an Isthmian policy." A year later Mahan was teaching at the Naval War College, determined to draw "lessons" from the past and "to raise the profession" of the Navy through the study of the history of sea power.[28]

The "New Navy" would not only restore status to its officers, it would also serve as a sanctuary for American asceticism—a place where men could seek confirmation of self-worth in strenuous activity, control the body and its emotional needs, and maintain strict self-discipline. The Navy would make certain men were what American culture expected them to be.

A man of great self-control, Mahan was an embodiment of the culture's expectation. As a young boy, he had been trained by his father to admire self-discipline. A West Point professor, Dennis Mahan appreciated war as an "art" which exercised "a prominent influence on the well-being of society" as the "most cursory glance at the grand military epochs" of history would show. He inspired in his son a great interest in military history, and inculcated in him the values of self-control and ambitious activity. "I trust," he wrote to his son, then a midshipman at the Annapolis Academy, "you will keep before your mind the nearness of your Academic Goal; the importance of the stake to your future professional position; and . . . like a good racer, you will put forth your efforts to distance your competitors. . . ." Urging his son to become "more your own master," he declared: "The hardest restraint is self-restraint, but it alone is truly valuable. To oblige one's self to do, and to be obliged by some one else to do, lie at the two extremes of government—one is the moral the other the physical code."[29]

Alfred Mahan matured into a person who would not show his feelings; he believed their expression to be a "feminine quality." Emotions should be "managed, economized, guided, and disciplined," not allowed to run "waste." The metaphor he used to describe what he called "self-repression" strikingly reflected the pervasiveness of technology in American culture: "Emotion harnessed and guided is steam controlled in a boiler, with pipes connecting to the engine which it is to drive. The steam is no less a force if it be allowed to escape; it simply becomes a force wasted unimproved." Mahan was not one to "waste" his force. To some of his fellow officers, he appeared stern and entirely lacking in humor: He bore himself with "dignity" and rarely joked. As a father, he instructed his children to strive for excellence, improve themselves, and develop self-discipline. "Nothing," he said, "can take the place of one's own individual, solitary, struggle."[30]

Mahan's "self-repression" compelled him to split off his emotional life and make it secret. While at the Annapolis Academy, young Mahan developed a close and affectionate relationship with a fellow student, Samuel Ashe. In the correspondence between the two men, which continued for more than forty years, we find Mahan expressing emotions, particularly those of softness. Due to illness, Ashe was forced to return home, and, on October 23, 1858, Mahan wrote to Ashe:

> For I cannot believe, Sam, that our love for each other is to be broken, your letter must have miscarried or you are sick. Averett said to me when you left, "Mahan, you would hardly miss your wife more, would you?" "Old man," said I, "if I am to miss my wife so much, I will never get married." And now dearest, I must stop. And lest you think I have been letting my angry feelings and jealousy run away from me, I will tell you the oft repeated tale—I love you dearly, deeply and sincerely, dear, dear Sam.
>
> Your most affectionate friend,
A. T. M.

A few days later, Mahan, deeply missing his friend, wrote to Ashe again:

> I have not yet fully realized that you are gone, it seems only as if you were not in my room; if I could feel it in its full length and breadth it would almost kill me. . . . I lay in bed last night, dear Sam, thinking of the gradual rise and growth

of our friendship. My first visit even to your room is vividly before me, and how as I went up there from night to night I could feel my attachment to you growing and see your own love for me showing itself more and more every night. After all what feeling is more delightful than that of loving and being loved, even though it be only man's love for man? . . . One night in particular; it has perhaps escaped your recollection, but I remember it as yesterday and prize the recollection most dearly. The happiness that I felt that night I will never forget.

In other letters to Ashe, Mahan insisted that he did not want to be "tied" down; he wanted the freedom that the frontier—now the sea—offered. "Ladies' society," he admitted, made him "temporarily feel in good spirits." But, he added, "I do not expect fully to enjoy myself again until I get to sea. I am more at home on a ship than any where else; my health and spirits are always good and the very air of the sea inspires a man with a sort of 'insouciance' that all the ladies in God's world can not give; indeed, the dear creatures, I think, rather have a tendency to multiply the cares and vex the spirits of men."After graduation from Annapolis, Mahan was sent to Japan, and there he became "intimate" with a fellow serviceman from another ship. He wrote to Ashe, insisting he did not feel the same "attachment" to this new friend as he did to Ashe. Then he "confess[ed] candidly" that he preferred men to women: "When you come to a simple question of sex, on the whole commend me to men."[31]

With his emotional self located in fraternity, Mahan elevated his rationality to power in his anxious struggle to perfect his self-control. He worried about the need to regulate conduct, which he considered "coincident with every moment of conscious life," requiring continuous effort to control. "We all have experience," he wrote, "in ourselves . . . of subduing the natural impulse" where particular actions are the suppression rather than the expression of the "inward feeling or mood. But we also know what a labor this involves, where the permanent natural disposition is contrary; or where the opposition proceeds from those temporary conditions we call moods, which themselves depend largely upon bodily conditions, the transient derangements of the natural life." The problem for Mahan was whether "human watchfulness" could equal the "sustained strain" involved in the effort to guard every action continuously.[32]

The strain on Mahan was enormous. He suffered from frequent painful headaches, and went through "seasons of great apprehension," believing that his family had an hereditary tendency toward disease and a disposition to "nervous and mental excitement and worry." Even as a young officer, he complained in a letter to his sister: "Tell mother that I am beginning to feel a tendency toward nervous headaches." Exercise, he hoped, would cure him. Years later, in the 1890s, Mahan's nervousness intensified. He feared he would "break down" from the strain on his brain and nerves, and told his wife that his "whole nervous system" was in "a state of exasperation."[33]

But Mahan only perpetuated his suffering and its sources as he promoted the "New Navy" as a sanctuary of American asceticism. Three years before the war against Spain, in an essay, "The Navy as a Career," Mahan wrote an eloquent statement on the purpose of the "New Navy." Describing the ascetic life and "suffering of emotions" a naval officer had to accept, he explained how the profession required "long breaks—two or three years—in the home life; the lack of habitude to home and its ways; husband and wife losing touch." American society, Mahan assured the men of the Navy, would ultimately appreciate their sacrifice. The consideration accorded to a profession, he observed, depended upon the general aims and pursuits of society. Due to a combination of circumstances, Americans had fastened their attention upon the "internal affairs" of the country and had attached paramount importance "to the making and having of money." But, he pointed out, money as the representative of power and "the means to gratification" had developed "external interests" or "business interests in foreign lands." While the "external interests" which supported the existence of the Navy still represented only a small proportion of Americans, the country was moving toward a broader view of national interests. "If this should come to pass," Mahan promised, "the Navy will undoubtedly gain that width of sympathy and recognition which, by the dignity it confers, is of itself no slight advantage to be considered in the choice of a profession. In no event will there be money in it; but there may always be honor and quietness of mind and worthy occupation,—which are better guarantees of happiness."[34]

Shortly before the actual outbreak of armed hostilities against Spain, Mahan praised, with even greater zeal, the high calling of the Navy. "Nothing is more ominous for the future of our race," he proclaimed as if he were giving a sermon, "than that tendency . . . which refuses to recognize in the profession of arms, in war . . . that something which has made the soldier to all ages the type of heroism and of self-denial. When the religion of Christ, of Him who was led as a lamb to the slaughter, seeks to raise before its followers the image of self-control, and of resistance to evil, it is the soldier whom it presents."[35] Thus, as he helped to guide the United States toward international violence, Mahan called upon Americans to regard the profession of war as the highest moral expression of American asceticism.

In imperialism, Mahan integrated asceticism, violence, and masculinity. Like Theodore Roosevelt, he believed men should not behave "softly," for softness and gentleness were "womanly qualities." "A fool can trudge through life with kindness," Mahan scoffed, "but the great men of the world are those of unrelenting heart who tear away and break down every obstacle." To Mahan, history was the chronicle of commercial conflicts between nations and the use of war to resolve those conflicts. While he acknowledged that arbitration should be tried first to resolve such conflicts, he said he had no sympathy for those who held that war was never imperative. He believed force was "a faculty of national life," a necessity to protect Western civilization, "an oasis set in the midst of a desert of barbarism." He condemned "luxury" and the "worship of comfort, wealth, and general softness" as threats to civilization, and called for the maintenance of the "strong masculine impulse" and the "masculine combative virtues." As he assessed the Spanish-American War, Mahan boasted: "What means less violent than war would in a half-year have solved the Caribbean problem, shattered national ideas deep-rooted in the prepossessions of a century, and planted the United States in Asia?" Mahan was not ashamed to express his belief in "raw power"—"the mighty hand that crushes everything that stands in its way and the will that makes men giants." And he did not hesitate to support the crushing of Chinese resistance against American imperialism. Shortly after United States troops suppressed the Boxer Rebellion in 1900, Mahan declared that the Chinese were "children" and that children needed to be disciplined, given a "good shaking."[36]

In the search for a "wider field," a new frontier for the regeneration of the American spirit, expansionists like Mahan were seeking to control their own rebellion against the repression of the self; they were also seeking to criticize the world of bureaucratic corporate capitalism which threatened republican individualism and which had "concentrated" wealth and power in the hands of "a protected few." Tightening their lines of self-restraint, these expansionists had fastened around themselves even more securely the lines of corporate domination, and eventually fell under the rule of the demonic "iron cage."

This complex process was related to what historian David Rothman has described as the "discovery of the asylum" in the nineteenth century. In a society of individualism, institutions of social control and regimentation emerged—not only the asylum, but also the orphanage, the reformatory, and the penitentiary.[37] The method of social control, in which republican values were instilled into individuals, had two parts: the asylum and the family. In Dr. Rush's formulation, the two had a dialectical relationship. The first was public and curative, the second private and preventative. As institutions for cure were established, the educational function of the family was emphasized. Both the asylum and the family were intended to create "republican machines." As restrained republicans suffered from headaches or from what Dr. Beard diagnosed as "American nervousness," and as their bodies rebelled against rigid self-control, many of them sought to quash their private rebellions, rehabilitate themselves, and provide an institutional environment for self-discipline. This was what men like Mahan sought to achieve in the "New Navy."

But even more formidable institutions of social control came to power as the "iron cages" of republican ideology constructed by Rush, Jefferson, and other founding fathers gave way to the corporate "iron cage." Once again Americans had a king—an external authority, ruling from a distance, now omnipotent and disinterested. Their republican ideology, which had in Jackson's time demanded the destruction of the Bank and set in motion the mechanism of the market, precluded the possibility of challenging new corporate "monsters." As self-governing and autonomous Americans, or "self-sufficient monads," they lacked the community, the sense of collective identity and action, to respond effectively to the threat of corporate monopolies and to bring them into their service. Still, some of the leaders insisted, a reaffirmation of the republican faith was needed. This was Senator Albert Beveridge's point when he commented on the unlikelihood of United States citizenship for Filipinos: "Whips of scorpions could not lash the Filipinos to this land of fervid enterprise, sleepless industry, and rigid order." Americans had to lash themselves—to be self-governing men.[38]

Yet, as they aggressively proclaimed the power of will, expansionists were enlarging the power of the "iron cage" of monopoly capitalism. Ironically, even as Mahan sought to transform the Navy into a vital center for the restoration of republican asceticism and virtue, he reinforced the money-making society he hoped to reform. The Navy extended American markets into Asia; more than ever before, it existed to serve American corporate needs. As the interests of the military and American industry became integrated, the dignity and honor Mahan wished to confer on the Navy became measured in terms of annual appropriations. Thus, in the end, what Mahan helped to achieve in imperialism and the building of the "New Navy" was the dependency of the military upon the very "concentrations" of wealth and power which he scorned.

But a more pernicious and tragic development took place as the United States expanded into the Philippines and China. In the violence and destructiveness of imperialism, there emerged the third and final prison—the demonic "iron cage." In this new structure of thought and action, Thanatos ruled. War was viewed as moral, "raw power" as an expression of "virility," masculine combativeness as "virtuous," and forceful racial domination as paternalism and patriotism. Rational control and concern for profits yielded to irrational impulses which emphasized power, aggression, and death.[39]

In imperialism, Mahan had mistaken the solution for the problem, and the demonic zeal for destruction overwhelmed many Americans and drove them to carry death to Asia. The republican "iron cages," demanding the rational domination of the instinctual life, generated discontent and rage. The Spanish-American War and American military violence in Asia only perpetuated American nervousness. In American aggression, expansionists imputed to "primitive" Filipinos and "savage" Chinese the emotional self republicans sought to deny, and sublimated republican repression into the violent domination of the "undeveloped races." The relief from nervousness that international violence offered was only partial and temporary, for its causes—Protestant and republican self-control and asceticism—remained even more tightly woven into the fabric of American culture. And the corporate "iron cage," as it reduced republican men to political impotency, compelled them to reassert the "strenuous life" and recover their manhood and republican will through violence in Cuba and the Philippines. Seeking to conquer a "larger liberty," imperialists had only extended the "empire of necessity."

In imperialism, moreover, the expansionists' search for foreign markets did not take society toward a resolution of the problems of monopoly capitalism and class conflict; it only fostered a dependency on external safety valves to siphon off the pressures of social tensions. What Josiah Strong believed was the way out actually aggravated the crisis of "our country." Without a king and traditions to provide community in America, society in the 1890s was fragmenting even more under the pressures of urban-rural conflicts, the Populist revolt, nativist-immigrant divisions, and labor-capitalist warfare. The war with Spain rendered more remote the possibility of a radical reformation of America as it momentarily drew together antagonistic groups in a jingoistic crusade and directed outward the aggressive and destructive impulses which the republican and corporate "iron cages" had agitated and intensified.

As American expansionists became imprisoned in the demonic "iron cage," they offered shrill claims of new freedom and vigor. And as the American military ruthlessly suppressed Filipino leader Emilio Aguinaldo's resistance and built a pyramid of the skulls of his countrymen—16,000 dead Filipinos, based on combat "body-count," and as many as 250,000 due to direct hostilities, disease, and starvation—expansionists promised the restoration of republican virtues through violence.[40] After all, had not warfare against Indians been regenerative?

Six years after Frederick Jackson Turner had paused to wonder what the future would bring to a society whose basis of vitality and virtue had disappeared, Theodore Roosevelt dramatically located a new frontier, the new source of American strength in Asia. In his speech "The Strenuous Life," given before the Hamilton Club in Chicago on April 10, 1899, Roosevelt sought to define again who Americans should be. The events and developments of the nineties—the crisis of American capitalism during the depression, the violent Homestead and Pullman strikes, the threat from an industrial proletariat, the political and economic emasculation of his patrician class in an America under the hegemony of powerful trusts, the war against Spain, Commodore Dewey's attack on Manila, the charge up San Juan Hill, the annexation of the Philippines, and the emergence of the United States as a power in Asia—demanded the effort be made.

Here was the jeremiad of the nineties: Americans must not "be content to rot by inches in ignoble ease," Roosevelt declared; they must not allow themselves to sink into "scrambling commercialism," heedless of the "higher life." They must not busy themselves only with the daily wants of their "bodies." They must not lose their "manly" qualities. Like Rush and Strong, Roosevelt insisted the reformation of the self be extended to the reformation of the world:

> The timid man, the lazy man, the man who distrusts his country, the over-civilized man, who has lost the great fighting, masterful virtues, the ignorant man, and the man of dull mind, whose soul is incapable of feeling the mighty lift that thrills "stern men with empires in their brains"—all these, of course, shrink from seeing the nation undertake its new duties; shrink from seeing us build a navy and an army adequate to our needs; shrink from seeing us do our share of the world's work, by bringing order out of chaos in the great, fair tropic islands from which the valor of our soldiers and sailors has driven the Spanish flag.

As a world power, the United States must deal aggressively and firmly in international affairs, and bring "order out of chaos" in the Philippines. Rush had used bleeding, purging, and the tranquilizer chair to promote the empire of liberty; Roosevelt prescribed military power. In this call for decisive military action to suppress the Filipino insurrection against American annexation, the Rough Rider declared he had no patience with the humanitarians, who canted about the "consent of the governed" in order to "excuse themselves for their unwillingness to play the part of men." Like Hank Morgan, Roosevelt refused to drive out "a medieval tyranny" only to make room for "savage anarchy." "Savagery," whether in America or Asia, had to yield to civilization; white Americans had to expand their power into Indian territory as well as the Philippines. To condemn American expansion into the Far East, Roosevelt charged, would be to make it "incumbent upon us to leave the Apaches of Arizona to work out their own salvation, and to decline to interfere in a single Indian reservation." In his conduct toward Apaches or Filipinos, Roosevelt refused to condemn his "forefathers" for "ever having settled in these United States."[41]

CHAPTER XII

DOWN FROM THE GARDENS
OF ASIA

Down from the Gardens of Asia descending radiating,
Adam and Eve appear, then their myriad progeny after them,
Wandering, yearning, curious, with restless explorations,
With questionings, baffled, formless, feverish, with never-happy hearts,
With that sad, incessant refrain, Wherefore unsatisfied soul? *and*
    Whither O mocking life?

Ah who shall soothe these feverish children?
Who justify these restless explorations?
Who speak the secret of impassive earth?
Who bind it to us? What is this separate Nature so unnatural?
What is this earth to our affections? (unloving earth, without a throb
    to answer ours,
Cold earth, the place of graves.)

                            —*Walt Whitman*
                            "*Passage to India*"

The realm of "iron cages" was not without its critics. American society
contained currents of emotion and thought in counterpoint to the structures of domination. As we have seen, Richard Henry Dana, Mark Twain,
George Beard, and Henry Adams possessed the perspicacity to discern the
destructiveness which certain values and expectations of American culture
could have to self and society. Men like Thomas Jefferson, Andrew Jackson, George Armstrong Custer, and Alfred Thayer Mahan resisted self-
repression in unique and often private ways even as they reinforced domination. And in their contradictory, ambivalent, and self-disquieting racial
attitudes, Benjamin Rush, Robert Montgomery Bird, Henry Hughes, Hen-

ry W. Grady, and Bret Harte betrayed their own discontent—a profound dissatisfaction which sprang from the market-oriented and anomic nature of American society and from the severe restraints white men had to inflict on themselves as members of American civilization. But Walt Whitman, singing joyfully to nineteenth-century Americans, was the culture's most creative and threatening critic: For he offered a vision of possibility.

Whitman, like Jefferson and Benton before him and like Mahan and Strong after him, was searching for the "passage to India." Yet, in his quest, the poet sings of an America where people of all colors come together, mixing indiscriminately in a great democracy yet respecting each other's rich cultural heritage and diversity, where community exists in a society without a king, where love's body is polymorphous and undifferentiated, and where the self is complete and integrated. For Whitman, "not physiognomy alone nor brain alone is worthy for the Muse"; the soul is "clear and sweet" and so is all that is not the soul. The body is not to be governed, subordinated to the soul or mind. Male and female are "but the equal of the other," and he sings of the "Female equally with the Male." Like frontier historian Turner, Whitman sees the American people, restless and inventive, moving westward toward Asia and carrying with them like the ethereal white woman of *American Progress* the magic of technology. He recognizes that America possesses "wholesale engines of war" which can carry death to Asia; yet he views the railroad and the steamship as means for humankind to achieve a new intimacy and unity—where the lands are to be "welded" together and where "all races and cultures" are "to be accepted, to be saluted, not to be controlled or placed in hierarchy." And, here in America, all are to be welcomed—"Chinese, Irish, German, pauper or not, criminal or not—all, all, without exceptions." Ours is not to be a society for "special types" but for the "great mass of people—the vast, surging, hopeful army of workers."[1]

While Whitman was America's critic of hope, Herman Melville was the critic of despair. Each assessed American expansionism differently: Where Whitman saw possibilities for greater cultural enrichment and greater understanding among the peoples of the world, Melville perceived death and destruction. Nearly a half century before the Spanish-American War, he could discern America's dark future in Asia. Long before Dewey's battleship had entered the waters of Manila Bay, the American whaler had been cruising near the Philippines: Americans were in the Pacific killing whales and extracting sperm oil to be used to illuminate the lamps and lubricate the machines of American civilization. One of the country's chief industries during the Market Revolution, the American whaling business sailed "a navy upwards of seven hundred vessels; manned by eighteen thousand men; yearly consuming 4,000,000 of dollars; the ships worth, at the time of sailing, $20,000,000; and every year importing into our harbors a well reaped harvest of $7,000,000." Long before Commodore Matthew C. Perry had anchored his fleet in Yedo Bay, American whalers had been hunting in the "Japanese sea": "If that double-bolted land, Japan, is ever to become hospitable," Ishmael reports in *Moby-Dick,* "it is the whale-ship alone to whom the credit will be due; for already she is on the threshold."[2] Long before Admiral Mahan urged Americans to recover their manhood in overseas expansion, Captain Ahab had been seeking conquest beyond America's continental frontier: The masculine thrust toward Asia was foreshadowed symbolically by his quest for Moby Dick and the American captain's death in Asiatic waters.

In Melville's foreboding vision, the technology that fascinated Bigelow, Benton, Webster, and Mahan becomes a pervasive and sinister motif. Ahab represents American technology; inducting scientific knowledge into the service of his hunt for the great white whale, he studies the sets of all the tides and currents in order to calculate the driftings of the sperm whale's food and the seasons for whales to be in particular latitudes. Thus he is able to "arrive at reasonable surmises, almost approaching to certainties, concerning the timeliest day to be upon this or that ground in search of his prey."[3] With his charts and instruments, Ahab allows very little to mystify him in his struggle to exert mastery over nature.

If Ahab resembles an engineer, his ship is likened to a factory and his crew to factory operatives. The *Pequod* is a virtual miniature of industrial America. Not only are there references to canals, railroads, and factories with their boilers and try-pots and furnaces spouting fire and smoke, but the *Pequod*'s social divisions of production are linked to the labor structure of industrial society. As Ishmael reports, "not one in two of the many thousand men before the mast employed in the American whale fishery, are American born, though pretty nearly all the officers are. Herein it is the same with the American whale fishery as with the American army and military and merchant navies, and the engineering forces employed in the construction of the American Canals and Railroads. The same, I say, because in all these cases the native American liberally provides the brains, the rest of the world as generally supplying the muscles." A significant supply of the "muscles" on the *Pequod* has been drawn from workers of color—blacks, Indians, Pacific Islanders, and Asians. Thus, the social order aboard the ill-fated ship reflects the dichotomy between Prospero (mind) and Caliban (body): white (brains) and color (muscles), white masters and black slaves, Anglo mine owners and Mexican miners, white foremen and Chinese railroad workers. The social divisions within the *Pequod*'s labor force graphically represent the class/caste structure of American labor and society. While not all whites are officers, all officers or men on deck are white; all workers of color are below deck, serving the interests of Captain Ahab and capitalist investors.[4]

Yet, this class/caste order does not erode the community, the ubiquitous solidarity which the *Pequod* workers, representing the races of the world, feel as the labor process unites them in a relationship of dependency, mutual survival, and brotherhood. They are not Reverend Strong's "criminal" and "appetite"-dominated workers in the cities of "Our Country." Neither are they Charles Crocker's Chinese workers, his so-called "pets," nor Henry George's Knights of St. Crispin, placing race above class consciousness. Rather they are Whitman's "vast, surging, hopeful army of workers"; as they work, they are integrated, bound to each other. During one of the chases in the whale-boat, mate Flask is mounted on the shoulders of the gigantic black Daggoo so he can see better. Harmoniously, Daggoo rolls "his fine form" with every roll of the sea; together, white and black, they become effective. Nowhere is this kind of dependency and cooperation more graphically illustrated than in the "monkey-rope," which is fastened to both Ishmael and Queequeg. Lowered down to the water to secure the blubber-hook onto the dead whale, with vicious sharks swirling around it, Queequeg is held by a rope tied to Ishmael. The process is perilous for both men. "We two, for the time," Ishmael tells us, "were wedded; and should poor Queequeg sink to rise no more, then both usage and honor demanded, that instead of cutting the cord, it should drag me down in his wake." There is a noble class unity among the crew, and the working class aboard the *Pequod* is saluted. They may have been the "meanest mariners, and renegades and castaways"; still, to them are ascribed "high qualities" and "democratic dignity," around them woven "tragic graces," and an "ethereal light" shines on the "workman's arm."[5]

But under Captain Ahab's administration, the ship becomes for these workers an "iron cage" and a coffin. The men are caught in a larger process as they kill whales and extract from them energy for market civilization and as they are inducted into the mad hunt for Moby Dick and imprisoned in Ahab's lines of force. Their very work seems to manifest their tragic future. To boil the blubber, they use scraps of whale fat as fuel for the tryworks. The whale seems to be "a self-consuming misanthrope": He supplies the fuel used to burn his body. The crew appears destined to a similar fate: "The rushing Pequod, freighted with savages, and laden with fire, burning a corpse, and plunging into that blackness of darkness, seemed the material counterpart of her monomaniac commander's soul."[6] Only rebellion could have saved the workers.

Yet, they do not mutiny against their mad master. While they clearly have the courage other workers would demonstrate in the Pullman Strike and the Homestead Strike and while they have the physical power to revolt, they do not seize command of the ship. They actually have the right to overthrow Ahab, for the captain "had indirectly laid himself open to the unanswerable charge of usurpation; and with perfect impunity, both moral and legal, his crew if so disposed . . . could refuse all further obedience to him, and even violently wrest from him the command." Significantly, the crew is not "so disposed." They do not feel the need for collective resistance—what Henry W. Grady would denounce as the "societies of socialism" and what George Washington Cable would condemn as the "evil charms of unions." Although Captain Ahab is never able to make them totally a part of his monomania, he controls their behavior and incorporates the bodies of all the workers into the machine-factory of the *Pequod*. Although he is unable to transform his men into Henry Hughes's "happy warrantees" or Booker T. Washington's "patient" and "faithful" workers, Ahab draws them into the rituals of the delirious hunt. He shares with them the "phantoms" of his mind—his Promethean conceptions of life and the universe—in order to legitimatize his control and to base his domination on consent rather than coercion. In short, he "manufactures" their cooperation. Charismatic and powerful, Captain Ahab extracts from his crew what Antonio Gramsci has called the "spontaneous loyalty" of the workers for their master. His power centralized, Ahab is an awesome administrator/leader—a greater Benjamin Rush and a more formidable scientific manager than Francis Amasa Walker. While Rush and Walker relied on authority to exercise control over mental patients and Indians respectively, Ahab uses the magnetic force of his personality, his power of persuasion, to dominate his men. He is able to charm them, make them want to obey his commands, and even feel the excitement of the chase.[7]

Under their captain's hegemony, the *Pequod* workers are unable to do what the slave Babo of the story *Benito Cereno* knows he must do in order to survive and to be free. Unlike Babo, the leader of a black rebellion on board the slaver *San Dominick,* they do not outwardly follow the orders of their master while carrying the knife of revolution. Neither do they do what Bartleby does—refuse to work. Had they, like the scrivener portrayed in Melville's short story, declared their great refusal, saying they "preferred not" to chase the great white whale, they would have torpedoed Ahab's mission. But they are unable even to commit civil disobedience, for they lack the political consciousness—the awareness of their own class interests as well as the recognition of Ahab's madness—necessary for resistance. Where Bartleby understands his oppression—his "mechanical" labor in a law office which is likened to a factory—and hence is able to rebel against a world of legal forms and dead letters, the *Pequod* crew, except for Starbuck and Ishmael, are blind to the disaster awaiting them and hence are unable to save themselves. To paraphrase historian Gabriel Kolko, they cannot choose alternatives as long as none is seriously proposed, and they cannot propose a relevant measure of fundamental opposition to Captain Ahab as long as they have no critical understanding of what is occurring on their ship. But their situation, even more than Bartleby's, demands that they respond: Bartleby merely opposes the absurd, while they face the demonic.[8]

In many respects, Captain Ahab personifies Tocqueville's nervous American, Bird's "houseless Nathan," and Twain's Connecticut Yankee. He, too, is a man in motion, restless, unattached; a boy harpooner at the age of eighteen, he has whaled continuously for forty years. He is an ascetic, lacking the "low, enjoying power"—Jefferson's strong "human passions" and Lawrence's "dark gods." Ahab holds "in check" what Dr. George Beard would describe as "atomic forces" and restrains his "normal feelings." He is a loner: When he was past fifty, he wedded a "young-girl wife" only to leave her with "but one dent" in the marriage pillow. And, in the same way Commander Jackson disciplines his body to destroy the Creeks, the "monsters" of the wilderness, Ahab dominates his physical self, forcing his "bowed," "humped," "tired," and "weary" body to press forward in pursuit of Moby Dick, the "monster" of the ocean. An incomplete man—without a leg, without his "wholeness," Ahab is an archetype of supreme "self-renunciation." Indeed, the "less" Ahab "is," the greater his "alienation." He is hardened, incapable of joy: His must be total and constant control. The totality of his self-domination is demonstrated in the "symphony," the moment of peace before the final and terrible confrontation. On that steel-blue day, the firmaments of sky and sea are one, blending in an all-pervading azure; the air is pensive, "transparently pure and soft, with a woman's look." And the "lovely aromas" in that "enchanted air" seemed at last to dispel for a moment "the cankerous thing in his soul." The situation moves Ahab. He drops a "tear into the sea," and sadly confesses: "What a forty years' fool—fool—old fool, has old Ahab been!"[9] But his emotions fail to overwhelm him as he recomposes himself and turns again to the hunt.

Like Nathan Quaker/Slaughter, Ahab has a scar which has deformed his being: Nathan has been scalped and Ahab has lost a leg. And as Ahab cherishes a "wild vindictiveness" against the great white whale, he associates Moby Dick with "all his bodily woes" and "all his intellectual and spiritual exasperations." For him, the whale becomes the "monomaniac incarnation of all those malicious agencies which some deep men feel eating in them, till they are left living on with half a heart and half a lung." Deliriously transferring "that intangible malignity" to the "abhorred white whale," Ahab pits himself, "all mutilated," against the animal. All evil, to him, is visibly personified and made "practically assailable" in Moby Dick, and he piles upon the "whale's white hump the sum of all the general rage and hate felt by his whole race from Adam down. . . ." Here, Ahab is like Prospero or like the Englishmen described in Winthrop Jordan's *White over Black:* The commander has imputed evil to the white whale as Prospero assigned darkness to Caliban and as Englishmen in colonial America used Africans to deny the "black bucks" within themselves.[10] And in his monomaniac struggle to conquer the parts of the self he has split off and hates, Ahab relentlessly seeks to destroy the great white whale.

Reduced to pure destructive and impulsive rage, Ahab becomes so one-dimensional and so rigid that he is described as a machine-man. Nothing is able to bend the "welded iron" of his soul, his "heart of wrought steel"; his "high, broad form" seems made of "solid bronze," and the life force within him is described as "magnetic." His brain seems to beat against "solid metal," his "iron brow," his "steel skull." Indeed, Ahab is actually part "mechanical," for one of his legs, constructed of ivory, is a replaceable part; thus, when the whale snaps it off, Ahab orders his carpenter to make him another. "By heaven," he shouts, "this dead wood has the better of my live flesh every way." He declares he would be happier yet if his whole physical self, not just his leg, could be rebuilt; then he would order a "complete man," fifty feet tall with a chest modeled after the Thames Tunnel, a brass forehead, and "no heart at all." Such a man would be like the Indian-hater in *The Confidence-Man*—an ocean-roving Colonel Moredock, with a finger like a "trigger" and nerves like "electric wires." Completely rebuilt, Ahab would be Dr. Beard's "electric machine" with all his "lamps actively burning"; he would be the ultimate "republican machine." Time and again Ahab is described in terms of a machine, particularly a steam engine, a locomotive. His blood reaches the "boiling point," and he has a "smoking brow." His ship, an extension of himself, leaves a wake which resembles train tracks, and the path to his "fixed purpose" is laid with "iron rails," whereon his soul is "grooved" to run. His eyes "glowing like coals," he moves mechanically, and "naught's an obstacle, naught's an angle to the iron way!" Gears and wheels become pervasive metaphors. In his relationship to his crew, Ahab's "one cogged circle fits into all their various wheels, and they revolve." Transformed into parts of Ahab's mechanical body, the workers on the *Pequod* are like Walker's factory laborers who are "connected" to the machinery and made to "conform" to its movements, and like the women in Melville's "Tartarus of Maids"—the exploited female factory operatives who do not so much seem "accessory wheels to the general machinery as mere cogs to the wheels." On the quarterdeck, Ishmael hears Ahab "lowly humming to himself, producing a sound so strangely muffled and inarticulate that it seemed the mechanical humming of the wheels of his vitality in him."[11] Again, governed by his single drive, Ahab paces the deck with his mechanical leg, his motions repetitive, as he scans the horizons of Asiatic waters.

In his search-and-destroy mission, Captain Ahab is so possessed by his monomania that he diverts his activities from the rational capitalist accumulation of sperm oil to the consuming and ultimately self-destructive hunt for his single enemy. Thus, when Starbuck discovers sperm oil leaking in the hold, he advises his captain to stop and make repairs: "Either do that, sir, or waste in one day more oil than we make good in a year. What we come twenty thousand miles to get is worth saving, sir." But Ahab is clearly thinking of something else as he responds: "So it is, so it is; if we get it." Starbuck, still concerned about profits, the leaking oil, tries to correct Ahab: "I was speaking of the oil in the hold, sir." "And I was not speaking or thinking of that at all. Begone! Let it leak!" explodes Ahab, blasting both Starbuck and the owners of the *Pequod.*[12] Thus, while Starbuck represents the rational self-interest of both the republican "iron cage" and the corporate "iron cage," Ahab is the embodiment of the demonic "iron cage." Already partially unveiled in Dr. Rush's "tranquilizer chair," Jefferson's "perpetual exercise of the most boisterous passions," Nathan Quaker/Slaughter's bloody carvings, and Jackson's massacre of Creeks at Horse Shoe Bend, the demonic "iron cage" is completely unshrouded in Ahab. Indeed, Ahab is a Hank Morgan without the deadly humor and humanitarian rhetoric; and like Morgan at the Battle of the Sand Belt, Ahab will destroy everything around him. Soon to assert its hegemony in American society after the Civil War, this final cage would appear again in Mahan's "New Navy" and American military violence in Asia, and subordinate the primacy of profits to the irrational quest for power and destruction.

Ahab's hunt is symbolic of the American thrust toward Asia. His ship, the *Pequod,* is "penetrating further and further into the heart of the Japanese cruising ground," into Asiatic "watery prairies"—Jefferson's "vacant lands," Custer's "ocean" of undulating grass, and Turner's "wider field," where Strong, Mahan, Roosevelt, and other "stern men with empires in their brains" would later urge Anglo-Saxon Americans to seek regeneration through violence. Much violence has already occurred in the American experience, as the name of the ship suggests: The Pequots were a tribe of Connecticut Indians destroyed by whites in the seventeenth century. The extinction of the Pequots, it becomes clear in the discussion on "Loose-Fish," must be viewed within the context of European and white American expansionism. "What was America in 1492 but a Loose-Fish, in which Columbus struck the Spanish standard by way of waifing it for his royal master and mistress?" observed Ishmael. Writing shortly after the American war against Mexico and after California had been placed in "the hands of an enterprising people," Melville has Ishmael ask: "What at last will Mexico be to the United States? All Loose-Fish."[13] More violence will occur, as the United States expands westward toward Asia—a "Loose-Fish."

The significance of Asia in the irrational and demonic hunt for the great white whale may be seen not only in the location of the *Pequod* in the "Japanese sea" but also in the relationship between Ahab and Fedallah. An Asian, Fedallah stands in Ahab's shadow, as if he were the captain's extension. Accompanied by four companions "tiger-yellow" in complexion, Fedallah appears suddenly and mysteriously on board the *Pequod,* wearing a rumpled "Chinese" jacket of black cotton which invests him "funereally." For the longest hours, Ahab and Fedallah stand apart in the starlight, gazing fixedly upon each other, "as if in the Parsee Ahab saw his forethrown shadow, in Ahab the Parsee his abandoned substance." Both men seemed "yoked together, and an unseen tyrant driving them; the lean shade siding the sold rib." Ahab pledges he will slay Moby Dick and survive, and Fedallah responds: "Hemp only can kill thee." In an act of self-assurance, Ahab arrogantly exclaims: "The gallows, ye mean.—I am immortal then, on land and on sea." But hemp, a rope described as "a dusky, dark fellow, a sort of Indian [from India]," is also used for the whale line.[14]

Imprisoned in the demonic "iron cage," Ahab becomes an engine in the service of Thanatos as he destroys both society (the *Pequod* and the crew) and self in the "watery prairies" of Asia, near the "Manilla isles." As the future of America would be intertwined with Asia's during the Spanish-American War and after, the fate of Ahab is tied to Fedallah's. White and yellow, they are literally bound together—"fastened"—as they meet their deaths. Prophesying the death of his captain, the Asian tells Ahab: "Though it come to the last, I shall still go before thee thy pilot." Indeed, Fedallah dies first, as he becomes tangled in Ahab's whale line and is dragged into the ocean by Moby Dick. The violence is mechanical; technology becomes the metaphor for violent death. The line darts out, like the "manifold whizzings of a steam-engine," its "flying beam," "shaft," and "wheel" in full action. And the whale, pulling the line, resembles "the mighty iron Leviathan of the modern railway." Fedallah is tied to the machine-like "monster"; "sashed round and round to the fish's back, pinioned in the turns upon turns in which, during the past night, the whale had reeled the involutions of the lines around him. . . ."[15] Ahab, in turn, is caught around the neck by the "whizzing" and "smoking" whale line made of "hemp" and is shot out of the boat, spinning and twisting behind Fedallah lashed to the great white whale, his "Chinese" jacket frayed to shreds and his distended eyes turned full upon old Ahab.

Notes

Preface

1. Karl Marx, *The Economic and Philosophic Manuscripts of 1844* (New York, 1973, originally published in 1932), p. 150; Herman Melville, *Moby-Dick, or, the Whale* (Boston, 1956, originally published in 1851), p. 154. This fragmentization is reflected in works such as Eugene Genovese's *The Political Economy of Slavery: Studies in the Economy and Society of the Slave South* (New York, 1966); Roy Harvey Pearce's *Savagism and Civilization: A Study of the Indian and the American Mind* (Baltimore, 1967); Cecil Robinson's *With the Ears of Strangers: The Mexican in American Literature* (Tucson, Arizona, 1963); and Stuart C. Miller's *The Unwelcome Immigrant: The American Image of the Chinese, 1785-1882* (Berkeley, 1969). Except for Genovese's, these works also tend to study racial attitudes as intellectual history. Thomas F. Gossett's *Race: The History of an Idea in America* (Dallas, 1963) is a first step, though a small one, toward a comparative analysis of racism. For the colonial period, see Gary Nash's *Red, White, and Black* (Englewood Cliffs, N.J., 1975).

2. Ronald T. Takaki, *A Pro-Slavery Crusade: The Agitation to Reopen the African Slave Trade* (New York, 1971); Winthrop D. Jordan, *White over Black: American Attitudes Toward the Negro, 1550-1812* (Chapel Hill, N.C., 1968), p. xiv.

3. In his book, *Racial Oppression in America* (New York, 1972), Robert Blauner pointed out the need to approach American society as a "total structure." Acknowledging what he called "a major defect of my study," he wrote: "It lacks a conception of American society as a total structure beyond the central significance that I attribute to racism. Thus my perspective tends to suffer from the fragmented character of the approaches to American race relations that I have just criticized. . . . there is no systematic exposition of capitalist structure and dynamics; racial oppression and racial conflict are not satisfactorily linked to the dominant economic relations nor to the overall distribution of political power in America" (see p. 13).

4. Summary of Antonio Gramsci's concept of cultural hegemony by Gwynn Williams, "The Concept of 'Egemonia' in the Thought of Antonio Gramsci: Some Notes on Interpretation," *Journal of the History of Ideas,* vol. 21 (1960), p. 587. Many of Gramsci's important writings may be found in *The Modern Prince and Other Writings* (New York, 1972). See Ralf Dahrendorf, *Class and Class Conflict in Industrial Society* (Stanford, 1959), for a summary of Karl Marx's concept of the "superstructure"—the "various and peculiarly formed sentiments, illusions, modes of thought, and conceptions of life," p. 14. The terms *phantoms* and *subliminations* are from Marx. His discussion on ideology and hegemony may be found in *The German Ideology,* which he wrote with Friedrich Engels and which has been reprinted in part in Loyd D. Easton and Kurt H. Guddat, eds., *Writings of the Young Marx on Philosophy and Society* (New York, 1967), pp. 414-5, 438-40. For a reminder of the dialectical in Marx's materialism, read Eugene Genovese, *In Red and Black: Marxian Explorations in Southern and Afro-American History* (New York, 1971), especially pp. 32, 33, 40, 43. In his assessment of statements by Marx on the function of ideas in history, Gramsci observed: "The analysis of these statements, I believe, reinforces the notion of 'historical bloc,' in which the material forces are the content and ideologies the form—merely an analytical distinction since material forces would be historically inconceivable without form and since ideologies would have to be considered individual dabbling without material forces." (In Genovese, ibid., p. 32).

5. C. Wright Mills, *The Sociological Imagination* (New York, 1976), pp. 3-6, 134, 143, 161. See also Karl Mannheim, *Ideology and Utopia: An Introduction to the Sociology of Knowledge* (New York, 1936), p. 10. The importance of ideological consensus is noted in Gabriel Kolko, *The Triumph of Conservatism: A Reinterpretation of American History, 1900-1916* (New York, 1977), especially pp. 282-5. Such "class values," Kolko argues, formed a crucial basis for what he calls "political capitalism." For a study of the relationship between advertising and cultural hegemony in the twentieth century, see Stuart Ewen, *Captains of Consciousness: Advertising and the Social Roots of the Consumer Culture* (New York, 1976).

6. Walt Whitman, *Leaves of Grass and Selected Prose* (New York, 1958), p. 342.

7. Karl Marx, *The Economic and Philosophic Manuscripts of 1844,* p. 150; Melville, *Moby-Dick,* p. 154. See also Norman O. Brown, *Life Against Death: The Psychoanalytical Meaning of History* (Middletown, Conn., 1959), p. 9; Herbert Marcuse, *Eros and Civilization: A Philosophical Inquiry into Freud* (New York, 1955); Sigmund Freud, *Civilization and Its Discontents* (Garden City, N.Y., n.d.). The term *alienation* has different uses in this book. It is used to describe the condition of the capitalist: In his accumulation, his asceticism and self-renunciation, he represses many of his human needs and his wholeness. *Alienation* is also used to describe the condition of the

worker: Compelled to exchange his labor for wages and denied control over the process of his productive activity, he is separated from the ownership of the product or the objectification of his labor. In either case, the person—whether capitalist or worker—is less than the totality of his essential being. See Marx, "Estranged Labor" and "The Meaning of Human Requirements," in *Economic and Philosophic Manuscripts,* pp. 106-19, 147-64.

8. Max Weber, *The Protestant Ethic and the Spirit of Capitalism* (New York, 1958, originally published in 1930), pp. 181-2; and "Bureaucracy," in H. H. Gerth and C. Wright Mills, eds., *From Max Weber: Essays in Sociology* (New York, 1973), pp. 196-244. The term *iron cage* is Weber's. He uses it to describe the material and mechanical power which dominate people in the modern age of "victorious capitalism." I am using it to describe that form of domination as well as two other forms— the republican "iron cages" and the demonic "iron cage." See Weber, *The Protestant Ethic and the Spirit of Capitalism,* pp. 181-2. The use of the plural for republican "iron cages," which also distinguishes it from the "iron cage" (Weber's), is suggested by D. H. Lawrence, *Studies in Classic American Literature* (New York, 1964), p. 21. On the republican "iron cages," see Richard Sennett & Jonathan Cobb, *The Hidden Injuries of Class* (New York, 1973), for a glimpse of its persistence and depth (pp. 22, 78, 250). On imperialism and what I call the third, or demonic "iron cage," see Joseph Schumpeter, "The Sociology of Imperialisms," in *Imperialism and Social Classes* (New York, 1951). Although they do not call it a "demonic" condition, Betty and Theodore Roszak have noted the ubiquitous presence of militarism, imperialism, and racism in Western societies by the end of the nineteenth century. See their fine essay, "The Hard and the Soft: The Force of Feminism in Modern Times," in *Masculine/Feminine: Readings in Sexual Mythology and the Liberation of Women* (New York, 1969), pp. 87-106.

9. Walt Whitman, in Horace Traubel, *With Walt Whitman in Canada,* 2 vols. (New York, 1915), vol. 2, pp. 34-5; Weber, *Protestant Ethic,* p. 182. See also Richard Slotkin, *Regeneration Through Violence: The Mythology of the American Frontier, 1600-1860* (Middletown, Conn., 1973); Gabriel Kolko, *The Triumph of Conservatism: A Reinterpretation of American History, 1900-1916* (New York, 1963).

I. The "Iron Cage" in the New Nation

1. Herman Melville, epigraph to "The Bell-Tower," in Richard Chase, ed., *Herman Melville: Selected Tales and Poems* (New York, 1959), pp. 190-205; D. H. Lawrence, *Studies in Classic American Literature* (New York, 1966), p. 21; Walt Whitman, *Leaves of Grass and Selected Prose* (New York, 1958), p. 148. John Adams to Abigail Adams, September 22, 1776, and September 8, 1777, in L. H. Butterfield *et al.,* eds., *Adams Family Correspondence* (Cambridge, Mass., 1963-), vol. 2, pp. 131, 338; Richard Hofstadter, *America at 1750: A Social Portrait* (New York, 1971), p. 293. See also Edmund S. Morgan, "The Puritan Ethic and the American Revolution," *William and Mary Quarterly,* 3d ser., vol. 24 (January 1967), pp. 3-43; Gordon S. Wood, *The Creation of the American Republic, 1776-1787* (Chapel Hill, N.C., 1969), pp. 46-124; John R. Howe, Jr., "Republican Thought and the Political Violence of the 1790's," *American Quarterly,* vol. 19, no. 2 (Summer 1967), pp. 147-65; Max Weber, *The Protestant Ethic and the Spirit of Capitalism* (New York, 1958, originally published in 1930), p. 181.

2. Marc Egnal and Joseph A. Ernest, "An Economic Interpretation of the American Revolution," *William and Mary Quarterly*, 3d ser., vol. 29 (January 1972), pp. 3-32; John Kidd quoted therein, p. 16.

3. Thomas Paine, *Common Sense*, in Moncure D. Conway, ed., *The Writings of Thomas Paine*, 4 vols. (New York, 1894), vol. 1, p. 78; Wood, *American Republic*, pp. 52-3; *Boston Evening Post*, November 6, 1767, quoted in Morgan, "Puritan Ethic," p. 9, and in Wood, *American Republic*, p. 114; "The Association," October 20, 1774, reprinted in Samuel E. Morison, ed., *Sources and Documents Illustrating the American Revolution, 1764-1788 and the Formation of the Federal Constitution* (London, 1961), p. 124.

4. Bostonian, quoted in Neil Harris, *The Artist in American Society: The Formative Years, 1790-1860* (New York, 1970), p. 32; Samuel Adams to Samuel P. Savage, October 6, 1778, in H. A. Cushing, ed., *Writings of Samuel Adams*, 4 vols. (New York, 1904-8), vol. 4, pp. 67-8, and see also Wood, *American Republic*, pp. 64, 110.

5. Franklin to Joseph Galloway, February 25, 1775, reprinted in Morison, *Sources and Documents*, p. 137; John Adams, quoted in Wood, *American Republic*, p. 110; Paine, *Common Sense*, in Conway, *Writings*, vol. 1, p. 75.

6. Paine, *Common Sense*, in Conway, *Writings*, vol. 1, pp. 83-4, 113-4.

7. Ibid., pp. 93, 83, 86, 85, 92.

8. Perry Miller, "Jonathan Edwards and the Great Awakening," in Miller, *Errand into the Wilderness* (New York, 1964), pp. 153, 160, 166.

9. Paine, "Common Sense," in Conway, *Writings*, vol. 1, p. 99; D. H. Lawrence, *Studies in Classic American Literature* (New York, 1964), pp. 19, 5. See also Karl Marx, "On the Jewish Question," in Loyd D. Easton and Kurt H. Guddat, eds., *Writings of the Young Marx on Philosophy and Society* (New York, 1967), p. 236; Winthrop D. Jordan, "Familial Politics: Thomas Paine and the Killing of the King, 1776," *Journal of American History*, vol. 60, no. 2 (September 1973), pp. 294-308; Edwin G. Burrows and Michael Wallace, *The American Revolution: The Ideology and Psychology of National Liberation*, published as vol. 6 of *Perspectives in American History* (Cambridge, Mass., 1972). Jordan went even further, arguing that the Revolutioi. was a symbolic act of parricide in which colonists killed their father/king. Burrows and Wallace suggested that the Revolution reflected the decline of patriarchalism in both colonial society and the colonial family, a development which tended to produce more "autonomous personality types" (pp. 287-9). If their claim can be substantiated, the ideology which I describe and the psychology which Jordan delineated have a basis in the sociology of the family.

10. James Madison, quoted in Harris, *Artist in American Society*, p. 29; John Adams, quoted in Wood, *American Republic*, pp. 119-20; Samuel Adams, quoted in Wood, *American Republic*, p. 118.

11. William M. Smith, quoted in Wood, *American Republic*, p. 65; John Adams to Thomas Jefferson, December 21, 1819, in Lester J. Cappon, ed., *The Adams-Jefferson Letters*, 2 vols. (Chapel Hill, N.C., 1959), vol. 2, p. 187.

12. Lawrence, *Studies in Classic American Literature*, p. 148. See Johan Huizinga, *Homo Ludens: A Study of the Play Element in Culture* (Boston, 1955); R. D. Laing, *The Politics of Experience* (New York, 1971), p. 55; Karl Marx, *The Economic and Philosophic Manuscripts of 1844* (New York, 1973), pp. 138-9; John Adams to Zabdiel

Adams, June 21, 1776, quoted in Howe, "Republican Thought," p. 155; Fourth of July Oration, quoted in Harris, *Artist in American Society,* p. 29. See also Henry F. May, *The Enlightenment in America* (New York, 1976), pp. 337, 358, 359.

13. Paine, *Common Sense,* in Conway, *Writings,* vol. 1, pp. 113, 100.

14. Winthrop D. Jordan, *White over Black: American Attitudes Toward the Negro, 1550-1812* (Chapel Hill, N.C., 1968), p. xiv.

15. John Rolfe, quoted in Jordan, *White over Black,* p. 73; William Shakespeare, *The Tempest* (New York, 1971), Act I, scene II, lines 100-10, 183-5, 198-208, 273, 405-45; Act II, scene II, lines 25-36, 59-61; Act IV, scene I, lines 215-20. For analyses of *The Tempest* in terms of Prospero and Caliban, see K. M. Abenheimer, "Shakespeare's 'Tempest': A Psychological Analysis," *Psychoanalytic Review,* vol. 32 (1946), pp. 399-415; Leo Lowenthal, *Literature and the Image of Man: Studies of the European Drama & Novel, 1600-1900* (Boston, 1966), chapter 3; Philip Mason, *Prospero and Caliban: The Psychology of Colonization* (London, 1956).

16. Lawrence, *Classic American Literature,* pp. 16, 18; Jordan, *White over Black,* p. 579.

17. Lee, quoted in Jordan, *White over Black,* p. 309; Hugh Henry Brackenridge, letter to *Freeman's Journal* (1782), and Franklin to Peter Collinson, May 9, 1753, reprinted in Wilcomb E. Washburn, ed., *The Indian and the White Man* (New York, 1964), pp. 111, 60-1.

18. James Otis, *The Rights of the British Colonies Asserted and Proved* (1764), reprinted in Bernard Bailyn, ed., *Pamphlets of the American Revolution, 1750-1776* (Cambridge, Mass., 1965); Thomas Paine, "African Slavery in America," *Pennsylvania Journal,* March 8, 1775, reprinted in Conway, *Writings,* vol. 1, p. 8; Preamble to the Act Passed by the Pennsylvania Assembly, March 1, 1780, in Conway, *Writings,* vol. 2, pp. 29-30.

19. Benjamin Franklin, *Observations Concerning the Increase of Mankind* (1751), in Leonard W. Labaree, ed., *The Papers of Benjamin Franklin* (New Haven, Conn., 1959-), vol. 4, p. 234.

20. *Debates and Proceedings in the Congress of the United States, 1789-1791,* 2 vols. (Washington, D.C., 1834), vol. 1, pp. 998, 1284; vol. 2, pp. 1148-56, 1162, 2264.

21. Benjamin Rush, *Medical Inquiries and Observations upon the Diseases of the Mind* (Philadelphia, 1812); Thomas Jefferson, *Notes on the State of Virginia* (New York, 1964).

II. "Diseases" of the Mind and Skin

1. Walt Whitman, *Leaves of Grass and Selected Prose* (New York, 1958), p. 38; Jefferson, quoted in Daniel J. Boorstin, *The Lost World of Thomas Jefferson* (Boston, 1960), pp. 14-6; Thomas S. Szasz, *The Manufacture of Madness: A Comparative Study of the Inquisition and the Mental Health Movement* (New York, 1970), p. 138; Rush to Enoch Green, 1761, in L. H. Butterfield, ed., *Letters of Benjamin Rush,* 2 vols. (Princeton, N.J., 1951), vol. 1, p. 3.

2. Rush, in George W. Corner, ed., *The Autobiography of Benjamin Rush: His "Travels Through Life" together with his "Commonplace Book for 1789-1813"* (Princeton, N.J., 1948), p. 114; Rush, quoted in David F. Hawke, *Benjamin Rush: Revolutionary Gadfly* (Indianapolis, 1971), p. 128.

3. Rush, in Corner, *Autobiography of Rush,* pp. 12-3, 221-2.

4. Samuel Davies and Rush, quoted in Hawke, *Rush,* pp. 22 and 19; Rush to Enoch Green, 1761, in Butterfield, *Letters of Rush,* vol. 1, p. 4.

5. Rush to Mrs. Rush, September 18(?), 1776, to John Adams, August 8, 1777, and to William Gordon, December 10, 1778, in Butterfield, *Letters of Rush,* vol. 1, pp. 221-2, 152, 113. Rush to E. Hazard, August 2, 1764, in Butterfield, *Letters of Rush,* vol. 1, p. 7; Rush, "Address to the People of the United States on the Defects of the Confederation," reprinted in Harry G. Good, *Benjamin Rush and His Services to American Education* (Berne, Ind., 1918), pp. 198-9.

6. Rush, in Corner, *Autobiography of Rush,* p. 46.

7. Rush, "Defects of Confederation," in Good, *Rush and His Services,* p. 204; Rush, in Corner, *Autobiography of Rush,* p. 160; Rush to Richard Price, June 2, 1787, and to David Ramsey, March or April 1788, in Butterfield, *Letters of Rush,* vol. 1, pp. 418-9, 454.

8. Rush, in Corner, *Autobiography of Rush,* pp. 83-4, 90-2; Rush to Thomas Bradford, April 15, 1768, in Butterfield, *Letters of Rush,* vol. 1, p. 33; Rush, quoted in Hawke, *Rush,* pp. 37-8, 81; Rush, in Corner, *Autobiography of Rush,* p. 164; Rush to E. Hazard, quoted in Hawke, *Rush,* p. 41.

9. Rush, "Of the Mode of Education Proper in a Republic," in Rush, *Essays, Literary, Moral & Philosophical* (Philadelphia, 1798), p. 14; Rush, "An Address to the Ministers of the Gospel of Every Denomination in the United States, upon subjects interesting to morals" (June 21, 1788), in Rush, *Essays,* pp. 114-21.

10. Rush, "Mode of Education," in Rush, *Essays,* pp. 6-20; Rush, "To the Citizens of Philadelphia: A Plan for Free Schools," in Butterfield, *Letters of Rush,* vol. 1, p. 413.

11. Rush, "Mode of Education," in Rush, *Essays,* p. 19; Benjamin Rush, *Thoughts upon Female Education* (Philadelphia, 1787), pp. 5-6. See also John Adams, in L. H. Butterfield, ed., *Diary and Autobiography,* 4 vols. (Cambridge, Mass., 1961), vol. 4, p. 123; John Adams to Abigail Adams, August 28, 1774, in L. H. Butterfield *et al.,* eds., *Adams Family Correspondence* (Cambridge, Mass., 1963-), vol. 1, p. 145. For an expanded analysis of Adams's view of the mother's role in the republic, see Martin Van Buren, "The Indispensable God of Health: A Study of Republican Hygiene and the Ideology of William Alcott" (Ph.D. diss., University of California at Los Angeles, 1977), chapter 3.

12. Rush to Enoch Green, 1761, in Butterfield, *Letters of Rush,* vol. 1, p. 3; Rush to Granville Sharp, July 9, 1774, in John A. Woods, ed., "The Correspondence of Benjamin Rush and Granville Sharp, 1773-1809," *Journal of American Studies,* vol. 1, no. 1 (April 1967), p. 8.

13. Rush, "An Inquiry into the Influence of Physical Causes upon the Moral Faculty," delivered before the American Philosophical Society, February 27, 1786, in Rush, *Medical Inquiries and Observations,* 5 vols. (Philadelphia, 1794), vol. 1, pp. 93-124.

14. Rush to John C. Lettson, September 28, 1787, in Butterfield, *Letters of Rush,* vol. 1, pp. 443-4; Rush, *Medical Inquiries and Observations upon the Diseases of the Mind* (Philadelphia, 1812).

15. See Rush, quoted in Szasz, *Manufacture of Madness,* p. 139; Rush, *Diseases of the Mind,* pp. 347-56.

16. Rush, *Diseases of the Mind,* pp. 33, 351-5.

17. Ibid., pp. 223, 185-7; Rush to John R. Coxe, September 5, 1810, in Butterfield, *Letters of Rush,* vol. 2, p. 1059.

18. Rush to Mrs. Rush, August 23, 1786, in Butterfield, *Letters of Rush,* vol. 1, pp. 394-5.

19. Rush to Enos Hitchcock, April 24, 1789, in ibid., pp. 511-2.

20. Rush to John Rush, May 18, 1796, in ibid., vol. 2, pp. 776-7; see also Rush, in Corner, *Autobiography of Rush,* appendix, pp. 369-71; Rush, in Corner, *Autobiography of Rush,* p. 261.

21. Rush, in Corner, *Autobiography of Rush,* p. 288; Rush to Thomas Jefferson, January 2, 1811, in Butterfield, *Letters of Rush,* vol. 2, p. 1074.

22. Rush to Granville Sharp, November 28, 1783, in Woods, "Correspondence of Rush and Sharp," p. 20.

23. See Rush, "Mode of Education," in Rush, *Essays,* pp. 6-20.

24. Rush, "An Account of the Vices Peculiar to the Indians of North America," in Rush, *Essays,* pp. 257-62; Rush, *Diseases of the Mind,* p. 351; Rush, "An Inquiry into the Natural History of Medicine among the Indians of North America and a Comparative View of their Diseases and Remedies with those of Civilized Nations," paper read before the American Philosophical Society, February 4, 1774, published in Rush, *Medical Inquiries and Observations,* vol. 1, pp. 11, 20, 28, 57-8.

25. Rush, *An Address to the Inhabitants of the British Settlements in America upon Slave-Keeping* (Philadelphia, 1773), pp. 1-2, 3-7, 22, 30.

26. Rush to Granville Sharp, October 29, 1773, July 9 and November 1, 1774, in Woods, "Correspondence of Rush and Sharp," pp. 3, 13; Rush to Nathanael Greene, September 16, 1782, in Butterfield, *Letters of Rush,* vol. 1, p. 286.

27. Rush in Corner, *Autobiography of Rush,* p. 246; manumission statement, quoted in Hawke, *Rush,* p. 361.

28. Rush, "Observations intended to favour a supposition that the black color (as it is called) of the Negroes is derived from the LEPROSY," *Transactions of the American Philosophical Society,* vol. 4 (1799), pp. 289-97.

29. Ibid., p. 294.

30. Ibid., p. 295; Rush to Granville Sharp, November 28, 1783, in Woods, "Correspondence of Rush and Sharp," p. 20.

31. Rush, "Observations . . . LEPROSY," p. 295.

32. Ibid. (italics added).

33. Ibid., pp. 295-6.

34. Stanley Stanhope Smith, *Essay on Variety,* quoted in Winthrop D. Jordan, *White over Black: American Attitudes toward the Negro, 1550-1812* (Chapel Hill, N.C., 1968), pp. 513-7. Rush, "Observations . . . LEPROSY," p. 297. For a discussion on the Negro's blackness and the curse of Ham, see Jordan, *White over Black,* pp. 17-20.

35. Rush to Thomas Jefferson, February 4, 1797; to John Nicholson, August 12, 1793; to the president of the Pennsylvania Abolitionist Society, 1794, in Butterfield, *Letters of Rush,* vol. 2, pp. 786, 636, 755. See also Rush, "Paradise of Negro Slaves. A Dream," in Rush, *Essays,* pp. 314-20.

36. Rush to Charles Nisbet, December 5, 1783, in Butterfield, *Letters of Rush,* vol. 1, pp. 315-6.

37. Rush, "Mode of Education," in Rush, *Essays,* pp. 8, 14; Rush, "Address to Ministers," in Rush, *Essays,* p. 118; Rush, "Observations . . . LEPROSY," p. 292; Samuel Davies, quoted in Hawke, *Rush,* p. 22; Rush to David Ramsey, March or April 1788, and to John Adams, August 8, 1777, in Butterfield, *Letters of Rush,* vol. 1, pp. 454, 152; Rush, "Defects of Confederation," in Good, *Rush and His Services,* p. 296; Rush to Granville Sharp, July 9, 1774, in Woods, "Correspondence of Rush and Sharp," p. 8; Rush to John Adams, August 6, 1811, in Butterfield, *Letters of Rush,* vol. 2, p. 1092.

III. Within the "Bowels" of the Republic

1. Thomas Jefferson, *Notes on the State of Virginia* (New York, 1964, written in 1781), p. 119; Jefferson to James Monroe, November 24, 1801, in Paul L. Ford, ed., *The Works of Thomas Jefferson,* 10 vols. (New York, 1892-99), vol. 9, p. 317.

2. Jefferson to Brother John Baptist de Coigne, Chief of Kaskaskia, June 1781, in Andrew A. Lipscomb and Albert E. Bergh, eds., *Writings of Thomas Jefferson,* 20 vols. (Washington, D.C., 1904), vol. 16, p. 372; Jefferson to Benjamin Franklin, August 3, 1777, in Julian Boyd, ed., *The Papers of Thomas Jefferson,* 18 vols. (Princeton, N.J., 1950-65), vol. 2, p. 26; Jefferson, *Notes,* p. 143; Jefferson, *Autobiography of Thomas Jefferson, 1743-1790* (New York, 1914), p. 77.

3. Jefferson, *Notes,* pp. 70, 127; Jefferson, in Edwin M. Betts, ed., *Thomas Jefferson's Farm Book* (Princeton, N.J., 1953), p. 10. For Jefferson's belief in moral sense, see John Chester Miller, *The Wolf by the Ears: Thomas Jefferson and Slavery* (New York, 1977), pp. 90-8; and Garry Wills, *Inventing America: Jefferson's Declaration of Independence* (Garden City, N.Y., 1978), especially pp. 167-258. "All students of Jefferson's philosophy," observed Wills, "have known that he believed in the moral sense as a separate faculty, but they have underestimated the importance of that fact. They do not see how central the moral sense was to the whole British-American philosophical endeavor by the middle of the eighteenth century—central to politics and 'political economy' as well as to epistemology and aesthetics" (p. 199).

4. Jefferson to Uriah Forrest, December 31, 1787, in Boyd, *Papers,* vol. 12, p. 478; Jefferson to Benjamin Rush, September 23, 1800, in Paul L. Ford, *Works,* vol. 9, p. 147; Jefferson, *Notes,* pp. 157-8.

5. Jefferson to John Adams, October 28, 1813, in Adrienne Koch and William Peden, eds., *The Life and Selected Writings of Thomas Jefferson* (New York, 1944), p. 633. For an analysis of Jefferson and Lockean theory, see Roy Harvey Pearce, *Savagism and Civilization: A Study of the Indian and the American Mind* (Baltimore, 1967), p. 67. For an emphasis on the influence of Francis Hutcheson *vis-à-vis* John Locke in the development of Jefferson's thinking, see Wills, *Inventing America.* In understanding Jefferson's philosophy, it would be a mistake, I think, to approach it too literally and require Jefferson to have actually read Locke's *Of Civil Government Second Treatise* in order to conclude he was influenced by Locke's ideas. See Wills, p. 174. My suspicion is that Jefferson, like many of us, worked with more than one set of ideas, which, for him, meant both Hutcheson's moral sense and Locke's social contract.

6. Jefferson, *Notes,* pp. 83-4.

7. Ibid., pp. 139-40, 141, 143.

8. Jefferson to Mr. Littlepage, May 8, 1789; to Dr. James Currie, August 4, 1787; to John Page, May 4, 1786; and to A. Stuart, January 25, 1786, in Lipscomb and Bergh, *Writings,* vol. 7, p. 339; vol. 6, p. 229-30; vol. 5, p. 305; and vol. 5, p. 259.

9. Jefferson to Martha Jefferson, March 28, 1787, in Boyd, *Papers,* vol. 11, p. 250; Edwin M. Betts, ed., *Thomas Jefferson's Farm Book,* p. xiii; Jefferson to Martha Jefferson, May 5 and March 28, 1787, in Boyd, *Papers,* vol. 11, pp. 349, 250; Jefferson to Peter Carr, August 10, 1787, in Lipscomb and Bergh, *Writings,* vol. 6, p. 262.

10. Jefferson to John Bannister, Jr., October 15, 1785, in Boyd, *Papers,* vol. 8, pp. 635-7; Jefferson, in Lipscomb and Bergh, *Writings,* vol. 17, pp. 279-80; Jefferson to James Madison, December 16, 1786, in Boyd, *Papers,* vol. 10, p. 604. See also Jordan, *White over Black,* pp. 462-4.

11. Jefferson to Anne Willing Bingham, May 11, 1788, in Boyd, *Papers,* vol. 13, pp. 151-2; Jefferson to Samuel Kercheval, September 5, 1816, in Lipscomb and Bergh, *Writings,* vol. 15, p. 72.

12. Jefferson to Robert Smith, in W. C. Ford, ed., *Thomas Jefferson's Correspondence, Printed from the Originals in the Collection of William K. Bixby,* quoted in Fawn M. Brodie, *Thomas Jefferson: An Intimate History* (New York, 1974), p. 375; Jefferson to Maria Cosway, January 14, 1789; April 24, 1788; and October 12, 1786, in Boyd, *Papers,* vol. 14, p. 446; vol. 13, pp. 103-4; and vol. 10, pp. 444, 446-8. For a detailed analysis of the Jefferson/Cosway relationship, see Brodie, *Jefferson,* pp. 199-215.

13. Samuel Johnson, quoted in Brodie, *Jefferson,* p. 96; Jefferson to Edward Coles, August 25, 1814, in Paul L. Ford, *Works,* vol. 11, p. 416; Jefferson to Francis Eppes, July 30, 1787, in Boyd, *Papers,* vol. 10, p. 653.

14. Jefferson, *Notes,* pp. 155.

15. Jefferson, *Autobiography,* p. 7; Jefferson, *Notes,* p. 132; Jefferson to Brissot de Warville, February 11, 1788, in Boyd, *Papers,* vol. 12, pp. 577-8.

16. Jefferson to Nicholas Lewis, July 29, 1787, in Boyd, *Papers,* vol. 11, p. 640.

17. Jefferson to Daniel Bradley, October 6, 1805, to Thomas M. Randolph, June 8, 1803, in Betts, *Jefferson's Farm Book,* pp. 21, 19.

18. Jefferson, *Notes,* p. 167; Jefferson to John Jordan, December 21, 1805; to W. Eppes, June 30, 1820; and to Joel Yancey, January 17, 1819, in Betts, *Jefferson's Farm Book,* pp. 21, 43.

19. Jefferson to John Holmes, April 22, 1820, and to Jared Sparks, February 4, 1824, in Paul L. Ford, *Works,* vol. 13, p. 159, and vol. 12, p. 334-9.

20. Jefferson to John Lynch, January 2, 1811, and to Rufus King, July 13, 1802, in ibid., vol. 11, p. 178, vol. 4, pp. 383-5. See also Jefferson to James Monroe, November 24, 1801, in ibid., vol. 9, p. 317.

21. Jefferson, *Notes,* pp. 132-3; Jefferson to John Holmes, April 22, 1820; to James Monroe, July 14, 1793; to St. George Tucker, August 28, 1797; and to James Monroe, September 20, 1800, in Paul L. Ford, *Works,* vol. 13, p. 159; vol. 7, pp. 449-59; vol. 8, p. 335; and vol. 9, p. 147; Jefferson to William Burwell, January 28, 1805, in Betts, *Jefferson's Farm Book,* p. 20; Jefferson to Edward Coles, August 25, 1814, in

Paul L. Ford, *Works,* vol. 11, pp. 417-8; Jefferson to John Adams, January 22, 1821, in Lester J. Cappon, ed., *The Adams-Jefferson Letters,* 2 vols. (Chapel Hill, N.C., 1959), vol. 2, p. 570.

22. Jefferson, *Notes,* pp. 155-6.

23. Jefferson, *Notes,* p. 127; Jefferson to Dr. Edward Bancroft, January 16, 1788, in Betts, *Jefferson's Farm Book,* p. 10. The relationship between moral sense and reason, as it applied to blacks in Jefferson's thinking, was perceptively noted by David Brion Davis in his review of Wills, *Inventing America, The New York Times Book Review,* vol. 83, no. 27 (July 2, 1978), pp. 1, 17. Jefferson, *Notes,* p. 133.

24. Jefferson, *Notes,* p. 138; Jefferson to Henry Gregoire, February 25, 1809, in Paul L. Ford, *Works,* vol. 11, pp. 99-100; to Benjamin Banneker, August 30, 1791, vol. 6, pp. 309-10; and to the Marquis de Condorcet, August 30, 1791, vol. 6, pp. 310-11.

25. Jefferson to Joel Harlow, October 8, 1809, in Paul L. Ford, *Works,* vol. 11, p. 121; Jefferson, *Notes,* pp. 137, 141.

26. Jefferson, *Notes,* pp. 138-9.

27. Jefferson to James Monroe, November 24, 1801, in Paul L. Ford, *Works,* vol. 9, p. 317; Jefferson, *Notes,* pp. 85-6.

28. Jefferson, *Notes,* pp. 138-9.

29. Jefferson to Coles, August 25, 1814, in Betts, *Jefferson's Farm Book,* p. 38.

30. Callender, in *Richmond Recorder,* September 1, 1802, quoted in Brodie, *Jefferson,* p. 349; Thomas M. Randolph, in appendix, Milton E. Flower, *James Parton: The Father of Modern Biography* (Durham, N.C., 1951), p. 237. For detailed analyses of the Jefferson/Hemings relationship, see Brodie, *Jefferson,* pp. 228-34, 349-63; Winthrop D. Jordan, *White over Black: American Attitudes toward the Negro, 1550-1812* (Chapel Hill, N.C., 1968), pp. 461-9.

31. Jefferson to James Monroe, May 29, 1801, in W. C. Ford, "Thomas Jefferson and James Thomson Callender," *New England Historical and Genealogical Register* (1896-97), vol. 2, p. 157; Thomas J. Randolph, in appendix, Flower, *Parton,* p. 237.

32. Thomas J. Randolph, in appendix, Flower, *Parton,* pp. 236-9; Fawn M. Brodie, "Jefferson Biographers and the Psychology of Canonization," *Journal of Interdisciplinary History,* vol. 2, no. 1 (Summer 1971), p. 169; Thomas J. Randolph, in appendix, Flower, *Parton,* p. 238; Brodie, *Jefferson,* p. 440.

33. Brodie, *Jefferson,* p. 296; Madison Hemings, "Life among the Lowly, No. 1," *Pike County* (Ohio) *Republican,* March 13, 1873, reprinted in Brodie, *Jefferson,* appendix, pp. 471-6. Callender, in *Richmond Recorder,* September 1, 1802, quoted in Brodie, *Jefferson,* p. 349. See also Brodie, *Jefferson,* pp. 291-2: "It may also be evidence that Jefferson chose to consider him free from birth, either because he had been conceived on the free soil of France, or because Jefferson had so promised his mother."

34. *Boston Gazette,* reprinted in *Richmond Recorder,* December 1, 1802, quoted in Jordan, *White over Black,* p. 468; Isaac Jefferson, *Memories of a Monticello Slave,* reprinted in James A. Bear, Jr., ed., *Jefferson at Monticello* (Charlottesville, Va., 1967), p. 4; *Boston Gazette,* reprinted in *Philadelphia Port Folio,* October 2, 1802, quoted in Brodie, *Jefferson,* p. 355; *Frederick-Town* (Virginia) *Herald,* reprinted in the *Richmond Recorder,* September 29, 1802, quoted in Brodie, *Jefferson,* p. 352; *Richmond Recorder,* September 22, 1802, quoted in Jordan, *White over Black,* p. 469.

35. *Richmond Examiner,* September 18, 25, 1802.

36. *Boston Gazette,* reprinted in *New York Evening Post,* December 8, 1802.

37. Jefferson to Brother John Baptist de Coigne, chief of Kaskaskia, June 1781, and to John Page, August 5, 1776, in Lipscomb and Bergh, *Writings,* vol. 16, p. 372, and vol. 4, pp. 270-1.

38. Jefferson to Miamis, Powtewatamies, and Weeauks, January 7, 1802, in Lipscomb and Bergh, *Writings,* vol. 16, pp. 390-1; Jefferson, quoted in Pearce, *Savagism and Civilization,* pp. 106-7; Jefferson to chiefs of the Shawanee Nation, February 19, 1807; to Governor James Jay, April 7, 1809; and to chiefs of the Ottawas, Chippewas, Powtewatamies, Shawanese, and Wyandots, January 18, 1809, in Lipscomb and Bergh, *Writings,* vol. 16, p. 424; and vol. 16, p. 469.

39. Jefferson to Charles Carroll, April 15, 1791, in Lipscomb and Bergh, *Writings,* vol. 8, pp. 177-8; Jefferson, Second Inaugural Address, March 4, 1805; Fourth Annual Message to Congress, November 8, 1804; and Seventh Annual Message to Congress, October 27, 1807, in James D. Richardson, ed., *A Compilation of the Messages and Papers of the Presidents, 1789-1897* (Washington, D.C., 1897), vol. 1, pp. 380, 371-2, 427-8.

40. Jefferson to William Ludlow, September 6, 1824, in Lipscomb and Bergh, *Writings,* vol. 16, pp. 74-5.

41. Jefferson, *Notes,* p. 70; Jefferson to the Marquis de Chastellux, June 7, 1785, in Boyd, *Papers,* vol. 8, pp. 185-6. Jefferson's assertions regarding the Indian's "equality" were so strikingly aggressive and apologetic they revealed his need to defend white Americans against the claims of Count Buffon and Abbe Raynal—European detractors of American culture and intellectual achievements. "They have supposed," Jefferson declared in his *Notes,* "there is something in the soil, climate, and other circumstances of America, which occasions animal nature to degenerate, not excepting even the man, native or adoptive, physical or moral." What irritated Jefferson was the application of this "theory" to the "race of whites transplanted from Europe." In their remarks on the ability of the "adopted" Americans, in which they noted that America had not produced one able mathematician or one man of genius in a single art or science, Buffon and Raynal were belittling even Jefferson himself. The genius of the "native" had to be defended and "proofs" offered in order for Jefferson to refute their insinuations about the "adoptive" man and to deny charges implying his own degeneracy. See Jefferson, *Notes,* pp. 209-10, 64, 199-200, 56. Jefferson, *Notes,* pp. 134-5, 60-1; Jefferson to the Marquis de Chastellux, June 7, 1785, in Boyd, *Papers,* vol. 8, pp. 185-6. One of Buffon's claims which Jefferson singled out for rebuttal involved the Indian male's sexual impotency. According to Jefferson, Buffon had stated that the "organs of generation" of Indian men were "smaller and weaker than those of Europeans." Unable to let this remark pass unchallenged, Jefferson queried sharply: "Is this a fact?" And added that he believed it was not. Still he agreed with Buffon that Indian men had "no ardor for their females." But the reason for this, Jefferson contended, was not due to the conditions of the American continent. As warriors Indian men were wholly bent upon war, he explained, and as hunters they pursued "game with ardor." Thus the "seeming frigidity" of the men was the effect of manners and not a defect of nature. Furthermore, the Indian male was "neither more defective in ardor, nor more impotent with his female, than the white reduced to the same diet and exercise. . . ." Clearly, the Indian male's problem

could be cured with civilization and a proper diet. See Jefferson, *Notes,* pp. 199-200, 56.

42. Jefferson to Delawares, Mohicans, and Munries, December 21, 1808, and to Colonel Benjamin Hawkins, February 18, 1803, in Lipscomb and Bergh, *Writings,* vol. 16, p. 452, and vol. 10, pp. 362-3.

43. Jefferson, *Notes,* pp. 184, 91; James Madison, quoted in Michael Paul Rogin, *Fathers and Children: Andrew Jackson and the Subjugation of the American Indian* (New York, 1975), p. 319. On the classification of mulatto as "Negro," see Jordan, *White over Black,* pp. 167-78.

44. Jefferson, *Notes,* p. 91.

45. Jefferson to chiefs of the Upper Cherokees, May 4, 1808, in Lipscomb and Bergh, *Writings,* vol. 16, p. 434; Jefferson to John Baptist de Coigne, June 1781, in Boyd, *Papers,* vol. 6, pp. 60-3; Jefferson to Delawares, Mohicans, and Munries, December 21, 1808, in Lipscomb and Bergh, *Writings,* vol. 16, p. 452.

46. Jefferson to Choctaw Nation, December 17, 1803, and to chiefs of the Ottawas, Chippewas, Powtewatamies, Wyandots, and Senecas of Sandusky, April 22, 1808, in Lipscomb and Bergh, *Writings,* vol. 16, pp. 401, 429; Jefferson, "Confidential Message Recommending a Western Exploring Expedition," January 18, 1803, in Lipscomb and Bergh, *Writings,* vol. 3, pp. 489-90.

47. Jefferson to Andrew Jackson, February 16, 1803, and to Governor William H. Harrison, February 27, 1803, in Lipscomb and Bergh, *Writings,* vol. 10, pp. 357-9, 370-3.

48. Jefferson to Horatio Gates, July 11, 1803, in Paul L. Ford, *Works,* vol. 10, p. 13; Jefferson, draft of an amendment to the Constitution, July 1803, in Paul L. Ford, *Works,* vol. 8, pp. 241-8; Jefferson to Cherokees, January 9, 1809, in Lipscomb and Bergh, *Writings,* vol. 16, pp. 458-9.

49. Jefferson to Governor William H. Harrison, February 27, 1803; to Chiefs of the Ottawas, Chippewas, Powtewatamies, and Senecas, April 22, 1808; and to Chiefs of the Wyandots, Ottawas, Chippewas, Powtewatamies, and Shawanese, January 10, 1809, in Lipscomb and Bergh, *Writings,* vol. 10, pp. 370-3; vol. 16, pp. 431-2; and vol. 16, p. 463.

50. Jefferson to John Adams, June 11, 1812, in Cappon, *Adams-Jefferson Letters,* vol. 2, pp. 307-8.

51. Jefferson, *Notes,* p. 129; Jefferson to John Hollins, May 5, 1811, in Lipscomb and Bergh, *Writings,* vol. 13, p. 58; Jefferson to John Adams, September 12, 1821, in Cappon, *Adams-Jefferson Letters,* vol. 2, p. 575.

IV. Beyond Primitive Accumulation

1. Marx, *Economic and Philosophic Manuscripts of 1844* (New York, 1973, originally published in 1932), p. 150; Rosa Luxemburg, *The Accumulation of Capital* (New Haven, 1951), pp. 369-70; Jefferson, *Notes on the State of Virginia* (New York, 1964, written in 1781), p. 154; Rush to John Adams, June 13, 1808, in John A. Schutz and Douglass Adair, eds., *The Spur of Fame: Dialogue of John Adams and Benjamin Rush, 1805-1813* (San Marino, Calif., 1966), p. 109.

2. Rush, "Address to the People of the United States on the Defects of the Confederation," in Henry G. Good, *Benjamin Rush and His Services to American Education* (Berne, Ind., 1918), pp. 205-6; John Adams to Thomas Jefferson, December 21, 1819, in Lester J. Cappon, ed., *The Adams-Jefferson Letters,* 2 vols. (Chapel Hill, N.C., 1959), vol. 2, p. 551.

3. Alexis de Tocqueville, *Democracy in America,* 2 vols. (New York, 1945, originally published in 1835), vol. 1, p. 3; Edward Pessen, *Riches, Class, and Power before the Civil War* (Lexington, Mass., 1973), pp. 313, 305. See Lawrence J. Friedman, "A Note on Tocqueville's 'Tyranny of the Majority,'" in Friedman, *Inventors of the Promised Land,* appendix, pp. 307-14, for a discussion on the importance of perception in Jacksonian society.

4. Tocqueville, *Democracy in America,* vol. 1, pp. 5-6, 9, 58.

5. Ibid., vol. 2, p. 105; vol. 1, p. 105; vol. 1, p. 205; vol. 2, pp. 204-5; vol. 2, pp. 202-3.

6. Ibid., vol. 2, pp. 23, 239, 137.

7. Ibid., pp. 214, 146, 237, 147, 144.

8. Ibid., pp. 140, 161; vol. 1, pp. 308, 140-1; vol. 2, p. 258; vol. 1, pp. 140-1.

9. Ibid., vol. 1, p. 299; vol. 2, pp. 232-5, 244; vol. 1, pp. 300-1; vol. 2, pp. 88, 232.

10. Karl Marx, *The Economic and Philosophic Manuscripts of 1844* (New York, 1973, originally published in 1932), pp. 150, 151; Marx, "On the Jewish Question," in Loyd D. Easton and Kurt H. Guddat, eds., *Writings of the Young Marx on Philosophy and Society* (New York, 1967), pp. 236-7; C. B. MacPherson, *The Political Theory of Possessive Individualism: Hobbes to Locke* (Oxford, 1962), p. 3. See also Norman O. Brown, *Life against Death: The Psychoanalytical Meaning of History* (Middletown, Conn., 1959), pp. 237-8: "The alienated consciousness is correlative with a money economy. Its root is the compulsion to work. This compulsion to work subordinates man to things. . . . Capitalism has made us so stupid and one-sided that objects exist for us only if we can possess them or if they have utility."

11. Rosa Luxemburg, *The Accumulation of Capital* (New Haven, 1951), pp. 369-70; George R. Taylor, *The Transportation Revolution, 1815-1860* (New York, 1962); Douglass C. North, *The Economic Growth of the United States, 1790-1860* (New York, 1966). For a study of the development of capitalism from a world perspective, see Immanuel Wallerstein, *The Modern World System: Capitalist Agriculture and the Origins of the European World Economy in the Sixteenth Century* (New York, 1974).

12. Taylor, pp. 3, 133, 135; North, pp. 17, 33; U.S. Bureau of the Census, *A Statistical Abstract Supplement: Historical Statistics of the United States, Colonial Times to 1957* (Washington, D.C., 1961), p. 14.

13. U.S. Bureau of the Census, *Historical Statistics,* p. 14; J. Potter, "The Growth of Population in America, 1700-1860," in D. V. Glass and D. E. C. Eversley, *Population in History* (Chicago, 1965), pp. 635, 666, 667; Stuart Bruchey, *The Roots of American Economic Growth, 1607-1861* (London, 1965), p. 79.

14. North, pp. 102, 103.

15. Ibid., pp. 50, 250, 233, 257, 262, 136, 141, 151.

16. Michael Paul Rogin, *Fathers and Children: Andrew Jackson and the Subjugation of the American Indian* (New York, 1975), p. 165; Arthur H. DeRosier, Jr., *The Removal*

of the Choctaw Indians (New York, 1972), p. 124; North, *Growth of the United States,* pp. 119, 124, 256, 257, 232, 233.

17. U.S., Congress, House, *Preliminary Report on the Eighth Census, 1860* (Washington D.C., 1862), pp. 126-33, in North, *Growth of the United States,* p. 129; Taylor, *Transportation Revolution,* p. 133; North, *Growth of the United States,* pp. 52, 75, 67, 68, 69, 75, 233; Mario Barrera, "Colonial Labor and Theories of Inequality: The Case of International Harvester," *Review of Radical Political Economics,* vol. 8, no. 2 (Summer 1976), pp. 1-18; Robert Blauner, *Racial Oppression in America* (New York, 1972).

18. James Madison, quoted in Rogin, p. 319.

V. The Metaphysics of Civilization: "The Red Race on Our Borders"

1. James Madison, quoted in Michael Paul Rogin, *Fathers and Children: Andrew Jackson and the Subjugation of the American Indian* (New York, 1975), p. 319; James Fenimore Cooper, *The Pathfinder* (New York, n.d., originally published in 1840), p. 107; Alexis de Tocqueville, *Democracy in America,* 2 vols. (New York, 1945, originally published in 1835), vol. 1, pp. 352-3, 364.

2. Herman Melville, *The Confidence-Man: His Masquerade* (New York, 1964, originally published in 1857), p. 136; David Brion Davis, *The Slave Power Conspiracy and the Paranoid Style* (Baton Rouge, 1969), pp. 25-31.

3. Melville, *Confidence-Man,* pp. 147-66. See also Roy Harvey Pearce, "The Metaphysics of Indian-Hating," *Ethnohistory,* vol. 4 (Winter 1957), pp. 27-40, and "Melville's Indian-Hater: A Note on a Meaning of the Confidence-Man," *Publications of the Modern Language Association,* vol. 67 (1952), pp. 942-8.

4. Lewis Cass, "Policy and Practice of the United States and Great Britain in Their Treatment of Indians," *North American Review,* LV (April 1827), pp. 365-442, especially 391-2; Cass, "Removal of the Indians," ibid., XXX (January 1830), pp. 64-109.

5. See Robert Montgomery Bird, *Nick of the Woods, or the Jibbenainosay, A Tale of Kentucky* (New York, 1853, originally published in 1837). For analyses of Bird and his novel, see R. W. B. Lewis, *The American Adam: Innocence, Tragedy, and Tradition in the Nineteenth Century* (Chicago, 1968), pp. 105-9; Richard Slotkin, *Regeneration through Violence: The Mythology of the American Frontier, 1600-1860* (Middletown, Conn., 1973), pp. 509-15. For biographies of Bird, see Curtis Dahl, *Robert Montgomery Bird* (New York, 1963) and Mary Mayer Bird, *Life of Robert Montgomery Bird* (Philadelphia, 1945).

6. Mary Bird, *Life of Bird,* p. 32; Dahl, *Bird,* p. 17; Clement E. Foust, *The Life and Dramatic Works of Robert Montgomery Bird* (New York, 1919), p. 52; Bird to Mary and Caroline Mayer, June 25, 1834, Bird Papers, University of Pennsylvania Library.

7. Bird, fragmented note on "The Disadvantages under which an American novelist must labour," and draft of an essay on national literature, Bird Papers.

8. Bird, fragmented note on Indian names, Bird Papers.

9. Bird, Notebooks, April 3, 1833; Bird to Mary Mayer, May 8, 1833; and Bird to Frost, May 18, 1833, Bird Papers.

10. Bird, "The White-Washed Cottage of the Susquehanna, an Indian Story," Bird Papers.

11. Bird, "Awossagame or the Seal of the Evil One," Bird Papers.

12. Bird, *Nick of the Woods,* preface, p. 7.

13. Ibid., pp. 7-10, 318.

14. Ibid., p. 232. Curiously, Bird himself displayed a duality in his own personality. During his early years in school, he encountered a strict and brutal teacher and suffered almost daily beatings at school. The punishment left him with deep emotional scars. According to Mary Bird many years later, he felt a combination of fear and resentment, hate and thirst for vengeance. The cruelties inflicted on him changed "the innocent child into a revengeful demon," driving him into such a great rage that he took on bended knee "a solemn oath to kill his persecutor as soon as he was old and strong enough to do so. . . ." His violent anger was not, in her judgment, merely "the impotent exhibition of baby wrath." "The current testimony of those who knew him best proves him to have been unusually gentle and tractible, enduring ordinary ills with great good nature; tho' roused, even then, as at subsequent periods of life, by repeated injustice or outrage, to an intensity of feeling few can comprehend or appreciate." See Mary Mayer Bird, *Life of Robert Montgomery Bird,* p. 9.

15. Bird, *Nick of the Woods,* pp. 145, 250-5.

16. Bird, *Nick of the Woods,* pp. 250-1.

17. Washington McCartney, "Eulogy," quoted in John William Ward, *Andrew Jackson: Symbol for an Age* (New York, 1962), p. 1; John Ross, quoted in Michael Paul Rogin, *Fathers and Children: Andrew Jackson and the Subjugation of the American Indian* (New York, 1975), p. 231. For this section on Jackson and Indian removal, I am indebted to Michael Paul Rogin's thoughtful and penetrating study, *Fathers and Children.*

18. Jackson, First Annual Message to Congress, December 8, 1829, in James D. Richardson, ed., *A Compilation of the Messages and Papers of the Presidents, 1789-1897* (Washington, D.C., 1897), vol. 2, p. 457.

19. Jackson to George W. Campbell, October 15, 1812, in John Spencer Bassett, ed., *Correspondence of Andrew Jackson,* 6 vols. (Washington, D.C., 1926), vol. 1, pp. 236-7; Marvin Meyers, *The Jacksonian Persuasion: Politics and Belief* (New York, 1960).

20. Eulogist and Mrs. Jackson, quoted in Rogin, *Fathers and Children,* pp. 40, 44; S. Putnam Waldo, *Memoirs of Andrew Jackson* (Hartford, Conn., 1820), quoted in Rogin, *Fathers and Children,* p. 40; Jackson to Richard Call, November 15, 1821, quoted in Rogin, *Fathers and Children,* p. 40; Jackson to George Campbell, October 15, 1812, in Bassett, *Correspondence,* vol. 1, pp. 236-7.

21. Old resident, quoted in Rogin, *Fathers and Children,* p. 52.

22. Jackson, quoted in Rogin, *Fathers and Children,* pp. 159, 286; Jackson to A. J. Donelson, February 24, 1817, and to Willie Blount, July 10, 1812, in Bassett, *Correspondence,* vol. 2, pp. 275-6, and vol. 1, pp. 231-2.

23. Jackson, Division Orders, March 12, 1812, quoted in Rogin, *Fathers and Children,* pp. 140-1; Jackson to Reverend Gideon Blackburn, December 3, 1813, and to Mrs.

Jackson, October 21, 1814, in Bassett, *Correspondence*, vol. 1, pp. 365-6, and vol. 2, p. 79; Slotkin, *Regeneration through Violence.*

24. Observer, quoted in Rogin, *Fathers and Children*, p. 162. See also ibid., pp. 155, 157, 145, 149.

25. Jackson to Willie Blount, July 10, 1812, in Bassett, *Correspondence*, vol. 1, pp. 231-2.

26. Jackson, General Orders, September 19, 1813, and General Order, December 15, 1813, in Bassett, *Correspondence*, vol. 1, pp. 319-20, 429-30; Jackson to Thomas Pinckney, February 16 and 17, 1814, in Bassett, *Correspondence*, vol. 1, pp. 463-5. See also H. S. Halbert and T. H. Ball, *The Creek War of 1813 and 1814* (Chicago, 1895), pp. 276-7.

27. Jackson to Thomas Pinckney, May 18, 1814; to George Campbell, October 15, 1812; and to Willie Blount, July 10, 1812, in Bassett, *Correspondence*, vol. 2, pp. 2-3; vol. 1, pp. 236-7, 231-2.

28. For information on Indian removal, see Rogin, *Fathers and Children,* especially pp. 165-250; Mary E. Young, *Redskins, Ruffleshirts, and Rednecks* (Norman, Okla., 1961); Arthur H. DeRosier, Jr., *The Removal of the Choctaw Indians* (New York, 1972); and Grant Foreman, *Indian Removal: The Emigration of the Five Civilized Tribes of Indians* (Norman, Okla., 1972).

29. Jackson, Special Message to the Senate, February 22, 1831, in Richardson, *Papers of the Presidents,* vol. 2, p. 541; Rogin, *Fathers and Children,* p. 213.

30. General John Coffee to Jackson, February 3, 1830, quoted in Mary E. Young, "Indian Removal and Land Allotment: The Civilized Tribes and Jacksonian Justice," *American Historical Review,* vol. 64 (October 1958), p. 36.

31. Jackson to Major David Haley, October 15, 1829, quoted in Annie Heloise Abel, *The History of Events Resulting in Indian Consolidation West of the Mississippi* (Washington, D.C., 1906). See also Jackson, Speech to Chickasaws, August 23, 1830, Executive Document no. 512, 23rd Cong., 1st Sess. (Washington, D.C., 1835), vol. 2, pp. 240-1; John Eaton to William Carroll, May 30, 1829, reprinted in Abel, *Indian Consolidation,* p. 371.

32. See Young, "Indian Removal and Land Allotment," pp. 38-45; DeRosier, *Removal of the Choctaw Indians,* p. 125; Rogin, *Fathers and Children,* pp. 228-30.

33. Lewis Cass to R. J. Meigs, October 31, 1834, quoted in Rogin, *Fathers and Children,* p. 230.

34. Jackson to General John Coffee, April 7, 1832, in Bassett, *Correspondence*, vol. 4, p. 430.

35. Reverend J. F. Schermerhorn to Lewis Cass, quoted in Rogin, *Fathers and Children,* p. 227. See also Foreman, *Indian Removal,* pp. 264-78.

36. Major W. M. Davis to Lewis Cass, quoted in Foreman, *Indian Removal,* p. 270.

37. Jackson, First Annual Message to Congress, in Richardson, *Papers of the Presidents,* vol. 2, pp. 456-8; Jackson, Speech to Chickasaws, p. 241.

38. Jackson, Second Annual Message to Congress, December 6, 1830, in Richardson, *Papers of the Presidents,* vol. 2, pp. 520-2; Jackson, Speech to Chickasaws, pp. 241-2.

39. Jackson to Captain James Gadsden, October 12, 1829, in Bassett, *Correspondence*, vol. 4, p. 81; Jackson to Major David Haley, October 15, 1829, quoted in Abel,

Indian Consolidation, p. 373; Jackson, Speech to Chickasaws, p. 241; Jackson, Special Message to Senate, in Richardson, *Papers of the Presidents,* vol. 2, p. 541.

40. Jackson, Letter to the Seminoles, 1835, reprinted in Paul Jacobs, *To Serve the Devil* (New York, 1971), vol. 1, pp. 63-4.

41. Jackson, Memorandum on the Florida Campaign, April (?) 1837, in Bassett, *Correspondence,* vol. 5, p. 468, Jackson to Secretary of War Joel Poinsett, October 1, 1837, in Bassett, *Correspondence,* vol. 5, p. 512. See also Rogin, *Fathers and Children,* p. 239.

42. Jackson, Proclamation, April 2, 1814, Fort Williams, in Bassett, *Correspondence,* vol. 1, p. 494; Jackson, Second Annual Message, in Richardson, *Papers of the Presidents,* vol. 2, pp. 520-2.

43. Jackson, Seventh Annual Message to Congress, December 7, 1835, in Richardson, *Papers of the Presidents,* vol. 3, p. 165; Jackson, quoted in Rogin, *Fathers and Children,* p. 289.

44. Jackson, General Orders, March 24(?), 1814, and Proclamation, April 2, 1814, in Bassett, *Correspondence,* vol. 1, pp. 487-8, 494; Jackson, Veto Message, July 10, 1832; Jackson, Seventh Annual Message to Congress, December 7, 1835; Jackson, Eighth Annual Message to Congress, December 5, 1836; Jackson, Farewell Address, March 4, 1837, in Richardson, *Papers of the Presidents,* vol. 2, p. 590; vol. 3, pp. 165, 246, 295-7.

45. Jackson, Veto Message; Seventh Annual Message; and Farewell Address; in ibid., vol. 2, p. 590; vol. 3, p. 166; vol. 3, pp. 305-6; Jackson, Fifth Annual Message to Congress, December 3, 1833, and First Annual Message, in Richardson, *Papers of the Presidents,* vol. 3, pp. 32-3, and vol. 2, p. 458; Jackson, draft of First Annual Message, December 8, 1829, in Bassett, *Correspondence,* vol. 4, p. 103. See also Meyers, *Jacksonian Persuasion,* pp. 16-32.

46. Nicholas Biddle, quoted in Rogin, *Fathers and Children,* p. 281; Jackson, quoted in Rogin, *Fathers and Children;* pp. 198, 289, 291; Jackson, Farewell Address, in Richardson, *Papers of the Presidents,* vol. 3, pp. 303-4; Jackson, Proclamation, in Bassett, *Correspondence,* vol. 1, p. 494.

47. Jackson to Mrs. Jackson, April 1, 1814, in Bassett, ed., *Jackson Correspondence,* I, p. 493; D. H. Lawrence, *Studies in Classic American Literature* (New York, 1966), p. 59. For a full analysis of the metaphor of a "pyramid of skulls," see Slotkin, *Regeneration through Violence.*

VI. The Metaphysics of Civilization: "The Black Race Within Our Bosom"

1. Herman Melville, quoted in Ann Douglas, *The Feminization of American Culture* (New York, 1977), p. 11; Karl Marx, *Capital: A Critique of Political Economy* (New York, 1906), p. 329; Alexis de Tocqueville, *Democracy in America* (New York, 1945, originally published in 1835), vol. 1, pp. 344, 347-8, 370.

2. Tocqueville, *Democracy in America,* vol. 1, pp. 373-4.

3. Leon Litwack, *North of Slavery: The Negro in the Free States, 1790-1860* (Chicago, 1961).

4. Leonard L. Richards, *"Gentlemen of Property and Standing": Anti-Abolition Mobs in Jacksonian America* (New York, 1970); black youth, quoted in Litwack, *North of*

Slavery, pp. 153-4; David Wilmot, quoted in Eugene H. Berwanger, *The Frontier against Slavery: Western Anti-Negro Prejudice and the Slavery Extension Controversy* (Urbana, Ill., 1967), pp. 24, 125-6. See Ronald T. Takaki, "Not Afraid to Die: Frederick Douglass and Violence" and "War upon the Whites: Black Rage in the Fiction of Martin Delany," in *Violence in the Black Imagination* (New York, 1972), pp. 17-36, 79-102.

5. See Robert A. Warner, *New Haven Negroes: A Social History* (New Haven, Conn., 1940), p. 34; Tocqueville, *Democracy in America,* vol. 1, p. 373; Litwack, *North of Slavery,* pp. 66, 98, 155-6; Frank U. Quillan, *The Color Line in Ohio: A History of Race Prejudice in a Typical Northern State* (Ann Arbor, Mich., 1913), p. 55.

6. See Litwack, *North of Slavery,* p. 167; Berwanger, *Frontier against Slavery,* p. 53; Emma Lou Thornbrough, *The Negro in Indiana: A Study of a Minority* (n.p., 1957), p. 62.

7. See Tocqueville, *Democracy in America,* vol. 1, p. 373; Berwanger, *Frontier against Slavery,* pp. 20, 36; quoted in Litwack, *North of Slavery,* p. 77.

8. Indiana abolitionists, quoted in Thornbrough, *Negro in Indiana,* pp. 127, 163; Lincoln, speech at Springfield, Illinois, June 26, 1857, in Roy P. Basler, ed., *The Collected Works of Abraham Lincoln,* 9 vols. (New Brunswick, N.J., 1953), vol. 2, pp. 408-9. For the best study of abolitionist thought, which relates abolitionists' ideas on slavery and race to their attitudes toward sexuality, family, religion, civilization, and union, see Ronald G. Walters, *The Antislavery Appeal: American Abolitionism after 1830* (Baltimore, 1976). The Republican party's views on race were complex, as Eric Foner showed in *Free Soil, Free Labor, Free Men: The Ideology of the Republican Party before the Civil War* (New York, 1970), pp. 261-300. The party included supporters of rights for blacks, yet racism was also pervasive within it.

9. See Michael B. Katz, *The Irony of Early School Reform: Educational Innovation in Mid-Nineteenth Century Massachusetts* (Boston, 1972), pp. 124, 120-1, 123, 42, 172, 41, 88, 43; Herbert G. Gutman, *Work, Culture & Society in Industrializing America* (New York, 1977), pp. 19, 20, 27, 71; David J. Rothman, *The Discovery of the Asylum: Social Order and Disorder in the New Republic* (Boston, 1971), pp. 290, 284, 162; Herbert G. Gutman, *The Black Family in Slavery and Freedom, 1750-1925* (New York, 1976), pp. 295-301; J. H. Plumb, "Slavery, Race, and the Poor," *New York Review of Books,* vol. 12 (March 13, 1969), pp. 3-5.

10. Stanley M. Elkins, *Slavery: A Problem in American Institutional and Intellectual Life* (New York, 1963), pp. 81-139. For recent criticisms of Elkins's thesis on Sambo, see Lawrence W. Levine, "Slave Songs and Slave Consciousness," in Tamara K. Hareven, ed., *Anonymous Americans: Explorations in Nineteenth-Century Social History* (Englewood Cliffs, N.J., 1971), and Gutman, *Black Family,* pp. 291-326.

11. See George Fitzhugh, *Sociology for the South,* in Harvey Wish, ed., *Antebellum: Writings of George Fitzhugh and Hinton Rowan Helper on Slavery* (New York, 1960), p. 88; Bertram W. Doyle, *Etiquette of Race Relations in the South* (Chicago, 1931), p. 54; Edward Pollard, *Black Diamonds Gathered in the Darkey Homes of the South* (New York, 1859), pp. 57-8.

12. See Fitzhugh, *Sociology for the South,* in Wish, *Antebellum,* p. 89; William Gilmore Simms, *The Yemassee* (New York, 1962), p. 392; John Hope Franklin, "The Enslave-

ment of Free Negroes in North Carolina," *Journal of Negro History,* vol. 29 (October 1944), p. 405.

13. *Charleston Mercury,* July 17, 1856, and June 2, 1858. See also *New Orleans Delta,* November 21, 1858, and Gutman, "A Brief Note on Late Nineteenth-Century Racial Ideology, Retrogressionist Beliefs, the Misperception of the Ex-Slave Family, and the Conceptualization of Afro-American History," in *Black Family,* pp. 531-44.

14. *Natchez Free Trader,* September 20, 1858. Gustave A. Breaux, Diary, January 1, 1859, Breaux Papers, Tulane University Library, New Orleans, La.

15. See Kenneth Stampp, *The Peculiar Institution: Slavery in the Ante-Bellum South* (New York, 1956), pp. 163, 146.

16. See Raymond and Alice H. Bauer, "Day to Day Resistance to Slavery," *Journal of Negro History,* vol. 27 (1942), pp. 388-419; Stampp, *Peculiar Institution,* p. 88; Frederick Douglass, *Life and Times of Frederick Douglass* (New York, 1962), pp. 64, 192.

17. J. J. Pettigrew, in *De Bow's Review,* vol. 25 (September 1858), p. 293; Roger Pryor, in ibid., vol. 24 (June 1858), p. 582; Benjamin F. Perry, in Lillian Kibler, *Benjamin F. Perry: South Carolina Unionist* (Durham, N.C., 1946), p. 282. Paternalism is the theme of Eugene Genovese, *Roll, Jordan, Roll: The World the Slaves Made* (New York, 1974).

18. Patrick Henry, quoted in J. F. Jameson, *The American Revolution Considered as a Social Movement* (Boston, 1963), p. 23; Governor Gerald Brandon, quoted in Edwin A. Miles, *Jacksonian Democracy in Mississippi* (Chapel Hill, N.C., 1960), p. 123; Edwin Holland and William Drayton, quoted in William W. Freehling, *Prelude to Civil War: The Nullification Controversy in South Carolina, 1816-1832* (New York, 1966), pp. 80, 76-7.

19. See Charles G. Sellers, *The Southerner as American* (Chapel Hill, N.C., 1960), p. 48; Stampp, *Peculiar Institution,* p. 424; Ernest T. Thompson, *Presbyterians in the South, 1607-1861* (Richmond, 1963), pp. 533-4; *Charleston Standard,* reprinted in *New York Weekly Tribune,* November 18, 1856.

20. *Galveston* (Tex.) *News,* December 6, 1856; *Charleston Mercury,* October 20, 1858; J. G. M. Ramsey to L. W. Spratt, April 23, 1858, Ramsey Papers, University of North Carolina Library.

21. *De Bow's Review,* vol. 14 (1853), p. 276 (italics added); quoted in Freehling, *Prelude to Civil War,* p. 59; T. R. Gray, *The Confessions of Nat Turner,* in Herbert Aptheker, *Nat Turner's Slave Rebellion* (New York, 1968), appendix, pp. 130-1; Frederika Bremer, *The Homes of the New World: Impressions of America,* 3 vols. (London, 1853), vol. 2, p. 451; Frances A. Kemble, *Journal of a Residence on a Georgia Plantation in 1838-1839* (New York, 1961), p. 342; *New Orleans Picayune,* December 24, 1856.

22. See Eugene D. Genovese, *The World the Slaveholders Made* (New York, 1969); Ulrich Bonnell Phillips, *Life and Labor in the Old South* (Boston, 1930), p. 177; Robert R. Russel, *Economic Aspects of Southern Sectionalism, 1840-1861* (New York, 1960), p. 35; *Edgefield* (South Carolina) *Advertiser,* June 13, 1855; Ulrich Bonnell Phillips, *American Negro Slavery* (Gloucester, 1959), p. 370; *Montgomery Journal,* reprinted in *Hunt's Merchants Magazine,* vol. 3 (April 1854), p. 500; U.S. Bureau of the Census, *A Statistical Abstract Supplement: Historical Statistics of the United*

States, Colonial Times to 1957 (Washington, D.C., 1960), p. 12; U.S. Census Office, *Eighth Census, 1860* (Washington, D.C. 1864), pp. 247-8.

23. Russel, *Economic Aspects,* p. 210; S. R. Cockrill, "Manufacture of Cotton by Its Producers," *De Bow's Review,* vol. 7 (October 1849), pp. 488-9; Charles S. Sydnor, *Slavery in Mississippi* (New York, 1933), p. 180; *Journal of the House of Representatives of South Carolina, 1849* (Columbia, 1849), pp. 48, 83; Frederick Law Olmsted, *A Journey through Texas* (New York, 1857), pp. 114, 220; *New Orleans Picayune,* December 11, 1856; Frederick Law Olmsted, *A Journey in the Back Country* (New York, 1863), pp. 180-1, and *A Journey in the Seaboard States in the Years, 1853-1854* (New York, 1904), vol. 2, p. 237; Ulrich Bonnell Phillips, ed., *Plantation and Frontier Documents: 1649-1863,* 2 vols. (Cleveland, 1909), vol. 2, pp. 367-8; *Jackson Semi-Weekly Mississippian,* January 24, 1859; *Little Rock Gazette and Democrat,* reprinted in *Jackson Eagle,* October 16, 1858; *Journal of the House of Representatives of South Carolina, 1854,* pp. 110, 156-7; *Journal of the House of Representatives of South Carolina, 1856,* p. 39; *Journal of the South Carolina Senate, 1854,* p. 110; *Journal of the South Carolina Senate, 1858,* p. 10; *Journal of the South Carolina Senate, 1859,* pp. 52, 97; *De Bow's Review,* vol. 26 (May 1859), p. 600; *Journal of the House of Representatives of the State of Alabama, 1859-1860* (Montgomery, 1860), pp. 81-2; *Journal of the House of Representatives of the State of Mississippi, 1859* (Jackson, 1859), p. 123; *Canton Citizen,* Canton, Mississippi, in *Brunswick Herald,* Brunswick, Georgia, June 23, 1858.

24. See Hinton Rowan Helper, *Impending Crisis of the South: How to Meet It* (New York, 1857), pp. 20, 24, 25, 43, 97, 120, 155.

25. Leonidas W. Spratt, "Report on the Slave Trade Made to the Southern Convention at Montgomery, Alabama," *De Bow's Review,* vol. 24 (June 1858), pp. 487, 602; *Edgefield Advertiser,* March 16, 1859; *De Bow's Review,* vol. 22 (January 1857), p. 217; Richard K. Cralle, ed., *The Works of John C. Calhoun,* 6 vols. (Charleston, S.C., 1851-56), vol. 4, pp. 532-3; *Mobile Daily Register,* September 18, 1857; George Fitzhugh, *Sociology for the South, or the Failure of Free Society* (Richmond, 1854), pp. 22-3, 39-40; idem., *Cannibals All! or Slaves Without Masters* (Cambridge, Mass., 1960), p. 31; idem., "Slavery Aggressions," *De Bow's Review,* vol. 28 (February 1860), p. 139; Leonidas W. Spratt, in *De Bow's Review,* vol. 27 (August 1859), p. 210. See also Richard Hofstadter, "John C. Calhoun: Marx of the Master Class," in his *The American Political Tradition* (New York, 1960), pp. 68-92.

26. Calhoun, in Cralle, *Works,* vol. 4, pp. 532-3; Henry Hughes, in *Port Gibson Southern Reveille,* Port Gibson, Mississippi, July 30, 1858; *Charleston Mercury,* June 2 and October 20, 1858; C. W. Miller, *Address on Reopening the Slave Trade* (Columbia, S.C., 1857), *Galveston Weekly News,* June 29, 1857; *New Orleans Delta,* February 14, 1858; Governor James Adams, "Message to the Legislature," in Edward B. Bryan, *Report of the Special Committee of the House of Representatives of South Carolina . . . As Relates to Slavery and the Slave Trade* (Columbia, S.C., 1857), p. 48; *Charleston Mercury,* reprinted in *Edgefield Advertiser,* November 16, 1854; Spratt, "Report on Slave Trade," pp. 487, 602. See also Hofstadter, *American Political Tradition,* pp. 68-92; Marx, *Capital,* pp. 689-703.

27. Special Committee of the Ohio Legislature, quoted in Frank U. Quillan, *The Color Line in Ohio: A History of Race Prejudice in a Typical Northern State* (Ann Arbor, Mich., 1913), p. 55; Thomas R. Dew, *Review of the Debate in the Virginia Legislature*

of 1831 and 1832, in Eric McKitrick, *Slavery Defended: The Views of the Old South* (Englewood Cliffs, N.J., 1963), p. 30 (italics added).

28. *Harper's New Monthly Magazine,* quoted in Stuart Bruchey, *The Roots of American Economic Growth, 1607-1861* (London, 1965), pp. 190-1.

29. Kai Erikson, *Wayward Puritans: A Study in the Sociology of Deviance* (New York, 1966), pp. 13, 64.

30. Michel Foucault, quoted in David Rothman, *The Discovery of the Asylum: Social Order and Disorder in the New Republic* (Boston, 1971), p. xvii; Harry Braverman, *Labor and Monopoly Capital: The Degradation of Work in the Twentieth Century* (New York; 1974), pp. 279-80. See also Michael B. Katz, "Origins of the Institutional State," *Marxist Perspectives,* vol. 1, no. 4 (Winter 1978), pp. 6-23.

31. Benjamin P. Thomas, *Theodore Dwight Weld: Crusader for Freedom* (New Brunswick, N.J., 1950), p. 255; Hofstadter, *American Political Tradition,* pp. 68-92; Karl Mannheim, *Ideology and Utopia: An Introduction to the Sociology of Knowledge* (New York, 1936), p. 10; "St. Henry" Letters, published in the *Jackson Semi-Weekly Mississippian,* October 4, 1859, February 3, 1860, and April 24, 1860; also in the *Port Gibson Southern Reveille,* July 30, 1858.

32. Hughes, Diary of Henry Hughes, in Henry Hughes Papers, Mississippi State Archives, Jackson, Mississippi; Doyle, *Etiquette of Race Relations,* p. 16; Hughes, letter to nephew, quoted in Richard M. Guess, "Henry Hughes, Sociologist, 1829-1862" (M.A. thesis, University of Mississippi, 1930), p. 15.

33. Joseph G. Baldwin, *The Flush Times of Alabama and Mississippi* (New York, 1957), p. 60; Sydnor, *Slavery in Mississippi,* pp. 185-6; Miles, *Jacksonian Democracy,* p. 123; U.S. Census Office, *Fifth Census, 1830* (Washington, D.C., 1832), p. 103, and *Sixth Census, 1840* (Washington, D.C., 1841), p. 58.

34. A Mississippian, quoted in Miles, *Jacksonian Democracy,* p. 124; Henry S. Foote, quoted in Clement Eaton, *The Freedom-of-Thought Struggle in the Old South* (New York, 1964), p. 97.

35. Governor of Mississippi, quoted in Miles, *Jacksonian Democracy,* pp. 123-4; Mississippi state legislative committee, quoted in Sydnor, *Slavery in Mississippi,* pp. 242-4.

36. Hughes, Diary, January 1, 1848.

37. Ibid., June 16, 1850.

38. Ibid., March 14, 1852, May 16, 1852, December 28, 1851, and February 29, 1852; Erik Erikson, *Young Man Luther: A Study in Psychoanalysis and History* (New York, 1959), p. 14.

39. Hughes, Diary, January 9, 1848, May 21, 1848, January 1, 1848, and November 30, 1851.

40. Ibid., July 9, 1848, January 9, 1848, January 16, 1848, January 9, 1853, and February 27, 1848.

41. Ibid., February 22, 1852, October 15, 1848, July 4, 1852, and September 15, 1850.

42. Ibid., July 11, 1852, and June 11, 1848.

43. Ibid., April 13, 1851.

44. Ibid., August 31, 1851, August 15, 1852, and October 24, 1852.

45. William Gilmore Simms, in *Port Gibson Southern Reveille,* December 30, 1854, in Hughes Scrapbook, Hughes Papers; review, unidentified newspaper clipping, in Hughes Scrapbook; Fitzhugh to G. F. Holmes, March 27, 1855, Holmes Letterbook, Duke University Library, Durham, N.C., quoted in Eugene Genovese, *The World the Slaveholders Made,* p. 130; *Port Gibson Southern Reveille,* December 30, 1854, in Hughes Scrapbook.

46. Hughes, Diary, March 16, 1851, May 2, 1852, and May 23, 1852.

47. Hughes, *Treatise on Sociology* (Philadelphia, 1854), pp. 237-40, 264-5, 241, 288, 242-3.

48. Ibid., pp. 286, 289-90, 167-8, 220-1, 280, 286-7.

49. Ibid., p. 292.

50. Tocqueville, *Democracy in America,* vol. 2, pp. 225, 209. See also Burton J. Bledstein, *The Culture of Professionalism: The Middle Class and the Development of Higher Education in America* (New York, 1976).

51. Childs to Holmes, December 12, 1850, Martin Delany file, Countway Library, Harvard Medical School; Records of the Medical Faculty of Harvard University, vol. 2, Minutes for November 4, 23, 1850, Countway Library.

52. Records of the Medical Faculty, vol. 2, Minutes for December 26, 1850, Countway Library; drafts of letters of the Massachusetts Colonization Society and to Abraham R. Thompson, Countway Library; letter signed "E. D. L.," published in the *Boston Evening Transcript,* January 1, 1851; Records of the Medical Faculty, vol. 2, Minutes for December 13, 1850, Countway Library.

53. Erikson, *Wayward Puritans,* p. 64. See also Winthrop D. Jordan, *White over Black: American Attitudes Toward the Negro, 1550-1812* (Chapel Hill, N.C., 1968).

54. Holmes to Morton, November 27, 1849, quoted in Thomas F. Gossett, *Race: The History of an Idea in America* (Dallas, Tex., 1963), p. 59. For an informative study of science and race, see William Stanton, *The Leopard's Spots: Scientific Attitudes toward Race in America, 1815-1859* (Chicago, 1960).

55. See Delany, *North Star,* April 28, 1848, and March 30, 1849; student petition, December 10, 1850; letter signed "Common Sense," published in the *Boston Journal,* clipping in Delany file, Countway Library. There was a student counterpetition favoring admission of the blacks, but even there students admitted that "their prejudices would perhaps lead them to wish that no occasion had occurred for the agitation of this question" (student petition, December 11, 1850, Countway Library).

56. Quote on size of woman's brain, in Eleanor Flexnor, *Century of Struggle: The Women's Rights Movement in the United States* (New York, 1968), p. 23; Dr. Charles Meigs, quoted in Richard H. Shryock, *Medicine and Society in America, 1660-1860* (New York, 1960), p. 121; Holmes, *Pages From an Old Volume of Life* (Cambridge, Mass., 1892), pp. 243-4.

57. Harriot K. Hunt, *Glances and Glimpses* (Boston, 1856), pp. 217, 263-4; letter from Hunt to the Harvard Medical Faculty, November 12, 1850, reprinted in *Boston Evening Transcript,* January 7, 1851. See also student resolutions, in letter signaled "Scapel," published in *Boston Evening Transcript,* January 3, 1851; Hunt to Elizabeth Cady Stanton, June 30, 1852, Stanton Papers, Library of Congress, Washington,

D.C. and "Protest of Harriot K. Hunt, M.D.," in *Frederick Douglass's Paper*, November 25, 1853.

58. *Monthly Religious Magazine* (1860), quoted in William E. Bridges, "Family Patterns and Social Values in America, 1825-1875," *American Quarterly*, vol. 17 (Spring 1965), p. 8. See also Carl N. Degler, "Revolution without Ideology: The Changing Place of Women in America," in R. J. Lifton, ed., *The Woman in America* (Boston, 1967), p. 194.

59. See the well-documented study by Barbara Welter, "The Cult of True Womanhood, 1820-1860," *American Quarterly*, vol. 18 (Summer 1966), pp. 151-74. See also Lawrence Friedman, *Inventors of the Promised Land* (New York, 1976), part two, "Woman's Role in the Promised Land," for a sophisticated study of the subtle and complex roles assigned to the "true woman." The subject has recently been given a full-scale treatment in Ann Douglas, *The Feminization of American Culture* (New York, 1977).

60. John T. Morse, Jr., *Life and Letters of Oliver Wendell Holmes*, 2 vols. (Boston, 1896), vol. 1, pp. 170-1 (italics added); Holmes to Harriet Beecher Stowe, March 31, 1872, in Morse, *Life and Letters*, vol. 2, pp. 233-4.

61. *Monthly Religious Magazine*, in Bridges, "Family Patterns," p. 8; Tocqueville, *Democracy in America*, vol. 2, p. 213.

62. John Ware, *Success in the Medical Profession: An Introductory Lecture delivered at the Massachusetts Medical College, November 6, 1850* (Boston, 1851), pp. 24-5 (italics added).

63. Horace Bushnell, "American Politics," *The American National Preacher* (1840), quoted in Ronald W. Hogeland, "Horace Bushnell's Concept of the American Woman: A Case Study in Masculine Ambivalence," paper read at the American Historical Association Meeting, December 1969; Holmes, *Elsie Venner—A Romance of Destiny* (Boston, 1888, originally published in 1859), p. 172.

64. "Common Sense," *Boston Journal*, clipping in Delany file, Countway Library.

65. Holmes, *Elsie Venner*, p. 240.

66. Douglass, *North Star*, June 13, 1850.

67. Holmes, *The Benefactors of the Medical School of Harvard University* (Boston, 1850), p. 10; Ware, *Success in the Medical Profession*, pp. 3-4; Hunt, *Glances and Glimpses*, p. 271. See also Shryock, *Medicine and Society in America*, p. 147; Holmes, *An Introductory Lecture delivered at the Massachusetts Medical College, November 3, 1847* (Boston, 1847), pp. 8-9. On the rise of male domination in the field of gynecology, see Graham John Barker-Benfield, *The Horrors of the Half-Known Life: Male Attitudes toward Women and Sexuality in Nineteenth-Century America* (New York, 1976). On the question of examination of women by male doctors, see Holmes's comment, in Holmes, *The Position and Prospects of the Medical Student* (Boston, 1844), pp. 20-1.

68. See Bledstein, *Culture of Professionalism*. The induction of professionalism, particularly the scientific and technical fields into the service of corporations, is studied in David F. Noble, *America by Design: Science, Technology, and the Rise of Corporate Capitalism* (New York, 1977).

VII. An American Prospero in King Arthur's Court

1. Karl Marx, *Capital; A Critique of Political Economy* (New York, 1906), pp. 416-7; Walt Whitman, *Leaves of Grass and Selected Prose* (New York, 1958), pp. 399-400; Jacob Bigelow, *Elements of Technology, Taken Chiefly from a Course of Lectures Delivered at Cambridge, on the Application of the Sciences to the Useful Arts* (Boston, 1829), pp. iv, v, 4-7, 29.

2. Karl Marx, *The Economic and Philosophic Manuscripts of 1844* (New York, 1973), p. 150. See also Hans Sachs, "The Delay of the Machine Age," *Psychoanalytic Quarterly*, vol. 2 (July-October 1933), pp. 404-24; Johan Huizinga, *Homo Ludens: A Study of the Play Element in Culture* (Boston, 1955); Harvey Cox, *The Feast of Fools: A Theological Essay on Festivity and Fantasy* (New York, 1970); Norman O. Brown, *Life against Death: The Psychoanalytical Meaning of History* (Middletown, Conn., 1959), pp. 32-9.

3. Jackson, Third Annual Message to Congress, 1831, in James D. Richardson, ed., *A Compilation of the Messages and Papers of the Presidents, 1789-1897* (Washington, D.C., 1897), vol. 2, p. 545; Joseph Ingersoll, quoted in Perry Miller, *Life of the Mind in America: From the Revolution to the Civil War* (New York, 1965), p. 269.

4. "Railroads of the United States," *Hunt's Merchants Magazine*, vol. 3 (October 1840), p. 288; "The Spirit of the Times; or the Fast Age," *Democratic Review*, vol. 33 (September 1853), pp. 260-1; Theodore Parker, quoted in Perry Miller, "The Responsibility of Mind in a Civilization of Machines," *American Scholar*, vol. 31 (Winter 1961), p. 62.

5. Miller, *Life of the Mind*, p. 293; J. A. Meigs, quoted in Miller, "Responsibility of Mind," p. 62; William M. Hall, quoted in Graham John Barker-Benfield, *The Horrors of the Half-Known Life: Male Attitudes toward Women and Sexuality in Nineteenth-Century America* (New York, 1976), p. 16; Henry Nash Smith, *Virgin Land* (New York, 1961).

6. Charles Fraser, "The Moral Influence of Steam," *Hunt's Merchants Magazine*, vol. 14 (June 1846), p. 513; Daniel Webster, "The Boston Mechanics Institution," lecture delivered on November 12, 1828, in Webster, *The Writings and Speeches of Daniel Webster*, 18 vols. (Boston, 1903), vol. 2, pp. 35-6, 25.

7. Charles Caldwell, M.D., "Thoughts on the Moral and Other Indirect Influences of Railroads," *New England Magazine*, vol. 2 (April 1832), pp. 292-7.

8. "Address of the Memphis Convention to the People of the United States," in *De Bow's Review*, vol. 13 (March 1850), p. 219.

9. See George R. Taylor, *The Transportation Revolution, 1850-1860* (New York, 1962), pp. 63-4, 79, 207, 212, 228, 249; Marvin M. Fisher, *Workshops in the Wilderness: The European Response to American Industrialism, 1830-60* (New York, 1967), pp. 5, 12; Edward C. Kirkland, *Industry Comes of Age: Business, Labor, and Public Policy, 1860-1897* (New York, 1961), p. 46; Robert Higgs, *The Transformation of the American Economy, 1865-1914: An Essay in Interpretation* (New York, 1971), pp. 47, 59; Peter Temin, *Iron and Steel in Nineteenth-Century America: An Economic Inquiry* (Cambridge, Mass., 1964), pp. 166-7, 274. Information on transformation of labor in America is based on statistics from U.S. Bureau of the Census, *Historical Statistics of the United States: Colonial Times to 1957* (Washington, D.C., 1960), p. 74.

10. Karl Marx, *Capital,* pp. 460-3. See also Stanley Aronowitz, *False Promises: The Shaping of American Working Class Consciousness* (New York, 1974), and Harry Braverman, *Labor and Monopoly Capital: The Degradation of Work in the Twentieth Century* (New York, 1974); Karl Marx, "Estranged Labor," in *Economic and Philosophic Manuscripts of 1844,* pp. 106-19; Gary Kulik, "Pawtucket Village and the Strike of 1824: The Origins of Class Conflict in Rhode Island," *Radical Labor History,* vol. 17 (Spring 1978), pp. 11, 13, 14, 28.

11. E. P. Thompson, "Time, Work-Discipline, and Industrial Capitalism," *Past and Present,* vol. 38 (1967), pp. 56-97; poem on "The clock in the workshop," reprinted in Herbert Gutman, *Work, Culture and Society in Industrializing America* (New York, 1977), pp. 23-4.

12. Testimony of shoe worker, 1899, reprinted in Leon Litwack, *The American Labor Movement* (Englewood Cliffs, N.J., 1964) pp. 6-7; description of factory life, quoted in Paul Buhle, "The Knights of Labor in Rhode Island," *Radical History Review,* vol. 17 (Spring 1978), pp. 44-5; David Rothman, *The Discovery of the Asylum: Social Order and Disorder in the New Republic* (Boston, 1971), pp. 105-7.

13. *Southern Quarterly Review,* vol. 2 (November 1828), p. 545; Jackson, Third Annual Message, in Richardson, *Papers of the Presidents,* p. 545.

14. Thomas Hart Benton, *Selections of Editorial Articles From the St. Louis Enquirer, on the Subject of Oregon and Texas, as Originally Published in that Paper in the Years 1818-19* (St. Louis, 1844), pp. 5, 23; Thomas Hart Benton, Speech on the Oregon Question, May 28, 1846, U.S. Congress, Senate, *Congressional Globe,* 29th Cong., 1st sess. (Washington D.C.), 1846, p. 915; idem., on railroad bill, U.S. Congress, Senate, *Congressional Globe,* 30th Cong., 2nd sess., February 7, 1849, pp. 473-4.

15. Benton, Speech on Oregon Question, *Congressional Globe,* pp. 917-18.

16. Benton, Speech on the Pacific Railroad Bill, January 26, 1855, in Charles W. Dana, *The Great West, or the Garden of the World* (Boston, 1858), pp. 383-8; Benton, on railroad bill, *Congressional Globe,* p. 470.

17. For Anglo-American depictions of Mexicans which preceded Dana's, see William Shaler, *Journal of a Voyage between China and the North-Western Coast of America in 1804* (Claremont, Calif., 1935, originally published in 1808), pp. 21, 45, 46, 59, 75-7, and Joel Roberts Poinsett, *Notes on Mexico Made in the Autumn of 1822* (New York, 1969, originally published in 1824), pp. 40, 120-2. For a survey of Anglo-American attitudes toward Mexicans, see Philip Anthony Hernandez, "The Other North Americans: The American Image of Mexico and Mexicans, 1550-1850" (Ph.D. thesis, University of California, Berkeley, 1974).

18. Richard Henry Dana, *Two Years Before the Mast* (New York, 1963, originally published in 1840), pp. 293-4.

19. Ibid., p. 36.

20. Ibid., pp. 39, 60-1.

21. Ibid., pp. 136-7.

22. Ibid., p. 106.

23. Ibid., p. 61.

24. Ibid., pp. 187-8, 114-6.

25. Ibid., p. 59; Benton Speech on Oregon Question, *Congressional Globe,* p. 915; James K. Polk, quoted in Norman Graebner, *Empire on the Pacific: A Study in American Continental Expansion* (New York, 1955), pp. 48-50. See also Taylor, *Transportation Revolution,* pp. 179, 199; Walter S. Tower, *A History of the American Whale Fishery* (Philadelphia, 1907), pp. 51, 53, 59.

26. "The Conquest of California," *Southern Quarterly Review,* vol. 15 (July 1849), pp. 411-5.

27. "American Genius and Enterprise," *Scientific American,* vol. 2 (September 1847), p. 397; Barrington Moore, Jr., *Social Origins of Dictatorship and Democracy: Lord and Peasant in the Making of the Modern World,* pp. 433 ff.

28. Carey McWilliams, *North from Mexico: The Spanish-Speaking People of the United States* (New York, 1968), pp. 169, 144; Andres E. Jimenez Montoya, "Political Domination in the Labor Market: Racial Division in the Arizona Copper Industry," Working Paper # 103, Institute for the Study of Social Change, University of California, Berkeley (1977); Mario Barrera, *Class Segmentation and Internal Colonialism: A Theory of Racial Inequality Based on the Chicano Experience,* chapter 3: "The Nineteenth Century, Part II. The Establishment of a Colonial Labor System" (manuscript in preparation for publication).

29. Barrera, *op. cit.,* Sylvester Mowry, *The Geography and Resources of Arizona and Sonora* (San Francisco, 1863), p. 67, quoted in Jimenez Montoya, p. 20, see also p. 22. Table on pay scales for Anglo and Mexican miners, 1860-1890, based on information from Joseph F. Park, "The History of Mexican Labor in Arizona During the Territorial Period" (M. A. Thesis, University of Arizona, 1961), p. 245.

30. Perry Miller, *Errand into the Wilderness,* pp. 204-16; *Literary World,* quoted in ibid., pp. 205-6; Fraser, "Influence of Steam," p. 514.

31. Henry Adams, *The Education of Henry Adams* (New York, 1931), pp. 72-3, 380, 383-5.

32. George M. Beard, *American Nervousness* (New York, 1881), pp. vi, 103, 113, 122, 106-7, 20, 26, 96, 115, 98-9, 118, 120-1, 128, 130-2, 127, 189-90, 175. See also Sigmund Freud, *Civilization and Its Discontents;* Brown, *Life Against Death,* pp. 82-3.

33. Edward Everett, *An Address Delivered Before the Massachusetts Charitable Mechanics Association* (Boston, 1837); *Mechanic's Register,* I (February 22, 1837), pp. 22-3; "American Genius and Enterprise," *Scientific American,* p. 397.

34. Mark Twain, *A Connecticut Yankee in King Arthur's Court* (New York, 1963), pp. 14-5, 19, 65, 89, 152. See John F. Kasson's interpretation of Twain's novel in *Civilizing the Machine: Technology and Republican Values in America* (New York, 1976), pp. 205-15, which I read after I had written this chapter. Henry Nash Smith's lectures on Twain in his course on the American novel, which I took as a graduate student, influenced my understanding of this novel.

35. Twain, *A Connecticut Yankee,* pp. 47, 34, 98, 99, 70-80, 301-14.

36. Twain, *Connecticut Yankee,* pp. 80-1, 53, 92-3, 38-9, 74, 26, 68, 290. On the relationship between professionalism and lay incompetence, see Christopher Lasch, "The

Siege of the Family," in *New York Review of Books,* vol. 24, no. 19 (November 24, 1977), pp. 15-7.

VIII. The Iron Horse in the West

1. Ulysses S. Grant, First Annual Message, 1869, in James Richardson, *Messages and Papers of the Presidents, 1789-1897* (Washington, D.C., 1897), vol. 9, p. 3993; Chief Red Cloud, quoted in E. L. Sabin, *Building the Pacific Railway* (Philadelphia, 1919), p. 233; *American Progress,* in the Prints and Photographs Division, Library of Congress, Washington, D.C.

2. See Frederick Jackson Turner, "The Significance of the Frontier in American History," in *The Early Writings of Frederick Jackson Turner* (Madison, Wis., 1938), pp. 180-205.

3. *Cheyenne Leader* and J. D. Cox, quoted in Robert G. Athearn, *William Tecumseh Sherman and the Settlement of the West* (Norman, Okla., 1956), pp. 324-5.

4. Act quoted in Francis A. Walker, *The Indian Question* (Boston, 1874), p. 5; attorneys quoted in Ira G. Clark, *Then Came the Railroads: The Century from Steam to Diesel in the Southwest* (Norman, Okla., 1958), pp. 121, 128.

5. Clark, *Then Came the Railroads,* pp. 120-1, 169, 161-73, 183; D. S. Otis, *The Dawes Act and the Allotment of Indian Lands* (Norman, Okla., 1973, originally published in 1934), pp. 23-4; General William Sherman, quoted in Athearn, *Sherman,* p. 344.

6. Alfred L. Riggs, "What Shall We Do with the Indians?" *The Nation,* vol. 67 (October 31, 1867), p. 356.

7. Buffalo Bill, quoted in Jay Monaghan, *Custer: The Life of General George Armstrong Custer* (Boston, 1959), p. 395; *Bismarck Weekly Tribune,* quoted in Henry E. Fritz, *The Movement for Indian Assimilation, 1860-1890* (Philadelphia, 1963), p. 176. For a study of the ambivalence officers experienced, see Thomas C. Leonard, "Red, White and the Army Blue: Empathy and Anger in the American West," *American Quarterly* (1974), pp. 176-90.

8. James Fenimore Cooper, *The Pathfinder* (New York, n.d.), p. 419; George A. Custer, *Wild Life on the Plains and Horrors of Indian Warfare* (St. Louis, 1891), pp. 31, 28.

9. Custer, *Wild Life,* pp. 13, 21-2, 215, 226; Custer to Mrs. Custer, April 14, 1867, in Elizabeth Custer, *Tenting on the Plains, or General Custer in Kansas and Texas* (New York, 1889), pp. 556-9; ibid., pp. 628-9, 24; Elizabeth Custer, *"Boots and Saddles"; or Life In Dakota with General Custer* (New York, 1885), p. 245.

10. Custer, "The Red Man," Custer Papers, Custer Battlefield National Monument, Crow Agency, Montana; Custer, *Wild Life,* p. 28.

11. Custer, *Wild Life,* pp. 31, 139-40.

12. Ibid., pp. 70, 98; Custer, quoted in Monaghan, *Custer,* p. 266; Custer to Libbie Custer, July 19, 1873, in Elizabeth Custer, *"Boots and Saddles,"* p. 278; Elizabeth Custer, *Tenting on the Plains,* pp. 111-2.

13. Elizabeth Custer, *Tenting on the Plains,* pp. 592, 528, 579.

14. Custer to Libbie Custer, July 19, 1873, in Custer, *"Boots and Saddles,"* p. 278; Custer, *Wild Life,* pp. 21, 14; Elizabeth Custer, *Tenting on the Plains,* p. 694.

15. Custer, *Wild Life,* p. 42.

16. For the modernization of the military, see William B. Skelton, "Professionalization in the U.S. Army Officer Corps During the Age of Jackson," *Armed Forces & Society,* vol. 1, no. 4 (Summer 1975), pp. 443-71.

17. Bernard Newton, *The Economics of Francis Amasa Walker: American Economics in Transition* (New York, 1968), p. 175. See also James P. Munroe, *A Life of Francis Amasa Walker* (New York, 1923); Massachusetts Institute of Technology, *Meetings Held in Commemoration of the Life and Services of F. A. Walker* (Boston, 1897).

18. Munroe, *Walker,* pp. 10-4, 23; Walker, "Legal Interference with the Hours of Labor," *Lippincott's Magazine* (November 1868), p. 532; Walker, *Political Economy* (New York, 1888), p. 9.

19. Walker, *The Making of the Nation, 1783-1817* (New York. 1905, originally published in 1895), pp. 65, 69-70.

20. Ibid., pp. 72, 206, 265-7.

21. Walker, "Legal Interference," pp. 530-2.

22. George M. Frederickson, *The Inner Civil War: Northern Intellectuals and the Crisis of the Union* (New York, 1968), pp. 202-5; Walker, quoted in Sidney Fine, *Laissez Faire and the General-Welfare State: A Study of Conflict in American Thought, 1865-1901* (Ann Arbor, Mich., 1964), pp. 73, 79; Walker, quoted in Munroe, *Walker,* pp. 304-5; Walker, "Our Population in 1900," *Atlantic Monthly,* vol. 32 (1873), pp. 490, 494-5; Walker, "Restriction of Immigration," *Atlantic Monthly,* vol. 77 (1896), pp. 822-9.

23. Walker, quoted in Munroe, *Walker,* pp. 131-2; Walker, "The Indian Problem, review of De B. R. Keim's *Sheridan's Troopers on the Borders," The Nation,* vol. 10 (June 16, 1870), pp. 389-90.

24. Walker, *Indian Question,* p. 17.

25. Ibid., pp. 34-5, 99.

26. Ibid., pp. 113-4, 38.

27. Walker, "Our Indians and Mr. Wells," *The Nation,* vol. 15 (August 1, 1872), p. 73; Walker, *Indian Question,* pp. 10, 62-3, 64-7.

28. Walker, *Annual Report of the Commissioner of Indian Affairs to the Secretary of the Interior for the Year 1872* (Washington, D.C., 1872), pp. 11, 63, 64, 77-9, 94, 95. See also David Rothman, *The Discovery of the Asylum: Social Order and Disorder in the New Republic* (Boston, 1971).

29. Walker, quoted in Munroe, *Walker,* pp. 135, 25; Walker, *Annual Report,* p. 11; Walker, *Indian Question,* pp. 79-80.

30. Walker, *Annual Report,* p. 9; Walker, *Indian Question,* pp. 91-2.

31. Quoted in Otis, *Dawes Act,* pp. x, 57. For studies of the Dawes Act, see Fritz, *Indian Assimilation;* Loring Benson Priest, *Uncle Sam's Stepchildren: The Reformation of United States Indian Policy, 1865-1887* (New York, 1972); Robert Winston Mardock, *The Reformers and the American Indian* (Columbia, Mo., 1971); and especially Otis, *The Dawes Act and the Allotment of Indian Lands.*

32. Otis, *Dawes Act,* pp. 3,6; Fritz, *Indian Assimilation,* p. 206; Mardock, *Reformers,* p. 211; Helen Hunt Jackson, *A Century of Dishonor: A Sketch of the United States*

Government's Dealings with Some of the Indian Tribes (Boston, 1886, originally published in 1881), p. 4; Thomas Jefferson and T. Hartley Crawford, quoted in F. P. Prucha, Introduction, Otis, *Dawes Act*, pp. ix-x.

33. *U.S. Statutes at Large*, vol. 24, pp. 388-91. The term *assimilation* was used in the debates in Congress. See U.S., Congress, Senate, *Congressional Record*, 49th Cong., 1st sess., 1886, vol. 12, p. 1634.

34. Otis, *Dawes Act*, pp. 17, 18, 86, 87; Wilcomb E. Washburn, *Red Man's Land/White Man's Law: A Study of the Past and Present Status of the American Indian* (New York, 1971), p. 145; Otis, *Dawes Act*, pp. 24, 26; Priest, *Uncle Sam's Stepchildren*, p. 223.

35. Quoted in Otis, *Dawes Act*, pp. 4, 5, 9, 10, 11, 38, 55; Mardock, *Reformers*, p. 212; Jackson, *Century of Dishonor*, pp. 1-4.

36. For the House debate on the Dawes Bill, see U.S., Congress, House, *Congressional Record*, 49th Cong., 2nd sess., 1887, vol. 18, pp. 189-92, 224-6, 973-4; Senate debate, see U.S. Congress, Senate, *Congressional Record*, 49th Cong., 1st sess., 1887, vol. 17, p. 1634.

37. Reverend Lyman Abbott, speech reprinted in Francis Paul Prucha, *Americanizing the American Indians: Writings by the "Friends of the Indian": 1800-1900* (Cambridge, Mass., 1973), p. 34; agent quoted in Otis, *Dawes Act*, p. 29; Senate debate, *Congressional Record*, vol. 17, p. 1762.

38. Senator Dawes, speech at Lake Mohonk Conference, 1887, published in Prucha, *Americanizing the American Indians*, pp. 108-9.

IX. Civilization in the "New South"

1. Karl Marx, *Capital: A Critique of Political Economy* (New York, 1906), p. 463; Eugene D. Genovese, *Roll, Jordan, Roll: The World the Slaves Made* (New York, 1974), pp. 3-7.

2. *New Orleans Picayune*, September 4, 1858.

3. Editor, quoted in F. A. P. Barnard, *An Oration Delivered before the Citizens of Tuscaloosa, Alabama, July 4, 1851*, p. 12, also quoted in Robert R. Russel, *Economic Aspects of Southern Sectionalism, 1840-1861* (New York, 1960), p. 48; Augusta Constitutionalist, reprinted in *De Bow's Review*, vol. 8 (January 1850), pp. 75-6; W. Sykes, "The Development of Southern Resources the Best Guaranty for the Protection of Southern Rights," *De Bow's Review*, vol. 12 (May 1852), pp. 540-2. See also George Fitzhugh, *Sociology for the South, or the Failure of Free Society* (Richmond, Va., 1854), pp. 93-4.

4. *Republican Banner and Nashville Whig*, June 12 and 17, 1858; Leonidas W. Spratt, "Report on the Slave Trade Made to the Southern Convention at Montgomery, Alabama," in *De Bow's Review*, vol. 24 (June 1858), p. 484; *Knoxville Southern Citizen*, reprinted in *Jackson Semi-Weekly Mississippian*, January 12, 1858; I. N. Davis, quoted in *Jackson Semi-Weekly Mississippian*, April 26, 1859.

5. Jackson *Semi-Weekly Mississippian*, May 23, 1859. See also *New Orleans Picayune*, October 16 and November 12, 1858, January 13 and April 27, 1859; *Nashville Union and American*, February 6 and 20, 1858; Kathleen Bruce, *Virginia Iron Manufacture in the Slave Era* (New York, 1931); *De Bow's Review*, vol. 6 (October and November

1848), p. 291; vol. 7 (October 1849), p. 458; vol. 8 (January 1850), pp. 75–6; vol. 14 (June 1853), p. 623; vol. 18 (April 1855), p. 530; vol. 19 (August 1855), p. 194; vol. 25 (December 1858), p. 717; and vol. 26 (March 1859), p. 319; Frederick Law Olmsted, *A Journey in the Seaboard States in the Years, 1853–1854,* (New York, 1904), vol. 1, pp. 183–4; and vol. 2, p. 53, and *A Journey through Texas* (New York, 1857), pp. 19, 32; Frederika Bremer, *The Homes of the New World: Impressions of America,* 3 vols. (London, 1853), vol. 3, p. 315; *Charleston* (S.C.) *Mercury,* February 26 and October 21, 1858; *Newbern* (N.C.) *Daily Progress,* January 12, 1859; Robert S. Starobin, *Industrial Slavery in the Old South* (New York, 1970), pp. 11–5; Charles B. Dew, *Ironmaker to the Confederacy: Joseph R. Anderson and the Tredegar Iron Works* (New Haven, Conn., 1966), pp. 26, 250; Richard C. Wade, *Slavery in the Cities: The South, 1820–1860* (New York, 1964). For the "natural limits" thesis, see Charles W. Ramsdell, "The Natural Limits of Slavery Expansion," *Mississippi Valley Historical Review,* vol. 16 (1929), pp. 151–71.

6. Edwin De Leon, "The New South: What It Is Doing, and What It Wants," *Putnam's Magazine,* vol. 15 (April 1870), pp. 458–64; *New Orleans Times-Democrat,* quoted in C. Vann Woodward, *Origins of the New South, 1877–1913* (Baton Rouge, 1951), p. 112. For studies of the "New South," see Paul M. Gaston, *The New South Creed: A Study in Southern Mythmaking* (New York, 1970), and Woodward, *Origins of the New South.*

7. See Woodward, *Origins of the New South,* pp. 126–32, 136; Raymond B. Nixon, *Henry W. Grady: Spokesman of the New South* (New York, 1943), pp. 94–5; Charles H. Wesley, *Negro Labor in the United States, 1850–1925* (New York, 1967, originally published in 1927), p. 226; Paul B. Worthman, "Working Class Mobility in Birmingham, Alabama, 1880–1914," in Tamara K. Hareven, ed., *Anonymous Americans: Explorations in Nineteenth-Century Social History* (Englewood Cliffs, N.J., 1971), p. 174; Richard J. Hopkins, "Occupational and Geographic Mobility in Atlanta, 1870–1896," *Journal of Southern History,* vol. 24 (May 1968), p. 200.

8. Richard H. Edmonds, quoted in Gaston, *New South Creed,* p. 147. See also Broadus Mitchell, *The Rise of Cotton Mills in the South* (Baltimore, 1921), p. 214; Wesley, *Negro Labor,* pp. 243–5, 234; Woodward, *Origins of the New South,* p. 360; Sterling D. Spero and Abram L. Harris, *The Black Worker: The Negro and the Labor Movement* (Port Washington, 1966), p. 246; Worthman, "Working-Class Mobility in Birmingham," p. 175.

9. Woodward, *Origins of the New South,* pp. 364–5; Spero and Harris, *Black Worker,* pp. 247, 363–6.

10. For these developments in the antebellum urban South, see Wade, *Slavery in the Cities.*

11. Andrew Carnegie, undated telegram, in Nixon, *Grady,* p. 332; *New York World* and *Louisville Post,* on Grady, reprinted in Harris, *Grady,* pp. 443–4, 519. See also Nixon, *Grady;* Joel Chandler Harris, ed., *Life of Henry W. Grady, Including His Writings and Speeches* (New York, 1890); Woodward, *Origins of the New South,* pp. 146–7.

12. Grady, "The South and Her Problems," reprinted in Edna L. Turpin, ed., *The New South and Other Addresses by Henry Woodfin Grady* (New York, 1904), p. 37.

13. Grady, "In Plain Black and White: A Reply to Mr. Cable," *Century Magazine,* vol. 29 (April 1885), pp. 909–17; idem., *The New South* (New York, 1890), p. 146; idem.,

Boston Banquet Speech, reprinted in Harris, *Life of Henry W. Grady*, p. 184; idem., "South and Her Problems," in Turpin, *New South and Other Addresses*, pp. 101-2.

14. Grady, "Where to Draw the Line," quoted in Nixon, *Grady: Spokesman of the New South*, p. 213; Grady, "South and Her Problems," in Turpin, *New South and Other Addresses*, p. 96.

15. Grady, *New South*, p. 146; Grady, "New South," in Turpin, *New South and Other Addresses*, p. 47; Grady, "Before the Bay State Club," in Harris, *Life of Henry W. Grady*, pp. 204-5.

16. Ibid., Grady, "Before the Bay State Club," pp. 204-5.

17. Grady, "Against Centralization," speech at the University of Virginia, June 25, 1889, reprinted in Edwin D. Shurter, ed., *The Complete Orations and Speeches of Henry W. Grady* (Norwood, 1910), pp. 138-9; Grady, "Cotton and Its Kingdom," *Harper's* (October 1881), reprinted in Harris, *Life of Henry W. Grady*, pp. 281-2; Grady, *New South*, pp. 190-1.

18. Grady, *New South*, pp. 190-1.

19. Grady, "In Plain Black and White," pp. 914-7.

20. Grady, "The Farmer and the Cities," speech at Elberton, Georgia, June 1889, reprinted in Shurter, *Complete Orations*, pp. 167-70.

21. Grady, *New South*, pp. 145, 148-9, 152-3; Grady, "Cotton and Its Kingdom," in Harris, *Life of Henry W. Grady*, pp. 271-2; Grady, "South and Her Problems," in Turpin, *New South, and Other Addresses*, p. 48; Grady, Boston Banquet, in Harris, *Grady*, p. 195. On Grady's childhood, see Harris, *Grady*, pp. 21-2.

22. Grady, "In Plain Black and White," pp. 911, 914-7; Grady, *New South*, pp. 89, 152-3, 244-5, 249-50; Grady, Boston Banquet Speech, in Harris, *Life of Henry W. Grady*, pp. 187-8; Grady, "The Farmer and the Cities," in Shurter, *Complete Orations*, pp. 167-70.

23. For this section on Cable, I am indebted to Lawrence J. Friedman, "Heresy in the New South: The Case for George W. Cable," in *The White Savage: Racial Fantasies in the Postbellum South* (Englewood Cliffs, N.J., 1970), pp. 99-118.

24. Cable, "The Negro Question," in Arlin Turner, ed., *The Negro Question, A Selection of Writings on Civil Rights in the South* (New York, 1968), p. 148; Cable to Moffat, May 11, 1888, and to wife, July 31, 1887, Cable Papers, photostats on file at Bowling Green State University, Popular Culture Center, Bowling Green, Ohio; Cable, quoted in Friedman, *White Savage*, p. 105.

25. Cable to wife, June 14, 1881, Cable Papers; William Lloyd Garrison, Jr., to Cable, n.d., and W. E. B. DuBois to Cable, February 23, 1890, Cable Papers; William B. Edwards, quoted in Friedman, *White Savage*, p. 100.

26. Cable, "Literature in the Southern States," in Turner, *Negro Question*, p. 44; Cable, "What Makes the Color Line," in Turner, *Negro Question*, p. 187; Cable quoted in Friedman, *White Savage*, p. 104; Cable to wife, April 2, 1884, Cable Papers; Cable, Diary, December 10, 1888, Cable Papers; Cable, quoted in Lucy C. Bikle, *George W. Cable: His Life and Letters* (New York, 1928), p. 4; Cable to wife, September 4, 1881, November 11, 1888, and March 3, 1886, Cable Papers.

27. Cable, *The Grandissimes* (New York, 1957), pp. 143, 141, 142, 191; Cable, *The Creoles of Louisiana* (New York, 1884), p. 39.

28. Cable to wife, July 31, 1887, Cable Papers; Cable, "Segregation in the Schools," in Turner, *Negro Question*, p. 29; Cable, *Grandissimes*, p. 186; Cable, "Creole Slave Dances: The Dance in Place Congo," *Century Magazine*, vol. 31 (February 1886), pp. 520-2, 525; Cable, "Creole Slave Songs," *Century Magazine*, vol. 31 (April 1886), p. 810.

29. Cable, "Negro Question," in Turner, *Negro Question*, p. 148; Cable, "The Silent South," in Turner, *Negro Question*, p. 83; Cable, "Segregation in the Schools," *New Orleans Bulletin*, September 26, 1875, reprinted in Turner, *Negro Question*, pp. 27, 31; Cable, quoted in Friedman, *White Savage*, p. 111.

30. Grady, "In Plain Black and White," p. 910; Cable to Miss Ford, December 27, 1889, Cable Papers; Cable, "Silent South," in Turner, *Negro Question*, p. 117.

31. Cable, "Negro Question," in Turner, *Negro Question*, p. 145; Cable, "Madame Delphine" and " 'Tite Poulette," in Cable, *Old Creole Days* (New York, 1920, originally published in 1879), pp. 62, 223; Cable, "My Politics," in Turner, *Negro Question*, p. 8.

32. Cable, in Turner, *Negro Question:* "Negro Question," p. 126; "Segregation in the Schools," p. 29; "My Politics," p. 9, and "Silent South," pp. 89, 111-2; Cable, quoted in Friedman, *White Savage*, pp. 101-2, 113.

33. Chesnutt to Cable, May 23, 1890; Cable to R. W. Gilden, February 19, 1887; Cable to wife, November 3, 1889; Chesnutt to Cable, October 4, 1889; Cable to Chesnutt, n.d.; Chesnutt to Cable, April 10, May 24, 1889; Cable to Chesnutt, June 17, 1890; and Chesnutt to Cable, April 11, 1895, Cable papers.

34. Cable to wife, July 31, 1887, Cable Papers; Cable, "Silent South," in Turner, *Negro Question*, pp. 115-6.

35. James Creelman, in *New York World*, September 18, 1895, reprinted in Louis R. Harlan, ed., *The Booker T. Washington Papers*, 4 vols. (Urbana, Ill., 1975), vol. 4, pp. 13, 14. See also Samuel R. Spencer, Jr., *Booker T. Washington and the Negro's Place in American Life* (Boston, 1955), p. 98; Booker T. Washington, *Up From Slavery* (New York, 1963, first published in 1901), p. 147. Of course, Washington and his politics were enormously complicated, for he used his "accommodation" to conceal his defiance and protest; indeed, the address itself was a way of "puttin' on massa." See Louis R. Harlan, *Booker T. Washington: The Making of a Black Leader, 1856-1901* (New York, 1972); August Meier, *Negro Thought in America, 1880-1915* (Ann Arbor, Mich., 1966). The danger of this dual role to the self was analyzed in Lawrence J. Friedman, "Life 'in the Lion's Mouth': Another Look at Booker T. Washington," *Journal of Negro History*, vol. 59, no. 4 (October 1974), pp. 337-51. *Chicago Inter Ocean*, October 2, 1895, reprinted in Harlan, *Booker T. Washington Papers*, vol. 4, pp. 38, 13, 41.

36. Washington, *Up From Slavery*, p. 148. See also Gaston, *New South Creed*, p. 208; Rayford W. Logan, *The Betrayal of the Negr. : From Rutherford B. Hayes to Woodrow Wilson* (New York, 1965), p. 276; Jack Abramowitz, "The Emergence of Booker T. Washington as a National Negro Leader," *Social Education*, vol. 32 (May 1968), pp. 447-9; Harlan, *Booker T. Washington*, p. 227.

37. Washington, in *New York World*, September 20, 1895, reprinted in Harlan, *Booker T. Washington Papers*, vol. 4, pp. 15-6; Washington, Atlanta Address, in *Up From Slavery*, pp. 153-8.

38. James Creelman, in *New York World,* reprinted in Harlan, *Booker T. Washington Papers,* vol. 4, pp. 3, 9. 10, 16.

39. Ibid., p. 7.

X. The "Heathen Chinee" and American Technology

1. Karl Marx, *Capital: A Critique of Political Economy* (New York, 1906), pp. 693-4; Hinton Rowan Helper, *The Land of Gold: Reality Versus Fiction* (Baltimore, 1855), p. 96.

2. John Todd, *The Sunset Land* (Boston, 1870), p. 303.

3. Mary Coolidge, *Chinese Immigration* (New York, 1969, originally published in 1909), p. 425.

4. Dan Caldwell, "The Negroization of the Chinese Stereotype in California," *Southern California Quarterly,* vol. 53 (June 1971), pp. 123-32; *New York Times,* September 3, 1865, quoted in Stuart C. Miller, *The Unwelcome Immigrant: The American Image of the Chinese, 1785-1882* (Berkeley, Calif., 1969), p. 170; *San Francisco Chronicle,* March 6, 1879, quoted in Elmer C. Sandmeyer, *The Anti-Chinese Movement in California* (Urbana, Ill., 1939), p. 26; John T. Morgan, U.S. Cong., *Congressional Record,* 47th Cong., 1st sess., 1882, p. 3266; Governor Henry Haight, "Inaugural Remarks," reprinted in H.J. West, *The Chinese Invasion* (San Francisco, 1873), pp. 86-7.

5. *San Francisco Alta,* June 4, 1853; *Hutching's California Magazine,* vol. 1 (March 1857), p. 387, quoted in Caldwell, "Negroization of the Chinese Stereotype," pp. 123, 128; *Report of the Joint Special Committee to Investigate Chinese Immigration,* Senate Report No. 689, 44th Cong., 2nd sess., 1876-7, p. vi; *New York Times* and Sarah E. Henshaw, quoted in Miller, *Unwelcome Immigrant,* pp. 76, 184, 185, 198; *The Wasp Magazine,* vol. 30 (January-June 1893), pp. 10-1; *Report of the Committee to Investigate Chinese Immigration,* p. 688.

6. Charles W. Brooks, "The Chinese Labor Problem," *Overland Monthly,* vol. 3 (November 1869), p. 413; Frank Norton, "Our Labor System and the Chinese," *Scribner's Monthly,* vol. 2 (May 1871), pp. 61-6; A. W. Loomis, "How Our Chinamen Are Employed," *Overland Monthly,* vol. 2 (March 1869), pp. 238-9; Planters' convention report, reprinted in John R. Commons, *et al.,* eds., *A Documentary History of American Industrial Society* (Cleveland, Ohio, 1910-11), vol. 9, p. 81; *Vicksburg* (Miss.) *Times,* June 30, 1869, in James W. Loewen, *The Mississippi Chinese: Between Black and White* (Cambridge, Mass., 1971), p. 22; John Todd, *The Sunset Land,* pp. 284-5. See also Charles H. Wesley, *Negro Labor in the United States, 1850-1925* (New York, 1967), p. 197.

7. *California Marin Journal,* April 13, 1876, quoted in Sandmeyer, *Anti-Chinese Movement in California,* p. 38; Horatio Seymour, letter to a workingmen's association, in *New York Times,* August 6, 1870; *The Nation,* vol. 9 (July 15, 1869), p. 445; Morgan, *Congressional Record,* 47th Cong., 1st sess., p. 3267.

8. California Supreme Court, *The People* v. *Hall,* October 1, 1854, in Robert F. Heizen and Alan F. Almquist, *The Other Californians* (Berkeley, 1971), p. 229; superintendent of education, quoted in Franklin Odo, *et al., Roots: An Asian-American Reader* (Los Angeles, 1971), p. 175; Hayes, quoted in Miller, *Unwelcome Immigrant,* p. 190.

9. Henry Grimm, *"The Chinese Must Go": A Farce in Four Acts* (San Francisco, 1879), pp. 3, 4, 8, 19.

10. Miller, *Unwelcome Immigrant,* p. 189; *Congressional Record,* 47th Cong., 1st sess., pp. 2973-4; *U.S. Statutes at Large,* vol. 22, pp. 58-61. See debate, *Congressional Record,* 47th Cong., 1st sess., pp. 2033, 3310, 3265, 3268; appendix, pp. 48, 89, 21.

11. *The Nation* (March 16, 1882), p. 222; Bret Harte, "Plain Language from Truthful James," *Overland Monthly,* vol. 5 (September 1870), pp. 287-8.

12. Mark Twain, quoted in Margaret Duckett, *Mark Twain and Bret Harte* (Norman, Okla., 1964), p. 52; *New York Globe,* January 7, 1871, quoted in George R. Stewart, Jr., *Bret Harte: Argonaut and Exile* (Boston, 1931), p. 180; *Springfield Republican,* quoted in Duckett, *Mark Twain and Bret Harte,* p. 38.

13. See Miller, *Unwelcome Immigrant;* Alexander Saxton, *The Indispensable Enemy: Labor and the Anti-Chinese Movement in California* (Berkeley, Calif., 1971); Robert McClellan, *The Heathen Chinee: A Study of American Attitudes toward China, 1890-1905* (Columbus, Ohio, 1971); Frederick Rudolph, "Chinamen in Yankeedom: Anti-Unionism in Massachusetts in 1870," *American Historical Review,* vol. 53, no. 1 (October 1947), pp. 1-29.

14. Harte, "Plain Language," pp. 287-8.

15. Harte to Mrs. M. Sherwood, in *New York Times,* May 10, 1902; and Harte, in S. R. Elliot, "Glimpses of Bret Harte," *The Reader* (July 1907), both quoted in Stewart, *Bret Harte,* p. 181.

16. See William P. Fenn, *Ah Sin and His Brethren in American Literature* (Peking, 1933), p. xi; Stewart, *Bret Harte,* pp. 183, 208, 210-1; Duckett, *Mark Twain and Bret Harte,* p. 32.

17. Harte to Nan Harte, September 13, 1879; August 17, 1885; and November 28, 1887; in Geoffrey Bret Harte, ed., *The Letters of Bret Harte* (London, 1926), pp. 154, 285-6, 322.

18. Harte, "Wan Lee, the Pagan" in Harte, *Harte's Complete Works,* 20 vols. (Boston, 1929), vol. 3, pp. 262-79.

19. Harte, "See Yup," in ibid., vol. 7, pp. 144-60.

20. Aaron H. Palmer, *Memoir, geographical, political, and commercial, on the present state, productive resources, and capabilities for commerce, of Siberia, Manchuria, and the Asiatic Islands of the Northern Pacific Ocean; and on the importance of opening commercial intercourse with those countries,* March 8, 1948. U.S. Cong., Senate, 30th Cong., 1st sess., Senate misc. no. 80, pp. 1, 52, 60, 61.

21. Henry Robinson, "Our Manufacturing Era," *Overland Monthly,* vol. 2 (March 1869), pp. 280-4.

22. See Saxton, *Indispensable Enemy,* pp. 60-6; Coolidge, *Chinese Immigration,* p. 63; B. P. Avery, "Building the Iron Road," *Overland Monthly,* vol. 2 (March 1869), p. 232.

23. Albert P. Richardson, *Beyond the Mississippi: From the Great River to the Great Ocean. Life and Adventure on the Prairies, Mountains, and Pacific Coast, 1857-1867* (Hartford, Conn., 1867), p. 462; company official, quoted in Saxton, *Indispensable Enemy,* p. 65. See Charles W. Brooks, "The Chinese Labor Problem," *Overland Monthly,* vol. 3 (November 1869), p. 408; Wesley S. Griswold, *A Work of Giants:*

Building the First Transcontinental Railroad (New York, 1962), p. 196; E. L. Sabin, *Building the Pacific Railway* (Philadelphia, 1919), p. 121.

24. *San Francisco Alta,* July 1 and 3, 1867; Leland Stanford, quoted in Sabin, *Building the Pacific Railway,* p. 111.

25. Palmer, *Memoir,* p. 1; F. F. Victor, "Manifest Destiny in the West," *Overland Monthly,* vol. 3 (August 1869), pp. 148-59; Frank Norton, "Our Labor System and the Chinese," *Scribner's Monthly,* vol. 2 (May 1871), p. 67; Leland Stanford, quoted in Saxton, *Indispensable Enemy,* p. 62.

26. Robert L. Harris, "The Pacific Railroad—Unopen," *Overland Monthly,* vol. 3 (September 1869), p. 252.

27. Loomis, "How Our Chinamen Are Employed," pp. 23-36; Reverend O. Gibson, *Chinaman or White Man, Which?* (San Francisco, 1873), p. 10; R. G. McClellan, quoted in Coolidge, *Chinese Immigration,* p. 357. See also Saxton, *Indispensable Enemy,* p. 4; Brooks, "Chinese Labor Problem," p. 408; Coolidge; *Chinese Immigration,* p. 359; *San Francisco Morning Call,* May 27, 1873, reprinted in Henry J. West, *The Chinese Invasion* (San Francisco, 1873); Ping Chiu, *Chinese Labor in California,* pp. 24-5, 32, 29, 64; *Report of the Committee to Investigate Chinese Immigration,* p. 252. The process of Chinese/white competition involved the expulsion of Chinese labor rather than of white. For example, in 1870 ninety percent of the cigarmakers in San Francisco were Chinese; a decade later, they constituted only thirty percent. See Coolidge, *Chinese Immigration,* p. 370.

28. For the full discussion of the North Adams event, see Rudolph's excellent article, "Chinamen in Yankeedom," pp. 1-29. See also Miller, *Unwelcome Immigrant,* pp. 175-84; Gunther Barth, *Bitter Strength: A History of the Chinese in the United States, 1850-1870* (Cambridge, Mass., 1964), pp. 197-202.

29. *Harper's New Monthly Magazine* (December 1870), p. 138; Rudolph, "Chinamen in Yankeedom," pp. 3, 4.

30. William Shanks, "Chinese Skilled Labor," *Scribner's Monthly,* vol. 2 (September 1871), p. 495; Washington Gladden, *From the Hub to the Hudson* (Greenfield, Wis., 1870), p. 107; *North Adams* (Mass.) *Transcript,* quoted in Rudolph, "Chinamen in Yankeedom," pp. 4, 8, 9; Shanks, "Chinese Skilled Labor," p. 495; Rudolph, "Chinamen in Yankeedom," p. 9; Marx, *Capital,* pp. 693, 696.

31. See Rudolph, "Chinamen in Yankeedom," pp. 10-5; Shanks, "Chinese Skilled Labor," p. 495.

32. See Rudolph, "Chinamen in Yankeedom," p. 14; *The Nation,* vol. 10 (June 23, 1870) and vol. 11 (July 14, 1870); *Harper's New Monthly Magazine* (December 1870), p. 138; Shanks, "Chinese Skilled Labor," pp. 495-6.

33. *The Nation,* vol. 10 (June 23, 1870), p. 397; *Boston Commonwealth,* June 25, 1870, and *Springfield* (Mass.) *Republican,* June 17, 1870, reprinted in Commons, *Documentary History of American Industrial Society,* vol. 9, pp. 84-6.

34. *The Nation,* vol. 10 (June 23, 1870), p. 397; *Harper's New Monthly Magazine* (December 1870), p. 138; Shanks, "Chinese Skilled Labor," pp. 495-6.

35. See Barth, *Bitter Strength,* pp. 202-9.

36. Samuel Bowles, *Our New West* (Hartford, Conn., 1869), p. 414.

37. *Report of the Committee to Investigate Chinese Immigration,* pp. 679, 680; Loomis, "How Our Chinamen Are Employed," p. 240; Brooks, "Chinese Labor Problem," p. 407; Bowles, *Our New West,* p. 414; *The Nation,* vol. 11 (July 14, 1870), pp. 18-9. See also Leigh Kagan, "Chinese in California (1850-1894): Migrant Labor or Immigrant?" (paper presented at the Asian Scholars on the Pacific Conference, University of Oregon, Eugene, Oregon, June 1977); Marx, *Capital,* pp. 689-703; Harry Braverman, *Labor and Monopoly Capital: The Degradation of Work in the Twentieth Century* (New York, 1974), pp. 382-401.

38. Ginn Wall, quoted in Victor G. and Brett De Bary Nee, *Longtime Californ': A Documentary Study of an American Chinatown* (New York, 1973), p. 27. See also Coolidge, *Chinese Immigration,* pp. 498, 501, 502.

39. Brooks, "Chinese Labor Problems," pp. 412-3; Loomis, "How Our Chinamen Are Employed," pp. 238-9; Robinson, "Our Manufacturing Era," p. 282.

40. Brooks, "Chinese Labor Problem," p. 412; Charles Crocker, testimony, *Report of the Committee to Investigate Chinese Immigration,* p. 667; E. L. Godkin, "Editorial," *The Nation,* vol. 10 (June 23, 1870), p. 397, and vol. 11 (July 14, 1870), pp. 18-9.

41. Abby Sage Richardson, "A Plea for Chinese Labor," *Scribner's Monthly,* vol. 2 (July 1871), pp. 286-90; *Boston Commonwealth,* June 25, 1870, in Commons, *Documentary History of American Industrial Society,* p. 496; *The Nation* (June 23, 1870), p. 397; "The Coming of the Barbarian," *The Nation* (July 15, 1869), p. 44.

42. *North Adams* (Mass.) *Transcript,* quoted in Rudolph, "Chinamen in Yankeedom," p. 23; *Harper's New Monthly Magazine* (December 1870), p. 139; Marx, *Capital,* pp. 693-4; Todd, *Sunset Land,* p. 283; Norton, "Our Labor System," p. 70.

43. *The Nation,* vol. 10 (June 30, 1870), p. 412; Henry George, speech, in *San Francisco Daily Examiner,* July 9, 1870, reprinted in West, *The Chinese Invasion,* p. 128. See also Rudolph, "Chinamen in Yankeedom," pp. 23-4.

44. Mother to George, August 15, 1858; father to George, September 18, 1858; and father to George, January 19, 1859, in George, Jr., *Life of Henry George,* pp. 76, 86. See also father to George, January 10, 1859, and George to father, January 4, 1859, Henry George Papers, New York Public Library, New York, New York. See also Henry George, Jr., *The Life of Henry George* (New York, 1930), pp. 1, 9-10.

45. George to sister Jennie, September 15, 1861, George Papers.

46. George, Diary, February 17, 1865, George Papers.

47. George, Jr., *Life of Henry George,* p. 149; George to father, August 8, 1866, George Papers; George, Jr., *Life of Henry George,* pp. 191-2; George to Reverend Thomas Dawson, February 1, 1883, in George, Jr., *Life of Henry George,* pp. 193, 311-2; George Speech in Cooper Union, October 5, 1886, George, Jr., *Life of Henry George,* pp. 468-70.

48. George, speech, February 4, 1890, in George, Jr., *Life of Henry George,* p. 100; George quoted in George, Jr., *Life of Henry George,* p. 210; George, speech, February 4, 1890, in George, Jr., *Life of Henry George,* p. 80.

49. George, Diary, February 21, 22, 1865; see also January 1, 1865; October 9, 1868; April 2, 1867; and December 1, 1869, George Papers.

50. George, "What the Railroad Will Bring Us," *Overland Monthly,* vol. 1 (October 1868), pp. 297-306.

51. George, "The Chinese on the Pacific Coast," *New York Tribune*, May 1, 1869, reprinted in A. M. Winn, *Valedictory Address, January 11, 1871, at Excelsior Hall, San Francisco, to the Mechanics' State Council of California* (San Francisco, 1871), pp. 13-9.

52. George to John Stuart Mill, August 22, 1869, and John Stuart Mill to George, October 23, 1869, George Papers; *Oakland* (Calif.) *Daily Transcript*, November 22, 1869.

53. *San Francisco Daily Herald*, May 24, 1869.

54. A. J. Steers to W. H. Appleton, 1880(?), in George Papers. See also George to Dr. Edward R. Taylor, January 4, 1881, George Papers, in which he wrote: "At last, it begins to look as though it had really taken hold." He felt that the book was "capable of an enormous sale.... Had a first class adv in the *Herald* this morning, and will have another in the *Sun* tomorrow. This is the *beginning*. For every day shows me that wherever the book goes it does attract attention. Every reader means more readers, and every buyer more buyers."

55. George, *Progress and Poverty: An Inquiry into the Cause of Industrial Depressions and of Increase of Want with Increase of Wealth. The Remedy.* (New York, 1879), pp. 3, 6, 280, 325, 326, 390, 388, 492, 475, 480, 496.

56. George, "Chinese Immigration," in John Lalor, *Cyclopedia of Political Science, Political Economy and of the Political History of the United States* (Chicago, 1883), pp. 409-14.

57. George, ibid., p. 414; George, "Chinese on the Pacific," p. 19; George, *Our Land and Land Policy, National and State* (San Francisco, 1871), pp. 26-7.

58. For more information on anti-Chinese violence, see Coolidge, *Chinese Immigration*, pp. 254-77; Saxton, *Indispensable Enemy*, pp. 200-13; William R. Locklear, "The Celestials and the Angels: A Study of the Anti-Chinese Movement in Los Angeles to 1882," *Historical Society of Southern California Quarterly*, vol. 42 (September 1960), pp. 239-56; Herbert Hill, "The Anti-Oriental Agitation and the Rise of Working-Class Racism" (paper delivered at Rutgers University, New Brunswick, N.J., October 1971).

59. George, *Social Problems* (New York, 1911, copyright 1883), p. 6; George, *Our Land and Land Policy*, pp. 44-5.

60. Ignatius Donnelly, *Caesar's Column: A Story of the Twentieth Century* (Cambridge, Mass., 1960, originally published in 1890), pp. 41, 96-7. See also Pierton W. Dooner, *Last Days of the Republic* (San Francisco, 1880).

XI. The Masculine Thrust Toward Asia

1. Walt Whitman, *Leaves of Grass and Selected Prose* (New York, 1958), p. 340; Max Weber, *The Protestant Ethic and the Spirit of Capitalism* (New York, 1958), pp. 181, 182; Max Weber, "Bureaucracy," in H. H. Gerth and C. Wright Mills, eds., *From Max Weber; Essays in Sociology* (New York, 1973), pp. 196-244. See also Guy Benveniste, *The Politics of Expertise* (San Francisco, 1972).

2. Lynn Marshall, "The Strange Stillbirth of the Whig Party," *American Historical Review*, vol. 72, no. 2 (January 1967), pp. 445-68; David F. Noble, *America by*

Design: Science, Technology, and the Rise of Corporate Capitalism (New York, 1977), pp. 3-65, 260-3; Henry David Thoreau, *Walden; or, Life in the Woods* (New York, 1957), p. 75. See also Matthew A. Crenson, *The Federal Machine: Beginnings of Bureaucracy in Jacksonian America* (Baltimore, 1975); Michael Paul Rogin, *Fathers and Children: Andrew Jackson and the Subjugation of the American Indian* (New York, 1975), pp. 294-5, and "Max Weber & Woodrow Wilson: The Iron Cage in Germany and America," *Polity: The Journal of the Northeastern Political Science Associations,* vol. 3, no. 4 (Summer 1971), pp. 562-4; Robert H. Wiebe, *The Search for Order, 1877-1920* (New York, 1968); Walter La Feber, *The New Empire: An Interpretation of American Expansion, 1860-1898* (Ithaca, N.Y., 1967). The importance of centralization and technology in the modern control of society is noted in C. Wright Mills, *The Power Elite* (New York, 1956), pp. 3-29, 298-324.

3. Charles R. Flint, quoted in Alfred D. Chandler, Jr., *Strategy and Structure: Chapters in the History of the Industrial Enterprise* (Cambridge, Mass., 1966), p. 33; Charles Francis Adams, Jr., quoted in Gabriel Kolko, *The Triumph of Conservatism: A Reinterpretation of American History, 1900-1916* (New York, 1977), p. 14.

4. Rogin, *Fathers and Children,* pp. 294-5; Kolko, *Triumph of Conservatism,* pp. 2-3, 22-3, 303.

5. Andrew Carnegie, paraphrased by La Feber, *New Empire,* p. 17; Carroll Wright, quoted in Josiah Strong, *Expansion Under New World Conditions* (New York, 1900), p. 80; Walter Gresham, quoted in La Feber, *New Empire,* p. 200; Brooks Adams, "The Struggle for Life Among Nations," in Adams, *America's Economic Supremacy* (New York, 1900), pp. 32, v-vi. See also Richard B. Du Boff, "Unemployment in the United States: An Historical Summary," *Monthly Review,* vol. 29, no. 6 (November 1977), p. 11.

6. Bureau of Foreign Commerce, State Department official, and *New York Commercial Advertiser,* quoted in La Feber, *New Empire,* pp. 21, 301-4, 310, 311, 353-4; Brooks Adams, *America's Economic Supremacy,* p. 20. See also Robert McClellan, *The Heathen Chinee: A Study of American Attitudes toward China, 1890-1905* (Columbus, Ohio, 1971); and Max Weber, "The Economic Foundations of 'Imperialism,' " in Gerth and Mills, eds., *From Max Weber,* pp. 162-70.

7. See Philip S. Foner, *History of the Labor Movement in the United States,* 2 vols. (New York, 1947, 1955), vol. 1, pp. 193, 468-74; vol. 2, pp. 103, 106, 114, 207-13, 262-7; Edward C. Kirkland, *Industry Comes of Age: Business, Labor, and Public Policy, 1860-1897* (New York, 1961), p. 366. The tensions between factory production and workers, particularly European immigrants, have been studied in Herbert G. Gutman, *Work, Culture, and Society in Industrializing America* (New York, 1976).

8. Josiah Strong, *Our Country: Its Possible Future and Its Present Crisis* (New York, 1885), pp. 2, 6-7, 70-3, 168.

9. Ibid., pp. 76, 174-5, 30, 40, 43, 44, 53, 57, 84-5, 94, 106, 126, 119, 139, 153, 14.

10. The influence of Alfred Thayer Mahan was acknowledged in the preface to this work. Strong informed the reader that Mahan had read several chapters and given "the benefit of his valuable criticism" (p. 10).

11. Ibid., pp. 23-4, 36.

12. Ibid., pp. 27, 19, 80, 86, 91, 99, 98, 86.

13. Strong, *The Times and Young Men* (New York, 1901), pp. 125, 127, 129-30; Strong, *The New Era; or, The Coming Kingdom* (New York, 1893), pp. 17, 228-9.

14. Strong, *The New Era*, p. 352.

15. Frederick Jackson Turner, "The Significance of the Frontier in American History," in *The Early Writings of Frederick Jackson Turner* (Madison, Wis., 1938), pp. 185-6, 220, 187, 188, 196. See Richard Slotkin, *Regeneration through Violence: The Mythology of the American Frontier, 1600-1860* (Middletown, Conn., 1973).

16. Turner, "Significance of Frontier," pp. 198, 202, 228.

17. John Winthrop, quoted in Roy Harvey Pearce, *Savagism and Civilization: A Study of the Indian and the American Mind* (Baltimore, 1967), p. 21. See also Perry Miller, "Nature and the National Ego," in *Errand into the Wilderness* (New York, 1964), pp. 204-16.

18. Turner, "The Significance of History," quoted in La Feber, *New Empire*, p. 66.

19. Theodore Roosevelt to Mahan, May 12, 1890, Alfred Thayer Mahan Papers, Library of Congress, Washington, D.C.; *Atlantic Monthly*, vol. 66 (October 1890), p. 567; *Blackwood's Magazine*, quoted in Julius W. Pratt, *Expansionists of 1898* (Baltimore, 1936), p. 22. See also William E. Livezey, *Mahan on Sea Power* (Norman, Okla., 1947), pp. 74-5.

20. Mahan to Admiral S. B. Luce, January 22, 1886, Mahan Papers; Mahan to Samuel Ashe, February 2 and September 8, 1887, Mahan-Ashe Papers, Duke University Library, Durham, North Carolina.

21. Alfred T. Mahan, *The Influence of Sea Power upon History, 1660-1783* (Boston, 1890), pp. 1, 25, 27, 28, 31, 33, 50, 57-8, 82-7.

22. Mahan to Theodore Roosevelt, May 1, 1897, quoted in Livezey, *Mahan on Sea Power*, p. 114; Mahan, *The Problem of Asia and Its Effect upon International Policies* (Boston, 1900); Mahan to Theodore Roosevelt, March 14, 1898, and Theodore Roosevelt to Mahan, March 21, 1898, Mahan Papers, Library of Congress.

23. Mahan, *The Interest of America in Sea Power, Present and Future* (Boston, 1898), p. 222; Mahan, *Influence of Sea Power*, p. 31; Mahan, *Retrospect and Prospect* (Boston, 1902), pp. 44, 34.

24. Mahan, *Problem of Asia*, pp. 15, 98; Mahan, *Interest of America in Sea Power*, pp. 165-6, 167; Mahan, *The Harvest Within: Thoughts on the Life of a Christian* (Boston, 1909), p. 118.

25. Mahan, *Problem of Asia*, pp. 191-2, 93; Mahan, *Interest of America in Sea Power*, pp. 251-2, 259; Mahan, *Lessons of the War with Spain* (Boston, 1899), p. 249.

26. La Feber, *New Empire*, p. 80.

27. Mahan to Samuel Ashe, April 30, [1879]; May 19, 1876; November 13, 1880; and December 21, 1882, Mahan-Ashe Papers; Mahan, quoted in Peter Karsten, *The Naval Aristocracy: The Golden Age of Annapolis and the Emergence of Modern American Navalism* (New York, 1972), p. 189.

28. Mahan, *Retrospect and Prospect*, pp. 17-8; Mahan, *From Sail to Steam: Recollections of Naval Life* (New York, 1907), pp. 324-5; Mahan to Samuel Ashe, July 26, 1884; March 12, 1880; March 11, 1885; and February 1, 1887, Mahan-Ashe Papers.

29. D. H. Mahan, *An Elementary Treatise on Advance-Guard. . . .* (New York, 1867,

originally published in 1847), p. 7; D. H. Mahan to A. T. Mahan, January 2 and February 7, 1859; October 14, 1858; and n.d., Mahan Papers. See also Mahan to Samuel Ashe, March 8, 1859, Mahan-Ashe Papers; W. D. Puleston, *The Life and Work of Captain Alfred Thayer Mahan* (New Haven, Conn., 1939), pp. 9-13. See also Robert Seager, "Ten Years before Mahan: The Unofficial Case for the New Navy, 1880-1890," *Mississippi Valley Historical Review,* vol. 40 (December 1953), p. 511; David M. Pletcher, *The Awkward Years: American Foreign Relations under Garfield and Arthur* (Columbia, Mo., 1962), p. 117.

30. Mahan, *Sail to Steam,* pp. xii-xiii; Mahan, *Harvest Within,* pp. 253-4, 1, 145, 194, 186-7; Mahan to daughter Ellen, August 3 and December 15, 1894; Mahan to wife, March 4, 1895; Mahan to sister, April 28, 1867, Mahan Papers, Library of Congress; Mahan to Samuel Ashe, April 13, 1876, Mahan-Ashe Papers. See also Charles C. Taylor, *The Life of Admiral Mahan, Naval Philosopher* (New York, 1920), p. 258; Puleston, *Mahan,* pp. 146, 86.

31. Mahan to Samuel Ashe, October 23 and 29, 1858; Mahan to Samuel Ashe, May 1 and April 18, 1859, October 10, 1868, Mahan-Ashe Papers. See also William Taylor and Christopher Lasch, "Two 'Kindred Spirits': Sorority and Family in New England 1839-1846," *New England Quarterly* (March 1963), pp. 23-41. For a discussion of the loss of sexual completeness, see Norman O. Brown, *Life against Death: The Psychoanalytical Meaning of History* (Middletown, Conn., 1959), pp. 131-4.

32. Mahan to Samuel Ashe, August 12, 1868, and February 12, 18(67?), Mahan-Ashe Papers; Mahan, *Harvest Within,* pp. 186-7.

33. Mahan to Samuel Ashe, April 13, 1876, Mahan-Ashe Papers; Mahan to sister, April 28, 1867; Mahan to wife, June 23 and August 8, 1894, and March 4, 1895, Mahan Papers.

34. Mahan, "The Navy as a Career," *The Forum* (November 1895), pp. 277-83.

35. Mahan, *Interest of America in Sea Power,* p. 268.

36. Mahan to Samuel Ashe, March 23, 1859; September 23, 1859; March 23, 1859, Mahan-Ashe Papers; Mahan, *Interest of America in Sea Power,* pp. 119-22; Mahan, *Lessons of the War with Spain,* p. 231; Mahan to B. Clark, December 19, 1900, Mahan Papers.

37. See David Rothman, *The Discovery of the Asylum: Social Order and Disorder in the New Republic* (Boston, 1971).

38. Albert Beveridge, quoted in Gossett, *Race: The History of an Idea in America* (Dallas, 1963), p. 337. The restrictions and restraints of the new order also generated a new athleticism in the 1890s. Outdoor activities became a rage: Competitive sports such as football and baseball swept college campuses throughout the country, and bicycling became a fad as the number of bicycles increased from one million in 1893 to ten million in 1900. This new athletic activism, historian John Higham observed, could only reform the rational structures and help Americans accommodate to life in a highly industrialized and bureaucratized society. See Higham, "The Reorientation of American Culture in the 1890s," in *Writing American History: Essays on Modern Scholarship* (Bloomington, Ind., 1970), pp. 73-104.

39. Mahan, *Problem of Asia,* pp. 191-2, 93; Mahan, *Lessons of the War with Spain,* pp. 231, 249; Mahan, *Interest of America in Sea Power,* pp. 119-22, 268; Mahan to B. Clark, December 19, 1900, Mahan Papers.

40. Strong, *Expansion,* pp. 244-6, 282, 296-7; Strong, *Our Country.* See also La Feber, *New Empire,* p. 286; Richard Hofstadter, "Manifest Destiny and the Philippines," in Daniel Aaron, ed., *America in Crisis* (New York, 1952), pp. 173-200; C. Vann Woodward, *Origins of the New South, 1877-1913* (Baton Rouge, 1951), p. 369; Gabriel Kolko, *The Triumph of Conservatism: A Reinterpretation of American History, 1900-1916* (New York, 1963); Henry F. Graff, *American Imperialism and the Philippine Insurrection* (Boston, 1969), p. xiv.

41. Theodore Roosevelt, "The Strenuous Life," in *The Strenuous Life: Essays and Addresses* (Philadelphia, 1903), pp. 3, 4, 6-8, 10-1, 19-20.

XII. Down from the Gardens of Asia

1. Walt Whitman, *Leaves of Grass and Selected Prose* (New York, 1958), pp. 1, 25, 18, 78, 83, 89, 399-400, 340, 121, 343; Walt Whitman, in Horace Traubel, *With Walt Whitman in Canada,* 2 vols. (New York, 1915), vol. 2, pp. 34-5. See also Norman O. Brown, "The Resurrection of the Body," in *Life against Death: The Psychoanalytical Meaning of History* (Middletown, Conn., 1959), pp. 307-22.

2. Herman Melville, *Moby-Dick, or the Whale* (Boston, 1956, originally published in 1851), pp. 100-1.

3. Ibid., p. 165.

4. Ibid., pp. 108, 325-9. For an analysis of the theme of the machine in *Moby-Dick,* see Leo Marx, *The Machine in the Garden: Technology and the Pastoral Ideal in America* (New York, 1967), pp. 287-319; also Henry Nash Smith, "The Image of Society in Moby-Dick," in Tyrus Hillway and Luther S. Mansfield, eds., *Moby-Dick: Centennial Essays* (Dallas, 1953), pp. 59-75. A discussion of Melville's thoughts on technology may be found in Marvin M. Fisher, " 'The Bell-Tower': Melville and Technology," *American Literature,* vol. 23 (1951-52), pp. 219-32; and Fisher, "Melville's 'Bell-Tower': A Double Thrust," *American Quarterly,* vol. 18 (Summer 1966), pp. 200-7. For another analysis of *Moby-Dick* in relation to American politics—this time to antebellum politics—see Alan Heimert, *"Moby-Dick* and American Political Symbolism," *American Quarterly,* vol. 15 (Winter 1963), pp. 498-534.

5. Melville, *Moby-Dick,* pp. 105, 182, 253, 322-3. For a fascinating analysis of the *Pequod's* crew as a brotherhood of workers and Ahab as a man of modern technology and a totalitarian, see C. L. R. James, *Mariners, Renegades, and Castaways: The Story of Herman Melville and the World* (New York, 1953). For a discussion of Melville's "Marxist" and "Freudian" writings, see Ann Douglas, "Herman Melville and the Revolt against the Reader," in *The Feminization of American Culture* (New York, 1977), pp. 289-326.

6. Melville, *Moby-Dick,* pp. 326-7.

7. Melville, *Moby-Dick,* pp. 176, 418. On Gramsci, see Eugene Genovese, "On Antonio Gramsci," in *In Red and Black: Marxian Explorations in Southern and Afro-American History* (New York, 1972), p. 406. The term *manufactures* is from Richard Lichtman, "Marx's Theory of Ideology," *Socialist Revolution,* vol. 23 (1975), pp. 46-7, where he observed: "Why has the working class failed to achieve power? Gramsci remarked that the appropriate objective conditions for revolution had been available for fifty years. . . . The growth of contemporary capitalism is inseparable from the increasing

domination of ideology. Direct force and the threat of violence are replaced by the prevalence of manufactured consent." For the concept of charisma, see Weber, "The Sociology of Charismatic Authority," in H. H. Gerth and C. Wright Mills, eds., *From Max Weber: Essays in Sociology* (New York, 1973), pp. 245-64. "Charisma," wrote Weber, "knows only inner determination and inner restraint. The holder of charisma seizes the task that is adequate for him and demands obedience and a following by virtue of his mission," p. 246. The term *phantoms* is from Marx, *German Ideology,* sections reprinted in Loyd D. Easton and Kurt H. Guddat, *Writings of Marx on Philosophy and Society* (New York, 1967), p. 415.

8. See Melville, "Bartleby the Scrivener," in Chase, ed., *Selected Tales,* pp. 92-131, and Gabriel Kolko, *The Triumph of Conservatism: A Reinterpretation of American History, 1900-1916* (New York, 1963), p. 304.

9. Melville, *Moby-Dick,* pp. 407-10, 142.

10. Melville, *Moby-Dick,* p. 154. See also Winthrop D. Jordan, *White over Black: American Attitudes Toward the Negro, 1550-1812* (Chapel Hill, N.C., 1968), p. 579.

11. Melville, *Moby-Dick,* pp. 104, 109, 141, 363, 364, 403, 404, 407, 409, 423-6, 142, 360, 136-8. See also Melville, "The Paradise of Bachelors and the Tartarus of Maids," in Chase, ed., *Selected Tales,* pp. 206-29.

12. Melville, *Moby-Dick,* p. 363.

13. Melville, *Moby-Dick,* pp. 368, 374, 309.

14. Melville, *Moby-Dick,* pp. 178, 179, 189, 259-60, 404, 224, 379.

15. Ibid., pp. 225, 226, 278-9, 377, 417, 422, 431.

Bibliography

For the conceptualization of the three "iron cages," the reader will, I hope, recognize my intellectual debt to Karl Marx, *Capital: A Critique of Political Economy* (New York, 1906) and Dirk J. Struik, ed., *The Economic and Philosophic Manuscripts of 1844* (New York, 1973), especially "Estranged Labor" and "The Meaning of Human Requirements," pp. 106-19 and 147-64; Max Weber, *The Protestant Ethic and the Spirit of Capitalism* (New York, 1958, originally published in 1930) and "Bureaucracy," in H. H. Gerth and C. Wright Mills, eds., *From Max Weber: Essays in Sociology* (New York, 1972), pp. 196-244; Sigmund Freud, *Civilization and Its Discontents* (Garden City, N.Y., n.d.); Walt Whitman, *Leaves of Grass and Selected Prose* (New York, 1958); and Herman Melville, *Moby-Dick, or the Whale* (Boston, 1956, originally published in 1851). To acknowledge both Marx and Whitman, or Weber, Freud, and Melville, or all five of them together should not be as bizarre as it may appear at first glance.

I. The "Iron Cage" in the New Nation

Recent scholarship has immensely deepened our understanding of the American Revolution in terms of its political ideology and psychology. Republicanism, which emerged in the struggle for independence from England, had origins in colonial Protestantism as well as the

Enlightenment, as we learn from Henry F. May, *The Enlightenment in America* (New York, 1976). The studies which I found seminal or useful for this chapter included Richard Hofstadter, *America at 1750: A Social Portrait* (New York, 1971); Edmund S. Morgan, "The Puritan Ethic and the American Revolution," *William and Mary Quarterly*, 3d ser., vol. 24 (January 1967), pp. 3-43; Gordon S. Wood, *The Creation of the American Republic, 1776-1787* (Chapel Hill, N.C., 1969); and Winthrop D. Jordan, "Familial Politics: Thomas Paine and the Killing of the King, 1776," *Journal of American History*, vol. 60, no. 2 (September 1973), pp. 294-308. Wood and Jordan together enabled me to see the relationship between republican self-government and the "killing" of the king. I also benefited from John R. Howe, Jr., "Republican Thought and the Political Violence of the 1790's," *American Quarterly*, vol. 19, no. 2 (Summer 1967), pp. 147-65; Neil Harris, *The Artist in American Society: The Formative Years, 1790-1860* (New York, 1970); Bernard Bailyn, *The Ideological Origins of the American Revolution* (Cambridge, Mass., 1973); David Tyack, "Forming the National Character: Paradox in the Educational Thought of the Revolutionary Generation," *Harvard Educational Review*, vol. 36, no. 1 (Winter 1966), pp. 29-41; Edmund S. Morgan, "Slavery and Freedom: The American Paradox," *Journal of American History*, vol. 59 (1972), pp. 5-29; and Edwin G. Burrows and Michael Wallace, *The American Revolution: The Ideology and Psychology of National Liberation*, published as vol. 6 of *Perspectives in American History* (Cambridge, Mass., 1972). Unfortunately, except for Morgan, all of the above studies fail to point out how republicanism conditioned not only the consciousness and character of the newly independent white Americans but also their racial attitudes.

For the colonial background, Winthrop Jordan, *White over Black: American Attitudes Toward the Negro, 1550-1812* (Chapel Hill, 1968), and Richard Slotkin, *Regeneration Through Violence: The Mythology of the American Frontier, 1600-1860* (Middletown, 1973) are indispensable. The problem of slavery is analyzed in a broad and comparative context in David Brion Davis, *The Problem of Slavery in Western Culture* (Ithaca, 1966). Slavery in colonial America had class dimensions and significance, as T. H. Breen, "A Changing Labor Force and Race Relations in Virginia, 1660-1710," *Journal of Social History*, vol. 7 (Fall 1973), pp. 3-25, and Edmund Morgan, *American Slavery, American Freedom: The Ordeal of Colonial Virginia* (New York, 1975) demonstrate. The material basis of slavery in colonial America is studied in Eric Williams, *Capitalism and Slavery* (New York, 1961).

For documents related to the American Revolution, see Bernard Bailyn, ed., *Pamphlets of the American Revolution, 1750-1776* (Cambridge, Mass., 1965); and Samuel E. Morison, ed., *Sources and Documents Illustrating the American Revolution, 1764-1788 and the Formation of the Federal Constitution* (London, 1961). For some of the Revolutionary leaders, see papers published in L. H. Butterfield *et al.*, eds., *Adams Family Correspondence* (Cambridge, Mass., 1963-); Gaillard Hunt, ed., *The Writings of James Madison*, 9 vols. (New York, 1900-10); Albert Henry Smyth, ed., *The Writings of Benjamin Franklin*, 10 vols. (New York, 1905-7); Moncure D. Conway, ed., *The Writings of Thomas Paine*, 4 vols. (New York, 1894); and Howard Fast, ed., *The Selected Work of Tom Paine* (New York, 1945). For the Naturalization Law of 1790, see *U.S. Statutes at Large*, vol. 1 (1790), p. 103, and *Debates and Proceedings in the Congress of the United States, 1789-1791*, vols. 1 and 2 (Washington, D.C., 1834), vol. 1, pp. 988, 1284; vol. 2, pp. 1148-64, 2264.

II. "Diseases" of the Mind and Skin

Benjamin Rush has been the subject of much controversy. The most critical assessment of Rush as the Father of American Psychiatry is Thomas S. Szasz, *The Manufacture of Madness:*

A Comparative Study of the Inquisition and the Mental Health Movement (New York, 1970). Favorable studies of Rush are Carl Binger, *Revolutionary Doctor: Benjamin Rush, 1746-1813* (New York, 1966); Harry G. Good, *Benjamin Rush and His Services to American Education* (Berne, Ind., 1918); Nathan G. Goodman, *Benjamin Rush, Physician and Citizen, 1746-1813* (Philadelphia, 1936); and David F. Hawke, *Benjamin Rush: Revolutionary Gadfly* (Indianapolis, 1971). To study Rush, however, one should consult his writings directly, especially L. H. Butterfield, ed., *Letters of Benjamin Rush,* 2 vols. (Princeton, N.J., 1951); and George W. Corner, ed., *The Autobiography of Benjamin Rush: His "Travels Through Life" together with his "Commonplace Book for 1789-1813"* (Princeton, N.J., 1948). See also D. D. Runes, ed., *The Selected Writings of Benjamin Rush* (New York, 1947); John A. Woods, ed., "The Correspondence of Benjamin Rush and Granville Sharp, 1773-1809," *Journal of American Studies,* vol. 1, no. 1 (April 1967), pp. 1-37; and John A. Schutz and Douglass Adair, eds., *The Spur of Fame: Dialogue of John Adams and Benjamin Rush, 1805-1813* (San Marino, Calif., 1966). Rush's published writings were prolific and touched on virtually every subject of his time: *An Address to the Inhabitants of the British Settlements in America upon Slave-Keeping* (Philadelphia, 1773); *Six Introductory Lectures* (Philadelphia, 1801); *Sixteen Introductory Lectures* (Philadelphia, 1811); *Medical Inquiries and Observations* (Philadelphia, 1794); *Medical Inquiries and Observations upon the Diseases of the Mind* (Philadelphia, 1812); *Thoughts upon Female Education* (Philadelphia, 1787); *The Way to Temperance, Health and Happiness: The Effects of Spirituous Liquors upon the Human Body* (Portland, Maine, 1793); *Essays, Literary, Moral & Philosophical* (Philadelphia, 1798); and "Observations intended to favour a supposition that the black Color (as it is called) of the Negroes is derived from the LEPROSY," *Transactions of the American Philosophical Society,* vol. 4 (1799), pp. 289-97.

III. Within the "Bowels" of the Republic

Three studies have taken us a long way toward an understanding of Thomas Jefferson and his attitudes toward blacks—Winthrop D. Jordan, *White over Black: American Attitudes Toward the Negro, 1550-1812* (Chapel Hill, N.C., 1968), especially chapter 12, "Thomas Jefferson: Self and Society," pp. 429-81; Fawn M. Brodie, *Thomas Jefferson: An Intimate History* (New York, 1974); and John Chester Miller, *The Wolf by the Ears: Thomas Jefferson and Slavery* (New York, 1977). Even so, Jordan only briefly relates Jefferson's racial attitudes to Indians, while Brodie virtually ignores this area of his life and thought. Of the three works, Miller's most effectively links Jefferson's racial views with his political and philosophical ideas. One should not read William W. Freehling, "The Founding Fathers and Slavery," *American Historical Review,* vol. 77, no. 1 (February 1972), pp. 81-93, which defends Jefferson and other founding fathers, without also reading William Cohen, "Thomas Jefferson and the Problem of Slavery," *Journal of American History,* vol. 56 (1969), pp. 503-26. Some problems involved in the study of Jefferson are delineated in Fawn M. Brodie, "Jefferson Biographers and the Psychology of Canonization," *Journal of Interdisciplinary History,* vol. 2, no. 1 (Summer 1971), pp. 155-71. For studies which attempt to place Jefferson in the context of his time and place, see Robert McColley, *Slavery and Jeffersonian Virginia* (Urbana, Ill., 1964) and Donald L. Robinson, *Slavery in the Structure of American Politics* (New York, 1971). Brodie's book is a study of "Jefferson and the life of the heart." But Jefferson's head was as important as his heart: To balance Brodie (and vice versa), one should read Adrienne Koch, *The Philosophy of Thomas Jefferson* (New York, 1943), Daniel J. Boorstin, *The Lost World of Thomas Jefferson* (Boston, Mass., 1960), and Garry Wills, *Inventing America: Jefferson's Declaration of Independence* (Garden City, N.Y., 1978). Wills offers a challenging interpretation of the origins of

Jefferson's ideas. And for a careful and informed assessment of Wills' argument, see Edmund Morgan, "The Heart of Jefferson" (a review of Wills' book), in *New York Review of Books*, vol. XXV, no. 13 (August 17, 1978), pp. 38-40.

Although much attention has been given to Jefferson and blacks, Jefferson had much to say about Indians and their place in America. Two differing views on Jefferson in this regard may be found in Bernard W. Sheehan, *Seeds of Extinction: Jeffersonian Philanthropy and the American Indian* (Chapel Hill, N.C., 1973) and Reginald Horsman, *Expansion and American Indian Policy, 1783-1812* (East Lansing, Mich., 1967). The best study of Jefferson's idea of the Indian is Roy Harvey Pearce, *Savagism and Civilization: A Study of the Indian and the American Mind* (Baltimore, 1967).

Jefferson's writings are both abundant and available. His one book—*Notes on the State of Virginia* (New York, 1964, written in 1781, originally published in 1785)—is indispensable for understanding his thoughts on race, politics, nature, religion, and the new nation. A useful anthology is Adrienne Koch and William Peden, eds., *The Life and Selected Writings of Thomas Jefferson* (New York, 1944). Jefferson's writings, public and personal, are collected and published in Paul L. Ford, ed., *The Works of Thomas Jefferson*, 10 vols. (New York, 1892-99), Andrew A. Lipscomb and Albert E. Bergh, eds., *Writings of Thomas Jefferson*, 20 vols. (Washington, D.C., 1904), and Julian Boyd, ed., *The Papers of Thomas Jefferson*, 18 vols. (Princeton, N.J., 1950-65). See also Thomas Jefferson, *Autobiography of Thomas Jefferson, 1743-1790* (New York, 1914); Edwin M. Betts, ed., *Thomas Jefferson's Farm Book* (Princeton, N.J., 1953); James D. Richardson, ed., *A Compilation of the Messages and Papers of the Presidents, 1789-1897* (Washington, D.C., 1897), vol. 1; Donald Jackson, ed., *Letters of the Lewis and Clark Expedition* (Urbana, Ill., 1962); Clarence E. Carter, ed., *The Territorial Papers of the United States* (Washington, D.C., 1937); Thomas Jefferson Randolph, ed., *Memoir, Correspondence, and Miscellanies from the Papers of Thomas Jefferson* (Charlottesville, Va., 1829); James A. Bear, Jr., and Edwin M. Betts, eds, *The Family Letters of Thomas Jefferson* (Columbia, Mo., 1966); and Lester J. Cappon, ed., *The Adams-Jefferson Letters*, 2 vols. (Chapel Hill, N.C., 1959).

IV. Beyond Primitive Accumulation

For the economic history of the first half of the nineteenth century, we have two very informative standard works—Douglass C. North, *The Economic Growth of the United States, 1790-1860* (New York, 1966); and George R. Taylor, *The Transportation Revolution, 1815-1860* (New York, 1962). The most important foreign commentator on American society during this period of economic growth was Alexis de Tocqueville, author of *Democracy in America*, 2 vols. (New York, 1945). These three works provide a firm basis for an understanding of United States history during this period and beyond.

V. The Metaphysics of Civilization: "The Red Race on Our Borders"

The key concept for this chapter is based on Herman Melville, *The Confidence-Man: His Masquerade* (New York, 1964, originally published in 1857). Roy Harvey Pearce has done much to help us understand this complex novel, especially in "The Metaphysics of Indian-Hating," *Ethnohistory*, vol. 4, no. 1 (Winter 1957), pp. 27-40; "Melville's Indian-Hater: A Note on a Meaning of the Confidence-Man," *Publications of the Modern Language Association*, vol. 67 (1952), pp. 942-8; and "The 'Ruines of Mankind': The Indian and the Puritan Mind," *Journal of the History of Ideas*, vol. 13, no. 2 (April 1952), pp. 200-17. A survey, which lacks the conceptualization present in Pearce's work, is Albert Keiser, *The Indian in American*

Literature (New York, 1953). One should also consult Robert F. Berkhofer, *Salvation and the Savage: Protestant Missions and American Indian Response, 1787-1862* (Lexington, Kentucky, 1965). Berkhofer's recently published *The White Man's Indian: Images of the American Indian from Columbus to the Present* (New York, 1978) is a useful survey of the various and contradictory white images of the "Indian." The most provocative interpretation of the Indian in the white imagination is Leslie A. Fiedler, *Love and Death in the American Novel* (New York, 1966) and *The Return of the Vanishing American* (New York, 1969). The main problem with studies of white attitudes toward Indians which depend on literary sources is their failure to relate the world of imagination to the economic substructure, specifically the Market Revolution.

Robert Montgomery Bird's *Nick of the Woods, or the Jibbenainosay, A Tale of Kentucky* (New York, 1853, originally published in 1837) offers us an opportunity to probe further the meaning of Indian-hating. It was reviewed in the *Southern Literary Messenger,* vol. 3 (April 1837), p. 209. For biographies of Bird, see Clement E. Foust, *The Life and Dramatic Works of Robert Montgomery Bird* (New York, 1919); Mary Mayer Bird, *Life of Robert Montgomery Bird* (Philadelphia, 1945); and Curtis Dahl, *Robert Montgomery Bird* (New York, 1963). R. W. B. Lewis has a short but interesting analysis of Bird in his *The American Adam: Innocence, Tragedy, and Tradition in the Nineteenth Century* (Chicago, 1968), pp. 105-9. Bird's novel involves the capture of "fair" Edith; the theme of captivity is analyzed in Roy Harvey Pearce, "The Significances of the Captivity Narrative," *American Literature,* vol. 19 (1947), pp. 1-20. Perry Miller has so much to say on so many relevant topics; one would do well here to read his essay "Nature and the National Ego," in *Errand into the Wilderness* (New York, 1964), pp. 204-16. The best way to understand Bird, his novel, and his Indian-hating is to examine the Robert Montgomery Bird Papers, at the University of Pennsylvania Library, Philadelphia, Pennsylvania: They contain important and revealing personal letters and drafts of unpublished stories, such as "Awossagame, or the Seal of the Evil One," and "The White-Washed Cottage of the Susquehanna, an Indian Story," in his school composition book.

In my study of Andrew Jackson, I have learned much from Michael Paul Rogin, *Fathers and Children: Andrew Jackson and the Subjugation of the American Indian* (New York, 1975). Provocative and insightful, this is no mere psychoanalytical investigation of Jackson: It is a remarkable and radical critique of the liberal tradition and capitalism in America. Readers of *Fathers and Children* will find it interesting to consult Rogin's early essay "Liberal Society and the Indian Question," *Politics and Society* (May 1971), pp. 269-312. To complement Rogin, one should read Richard Slotkin, *Regeneration through Violence: The Mythology of the American Frontier 1600-1860* (Middletown, Conn., 1973).

For white Americans' perceptions of Jackson, see John William Ward, *Andrew Jackson: Symbol for an Age* (New York, 1962), and Michael Fellman, "The Earthbound Eagle: Andrew Jackson and the American Pantheon," *American Studies,* vol. 12 (Fall 1971). Much of the symbolic Jackson was derived from his association with the West; for a study of the West in European and American white fantasy, see Loren Baritz, "The Idea of the West," *American Historical Review,* vol. 66 (April 1961), pp. 618-41.

For conflicting assessments of Jackson's role in the removal of Indians, one should read both Francis Paul Prucha, *American Indian Policy in the Formative Years* (Cambridge, Mass., 1962), and "Andrew Jackson's Indian Policy: A Reassessment," *Journal of American History,* vol. 56 (December 1969), pp. 527-39; and Mary E. Young, *Redskins, Ruffleshirts, and Rednecks* (Norman, Okla., 1961) and "Indian Removal and Land Allotment: The Civilized Tribes and Jacksonian Justice," *American Historical Review,* vol. 64 (October 1958), pp. 31-45. Other useful studies are Reginald Horsman, "American Indian Policy and the Origins of Manifest

Destiny," in Francis Paul Prucha, ed., *The Indian in American History* (New York, 1971); Grant Foreman, *Indian Removal* (Norman, Okla. 1932); Arthur H. DeRosier, Jr., *The Removal of the Choctaw Indians* (New York, 1972); Marian L. Starkey, *The Cherokee Nation* (New York, 1966); and Annie Heloise Abel, *The History of Events Resulting in Indian Consolidation West of the Mississippi, Report of Proceedings* (Washington, D.C., 1906). For information on atrocities committed against the Creeks by American troops, see H. S. Halbert and T. H. Ball, *The Creek War of 1813 and 1814* (Chicago, 1895).

So much of Jackson's attitudes toward the Indians is integrated in his language. Thus one should examine his writings, public and private. They are available in John Spencer Bassett, ed., *Correspondence of Andrew Jackson,* 6 vols. (Washington, D.C., 1926-33); Walter Lowrie and Walter S. Franklin, eds., *American State Papers* (Washington, D.C., 1834); and James D. Richardson, ed., *A Compilation of the Messages and Papers of the Presidents, 1789-1897* (Washington, D.C., 1897), vol. 2. Jackson's language is important for an understanding of political ideology and psychology, as Marvin Meyers shows us so skillfully in *The Jacksonian Persuasion: Politics and Belief* (New York, 1960). Unfortunately, Meyers fails to suggest that Jackson's attack on the Bank was related to his attack on the Indians. Both attacks, I argue, reflected a Jacksonian Persuasion: They instructed Americans who the "real people" were. This shortcoming in Meyers's study is part of the general failure to link political and cultural ideology to race.

VI. The Metaphysics of Civilization: "The Black Race Within Our Bosom"

The sectionalism which led to the Civil War has conditioned the way in which historians have approached the study of this period; yet, in reality, there were important areas of consensus in American society, North and South. One area involved anti-black antagonism. For northern society, Leon Litwack, *North of Slavery: The Negro in the Free States, 1790-1860* (Chicago, 1961), is an indispensable study, which is supplemented by Eugene H. Berwanger, *The Frontier against Slavery: Western Anti-Negro Prejudice and the Slavery Extension Controversy* (Urbana, Ill., 1967). For southern society, Kenneth Stampp, *The Peculiar Institution: Slavery in the Ante-Bellum South* (New York, 1956), is still the standard work on slavery. More recent studies by Eugene Genovese, *Roll, Jordan, Roll: The World the Slaves Made* (New York, 1974), and Herbert G. Gutman, *The Black Family in Slavery and Freedom, 1750-1925* (New York, 1976) have immensely enriched our understanding of black life and thought in the slave South. Stanley M. Elkins, *Slavery: A Problem in American Institutional and Intellectual Life* (New York, 1963), is still probably the most provocative and heuristic book on the subject. But where Elkins offers analogy to buttress his thesis, Lawrence W. Levine, in *Black Culture and Black Consciousness: Afro-American Folk Thought From Slavery To Freedom* (New York, 1978), provides research to demonstrate the complexity of black thought. For grace and subtlety, few books match William R. Taylor, *Cavalier & Yankee: The Old South and American National Character* (New York, 1963). We still need, however, a study of racism as a reflection of the national character of antebellum society. The study which comes closest to meeting this need is Lawrence J. Friedman, *Inventors of the Promised Land* (New York, 1975), which analyzes the multiple ways racism, sexism, and patriotism were dynamically interrelated as white men sought at once the moral perfection they hoped for and the rootedness they needed. George M. Frederickson, *The Black Image in the White Mind: The Debate on Afro-American Character and Destiny, 1817-1914* (New York, 1972), is a comprehensive study which analyzes racism as "a fluid pattern of belief, affected in significant and diverse ways by the same social, intellectual, and political currents influencing other basic aspects of American thought and experience," p. 320.

The southern defense of slavery is the subject of my *A Pro-Slavery Crusade: The Agitation to Reopen the African Slave Trade* (New York, 1971). See also Charles G. Sellers, "The Travail of Slavery," in Sellers, ed., *The Southerner as American* (Chapel Hill, N.C., 1960); and William W. Freehling, *Prelude to Civil War: The Nullification Controversy in South Carolina, 1816-1832* (New York, 1966). Another view is presented in Eugene Genovese, *The World the Slaveholders Made* (New York, 1969). The most durable study of the white South remains W. J. Cash, *The Mind of the South* (New York, 1941).

Women, like blacks and Indians, were assigned a place in American society, one defined by white men. For a general survey, read Carl N. Degler, "Revolution without Ideology: The Changing Place of Women in America," in R. J. Lifton, ed., *The Woman in America* (Boston, 1967). For the period under discussion, see Barbara Welter, "The Cult of True Womanhood, 1820-1860," *American Quarterly*, vol. 18 (Summer 1966), pp. 151-74; Gerda Lerner, "The Lady & the Mill Girl: Changes in the Status of Women in the Age of Jackson," *Midcontinent American Studies Journal*, vol. 10, no. 1 (Spring 1969), pp. 5-15; Charles E. Rosenberg, "Sexuality, Class and Role in 19th Century America," *American Quarterly*, vol. 25, no. 2 (May 1973), pp. 131-53; and Ann Douglas, *The Feminization of American Culture* (New York, 1977). The southern situation is the focus of Anne Firor Scott, *The Southern Lady: From Pedestal to Politics, 1800-1936* (Chicago, 1970). Surely the most provocative and dazzling study of white male oppression of women is Graham John Barker-Benfield, *The Horrors of the Half-Known Life: Male Attitudes toward Women and Sexuality in Nineteenth-Century America* (New York, 1976).

For the controversy at Harvard Medical School, one may wish to examine directly the papers of professors like Oliver Wendell Holmes, Jacob Bigelow, Henry Bigelow, and John Ware, which are housed in the Countway Medical School Library, Boston, Mass. Their lectures and essays are also informative, in terms of our purpose. See John Ware, *Hints to Young Men on the True Relation of the Sexes* (Boston, 1850), and *Success in the Medical Profession: An Introductory Lecture delivered at the Massachusetts Medical College, November 6, 1850* (Boston, 1851); and Oliver Wendell Holmes, *The Position and Prospects of the Medical Student* (Boston, 1844), and *Introductory Lecture delivered at the Massachusetts Medical College, November 3, 1847* (Boston, 1847). One should not overlook Holmes's novel, *Elsie Venner—A Romance of Destiny* (Boston, 1888, originally published in 1859). For the other side of the story, or rather for the view of the incident from the bottom up, see Harriot K. Hunt, *Glances and Glimpses* (Boston, 1856), and my essay, "War upon the Whites: Black Rage in the Fiction of Martin Delany," in *Violence in the Black Imagination: Essays and Documents* (New York, 1972), pp. 79-102.

VII. An American Prospero in King Arthur's Court

The three studies which greatly influenced the conceptualization of this chapter were Hans Sachs, "The Delay of the Machine Age," *Psychoanalytic Quarterly*, vol. 2 (July-October, 1933), pp. 404-24; Johan Huizinga, *Homo Ludens: A Study of the Play Element in Culture* (Boston, 1955); and Karl Marx, "Machinery and Modern Industry," in *Capital: A Critique of Political Economy* (New York, 1906), pp. 405-88. Herbert Marcuse, *One-Dimensional Man: Studies in the Ideology of Advanced Industrial Society* (Boston, 1966), also helped me reflect on the meaning of the American character in a technological society. Another suggestive work is

Keith Thomas, "Work and Leisure in Pre-Industrial Society," *Past and Present,* vol. 29 (1964), pp. 50-66. What Sachs, Huizinga, Marx, Marcuse, and Thomas analyze is the world we have as well as the one we have lost.

How this happened in America in the nineteenth century is the subject of Leo Marx, *The Machine in the Garden: Technology and the Pastoral Ideal in America* (New York, 1967) and Perry Miller, *The Life of the Mind in America: From the Revolution to the Civil War* (New York, 1965), *Nature's Nation* (Cambridge, Mass., 1965), and "The Responsibility of Mind in a Civilization of Machines," *American Scholar,* vol. 31 (Winter 1961), pp. 51-69. Unlike George R. Taylor and Douglass C. North, Marx and Miller are interested in the impact of technology on American culture and thought. As usual, Miller, I think, says more than he appears to be saying.

One may also wish to consult Arthur A. Ekirch, Jr., *The Idea of Progress in America, 1815-1860* (New York, 1944), a standard and conventional study; and John F. Kasson, *Civilizing the Machine: Technology and Republican Values in America, 1776-1900* (New York, 1976). Other studies include Charles L. Sanford, *The Quest for Paradise: Europe and the American Moral Imagination* (Urbana, Ill., 1961), and "The Intellectual Origins and New Worldliness of American Industry," *Journal of Economic History,* vol. 18 (1958), pp. 1-16; Marvin M. Fisher, *Workshops in the Wilderness: The European Response to American Industrialism, 1830-1860* (New York, 1967), "The Iconology of Industrialism, 1830-1860," *American Quarterly,* vol. 13 (Fall 1961), pp. 347-74, and "Melville's 'Bell-Tower': A Double Thrust," *American Quarterly,* vol. 18 (Summer 1966), pp. 200-7; Hugo A. Meier, "American Technology and the Nineteenth Century World," *American Quarterly,* vol. 10 (1958), pp. 116-30, and "Technology and Democracy, 1800-1860," *Mississippi Valley Historical Review,* vol. 43 (1957), pp. 618-40; Samuel Rezneck, "The Rise and Early Development of the Industrial Consciousness in the United States, 1760-1830," *Journal of Economic and Business History,* vol. 4 (August 1932), pp. 784-812; Lowell Lozer, "A Century of Progress, 1833-1933: Technology's Triumph Over Man," in Henning Cohen, ed., *The American Culture* (Boston, 1968), pp. 206-9; Clarence Mondale, "Daniel Webster and Technology," *American Quarterly,* vol. 14 (Spring 1962), pp. 37-47; Charles A. Fenton, "The Bell-Tower: Melville and Technology," *American Literature,* vol. 28 (May 1951), pp. 219-32; and John R. Betts, "The Technological Revolution and the Rise of Sport, 1850-1900," *Mississippi Valley Historical Review,* vol. 40 (1953-54), pp. 231-56. Economic statistics and information may be found in U.S. Bureau of the Census, *A Statistical Supplement: Historical Statistics of the United States: Colonial Times to 1957* (Washington, D.C., 1960); Edward C. Kirkland, *Industry Comes of Age: Business, Labor, and Public Policy, 1860-1897* (New York, 1962); and Robert Higgs, *The Transformation of the American Economy, 1865-1914: An Essay in Interpretation* (New York, 1971). For what happened afterward, one might begin with Samuel Haber, *Efficiency and Uplift: Scientific Management in the Progressive Era* (Chicago, 1964). Mark Twain and Henry Adams, two naysayers, are discussed in Henry Nash Smith, *Mark Twain's Fable of Progress: Political and Economic Ideas in "A Connecticut Yankee"* (New Brunswick, N.J., 1964); and Tony Tanner, "The Lost America—The Despair of Henry Adams and Mark Twain," *Modern Age,* vol. 5 (Summer 1961), pp. 299-310.

Here as elsewhere the original sources are invaluable. Mark Twain, *A Connecticut Yankee in King Arthur's Court* (New York, 1963, originally published in 1889) is no mere children's story, as I imply in this chapter. Henry Adams, *The Education of Henry Adams* (New York, 1931, originally published in 1918), explores the relationship between technology and progress in an introspective narrative of despair. Jacob Bigelow, *Elements of Technology, Taken Chiefly from a Course of Lectures Delivered at Cambridge, on the Application of the Sciences to the*

Useful Arts (Boston, 1829); and George M. Beard, *American Nervousness: Its Causes and Consequences, A Supplement to Nervous Exhaustion* (New York, 1881), should be read side by side. See also articles in magazines and journals of the nineteenth century: "American Genius and Enterprise," *Scientific American,* vol. 2 (September 1847), p. 397; Charles Fraser, "The Moral Influence of Steam," *Hunt's Merchants Magazine,* vol. 14 (June 1846), pp. 499-515; "Railroads of the United States," *Hunt's Merchants Magazine,* vol. 3 (October 1840), pp. 273-95; "American Manufacturers," *Hunt's Merchants Magazine,* vol. 5 (1841), p. 141; "What is the Golden Age," *Scientific American,* vol. 5 (December 1849), p. 109; "The Progress of Inventions and Inventors," *Scientific American,* vol. 8 (June 4, 1853), p. 301; "Progress of Science and Mechanical Art," *Scientific American,* vol. 3 (October 30, 1847), p. 45; "Effects of Machinery," *North American Review,* vol. 34 (January 1832), p. 229; Charles Caldwell, M.D., "Thoughts on the Moral and other Indirect Influences of Rail-Roads," *New England Magazine,* vol. 2 (April 1832), pp. 288-300; "Address of the Memphis Convention to the People of the United States," *De Bow's Review* (March 1850), pp. 217-32; and "The Spirit of the Times; or the Fast Age," *Democratic Review,* vol. 33 (September 1853), pp. 257-63.

Clearly a new radical scholarship on American labor history is emerging which is already helping to provide a fresh and critical perspective on our past and present. Stanley Aronowitz, *False Promises: The Shaping of American Working Class Consciousness* (New York, 1974), and Harry Braverman, *Labor and Monopoly Capital: The Degradation of Work in the Twentieth Century* (New York, 1974), are both seminal works, important particularly for their scope and application of Marxist theories. Herbert G. Gutman, *Work, Culture and Society in Industrializing America* (New York, 1977), offers us a fine heuristic essay to open the study, in which he notes that "nonwhite free laborers, mostly black and Asian immigrants" were "affected by the tensions that will be described here, a fact that emphasizes the central place they deserve in any comprehensive study of American work habits and changing American working-class behavior" (p. 13). Case studies have helped to advance much of our understanding of working-class culture and consciousness. See Gary Kulik, "Pawtucket Village and the Strike of 1824: The Origins of Class Conflict in Rhode Island," *Radical History Review,* 17 (Spring 1978), pp. 5-37; Paul Buhle, "The Knights of Labor in Rhode Island," *Radical History Review,* 17 (Spring 1978), pp. 38-62; Bruce Laurie, " 'Nothing on Compulsion': Life Styles of Philadelphia Artisans, 1820-1850," *Labor History,* vol. 15, no. 3 (1974), pp. 337-66; Paul Faler, "Cultural Aspects of the Industrial Revolution: Lynn, Massachusetts, Shoemakers and Industrial Morality, 1826-1860," ibid., pp. 367-94; David Montgomery, "The Shuttle and the Cross: Weavers and Artisans in the Kensington Riots of 1844," *Journal of Social History,* vol. 5, no. 4 (1972), pp. 411-46; Paul E. Johnson, *A Shopkeeper's Millennium: Society and Revivals in Rochester, New York, 1815-1837* (New York, 1978).

California was a colony of the United States long before it was formally annexed through act of war. For studies of American expansion into the West Coast, one should read John A. Hawgood, "The Pattern of Yankee Infiltration in Mexican Alta California, 1821-1846," *Pacific Historical Review,* vol. 27 (1958); Norman Graebner, *Empire on the Pacific: A Study in American Continental Expansion* (New York, 1955); and Frederick Merk, *Manifest Destiny and Mission in American History* (New York, 1963). Evidence of the penetration of the American whaling industry into the California coast may be found in Elmo P. Hohman, *The American Whaleman* (New York, 1928); and Walter S. Tower, *A History of the American Whale Fishery* (Philadelphia, 1907).

Carey McWilliams, *North from Mexico: The Spanish-Speaking People of the United States* (New York, 1968), is a classic; still, studies of Anglo attitudes toward Mexicans are inadequate, lacking the comprehensiveness and depth present in studies of white attitudes toward blacks or Indians. Philip Anthony Hernandez, "The Other North Americans: The American Image of Mexico and Mexicans, 1550-1850" (Ph.D. thesis, University of California, Berkeley, 1974), is a survey; Cecil Robinson, *With the Ears of Strangers: The Mexican in American Literature* (Tucson, Ariz., 1963), examines one set of documents. For the colonial period, see Raymond Paredes, "The Origins of Anti-Mexican Sentiment in the United States," *New Scholar,* vol. 6 (1977), pp. 139-65.

Until we have new studies of Anglo attitudes toward Mexicans, we will have to consult the sources directly. One may begin with William Shaler, *Journal of a Voyage between China and the North-Western Coast of America in 1804* (Claremont, Calif., 1935); Joel Robert Poinsett, *Notes on Mexico Made in Autumn of 1822* (New York, 1969, originally published in 1824); and Richard Henry Dana, *Two Years Before the Mast* (New York, 1963, originally published in 1840).

For studies of Mexican/Chicano labor in industrializing America, see Mario Barrera, *Class Segmentation and Internal Colonialism: A Theory of Racial Inequality Based on the Chicano Experience* (manuscript in preparation for publication); Andres E. Jiminez Montoya, "Political Domination in the Labor Market: Racial Division in the Arizona Copper Industry," Working Paper # 103, Institute for the Study of Social Change, University of California, Berkeley, 1977; Special Issue on Labor History and the Chicano, *Aztlan: International Journal of Chicano Studies Research,* vol. 6, no. 2 (1975); Joseph F. Park, "The History of Mexican Labor in Arizona During the Territorial Period" (M.A. thesis, University of Arizona, Tucson, 1961).

VIII. The Iron Horse in the West

The penetration of white civilization and technology into the western plains raised the question of the future of the Indian in an America where the frontier would soon disappear. Informative studies of some of the white responses to this question are Henry E. Fritz, *The Movement for Indian Assimilation, 1860-1890* (Philadelphia, 1963); Loring Benson Priest, *Uncle Sam's Stepchildren: The Reformation of United States Indian Policy, 1865-1887* (New York, 1972); and Robert Winston Mardock, *The Reformers and the American Indian* (Columbia, Mo., 1971). Francis Paul Prucha has published an important collection, *Americanizing the American Indians: Writings by the "Friends of the Indian": 1880-1900* (Cambridge, Mass., 1973). For information on the federal bureaucracy and the Indian, see Laurence F. Schmeckeluer, *The Office of Indian Affairs: Its History, Activities, and Organization* (Baltimore, 1927), and Edmund J. Danzinger, Jr., *Indians and Bureaucrats: Administering the Reservation Policy during the Civil War* (Urbana, Ill., 1975). For an examination of different responses to the question, one can read Alfred L. Riggs, "What Shall We Do With the Indians?" *The Nation,* vol. 5 (October 31, 1867), p. 356; E. L. Godkin, "Our Indian Wards," *The Nation,* vol. 23 (July 13, 1876), pp. 21-2, and "The Indian Difficulty," *The Nation,* vol. 7 (December 13, 1868), pp. 544-6; and Helen Hunt Jackson, *A Century of Dishonor: A Sketch of the United States Government's Dealings with Some of the Indian Tribes* (Boston, 1886, originally published in 1881). The railroad response is analyzed in Ira G. Clark, *Then Came the Railroads: The Century from Steam to Diesel in the Southwest* (Norman, Okla., 1958); and H. Craig Miner, *The Corporation and the Indian: Tribal Sovereignty and Industrial Civilization in Indian Territory, 1865-1907* (Columbia, Mo., 1976). Also consult *Report of W. T. Sherman, Oct. 27, 1883, Annual Report of the Secretary of War,* 48th Cong., 1st sess., House Exec. Doc. no. 1, part 2. For the Dawes Act, see D. S. Otis, *The Dawes Act and the Allotment of Indian Lands* (Norman, Okla., 1973, originally published in 1934); Wilcomb Washburn, *The Assault on Indian Tribalism: The General Allotment Law (Dawes Act) of 1887* (New York, 1975); and David Halford, "The Subversion of the Indian Land Allotment System, 1887-1934," *The Indian Historian,* vol. 8 (Spring 1975), pp. 11-21. For a contemporary view, see James B. Thayer, "The Dawes Bill and the Indians," *Atlantic Monthly,* vol. 66 (1888).

Francis Amasa Walker is remembered for his economic ideas rather than his attitudes toward the Indians; yet, as I have tried to show, the two were related. Sidney Fine, *Laissez Faire and the General-Welfare State: A Study of Conflict in American Thought, 1865-1901* (Ann Arbor, Mich., 1964); and Joseph Dorfman, *The Economic Mind in American Civilization* (New York, 1946-49), give attention to Walker as a political economist. George M. Frederickson, *The Inner Civil War: Northern Intellectuals and the Crisis of the Union* (New York, 1968) places Walker within the context of scientific management. For a study of Walker's economic ideas, see Bernard Newton, *The Economics of Francis Amasa Walker: American Economics in Transition* (New York, 1968). James P. Munroe has written *A Life of Francis Amasa Walker* (New York, 1923).

Walker's assessment of the Indian situation was published in *Annual Report of the Commissioner of Indian Affairs to the Secretary of the Interior for the Year 1872* (Washington, D.C., 1872), also published as *The Indian Question* (Boston, 1874). See also Walker, "Indian Citizenship," *International Review,* vol. 1 (May-June, 1874), pp. 305-26; "Letter from the Commissioner of Indian Affairs upon the Action of the Department relating to the Kansas Indian Lands in the State of Kansas," December 2, 1871, 42d Cong., 2d sess., Senate Misc. Doc., no. 10, vol. 1, p. 4; "The Indian Problem: Review of De B. R. Keim's *Sheridan's Troopers on the Borders," The Nation,* vol. 10 (June 16, 1870), p. 389-90; and "Our Indians and Mr. Wells," *The Nation,* vol. 15 (August 1, 1872), p. 73.

For Walker's thoughts on political economy, see his essays published in Davis R. Dewey, *Discussions in Economics and Statistics,* 2 vols. (New York, 1899); and in James P. Munroe, *Discussions in Education* (New York, 1899). Some of Walker's early publications indicate the direction of his analysis: "Why Are We Not a Manufacturing People?" *Washington National Era,* January 28, 1858; "More Thoughts on Hard Times," *Washington National Era,* October 28, 1857; and "Legal Interference with the Hours of Labor," *Lippincott's Magazine* (November 1868), pp. 527-33. For his later works, see Francis A. Walker, *Political Economy* (New York, 1888); "American Manufactures," *Princeton Review,* vol. 11 (March 1883), pp. 213-23; "Our Population in 1900," *Atlantic Monthly,* vol. 32 (1873), pp. 492-5; and *The Making of the Nation, 1783-1817* (New York, 1905).

For my analysis of George Armstrong Custer, I found helpful Thomas C. Leonard, "Red, White and the Army Blue: Empathy and Anger in the American West," *American Quarterly* (1974), pp. 176-90. Unfortunately I was not able to learn much about Custer from the many biographies, including Stephen E. Ambrose, *Crazy Horse and Custer* (New York, 1975); Jay Monaghan, *Custer: The Life of General George Armstrong Custer* (Boston, 1959); Frederick F. Van de Water, *Glory-hunter; a Life of General Custer* (Indianapolis, 1934); and Edgar Stewart, *Custer's Luck* (Norman, Okla., 1957).

The best way to understand Custer is to read the sources, especially Custer, *Wild Life on the Plains and Horrors of Indian Warfare* (St. Louis, 1891); and "Battling with the Sioux in the Yellowstone," *Galaxy,* vol. 22 (July 1876), pp. 91-102. For one of his earliest writings on the Indian, see Custer, "The Red Man," an essay written at West Point, now in Custer Papers, Custer Battlefield National Monument, Crow Agency, Montana. His letters to his wife, Elizabeth (Libbie), contain many references to Indians: See Marguerite Merington, ed., *The Custer Story: The Life and Intimate Letters of General George A. Custer and His Wife Elizabeth* (New York, 1950). Elizabeth Custer, one of the makers of the Custer myth, may have told us more than she intended in *Tenting on the Plains, or General Custer in Kansas and Texas* (New York, 1889); *"Boots and Saddles"; or Life in Dakota with General Custer* (New York, 1885); and *Following the Guidon* (New York, 1890). The George A. Custer Papers in the New York Public Library contain miscellaneous items of limited value.

IX. Civilization in the "New South"

Two brilliant studies of race relations in the postbellum South are W. J. Cash, *The Mind of the South* (New York, 1941); and Lawrence J. Friedman, *The White Savage: Racial Fantasies in the Postbellum South* (Englewood Cliffs, N.J., 1970). Friedman's work offers a significant critique of the interpretation of C. Vann Woodward, *The Strange Career of Jim Crow* (New York, 1960), and *Origins of the New South, 1877-1913* (Baton Rouge, 1951). See also Paul M. Gaston, *The New South Creed: A Study in Southern Mythmaking* (New York, 1970).

Information on blacks in southern industries may be found in Sterling D. Spero and Abram L. Harris, *The Black Worker: The Negro and the Labor Movement* (Port Washington, N.Y., 1966); Charles H. Wesley, *Negro Labor in the United States, 1850-1925* (New York, 1967, originally published in 1927); Broadus Mitchell, *The Rise of Cotton Mills in the South* (Baltimore, 1921); Victor S. Clark, *History of Manufactures in the United States, 1860-1914* (Washington, D.C., 1928); Homer B. Vanderblue and William L. Crum, *The Iron Industry in Prosperity and Depression* (Chicago, 1927); Ethel M. Armes, *The Story of Coal and Iron in Alabama* (Birmingham, 1910); Broadus Mitchell and George S. Mitchell, *The Industrial Revolution in the South* (Baltimore, 1930); Robert S. Starobin, *Industrial Slavery in the Old South* (New York, 1970); Charles B. Dew, *Ironmaker to the Confederacy: Joseph R. Anderson and the Tredegar Iron Works* (New Haven, Conn., 1966); Gunnar Myrdal, *An American Dilemma: The Negro Problem and Modern Democracy* (New York, 1944); and Paul B. Worthman, "Working Class Mobility in Birmingham, Alabama, 1880-1914," in Tamara K. Hareven, *Anonymous Americans: Explorations in Nineteenth-Century Social History* (Englewood Cliffs, N.J., 1971), pp. 172-213.

The apostle of the "New South" is the subject of Raymond B. Nixon, *Henry W. Grady: Spokesman of the New South* (New York, 1943). Also useful is Joel Chandler Harris, ed., *Life of Henry W. Grady, Including His Writings and Speeches* (New York, 1890). Many of Grady's speeches and essays have been collected and published in Edna L. Turpin, ed., *The New South and Other Addresses by Henry Woodfin Grady* (New York, 1904); Henry W. Grady, *The New South* (New York, 1890); and Edwin D. Shurter, ed., *The Complete Orations and Speeches of Henry W. Grady* (Norwood, 1910).

The best biography of George Washington Cable is Arlin Turner, *George W. Cable* (Durham, N.C., 1956). But one should also consult Lucy C. Bikle, *George W. Cable: His Life and Letters* (New York, 1928); and Helen M. Chesnutt, *Charles Waddell Chesnutt: Pioneer of the Color Line* (Chapel Hill, N.C., 1952). For Cable's writings, see especially *The Grandissimes* (New York, 1957, originally published in 1880); "We of the South," *Century Magazine,* vol. 29 (November 1884), pp. 151-2; "The Convict Lease System in the Southern States," *Century Magazine,* vol. 27 (February 1884), pp. 582-99; "Creole Slave Dances: The Dance in Place Congo," *Century Magazine,* vol. 31 (April 1886), pp. 807-28; *Old Creole Days: A Story of Creole Life* (New York, 1920, originally published in 1879); and *The Creoles of Louisiana* (New York, 1884). Cable's writings on race have been collected in Arlin Turner, ed., *The Negro Question, A Selection of Writings on Civil Rights in the South* (New York, 1968). A very useful photostated collection of the Cable Papers is available at the Popular Cultural Center of Bowling Green State University, Bowling Green, Ohio.

As I have tried to show, Booker T. Washington offered much to both the Cables and the Gradys of the "New South." For Washington, see August Meier, *Negro Thought in America, 1880-1915* (Ann Arbor, Mich., 1966); Samuel R. Spencer, Jr., *Booker T. Washington and the Negro's Place in American Life* (Boston, 1955); Louis R. Harlan, *Booker T. Washington: The Making of a Black Leader, 1856-1901* (New York, 1972); Jack Abramowitz, "The Emergence of Booker T. Washington as a National Leader," *Social Education,* vol. 32 (May 1968); Oliver C. Cox, "Leadership among Negroes in the United States," in Alvin W. Gouldner, ed., *Studies in Leadership* (New York, 1950), pp. 235-9; Rayford W. Logan, *The Betrayal of the Negro: From Rutherford B. Hayes to Woodrow Wilson* (New York, 1965); and Lawrence J. Friedman, "Life 'in the Lion's Mouth': Another Look at Booker T. Washington," *Journal of Negro History,* vol. 59, no. 4 (October 1974), pp. 337-51. For Washington's writings, see Louis R. Harlan, ed., *The Booker T. Washington Papers,* 4 vols. (Urbana, Ill., 1975).

X. The "Heathen Chinee" and American Technology

The study of the history of race relations in the United States is usually limited to those between blacks and whites. Recently, however, historians have given serious attention to racial developments as they affected Asians in this country. Two very valuable studies are Alexander Saxton, *The Indispensable Enemy: Labor and the Anti-Chinese Movement in California* (Berkeley, Calif., 1971); and Stuart C. Miller, *The Unwelcome Immigrant: The American Image of the Chinese, 1785-1882* (Berkeley, Calif., 1969). Dan Caldwell offers a provocative comparative analysis in "The Negroization of the Chinese Stereotype in California," *Southern California Quarterly,* vol. 53 (June 1971), pp. 123-32; and is criticized by Luther W. Spoehr in "Sambo and the Heathen Chinee: Californians' Racial Stereotypes in the Late 1870's," *Pacific Historical Review,* vol. 42 (May 1973), pp. 185-204. An older but still useful study is Elmer C. Sandmeyer, *The Anti-Chinese Movement in California* (Urbana, Ill., 1939). Gunther Barth, *Bitter Strength: A History of the Chinese in the United States, 1850-1870* (Cambridge, Mass., 1964), depends on sources written in English.

For more specific studies of the anti-Chinese agitation, see William R. Locklear, "The Celestials and the Angels: A Study of the Anti-Chinese Movement in Los Angeles to 1882," *Historical Society of Southern California Quarterly,* vol. 42 (September 1960), pp. 239-56; Frederick Rudolph, "Chinamen in Yankeedom: Anti-Unionism in Massachusetts in 1870," *American Historical Review,* vol. 53, no. 1 (October 1947), pp. 1-29, which is an important study of white reaction in New England and provides some balance to the concentration on California; Roger R. Olmsted, "The Chinese Must Go!" *California Historical Quarterly,* vol. 50, no. 3 (September 1971), pp. 285-94, which has a selection of anti-Chinese cartoons from the exclusion period; Rodman W. Paul, "The Origin of the Chinese Issue in California," *Mississippi Valley Historical Review,* vol. 25 (September 1938), pp. 181-96; Stuart W. Hyde, "The Chinese Stereotype in American Melodrama," *California Historical Quarterly* (December 1955), pp. 357-67; William P. Fenn, *Ah Sin and His Brethren in American Literature* (Peking, 1933); Jules A. Karlin, "The Anti-Chinese Outbreaks in Seattle, 1885-1886," *Pacific Northwest Quarterly,* vol. 39, no. 2 (April 1948), pp. 103-30, and "The Anti-Chinese Outbreak in Tacoma, 1885," *Pacific Historical Review,* vol. 23 (August 1954), pp. 271-83; B. P. Wilcox, "Anti-Chinese Riots in Washington," *Washington Historical Quarterly,* vol. 20, no. 3 (July 1929), pp. 207-11; Arthur Mann, "Samuel Gompers and the Irony of Racism," *Antioch Review,* vol. 13 (1953), pp. 203-14; W. M. Armstrong, "Godkin and Chinese Labor: A Paradox in Nineteenth Century Liberalism," *American Journal of Economics and Sociology,* vol. 12 (1962), pp. 91-102; Herbert Hill, "The Anti-Oriental Agitation and the Rise of Working Class

Racism" (paper delivered at Rutgers University, New Brunswick, N.J., October 1971); and John P. Young, "The Support of the Anti-Oriental Movement," *Annals of the Academy of Political and Social Science*, vol. 24, no. 2 (September 1909).

The Chinese were involved in virtually every aspect of labor in the West, as we learn from Ping Chiu, *Chinese Labor in California, 1850-1880: An Economic Study* (Madison, Wis., 1963). Mary Coolidge, *Chinese Immigration* (New York, 1969, originally published in 1909), is still a standard work which needs to be challenged by revisionist studies. Studies of the Chinese and the building of the railroad are inadequate; but among the better efforts are Wesley S. Griswold, *A Work of Giants: Building the First Transcontinental Railroad* (New York, 1962); E. L. Sabin, *Building the Pacific Railway* (Philadelphia, 1919); and John D. Galloway, *The First Transcontinental Railway* (New York, 1950). For Chinese in the mines, see also Rodman W. Paul, *California Gold, the Beginning of Mining in the Far West* (Cambridge, 1947); and John R. Commons, et al., eds., *A Documentary History of American Industrial Society* (Cleveland, Ohio, 1910-11), vol. 9. Discussions of the Chinese by white Americans can be found virtually everywhere—newspapers, magazines, legislative testimonies, plays, poems, novels, and travel narratives. For a sampling of this abundance, see Pierton W. Dooner, *Last Days of the Republic* (San Francisco, 1880); John Todd, *The Sunset Land* (Boston, 1870); A. W. Loomis, "The Old East in the New West," *Overland Monthly*, vol. 1 (1868), pp. 360-7; Reverend O. Gibson, *Chinaman or White Man, Which?* (San Francisco, 1873), and *The Chinese in America* (Cincinnati, 1877); Samuel Bowles, *Our New West* (Hartford, Conn., 1869); Hinton Rowan Helper, *The Land of Gold: Reality Versus Fiction* (Baltimore, 1855); James L. Bowen, "The Celestials in Sunday School," *Scribner's Monthly*, vol. 1 (March 1871), pp. 556-9; "The Chinese Invasion," *The Nation*, vol. 11 (July 14, 1870), p. 20; E. L. Godkin, "The Coming of the Barbarian," *The Nation*, vol. 9 (July 15, 1869), pp. 44-5; Henry J. West, *The Chinese Invasion* (San Francisco, 1873); Robert Wolter, *Short and True History of the Taking of California and Oregon by the Chinese in the Year A.D. 1899* (San Francisco, 1882); William Shanks, "Chinese Skilled Labor," *Scribner's Monthly*, vol. 2 (September 1871), pp. 494-7; Abby Sage Richardson, "A Plea for Chinese Labor," *Scribner's Monthly*, vol. 2 (July 1871), pp. 286-90; Henry Robinson, "Our Manufacturing Era," *Overland Monthly*, vol. 2 (March 1869), pp. 280-4; Frank Norton, "Our Labor System and the Chinese," *Scribner's Monthly*, vol. 2 (May 1871), pp. 61-70; A. W. Loomis, "How Our Chinamen Are Employed," *Overland Monthly*, vol. 2 (March 1869), pp. 231-40; Charles W. Brooks, "The Chinese Labor Problem," *Overland Monthly*, vol. 3 (November 1869), pp. 407-19; "Editor's Easy Chair," *Harper's*, vol. 42 (December 1870), pp. 137-9; Henry Grimm, *"The Chinese Must Go": A Farce in Four Acts* (San Francisco, 1879); *Report of the Joint Special Committee to Investigate Chinese Immigration*, Senate Report no. 689, 44th Cong., 2d sess., 1876-77; U.S. Congress, *Congressional Record*, 47th Cong., 1st sess., 1882, which contains the debate on the exclusion bill; Arthur H. Smith, *Chinese Characteristics* (New York, 1894); and Ignatius Donnelly, *Caesar's Column: A Story of the Twentieth Century* (Cambridge, Mass., 1960, originally published in 1890).

The author of the poem "The Heathen Chinee," or "Plain Language from Truthful James," *Overland Monthly*, vol. 5 (September 1870), pp. 287-8, is the subject of Margaret L. Keim, "The Chinese as Portrayed in the Works of Bret Harte," *Sociology and Social Research*, vol. 25 (May 1941), pp. 441-50; Margaret Duckett, "Plain Language from Bret Harte," *Nineteenth-Century Fiction*, vol. 11 (March 1957), pp. 241-60, and *Mark Twain and Bret Harte* (Norman, Okla., 1964); Richard O'Connor, *Bret Harte* (Boston, 1966); and George R. Stewart, Jr., *Bret Harte: Argonaut and Exile* (Boston, 1931). For Harte's writings, see Harte, *Harte's Complete Works*, 20 vols. (Boston, 1929); and Geoffrey Bret Harte, ed., *The Letters of*

Bret Harte (London, 1926). The Bret Harte Papers in the Bancroft Library of the University of California, Berkeley, contain the original manuscript for Harte's poem on the "Heathen Chinee."

Of all the many biographies of Henry George only two are worthwhile: Henry George, Jr., *The Life of Henry George* (New York, 1930); and Charles A. Barker, *Henry George* (New York, 1955). For an understanding of the author of *Progress and Poverty: An Inquiry into the Cause of Industrial Depressions and of Increase of Want with Increase of Wealth. The Remedy* (New York, 1879), one must read his early writings, especially "What the Railroad Will Bring Us," *Overland Monthly*, vol. 1 (October 1868), pp. 297-306; "The Chinese on the Pacific Coast," *New York Tribune*, May 1, 1869; the exchange between George and John Stuart Mill published in the *Oakland* (Calif.) *Daily Transcript*, November 20 and 22, 1869; and *Our Land and Land Policy, National and State* (San Francisco, 1871). For his other writings, see Henry George, Jr., *Complete Works of Henry George*, 10 vols. (Garden City, N.Y., 1911); and George, "The Kearney Agitation in California," *Popular Science Monthly*, vol. 17 (August 1880), p. 433, and "Chinese Immigration," in John Lalor, *Cyclopedia of Political Science, Political Economy and of the Political History of the United States* (Chicago, 1883). The Henry George Papers at the New York Public Library, New York City, is an enormous collection, containing diaries and letters of great interest.

I am grateful to Professor Ling-chi Wang for leading me to one of the key documents analyzed in this chapter—Aaron H. Palmer, *Memoir, geographical, political, and commercial, on the present state, productive resources, and capabilities for commerce, of Siberia, Manchuria, and the Asiatic Islands of the Northern Pacific Ocean; and on the importance of opening commercial intercourse with those countries,* March 8, 1848. U.S. Cong., Senate, 30th Cong., 1st sess., Senate misc. no. 80 (Washington, 1848).

For Chinese labor as a migrant industrial reserve army, see Leigh Kagan, "Chinese in California (1850-94): Migrant Labor or Immigrant?" (Paper presented at the Asian Scholars on the Pacific Conference, University of Oregon, Eugene, Ore., June 1977); Harry Braverman, *Labor and Monopoly Capital: The Degradation of Work in the Twentieth Century* (New York, 1974), pp. 382-401; and Karl Marx, "Progressive Production of a Relative Surplus-Population, or Industrial Reserve Army," in *Capital: A Critique of Political Economy* (New York, 1906), pp. 689-702.

XI. The Masculine Thrust Toward Asia

For an understanding of the economic and political context in which American expansionism developed, see Robert H. Wiebe, *The Search for Order, 1877-1920* (New York, 1968); Gabriel Kolko, *The Triumph of Conservatism: A Reinterpretation of American History, 1900-1916* (New York, 1963); Alfred D. Chandler, Jr., *Strategy and Structure: Chapters in the History of the Industrial Enterprise* (Cambridge, 1966), and David F. Noble, *America by Design: Science, Technology, and the Rise of Corporate Capitalism* (New York, 1977). The beginnings of modernization and bureaucracy in America are studied in Lynn Marshall's seminal essay, "The Strange Stillbirth of the Whig Party," *American Historical Review*, vol. 72, no. 2 (January 1967), pp. 445-68; and Richard D. Brown, "Modernization: A Victorian Climax," *American Quarterly*, vol. 27, no. 5 (December 1975), pp. 533-48. For some insights on what happened by the end of the nineteenth century, read John Higham, "The Reorientation of American Culture in the 1890s," in *Writing American History: Essays on Modern Scholarship* (Bloomington, Ind., 1970).

The most successful study of the relationship between ideology and economic interests in the development of American expansion is Walter La Feber, *The New Empire: An Interpreta-*

tion of American Expansion, 1860-1898 (Ithaca, N.Y., 1967). William A. Williams, *The Tragedy of American Diplomacy* (New York, 1962) is still provocative; the same is true for Richard Hofstadter, "Manifest Destiny and the Philippines," in Daniel Aaron, ed., *America in Crisis* (New York, 1952), pp. 173-200. Other important studies of this topic include Julius W. Pratt, *Expansionists of 1898* (Baltimore, 1936); Ernest R. May, *Imperial Democracy: The Emergence of America as a Great Power* (New York, 1961); Richard Hofstadter, *Social Darwinism in American Thought* (Boston, 1962, originally published in 1944); Charles S. Campbell, Jr., *Special Business Interests and the Open Door Policy* (New Haven, Conn., 1951); Thomas J. McCormick, *China Market: America's Quest for Informal Empire, 1893-1901* (Chicago, 1967); Robert E. Osgood, *Ideals and Self Interest in America's Foreign Relations* (Chicago, 1953); Charles A. Beard, *A Foreign Policy for America* (New York, 1940); Charles Vevier, "American Continentalism: The History of an Idea, 1845-1910," *American Historical Review*, vol. 65, no. 2 (January 1960), pp. 323-35; Paul A. Varg, *The Making of a Myth: The United States and China, 1897-1912* (East Lansing, Mich., 1968); and Marilyn B. Young, *The Rhetoric of Empire: American China Policy, 1895-1901* (Cambridge, Mass., 1968). Albert K. Weinberg, *Manifest Destiny: A Study of Nationalist Expansionism in American History* (Gloucester, Mass., 1958) is a classic; Robert McClellan, *The Heathen Chinee: A Study of American Attitudes toward China, 1890-1905* (Columbus, Ohio, 1971), tries to show the influence of American white images of Chinese on United States policy toward China. For anti-imperialism, see the differing interpretations by F. H. Harrington, "The Anti-Imperialist Movement in the United States, 1898-1900," *Mississippi Valley Historical Review*, vol. 22 (September 1935), pp. 211-30; and Christopher Lasch, "The Anti-Imperialists, the Philippines, and the Inequality of Man," *Journal of Southern History*, vol. 14 (August 1958), pp. 319-31.

Theories of imperialism are developed in Hannah Arendt, *The Origins of Totalitarianism* (New York, 1958); V. I. Lenin, *Imperialism, the Highest Stage of Capitalism* (Peking, 1970); Rosa Luxemburg, *The Accumulation of Capital* (New Haven, 1951); and J. A. Hobson, *Imperialism: A Study* (London, 1954). Some sources to examine are Frederick Jackson Turner, "The Significance of the Frontier in American History," in *The Early Writings of Frederick Jackson Turner* (Madison, Wis., 1938); Brooks Adams, *America's Economic Supremacy* (New York, 1900), and *The Law of Civilization and Decay: An Essay on History* (New York, 1943); and Theodore Roosevelt, *The Strenuous Life: Essays and Addresses* (Philadelphia, 1903). For a view from the other side, see Mark Twain, "To the Person Sitting in Darkness," *North American Review*, vol. 172 (February 1901), pp. 161-76.

Reverend Josiah Strong still lacks a biography. The closest to one is Dorothea R. Muller, "Josiah Strong and the Challenge of the City," Ph.D. diss., New York University, 1956. Author of *Our Country: Its Possible Future and Its Present Crisis* (New York, 1885), Strong also wrote *Expansion under New World-Conditions* (New York, 1900); *The Times and Young Men* (New York, 1901); *The New Era; or, The Coming Kingdom* (New York, 1893); and *The Challenge of the City* (New York, 1907).

Admiral Alfred Thayer Mahan, one of the key architects of America's imperial policy, has received much biographical attention. Charles C. Taylor, *The Life of Admiral Mahan, Naval Philosopher* (New York, 1920); and W. D. Puleston, *The Life and Work of Captain Alfred Thayer Mahan* (New Haven, Conn., 1939) are superficial; but William E. Livezey, *Mahan on Sea Power* (Norman, Okla., 1947) is informative. See also Harold and Margaret Sprout, *Rise of American Naval Power, 1776-1918* (Princeton, N.J., 1946); Robert Seager, "Ten Years before Mahan: The Unofficial Case for the New Navy, 1880-1890," *Mississippi Valley Historical Review*, vol. 40 (December 1953), pp. 491-512; Peter Karsten, *The Naval Aristocracy: The Golden Age of Annapolis and the Emergence of Modern American Navalism* (New York,

1972); and Walter La Feber, "A Note on the 'Mercantilistic Imperialism' of Alfred Thayer Mahan," *Mississippi Valley Historical Review,* vol. 48, no. 4 (March 1962).

Indispensable for an understanding of Mahan and also imperialist ideology are Mahan's writings, especially *The Influence of Sea Power upon History, 1660-1783* (Boston, 1890); *The Problem of Asia and Its Effect upon International Policies* (Boston, 1900); *The Interest of America in Sea Power, Present and Future* (Boston, 1898); *Lessons of the War with Spain* (Boston, 1899); and "The Navy as a Career," *The Forum* (November 1895), pp. 277-83. Mahan's personal life shaped his thoughts on the Navy and foreign policy: For autobiographical information, see Mahan, *The Harvest Within: Thoughts on the Life of a Christian* (Boston, 1909); and *From Sail to Steam; Recollections of Naval Life* (New York, 1907). The Alfred Thayer Mahan Papers at the Library of Congress, Washington, D.C., and the Mahan-Ashe Papers at Duke University, Durham, North Carolina, are revealing.

XII. Down from the Gardens of Asia

The completeness Whitman celebrates in *Leaves of Grass* is analyzed in different terms in Norman O. Brown, *Life against Death: The Psychoanalytical Meaning of History* (Middletown, Conn., 1959).

We can learn much about American society and imperialism from Herman Melville, *Moby-Dick, or the Whale* (Boston, 1956, originally published in 1851). Henry Nash Smith, "The Image of Society in *Moby-Dick,*" in Tyrus Hillway and Luther S. Mansfield, *Moby-Dick: Centennial Essays* (Dallas, 1953); and Leo Marx, *The Machine in the Garden: Technology and the Pastoral Ideal in America* (New York, 1967) are interesting, while black West Indian Marxist C. L. R. James, *Mariners, Renegades and Castaways: The Story of Herman Melville and the World* (New York, 1953), a little-known and hard-to-find book, is illuminating.

Index

A Note About the Author

Ronald T. Takaki was born in Honolulu, Hawaii, in 1939, and received his B.A. (1961) from the College of Wooster and his M.A. (1962) and Ph.D. (1967) in History from the University of California at Berkeley. A fellow of the National Endowment for the Humanities, 1970-71, he is the author of *A Pro-Slavery Crusade: The Agitation to Reopen the African Slave Trade* (1971) and *Violence in the Black Imagination: Essays and Documents* (1972). He has also written reviews for the *Journal of Ethnic Studies* and the *Journal of American History*. Between 1967 and 1972 he taught in the History Department at UCLA, where he offered the university's first courses on black history and the history of racial attitudes in America, and where he also helped to establish its Ethnic Studies Centers. Currently a member of the faculty at Berkeley, Takaki has served as chairperson of the Department of Ethnic Studies and teaches courses on the history of race and culture in America.

A Note on the Type

The text of this book was set in a face called Times Roman, designed by Stanley Morison for *The Times* (London), and first introduced by that newspaper in 1932.

Among typographers and designers of the twentieth century, Stanley Morison has been a strong forming influence, as typographical adviser to the English Monotype Corporation, as a director of two distinguished English publishing houses, and as a writer of sensibility, erudition, and keen practical sense.

Set via computer-driven cathode ray tube by Lehigh/Rocappi
from input provided by Random House, Inc.
Printed and bound by The Haddon Craftsmen, Inc., Scranton, Pennsylvania
Typography and binding design by Margaret Wagner